MAY 2011

Adam's Gift

Adam's Gift

·········◈·········

A MEMOIR OF A
PASTOR'S CALLING
TO DEFY THE CHURCH'S
PERSECUTION OF
LESBIANS AND GAYS

Jimmy Creech

Duke University Press
Durham and London 2011

© 2011 Duke University Press

All rights reserved

Printed in the United States of America
on acid-free paper ∞

Designed by Heather Hensley

Typeset in Arno Pro by Tseng Information
Systems, Inc.

Library of Congress Cataloging-in-
Publication Data appear on the last printed
page of this book.

For Chris — my lover, my friend

CONTENTS

ACKNOWLEDGMENTS

Adam's Gift is a memoir. It begins when a gay man's coming out inspired me to advocate for the rights and acceptance of lesbian, gay, bisexual, and transgender people in both the church and American society.

The book tells how I overcame the misinformation I'd learned about homosexuality and how the gay people who became my mentors transformed my fear of homosexuality into compassion. It describes how the parishioners of two very different congregations that I served as pastor, as well as bishops and church leaders throughout the nation, reacted to my ministry with gay people, some offering support and others demonstrating resistance and hostility.

But *Adam's Gift* is more than a personal story. It's a historical marker in the midst of a movement toward freedom, justice, and equality for lesbian, gay, bisexual, and transgender people, a movement that is inexorable and uncompromising.

My work on *Adam's Gift* began during a walk with my wife, Chris Weedy, on the beach of Ocracoke Island, North Carolina, in the summer of 1998. It was her idea that I tell the story that began with Adam in 1984, a story that was still unfolding when I started to write. It has taken me more than eleven years to finish this memoir. Without Chris's patience and encouragement, I could not have done it. My gratitude to her is immeasurable.

I'm also grateful to those who read part or all of the manuscript and gave me honest, helpful critiques: Ceil Cleveland, Bob Dorr, Elliot Engel, Rich Eychaner, Vic Ferrall, Jerry Footlick, Bill Jenks, Sonia Pabley, Donald Palmer, Mahan Siler, Dwight Smith, and Mel White. The encouragement of Betty Dorr, Mitchell Gold, Leila May, Gary Nixon, and Linda Smith sustained me while I wrote this book.

I am indebted to the leadership and staff of the First United Methodist Church of Omaha, Nebraska, for the grace they gave to my family and me, and for their courage and faithfulness during challenging times. And I'm immensely grateful for the witness for inclusion that the congregation continues to make.

Throughout the events that are recounted in this story, I received generous support from many people, some of them strangers I never met. They supported me because they believed in what I was doing. My deepest regret is that I have been unable to adequately express my gratitude to them. I continue to remember their generosity and grace with gratitude. Without Adam, there would be no story to tell. I give thanks for his integrity and willingness to trust me with his secret.

"I quit! I won't take it anymore. I'm leaving the church!" Adam[1] cried as he entered my office.

I quickly went to him and asked him to have a seat on the couch, taking a chair across from him. He was in obvious agony, his body shaking with anger and grief. His eyes were red and swollen from crying, and they moved nervously back and forth between mine and the floor. He leaned forward, elbows on his knees, hands clenched in front of him, fingers interlocked so tightly that his knuckles were white.

"Why, Adam? Tell me what's happened," I said gently, trying to calm and comfort him.

"I won't be a member of a church that thinks that I'm some kind of pervert, that doesn't want me."

I had no clue what he was talking about. "Adam," I said, "tell me who said that. Who in our church thinks you're a pervert? Who doesn't want you?"

"Didn't you read the paper this morning? Didn't you see what they did? I've been a Methodist since I was ten years old. I've given the church my time, my money—and what do I get?"

That Wednesday morning in May 1984 had been quiet before Adam appeared. As I drank my morning coffee at home, an hour or so earlier, I had read a newspaper report that the General Conference[2] of The United Methodist Church—gathered in Baltimore, Maryland, for its quadrennial meeting—had just passed a new policy prohibiting the ordination and appointment of "self-avowed practicing homosexuals." Because I didn't know anyone who was a self-avowed practicing homosexual, the news meant nothing to me. There'd been other reports on the General Conference's actions in the newspaper over the past week, and I'd grown indifferent to them. It seemed that nothing happening in Baltimore was particularly important or would affect my ministry. I was wrong.

"I don't want to be ordained," said Adam. "But I don't want to be told I can't be because I'm gay. I'm just as moral as anybody, just as good a Christian."

I'd first met Adam when I became pastor of the United Methodist church in Warsaw, North Carolina, three years earlier. Adam was in his late forties, and he was an educator at a nearby community college. Quiet and reserved, he often complimented me on my sermons — so, of course, I admired his intelligence. Comments people made about him showed me that he was highly respected by other members of the congregation. I didn't know Adam was gay until that Wednesday morning. It never crossed my mind that he might be. I assumed that everyone I knew was heterosexual.

That morning, Adam revealed to me a hidden world of oppression in which people who are gay, lesbian, transgender, or bisexual suffer an insidious violence disguised as Christian morality that attacks their very beings, their very souls. It's a reality created and sustained by the claim that gay people are sick, sinful, and criminal, a claim that is declared to be God's truth in pulpits, courtrooms, workplaces, and schoolrooms; on playgrounds, athletic fields, and street corners; and at family dinner tables. The cruelest aspect of this hidden world is that gay people internalize these demeaning proclamations and hate themselves for simply being who they are. It's a world they cannot escape and have little defense against, except to hide their sexuality and pretend to be someone they are not, or to end their lives.

Adam's words rushed from his soul like water pouring through a broken dam. I listened with rapt attention, losing all track of time, as he opened to me a whole new world. He told me that as a child he would hear preachers and others in the church talk about God's unconditional love, and then hear from those same people the irreconcilable message that God hates, rejects, and condemns homosexuals to hell. He shared the story of his painful struggle to discover, understand, and accept his sexuality, first running from the self he discovered and later trying — and failing — to be heterosexual. He talked about the shame and guilt he felt about simply being himself. He even told me that he had considered suicide, once thinking that was the only way he could escape his homosexuality and demonstrate true repentance for it. He said that finally, after hating God for condemning him, he had chosen to trust God's unconditional love. But this only made it possible to survive; it didn't ease his pain or end his shame.

I was so stunned by Adam's revelation of the abuse he'd experienced in the church that I no longer recall everything I said to him in response. But I do remember these reassuring words that came from the depths of my soul, from instinct if not reason: "Adam, God loves you and accepts who you are. You have every reason to respect yourself and to expect others to respect you." I was as sure of that as I had ever been sure of anything.

I also told him, "The church should never be a place where you feel attacked and scorned. I understand and support your decision to leave the church, not because I want you to leave, but because you shouldn't allow yourself to be mistreated. No one should tolerate an abusive relationship." And I said, "Thanks for telling me your story. Thanks for trusting me. I promise to be your pastor as long as you want me to be, even if you're not a member of this church."

After Adam's visit, I thought about all the stereotypes I had learned about "queers"—that they are dangerous people, psychologically sick, depraved, and immoral. Adam fit none of these stereotypes; in fact, he'd destroyed them for me. He was a healthy, responsible person of good character. He was a gentle person of faith, a thoughtful and practicing Christian. Who Adam was and my beliefs about homosexuality were incompatible. I was distraught.

I was devoted to The United Methodist Church. It had nurtured me in my faith journey from childhood into adulthood. I was committed to serve it as a pastor. Adam's revelation changed neither my feeling for The United Methodist Church, nor my commitment to it. But what he said troubled me greatly. While I knew the church did much good, I was not unaware of the harm it had done and could do. Because I'd seen how the church had supported and promoted racism in the South, anointing racial segregation and the myth of white supremacy as God's will, making God the enemy of racial equality and justice, the holy oppressor of black people, I knew that the church I loved was capable of the spiritual violence that Adam had described to me. I'd also witnessed Southern prejudice against Jews, Roman Catholics, and women, often supported by the church. These were injustices that I knew the church had acknowledged and repudiated. Now, however, Adam had revealed another injustice that the church had not acknowledged, one I had not known about before.

As a pastor, my mission was to help people overcome whatever damaged them spiritually; whatever diminished their capacity to trust God's love, to love others, and to love themselves. I'd never imagined sexuality to be an issue of justice, much less a spiritual one. In fact, I knew no clergy who did see it that way. Although I didn't realize it immediately, Adam's visit that Wednesday set the rest of my life and ministry on a new course. Adam launched me on a journey with no clear destination and with no guide or maps to follow, other than an intuitive sense of what was right, just, and compassionate. Before I could move forward, however, it was necessary for me to look back on my personal history to understand how my attitudes toward sexuality in general and homosexuality in particular had been formed.

I grew up in Goldsboro, North Carolina. Until I was ten years old, my family lived on a street lined with large oak trees and homes built in the early years of the twentieth century, just three blocks west of the center of town and one block east of the train station. I was the third of four children — Will and Frances were, respectively, nine and seven years older than I was, and Alice was six years younger. Each of us was born in the house where we lived, 105 South Virginia Street.

My father, Wilbur, owned Creech's Furniture, which was a walk of two and a half blocks from our home toward downtown. My mother, Frances, went to college in the 1920s to be a teacher, but she stayed at home to raise my sisters, brother, and me. Both my parents were active members of St. Paul Methodist Church, where Dad was on the Parsonage Committee — keeping the pastor's home well furnished with contributions from his store — and Mom taught an adult Sunday school class. Family Bible reading and prayer were part of our evening routine. In our home, every special event was an occasion for family devotions. On birthdays, we always had a large candle for Jesus in the center of the cake. On Christmas, before we opened any gifts, we read the nativity stories from the Gospels, lit a candle for Jesus, sang "Happy Birthday" to him, and said a prayer of thanksgiving for his life.

Although my mother and father were devout, they were not rigid in their beliefs. They taught me that our way isn't God's only way, but that there are a variety of people and religions in the world, all deserving as much respect as our own. While it wasn't unusual for Southerners to consider any religion other than Southern Protestant Christianity against God's will and un-American, Mom and Dad had friends who were Roman Catholics and Jews. When Jehovah's Witnesses and Mormons came by with their tracts, Mom would welcome them into our home like honored guests. Often she attended evening prayer meetings at a black church in a part of Goldsboro that white people called Colored Town, just a few blocks from our home.

The earliest memory I have of budding erotic desire and sensual pleasure was when I was four or five years old. One summer day, a family came from out of town to stay with Frank Samath, a neighbor who lived just down the street from my house. A girl in the family was my age. I don't remember her name, but I can't forget her beauty. She was gentle and sweet with olive skin, dark brown eyes, and long black hair. She was the first person for whom I felt that deep aching desire to be near and to touch.

In those hot and humid summer days, I was always barefoot and shirtless, wearing only a pair of shorts. She was always barefoot, too, and wore a light cotton dress or shorts and a T-shirt.

We played together day after day at Frank's house. We played under the hot sun and in the warm, gentle rain. The odor of her body, wet from the summer's heat or rain, was delicious. We picked dandelions, using the golden flowers to make crowns for our heads and blowing on the gray puff balls to make the seeds scatter on the breeze. At night, we caught lightning bugs, cupping them in our hands and thrilling at their pulsating glow between our fingers.

In Frank's backyard was a mimosa tree with branches high enough for us to play beneath, sometimes napping together in their cool shade, our legs and arms entwined. We especially loved the mimosa flowers, which last much of the summer. A slender stem is topped with thousands of delicate pink, mauve, and yellow fibers that spread into a fan. The flower has the subtle fragrance of ripe peaches. The little girl and I enjoyed lying in the grass beneath the tree, where we would take turns lightly stroking and tickling each other's body with these soft, fragrant flowers.

It was under the mimosa tree that I first became conscious of sensual pleasure and the physical desire to touch, smell, taste, and hold someone. I did not fully understand, of course; but erotic passion had wakened within me. In the pleasure and pleasuring of our play, I discovered at the most basic level that I was a sexual being who hungered for physical and emotional affection, and intimacy with another person.

Later, I wrestled with male friends in the grass under trees, and lay quietly next to them, with our backs on the ground and our eyes searching for the shapes of animals in clouds above. Their bodies had odors, too, but not like the little girl's. With my male friends, I felt no sensual longing to touch, no mystical desire to unite. Being with them was fun and entertaining, but it was not the same as being with her.

It was under the mimosa tree with my young girl friend that I sensed for the first time the desire to reach out of myself so as to unite in love and passion with someone else. This was a desire beyond reason for a mystical union that was both corporeal and spiritual.

Years later, when listening to lesbian, bisexual, and gay friends describe how they discovered their sexuality, I'd recall the mimosa tree. It is clear to me that being erotically attracted to someone, whether of your own gender or the other gender, is a normal step in the maturation process. It's so normal that most nongay people don't remember it, any more than they remember "discovering" their fingers and toes. For gay, lesbian, and bisexual people, however, the discovery soon becomes problematic, and consequently memorable, as they realize that they are different from most other people — if not from everyone they know — and that others do not accept, and may even condemn, their difference.

I never talked to my parents about what happened to me beneath the mimosa tree, about my erotic and sensual feelings. I had already learned that my feelings were not okay, that they were bad, and I shouldn't have them. I didn't know how to reconcile them with the moral lessons I was being taught, both directly and indirectly. I struggled with the shame of pleasure and the guilt of wanting to touch and hold a girl.

When I was growing up, in the late 1940s and the 1950s, there was very little open discussion about sexuality at home, church, or school. My friends and I were left to learn what we could on our own, and to share with one another what we knew — or thought we knew — about it. What I heard from older youth and adults made sex sound morally wrong and disgusting, so disconnected from what I had felt with my girl friend under the mimosa tree that I didn't even relate the two. There was always snickering when a conversation turned to sex, as if it were salacious and embarrassing.

I was six when my sister Alice was born, at the end of November. On Christmas Day, I was shooting a basketball with a friend in his backyard when he told me that there was no Santa Claus, that my parents had bought all those gifts under our tree, and that a stork hadn't brought Alice to live with us. My parents, he said, had had sex to make her, as well as my older sister and brother, and me. That's how babies are made, he insisted.

I was crushed that Santa Claus didn't exist, after all those years of believing in him. And I was shocked and disgusted at the thought of my mother and father having sex, after years of being told it was dirty and forbidden. I suspected my friend was telling the truth, but I held on to my disbelief until dinner that night. I wasn't ready to mention the stork, but I asked my parents about Santa Claus. Mom told me that "if you believe in him, he exists." I knew then that my friend was right. Mom and Dad weren't telling me the truth about Santa Claus. I knew, too, that they weren't telling me the truth about the stork. I didn't even need to ask.

My parents never did discuss sex with me, or with any of my siblings. Once, when I was in my late forties, I asked Mom why she had never talked to me about sex when I was a child or youth, and she replied: "Because I knew if I did, you might get interested in it." Her parents never talked to her about sex, apparently for the same reason. My father enjoyed telling the story of taking Mom back to her mother the day after their wedding, so that my grandmother could explain "how babies are born." It seems that my parents' wedding night was chaste, frustrating my father, who was nine years older than his bride. My mother claims that up until then, she thought that women got pregnant from sitting on toilet seats that men had used. She felt that not knowing had served her well until her wedding night, and that ignorance would serve me just as well.

My childhood playground was downtown Goldsboro and the area around the train station. I played on the roofs of buildings and explored the alleys between them. One block west of our house, just across the street from the train station, was a small brick building where a man operated a peanut roasting machine. From time to time, the man would open up the building and roast peanuts.

One day when I was about nine years old, lured by the irresistible aroma of the roasting peanuts permeating the neighborhood, I discovered a vacant store adjacent to the peanut roaster. I strained to see inside, through the dirty storefront glass. The floor was littered with old bricks, various kinds of business documents, and broken furniture, everything covered with thick gray dust that had long been undisturbed. Intrigued, I found a broken door in the back of the vacant store, squeezed myself inside, and explored the store's contents. Underneath a table, I found an old calendar with a large color photo at the top, the first time I'd ever seen a woman's unclothed body. Her head was tilted back to rest on her arm, her eyes were closed, and an innocent, dreamy smile was on her face. Her hair was long and flowed down over one shoulder. Her breasts were lifted, large, and firm, with nipples that were erect and enticing. I imagined her saying to me: "I'm yours. Touch me, taste me. It's okay."

I held the calendar and studied it carefully, frozen with fascination and fear. I felt my body aroused by the titillation—blood pounded in my head, my breathing was quick and shallow, my muscles were taut. We were alone, the woman in the calendar and I. I knew no one was watching, and no one would know what was going on. But my head was full of voices telling me that what I was doing—what I was feeling and wanting—was wrong, was bad. The sensual beauty of the woman and the erotic electricity of the moment were forbidden.

In panic, I put the calendar down and quickly left, sure that I had committed an awful sin. I tried to forget what I had seen, but I was obsessed with the woman's beauty, now vividly burned into my memory. Days later, when I could no longer resist, I returned in spite of my shame, driven to see the woman once again, carefully studying her as I had the first time. I repeated this private tryst over and over, each time leaving with an agonizing mix of humiliation and pleasure. One day, I found the broken door repaired and bolted. I never saw the calendar again.

What I remember most about the beautiful, sensual woman was her sweet, innocent smile that said sex wasn't as shameful or ugly as I'd been taught. I wondered how anyone so beautiful could be bad.

I first learned about homosexuality from what some older friends said about a classmate of theirs called Pee-Wee. They said he was a queer. Nobody explained to me what that meant, except that queers do "bad things to little boys like you." He was four or five years older than me. Somehow, I got the message that what he did was violent and sexual in nature.

But Pee-Wee wasn't a bully, always beating up younger boys. In fact, he was slightly built, quiet, and unobtrusive. I never saw him with anybody except his mother. Once, I spotted him walking toward me on a sidewalk. I crossed the street to avoid him. I never interacted with him or even spoke to him.

I saw him around town when I was at Virginia Street Elementary School. Then he moved away. I don't know where he went, and I haven't heard anything about him since. But for many years in Goldsboro, "Pee-Wee" was synonymous with "queer." In my preadolescent and teenage years, if you wanted to call a guy a queer, you called him "Pee-Wee."

I don't know if Pee-Wee was gay. People might have said he was because he was small and quiet, because he was different. Then again, he might have showed an interest in boys or behaved in some way to make people think he was gay. I never heard any stories about such incidents or about his actually harming "little boys." All I ever heard about Pee-Wee were accusations, which were enough to make me fear and avoid him. Because of my fear, I did not see him as someone struggling through adolescence just like me, and I felt no empathy for him.

The lasting image I have of Pee-Wee is of him walking down the street alone, shoulders stooped and head down. Whether or not he was gay, we isolated him because of what we imagined, fueled by fear and disgust. With rumor and innuendo, ridicule and humiliation, we drew an invisible but impenetrable barrier around him. We persecuted him because we feared him, because we were sickened by what we imagined he did, not because he ever harmed or made passes at us. We made him into a diabolical symbol upon which we projected our own pathological fear and disgust of sexuality. As long as we were not like him and did not associate with him, we were okay. He suffered because of us—and for us.

What we did to Pee-Wee, we did to every other young boy and girl in Goldsboro. Who would want to let anyone know or think that they were gay—were like what everyone said Pee-Wee was—when they knew what would happen to them, how they would be treated? All of us want desperately to be accepted, especially during adolescence. When we know we're different—especially in a way that we know is unacceptable—we instinctively try to hide our difference. But hiding leads to a fear of discovery, and living with fear is torture. We are always afraid of being exposed, revealed for who we really are. Hiding a part of ourselves ends up making us hate all of ourselves, and anyone who resembles who we really are. Some of my friends, I learned years later, people who laughed at and taunted Pee-Wee, were hiding the truth that they were what we said Pee-Wee was: queer. It seemed safe to hide behind expressions of hatred and disgust aimed at homosexuals. But the cost was living daily with self-hatred and fear of exposure.

This fear was on top of the pressure to conform to gender role expectations. Boys were expected to be emotionally tough and aloof, competitive, in control, and lusting after females. To be emotionally sensitive and responsive was to be like a girl — an association no young boy wanted — and put us in the category of sissy, making us pussies, which was equated with being queer. To be queer was to be weak, soft, and compliant, as well as sick, perverse, and disgusting. The fear and disgust of homosexuality in others and in ourselves, which was taught us in formal and informal ways, effectively socialized us into our heterosexist culture. It was social conditioning at its most effective. We had to be careful about our appearance, careful that we acted the way men should act.

I don't recall hearing comments about girls being queer. I never heard the words *dyke*, *butch*, and *lesbian* until years later, when I was in college.

We boys learned that sex was power: political, competitive, and aggressive, a sign of dominance and control, the measure of manhood. Females, the objects of our sexual prowess, were our means to manhood through both penetration and subjugation. Competition — in sports, business, politics, or war — was the only socially acceptable sexual relationship, the only permissible sexual behavior, between men. To love and be devoted to another man, to live in a mutually caring and nurturing relationship, was not what real men did in the culture in which I grew up.

At one time I projected my fear onto Pee-Wee, but now I project my guilt and shame because of the way we mistreated him. I grieve for what we did to Pee-Wee — the enforced isolation, the humiliation, the denial of his humanity. I pray for his forgiveness. I hope he is well and thriving. I hope he has friends who accept and love him. I hope he loves himself.

Ironically, I had what could be called a homosexual experience as a child, although I didn't know it at the time. When I was eight or nine, an older boy stayed at my home with his mother, while they were visiting Goldsboro. He slept in my bed with me. The first night, after the light was out, he whispered, "Can I stick my dick in your ass?" I'd never heard of such a thing and thought it was disgusting. "No," I said, "go to sleep!"

"Ah, come on, it feels good. You'll like it. It's fun," he pleaded. "No! Go to sleep!" I repeated. He did and never asked again.

I had no sense that what he wanted to do was morally bad or wrong. My only thought at the time was: "This kid is weird!" It didn't cross my mind that he might be gay because I didn't know that's what gay men liked to do. I didn't associate him with Pee-Wee because I saw no harm in the boy or what he wanted to do. He propositioned me in the same way he might have said, "Let's wrestle," or "Let's play cowboys and Indians." I wasn't afraid, just disgusted. My ass was for shitting, after all, not having someone's dick stuck in it. This kid wasn't queer, just weird. I feared Pee-Wee, because people told me he was queer; but I didn't fear this weird kid in my bed.

As I got older, references to sex in high school were always indirect, vague, and metaphorical. In church youth programs, sex was not discussed at all. There was enough in the cultural ethos to teach us what was expected of us as girls and boys. I learned that men and women were supposed to have sex, but that it was immoral unless you were married.

I learned that sex was filthy before marriage, but glorious afterward. It was mysterious and fearsome, eliciting powerful urges and fantasies that had to be controlled and disciplined. Unmarried people who were sexually active because they could not control these urges, or didn't care to, were contemptible, and their reputations were scarred for life. People who could control their urges were honorable and saintly. Sexuality, I learned, is the primary and most serious moral category in life, far ahead of honesty, charity, peace, and justice. Almost every other fault and sin can be overlooked or forgiven, but not the sins of sexual indiscretion.

Consequently, the erotic desires I had first discovered under the mimosa tree became mixed up over time with feelings of fear, shame, and guilt. I wrestled alone with the shame of pleasure and the guilt of wanting to touch and hold a girl, not knowing how to reconcile them with the moral lessons I had internalized. The way I unconsciously chose to control my inner conflict was to avoid being emotionally close to any girl.

In the ninth grade, I was crazy in love with Judi, a seventh grader. She was astonishingly beautiful, with a body developed well ahead of her age. We considered ourselves to be going steady. Once we went together to the public library to do homework. Between the book stacks, we stood close together, leaning our bodies against one another, our faces touching. I felt our bodies steaming. Judi closed her eyes and tilted her head back. I kissed her. My heart nearly stopped, and my body shivered with excitement. I was terrified.

I called Judi the next day to tell her I wanted to break up. I didn't explain why, just said I didn't want to go steady with her any longer. Naturally, my rejection hurt her. She thought it was her fault, thought she'd done something wrong or that something was wrong with her to make me stop liking her. I felt guilty. But I also felt safer. The truth was, she'd done something wonderful; she was wonderful, and I liked her too much. I couldn't handle the intense emotions and erotic passion I felt for her. I had to run away from them by leaving her.

I was incapable of having the experience I had freely and innocently enjoyed under the mimosa tree. That became a nostalgic remnant of childhood safely stored away in my memory. Even though I went on dates as a youth and young adult, I was careful to avoid intimacy and never had another steady girlfriend. The next girl with whom I allowed myself to become emotionally involved, I married.

It took much reading and hard rethinking as an adult to recover the innocence I experienced under the mimosa tree. When I was sexually intimate for the first time with the woman I married, all of the old negative scripts and conflicts about sex played out in my mind. Over time, however, I came to understand that sexual relations are essential to our emotional, psychological, and physical health, as well as to true marital intimacy and bonding. The historical association of sexuality with sin is not biblical, but the fault of Christian theology based on Greek philosophy (see the next chapter), which has caused much harm for over two millennia. This is the Christian church's original sin, blaspheming God's good creation.

Growing up, I spent so much time at St. Paul Methodist Church that it was like my second home. To this day, I can see the pictures of biblical stories and characters on the Sunday school walls, smell the odor of the fellowship hall, taste the Kool-Aid and vanilla wafers we'd have during summer Bible school, and feel myself once again in the mysteriously dark furnace room below the sanctuary, where Mr. West, the janitor, hung out. I'd often steal away to sit there with other children, when we should have been in choir or Sunday school, to hear his amazing stories about fighting in the First World War.

Sunday school teachers and pastors emphasized the golden rule, the story of the Good Samaritan, the stories of Jesus, and the Great Commandment: "Love God with all your heart, soul, mind, and strength; and your neighbor as yourself." In the midst of the Bible Belt, dominated by Southern Baptist evangelicalism, St. Paul Methodist Church conveyed to me the spirit of Methodism's founder, John Wesley, who gave priority to piety over dogma and doctrine, and to social responsibility over purity and personal salvation.

Because of this influence, as a young teenager I struggled to discern a purpose for my life that would contribute to a better world. Not knowing what that purpose was caused me much anguish. The more I thought about it, the more lost and frustrated I felt. Many nights I lay in bed staring in the dark, searching my mind and heart for an answer, and praying for guidance.

Then I discovered Dr. Tom Dooley, who became my hero. I read his books about his experiences as a doctor in Vietnam and Laos.[1] He went to South Vietnam in 1954 as a doctor in the U.S. Navy. There he supervised a medical assistance program for refugees fleeing North Vietnam. After he was discharged in 1956, he returned to Southeast Asia to set up hospitals and clinics. He founded the Medical International Cooperation Organization (MEDICO). In 1959, he was diagnosed with cancer, and he died in 1961 at the age of thirty-four. He was posthumously awarded the Congressional Gold Medal, the highest civilian award given by the U.S. Congress.

I was impressed that Dooley devoted his medical career to people who lived in a part of the world that was then little known to Americans. But, what most impressed me was the story he told about his struggle to decide what to do with his life. In one of his books, he described his sense of being adrift, of having no specific direction, purpose, or meaning for his life. Although all seemed to be going well for him on the outside, something on the inside made him uneasy and restless. Being a successful and wealthy doctor in the United States, in spite of the good he could do wherever he chose to practice, was not enough. In Southeast Asia he found his calling, and his search for purpose ended.

Dooley described what I was feeling and thus strengthened my yearning for a clear sense of purpose. Thanks to his books, I no longer felt alone in my struggle. Because he was able to find his purpose, I was able to relax and trust that somehow I, too, would discover the meaning and purpose of my life.

As I write about how important Tom Dooley was to me, reflecting on my journey and where I am today, I smile, remembering this young doctor who devoted his life to the people of Southeast Asia. I also grieve because, in doing research for my own book, I discovered that Dooley was given a dishonorable discharge by the U.S. Navy because he was gay.[2] Although he was publicly celebrated as an extraordinary example of generosity and mercy, the navy considered him undesirable and kicked him out. Dooley, a devout Roman Catholic and exemplary citizen of the world, suffered the hatred of a culture shaped by the Christian church's misguided teachings, policies, and practices about homosexuality.

There were others who were important influences in my youth, especially teachers, who I only discovered much later shared Tom Dooley's secret. They gave generously to me and other young people, encouraging us to embrace our humanity, develop our potential, and discover our places in life, all the while having to hide the truth about their own humanity and deny their full potential. No matter how honorable and giving they were, they would have been fired and ostracized if their homosexuality had been discovered. Along with Tom Dooley, they were victims of the same bigotry that I had used much earlier against Pee-Wee.

As I pondered what I was going to do with my life, I felt I had no special skills or talents. I didn't consider myself to be especially smart or creative. I didn't like public attention, and I certainly didn't like speaking in front of an audience. Whenever I had to make a presentation in class or at church, my mind would lock up and my body would shake; I felt that I couldn't think and speak at the same time. Not surprisingly, I never considered becoming a preacher.

However, that changed in the summer of 1962, before my senior year in high school, when my calling came out of the blue. I was one of six young people in a church-sponsored summer program that provided services to migrant farmworkers along the coast of North Carolina.

Each year, thousands of farmworkers migrated through the area picking cabbage, tobacco, and other cash crops. Farmworkers are the most economically oppressed people in the country, often living in virtual slavery. In 1962, those who worked the East Coast were almost exclusively African American (Latinos and Haitians wouldn't begin to supplant black farmworkers on the East Coast until the late 1970s).

Farmworkers traveled along the coast in old trucks or buses and lived in camps that usually consisted of dilapidated shacks, abandoned farmhouses, and barns. The ground around the housing was bare dirt, dusty during droughts and muddy when it rained. Well water for drinking and bathing was often contaminated with human waste from a nearby outhouse.

The work was hard, lasting from early morning until dark, six days a week. In the fields, the workers were exposed to blistering sun and oppressive humidity, as well as toxic insecticides and herbicides. They couldn't afford to get sick and miss work, and many workers ignored infected cuts and even broken bones. Tuberculosis, hepatitis, pneumonia, and abscessed teeth were common.

Migrant camps were located on remote rural roads, hidden from public view. Because the length of time the farmworkers stayed in any one place was brief—usually just one to two weeks at a time—they had no connection with local people or nearby small towns. No one, either black or white, reached out to invite them to church or community events. They were invisible and isolated amid people who required their labor yet ignored their existence.

During the ten days of the youth service program for migrants, we sorted clothing that had been sent for the farmworkers by church groups from all over the state. We traveled with a mobile medical unit, a van stocked with basic medical supplies and equipment, and staffed by local doctors and dentists who had volunteered their services. We also staffed a childcare center for the migrants' children.

On the second Sunday, near the end of the program, I went to a farmworkers' camp early in the morning with a black minister who was employed by the National Council of Churches to lead worship for the migrants. He drove a large station wagon that he had named the Harvester. Inside was a portable organ, a small table with a cross and Bible, a lectern, and an assortment of old, worn hymnals.

As we drove up the dirt road and the camp came into sight, men, women, and children spilled out of the buildings into the parking area to greet us. Many ran toward us while still dressing, pulling up pants, buttoning blouses, hopping on one foot while putting a shoe on the other. As they crowded around us, helping to unload the Harvester, the air was heavy with the sweet odor of cheap wine and fortified malt liquor. I realized the enthusiastic reception was partly because the farmworkers were drunk.

The leaders of the program had prepared us for this, explaining that when the farmworkers stopped work late on Saturday evenings, they routinely began to drink, mostly cheap wine and malt liquor bought from the crew leaders. They drank late into the night until they passed out, and they started drinking again when they woke in the morning. They drank to mask their bodies' pain and exhaustion from the week's punishing work, to numb the despair of their wretched existence, and to blunt the humiliation of being isolated and ignored by the rest of humanity. Intoxication was their survival, their salvation. And on that Sunday morning, it was the elixir of their spirits!

Many of them couldn't read, yet they held the hymnals like holy objects and sang with loud, unrestrained voices as the minister played the organ. He led the workers in the Lord's Prayer, which all of them could recite by heart. I read a passage from the Gospel of Matthew about the birds of the air and the lilies of the field, and how God takes care of them, feeds them, and clothes them. "Do not worry about tomorrow," I read, "today's trouble is enough for today."[3]

I felt good out there in the fields, far away from churches, stores, and nicely kept homes, surrounded by these hardworking people. The scripture's reassuring words for the moment glossed over the reality of the migrants' world for me, just as the alcohol had for them.

As we began to reload the Harvester, a tall, lean man emerged from the scattering farmworkers and approached me with a child I recognized from the childcare center. The man's clothes were dirty and ragged, the sleeves of his shirt tightly rolled above his elbows, exposing his lean, muscular arms. There was a somber expression on his face, no polite or apologetic smile. His eyes, bloodshot and jaundiced, fixed relentlessly on mine. His scarred and callused hands gripped the shoulders of the young boy now standing in front of him. He was completely earnest when he spoke directly to me, urgently pleading. "Save my son from this life."

I was stunned. God was speaking to me that morning in the passionate prayer of a black man whose breath reeked of wine, a profound irony for a privileged white Southern boy. I don't remember how I responded, or what I did. I suspect that if I could remember, I'd be embarrassed by my banality and ineptitude.

There would be other influences over following years that would confirm my vocation, but I remember this encounter as my call to ministry. I had been confronted with the truth that words without action, without flesh, were words without meaning, without hope. The message of God's love is pleasing to hear, but when there is suffering and no justice, freedom, mercy, or peace, that message sounds fanciful and false.

I returned home bursting with an evangelical passion, almost a mania, to tell everyone I could about the suffering of the migrant farmworkers and the need for the church to end it. One evening at the local dairy bar, I ran into the pastor of St. Luke Methodist Church, an offshoot of St. Paul Methodist Church on the prosperous eastern edge of Goldsboro. He greeted me cheerfully and asked about the summer program. I briefly described what I'd learned and what I believed the church should do to help the farm-workers. He listened politely until I asked if I could come to St. Luke and make a presentation. From crown to chin, his balding head grew beet red, his eyes widened with fear, and—quickly turning on his heel to leave—he stammered: "G-great idea! I'll . . . I'll get back with you about that." He never did. Migrant farmworkers provided cheap and dependable labor—and they didn't stay. The people of Goldsboro didn't want to know about their suffering, and they especially didn't want to be told they were responsible for it.

Of course, something else was involved in the minister's rush away from my suggestion, an issue that was always under the surface of nearly every injustice in the South: racism. Raising questions about the injustices that migrant farmworkers experienced risked raising larger questions about racial disparities and injustice. White Southerners were adept at not seeing the harsh realities that African Americans experienced.

St. Paul Methodist Church was a congregation of good, Christian people, all white. They taught me to sing: "Jesus loves the little children, all the children of the world. Red and yellow, black and white, they are precious in his sight." I didn't understand it at the time, but in spite of the love ethic the people of St. Paul taught and tried to live, they were blinded by racism and could not see their infidelity to the gospel of Jesus Christ.

I heard church ushers angrily declare: "If any colored people come to the church door, I won't let them in. They don't want to worship with us. They just want to cause trouble." I heard Sunday school teachers use the Bible to justify and defend slavery by referring to the Apostle Paul's statement that slaves should be obedient to their masters, and masters should treat their slaves kindly (Colossians 3:22–4:1). I heard church leaders argue that the black race had been condemned to slavery—a misreading of Genesis 9:22–27—that the races shouldn't mix, and that segregation is the will of God, using such scriptures as Leviticus 19:19 and chapters 9–10 of Ezra to support their claims.

In Goldsboro, every social institution was segregated: churches, schools, courts, hospitals. Even in death, whites and blacks were kept apart, buried in separate cemeteries. Because the reality I lived in was racially segregated,

I didn't question it or the justifications for it that I'd been taught. How could my parents, teachers, and ministers all be wrong about this?

The climate of race relations in Goldsboro was placid and noncontroversial in the early years of my life, but in the late 1950s, it began to change. The Reverend Dr. Martin Luther King Jr. and the civil rights movement fired up a passion for justice and equality in Goldsboro's black community. Even inundated by the media bombast of Southern racism, the eloquent dignity of black people, the righteousness of their cause, and the courage of their commitment was obvious. Southern culture, with its false underpinnings of religion, law, and custom, was being exposed to the nation, the world, and me.

The Southern media labeled King a rabble-rouser, a communist, and a threat to the national order. Yet I was fascinated by the dignity of this black preacher, who talked of love, nonviolence, justice, and equality. My experience in a stratified society showed me the truth of what he said. I was also inspired by the thousands of black people who rallied to his message of nonviolent protest in the face of violent white opposition. I was appalled by the lynchings, bombings, shootings, and beatings perpetrated by whites against blacks, believing them to be shameful and contrary to everything I understood about civil and Christian behavior. I heard people I respected and considered models of Christian virtue and civic responsibility condemn Dr. King and the blacks who followed him for violating the "will of God" and trying to change the "way it's always been." I saw the religion I knew to be a positive force for good used to justify prejudice, injustice, and even violence.

These white people were good people. They cared about the schools, churches, and community—at least, their schools, churches, and community. They loved their families and their neighbors. I never heard them speak harshly of others or threaten violence. But when the civil rights movement and racial equality came up in conversation, something awful and evil came out of their souls, and they spoke as if possessed. Anger, hatred, fear, and violent impulses contorted their faces, profaned their language, and controlled their behavior.

I often heard it said that those who fought for racial justice and equality deserved the violence they got in return. Even my father—a good, gentle, and kind person whom I loved and respected deeply—held this belief. I was shocked when his response to the brutal murders in 1964 of Andrew Goodman, James Chaney, and Michael Schwerner, civil rights workers in Mississippi, was: "It was their fault; they shouldn't have meddled." It was a sobering wake-up call for me. I learned that evil is perpetrated not only by malevolent people, but also by good people who resist change and protect the status quo. The evil that good people do because of fear and bigotry was a revelation to me, and it prepared me well to understand years later how the persecution of gay people is condoned and promoted by both church and society.

The church had been central to my life. It was the foundation for all I believed to be good and true. But during the civil rights struggle, I discovered it was also a defender of injustice and bigotry. The contradiction became more and more apparent to me. Nonetheless, I clung to the positive side of the church, hoping it could prevail over the adulterous side.

After high school, I enrolled at the University of North Carolina, Chapel Hill. I majored in biblical studies, with my goal being ordination as a minister. In my Old Testament classes, I discovered the prophetic literature in the Hebrew scriptures. As a youth, I had heard a lot about God's command for us to love, but I had not heard about God's requirement to "do justice" (Micah 6:8). I had not been instructed to "seek justice, correct oppression; defend the fatherless and plead for the widow" (Isaiah 1:17). I had not been told to "let justice roll down like waters, and righteousness like an ever-flowing stream" (Amos 5:24).

The Christian love I'd learned about as a child was a charitable love. It was a personal, one-on-one love of neighbor; a love that operated within the status quo, that treated the symptoms, not the causes, of suffering. Love's demand for justice was a new dimension to the divine love that Jesus embodied. Christian discipleship, I discovered, meant working to set people free from whatever holds them in bondage, whatever denies fullness of life, by dismantling the cultural systems and structures of injustice and by creating a community where all of God's children are welcomed and blessed. As I studied the prophets, I imagined that migrant farmworker standing before me like an Amos demanding justice, and I better understood why our encounter had affected me so.

I learned that the Hebrews, later to be called Jews, perceived the liberating and compassionate activity of the divine in the events of human history. They found the language of God in action — not philosophy, as the Greeks had done. The Hebrew God is no abstraction held captive in idols, whether of stone, wood, or words. This God is free, alive, and unpredictable, doing surprising deeds to create a just and compassionate world.

This is a God who hears the cry of the wretched, the poor, the oppressed, and the forsaken and responds to it. This is not a God who protects the status quo, for in the story of Israel, injustice and corruption always infect the institutions of power, from the palace and the market to the temple. This God champions not the wealthy and the powerful, but the poor and the weak. The biblical stories make it clear that the Holy is a subversive power constantly working to overthrow social systems of arrogance, injustice, and greed in favor of a community of equals. To be obedient is to work with God, to allow God to work through you, to make this community a reality.

In the summer of 1965, following my sophomore year at the University of North Carolina, I traveled to Syria, Lebanon, Jordan, and Israel to study with the Institute for Mediterranean Studies. There I was struck by the Middle Eastern cultural norms governing male and female relations. It was common to see two men strolling together holding hands, and kissing in greeting or at parting. Women always walked behind men, and men and women never had physical contact in public. With the cultural bias drummed into me that forbade men to show affection to men, this amazed me. I was not prepared for it. It shook my assumptions about gender roles and permissible physical contact.

One night, just outside Jerusalem's ancient walls, I went for a walk alone in the Kidron Valley. Out of the shadows, a man approached me. Wearing traditional Arabic garb — a robe and kaffiyeh of white cotton — he spoke in Arabic, mixed with some broken English and supplemented with dramatic gestures. He beckoned me to follow him toward something ahead of us just off the dirt path, hidden in the dark. Without hesitation, I followed him to a small stable, where two donkeys were secured for the night. A sign on the stable explained in Arabic, French, and English that this was the road on which Jesus had entered Jerusalem on Palm Sunday, riding a donkey like the ones in the stable.

Then the man took my hand in his. I froze in panic. He pulled insistently, urging me to come with him. My feet moved, tripping forward, even though I was afraid of what was about to happen. He led me up the hill toward the Garden of Gethsemane, still holding my hand. I could see lights in homes along the way, but the street was unlighted, and I felt completely vulnerable.

All the way up the steep road, my heart pounded inside my chest, yet I resisted my instinctive fear of danger, refusing to pull away and run.

When we reached the top of the hill, we walked to a large outcropping of rock, surrounded by ancient olive trees. The man let go of my hand and gently touched the surface of the rock, tracing a slight depression with his fingers. With dramatic gestures, he explained that this was where Jesus ascended after the resurrection, and that the depression was Jesus's final footprint.

He was pleased that he'd shown this sacred spot to me, as if he had shared a treasured secret. "Come tomorrow," he said, "and I'll show you more." I hardly knew what to do, having struggled all the way against fear and now discovering that this was a gracious gesture by an anonymous man in a foreign land. I expressed gratitude to my guide for showing me these sacred sites. He bowed his head, offered words of praise to Allah, and left me there alone.

I walked slowly back down the road to my hotel in the valley below. Stars sparkled in the moonless sky. I felt light, free of the fear I'd carried up the hill. I could still sense the man's hand holding my own. It no longer felt menacing.

Back in North Carolina for the fall semester of my junior year, I read a short story for an English class about a boy at camp. On the first day of camp, Mike's father goes with him to the cabin where he'll stay for the summer to help him put his things away and make his bed. As his father leaves, they shake hands and wish each other well for the summer.

Other boys arrive with their fathers and the same ritual is repeated, except that Mike's cabinmate hugs and kisses his father when he leaves, instead of just shaking hands. Mike is impressed by this display of affection. He and his father haven't hugged and kissed since Mike was a child, in spite of the fact that they love each other very much. He isn't sure about the propriety of a father and son kissing. He thinks such male intimacy is unseemly and childish, not manly.

Midway through the summer, Mike learns that his father has died. He's grief-stricken. The memory of his cabinmate's kissing his father good-bye has stayed with him, and now Mike regrets that he hadn't done the same with his father. He longs to see his father, to tell him how much he loves him, to hold and be held by him, and to kiss him.

I was deeply moved by the story and began to reflect on my relationship with my father, about how we did and didn't show each other affection. We shook hands and sometimes hugged, but that was about it. Perhaps, I thought, our conditioned fear of homosexuality was interfering with our freedom to express affection to one another. I decided that I would kiss my father to greet him and to say good-bye from then on. I also decided that, if I ever had a son, I would hug and kiss him as long as I lived, no matter what his age. I would not allow the fear of homosexuality to restrict me from showing affection to my father or to my son, should I have one.

On my next visit home, I greeted Dad with an embrace and a kiss on his cheek. I felt his body stiffen—I had caught him off guard. He made no comment. When I left a few days later to return to college, I did the same thing. Again, he stiffened, but he did not protest or resist. Over time, my father relaxed and learned to embrace me and accept my kiss on his cheek or forehead. He never kissed me in return, however. And we never talked about it.

Another work of literature that was important to me was James Baldwin's *Giovanni's Room*, a novel about two men's love for one another, set in Paris. Baldwin's sensitive, sympathetic portrayal of gay passion and heartbreak exposed me to the possibility of loving sexual intimacy between men. I found the story to be poignant and tragic, in no way repulsive. I didn't know that Baldwin was gay until years later, and in college I marveled at his compassionate portrayal of the kind of relationship that I had long thought to be perverse and taboo. While I considered the book purely fiction, having no immediate impact on my attitude about homosexuality, it planted a seed of doubt in my mind about the sinfulness of homosexuality that would fully mature later on.

After graduation from the University of North Carolina, I attended divinity school at Duke University from 1967 to 1970, a turbulent period in U.S. history. The Vietnam War was raging in Southeast Asia, and opposition to it was raging on college and university campuses around the country and in the streets of major cities. The struggle for racial justice continued unresolved, exacerbated by the assassinations of Dr. King and Robert Kennedy, economic discrimination, and the racism of the war. The Democratic national convention in Chicago stained the ideals of American democracy with violence and repression. Cambodia was bombed. The Soviet Union crushed a democratic reform movement, "Communism with a human face," in Czechoslovakia. This was the context, the state of the world, when my understanding of what God wanted me do, of what it means to follow

Jesus, and of ministry were being shaped at Duke Divinity School. This context, along with what I was learning in the classroom, convinced me that genuine ministry must be engaged with the real world, with its politics, injustice, and suffering. Again, the memory of the black farmworker spoke to me, calling me to a ministry of justice and compassion.

The theological priority of liberation was reiterated by Frederick Herzog, professor of systematic theology at Duke. Fred taught that the "text" of our faith (the Hebrew and Christian scriptures) and the "context" of our lives were in constant dialogue, each addressing the other with questions about what we should do, how we should act, to be faithful followers of Jesus. Fred believed the most important work in Christian theology at that time was being done by blacks in the United States, by those involved in the South African liberation movement, and in Latin America by the poor, the politically disenfranchised, and other persecuted and exploited people who could best understand and articulate the revolutionary, liberating message of the Christian gospel. "If God is not the God of the oppressed," Fred wrote, "he is not the God of the New Testament. [God] is struggling for new life among the oppressed and not among the affluent (especially the affluent churches)."[4] He also wrote: "There is only one point to human life on this earth: Participation in God's struggle for a life of justice . . . [W]hether the struggle for a just life is effective or ineffective is not the issue. The meaning of life is in the struggle."[5]

When I completed my studies at Duke Divinity School, I applied for ordination in the North Carolina Annual Conference[6] of The United Methodist Church. My application was not approved without controversy and resistance. Interestingly, this was not because of my theology. No one on the Board of Ordained Ministry seemed troubled by that, although I was told there was "too much horizontal and not much vertical" in my understanding of God and the church. What caused the board difficulty was the length of my hair. Considering that this was the early 1970s, my hair wasn't all that long, only covering my ears, but my sideburns were wide and full, running down to just above my chin. It took two interviews and a last-minute meeting with the board on the day of ordination before they finally gave me, my hair, and sideburns their approval. I was ordained a United Methodist minister by Bishop Robert Blackburn in June 1970.

My first appointment was to Edenton Street United Methodist Church, in Raleigh, as an associate pastor. The large, wealthy, and prestigious "Mother

Church" of eastern North Carolina, Edenton Street Church served as my finishing school, giving me the real-life experience that divinity school couldn't. But after three years there, I wanted the opportunity to serve a congregation on my own. At my request, I was appointed to the United Methodist church in a village of approximately five hundred people on Ocracoke, a remote island off the North Carolina coast. Bucking Methodist tradition, in which the average length of a pastor's tenure at one church is two years, I served the Ocracoke church for eight. Then, in 1981, the bishop appointed me to be the pastor of the United Methodist church in Warsaw, a small town in eastern North Carolina. It was there that I met Adam in 1984.

Before Adam's revelation, I was vaguely aware that there was a gay world somewhere, parallel to but distinct from my own. Adam brought the two worlds together for me, teaching me that the alien gay world I imagined was really a hidden and painful dimension of the world in which I lived. Until he opened my eyes, I was unaware that The United Methodist Church, and the Christian church in general, persecuted gay people. I'd given no attention to the hurtful language about homosexuality in *The Book of Discipline of The United Methodist Church*, which contains the rules and policies that govern the church to which I belonged.

Ultimately, my reaction to Adam moved from personal reflection to pastoral responsibility. If my response to him and other gay people was to be appropriate for a Christian minister, I needed to do a great deal of research and study. I needed to know and understand what the Bible said about homosexuality, what the Christian church had taught about it over the past two thousand years, and what the most current scientific studies on sexuality revealed.

Because it is basic to Christian belief, the Bible was the initial focus of my research. I had often heard people claim that the Bible says homosexuality is a sin, and I had simply accepted that claim without any critical thought. But I didn't know what evidence there was for the claim. The issue of homosexuality in a religious context never came up during my four years of biblical studies at the University of North Carolina or during my three at Duke Divinity School. So I had some research to do.

I first went to *The Interpreter's Dictionary of the Bible* (*IDB*)[1] and found unambiguous statements denouncing homosexuality, such as "in the legal codes homosexual relations are forbidden as an abomination worthy of death," and, "homosexuals are among those condemned by Paul." The entry for "sodomite" read: "An English common noun, derived from the story of SODOM in Genesis 18–19, meaning a male person who engages in sexual relations with another male. The men of Sodom demanded that Lot surrender his two male guests (angels) to them for sexual purposes: 'Bring them out to us, that we may know them' (Genesis 19:5). The wickedness of Sodom became proverbial."[2]

In addition, the IDB identified seven biblical passages[3] that it claimed specifically condemned homosexuality. This initial research seemed to confirm the claim that homosexuality is a sin, according to the Bible. Had it not been for Adam, my exploration of the scriptures' comments on homosexuality would have ended.

But I wasn't satisfied. If homosexual acts were violent, wicked, depraved, and unholy, as they were described in the IDB, then I had a problem. These words did not describe Adam. If the Apostle Paul had known Adam, on what basis could he have judged my friend to be unrighteous? I was not willing to consign Adam to this condemned company, to pronounce him a sinner because he was gay, and to say that God did not love people like him. I felt compelled to investigate further, to try to understand why homosexuality was considered so reprehensible by the biblical writers.

To gain a larger context for my study, I stepped outside of the biblical text and did some reading in the social sciences about human sexuality in general, and homosexuality in particular. While I had the words *homosexual* and *homosexuality* to guide my search through biblical reference works, I was not fully informed of their scientific meaning and history. All I had so far was the very limited description of same-gender sexual conduct in a very few verses of scripture.

In my reading, I found that homosexuality, bisexuality, and heterosexuality are words that were invented in the field of psychology to refer to these sexual orientations when, in the late 1800s, they were discovered to be natural and innate aspects of human sexuality. Prior to this time, there was no understanding of sexuality as a dimension of the human personality, or of the various sexual orientations within the human species. People do not choose their sexual orientation, whichever one it is. Rather, it is an essential, normal, and natural part of every person's identity, along with ethnicity, gender, and personality traits. Homosexuality is not a disorder or pathology that should be corrected, changed, or cured. It is a sexual orientation that is a natural, normal, and healthy aspect of being human.

Sexual orientation, I learned, is more than genital sexual behavior. People who are heterosexual sometimes engage in same-gender sexual behavior, and people who are homosexual sometimes engage in other-gender sexual behavior. It is not behavior that determines and defines a person's sexual orientation. Rather, sexual orientation is an essential aspect of personality that predisposes a person to be sexually attracted to one — or both, in the case of bisexuals — of the two genders, whether or not the person is sexually active. Just as a person can be heterosexual and a virgin, one can be homosexual and a virgin. Orientation does not begin and end with sex acts. It is a constant and vital part of who a person is, encompassing erotic attraction, affection, and bonding as well as genital activity. Which orientation one has is determined by a complex of factors, both genetic and environmental.

This study of human sexuality, here briefly summarized (I will present more information in chapter 10), helped me understand that the biblical writers had known just as little about sexual orientation as they did about nuclear fission or aerodynamics. In scripture, sex was understood solely as genital activity motivated by lust, love, or the desire to have a child; it was regulated by social custom, not by an innate aspect of the personality. In fact, the biblical languages of Hebrew, Aramaic, and Greek had no words for heterosexuality, bisexuality, and homosexuality, words that weren't invented until the late nineteenth century CE. I now understood that it could not be the orientation of homosexuality that the Bible condemns, but rather specific same-gender sexual behaviors. Consequently, I realized that the claim "the Bible says homosexuality is a sin" is misleading and inappropriate, since the biblical writers had no knowledge of sexual orientation in general, or of homosexuality in particular. They couldn't discuss, much less condemn, something they knew nothing about.

I went back to the Bible with a new set of questions: Why is the same-gender sexual activity described in the Bible condemned? What was objectionable or unethical about the acts described? Could any of these passages be interpreted as condemning loving same-gender sexual intimacy? These questions pushed me beyond the standard resources in my personal library. I discovered a body of scholarship that gave me a new understanding of the historical and cultural contexts of the biblical references to same-gender sexual acts (see the selected bibliography). Here's what I learned.

The legendary story of Sodom and Gomorrah (Genesis 19:1–29), often cited as evidence of God's wrathful rejection of homosexuality, is about an intended male-against-male gang rape of two strangers (actually angels in the guise of men) who had come out of the wilderness in search of shelter and safety (there is a similar but barely known story in Judges 19). In the ancient patriarchal culture of the Bible, the rape of men by men was especially humiliating because the male victim was thereby demoted to the inferior and subservient status of a woman. This violent behavior was motivated neither by sexual attraction nor lust, nor is it proof that the men of Sodom were homosexual. Rather, it was evidence of Sodom's xenophobia and inhospitality. Inhospitality, not homosexuality, was the sin of Sodom.

Along with Gomorrah, Sodom is known in the Hebrew and Christian scriptures as the preeminent example of divine judgment and punishment for inhospitality, greed, arrogance, and violence. Ezekiel, for example, says: "Behold, this was the guilt of your sister Sodom: she and her daughters had pride, surfeit of food, and prosperous ease, but did not aid the poor and needy. They were haughty and did abominable things before me; therefore, I removed them when I saw it" (16:49–50).[4]

Only one of the biblical references to Sodom's sin says it was primarily sexual in nature. That lone exception is Jude 7, but for a reason unrelated to same-gender sexual behavior. The passage reads: *"Sodom and Gomorrah . . .* acted immorally and *indulged in unnatural lust"* (emphasis added). The Greek words that are translated as "indulged in unnatural lust" actually mean "went after other flesh." Jude's concern is that the subjects of the intended rape are angels, who—by virtue of not being human—were of "other flesh." Consequently, Jude is not concerned with same-gender sexual behavior.

The terms *sodomy* and *sodomite*, derived from the story of Sodom in Genesis, are of medieval origin, coined to refer to same-gender sexual activity and those who engage in it.[5] They were also used to refer to all sex acts that were not procreative in nature, such as anal and oral sex between a woman and a man. But the story of Sodom is about intended male-against-male violent rape, not about healthy, caring, loving sexual intimacy. To equate sodomy, derived from a story of violence, with homosexuality violates logic and lacks scholarly integrity. It is also not biblical, but reads into the story of Sodom the popular prejudice against gays. The linguistic history of *sodomy* and *sodomite* demonstrates how prejudice becomes institutionalized and perpetuated through language—how words can carry the deadly viruses of ignorance, falsehood, fear, and bigotry. Biblical scholars have unwittingly perpetuated this prejudice by uncritically using these words, even in modern times, thereby misinforming seminarians, clergy, Sunday school teachers, and lay people for generations. Such words do violence to truth and people, while hiding behind tradition and piety.

Two passages in the book of Leviticus are regularly cited as condemning homosexuality: "you shall not lie with a male as with a woman; it is an abomination" (18:22), and "if a man lies with a male as with a woman, both of them have committed an abomination; they shall be put to death" (20:13). These passages are found within the cultic ritual and ethical laws known in biblical scholarship as "the Holiness Code" (Leviticus 17–20). The purpose for this collection of laws is explained in the text this way: "You shall not do as they do in the land of Egypt, where you dwelt, and you shall not do as they do in the land of Canaan, to which I am bringing you. You shall not walk in their statutes. You shall do my ordinances and keep my statutes and walk in them" (18:3–4).

When the Hebrews settled in the land of Canaan, their national identity and unique religion were threatened by assimilation with the indigenous culture of the Canaanites. These were crucial survival issues for a young nation that had been a nomadic tent-dwelling people dependent upon cattle, who were now adjusting to a sedentary, agrarian life. The concern, then, of the Leviticus verses quoted above was not a particular sexual ethic, but rather rules designed to maintain the distinct Hebrew cultural and religious identity.

The Canaanites, who were ultimately dominated by the Hebrews, possessed highly developed agricultural skills and understood the rhythms of the seasons and the fertility of the earth. Their god, Baal, was a divinity rooted in the mystical power of sexuality, whose greatest virtue was its predictable, cyclical nature—mirroring the reproductive cycles of birth, life, and death. Sexual intercourse in the temples of Baal with female as well as male prostitutes, known as "holy ones," was believed to ensure and enhance the fertility of the land.

The God of the Hebrews was a dynamic god who couldn't be pinned down, moving constantly into the future, doing and creating new and unpredictable things. This is just the kind of god who could lead you through a wilderness. But what power did the Hebrew God have in this new setting?

Baal was attractive to the Hebrews because he promised and seemingly delivered fruitful harvests. But succumbing to this foreign god would threaten the integrity and uniqueness of the religion of the Hebrews. Consequently, scholars explain, the men of Israel were forbidden to "lie with a man as with a woman," because doing so imitated the worship of Baal, which was idolatrous. An idolatrous act was called an "abomination" in the Bible because it was believed to be offensive to God, violating the second commandment: "You shall have no other gods before [or besides] me" (Exodus 20:3–6).

Another aspect of Hebrew culture that contributes to the Holiness Code is rigidly defined gender roles. Hebrew culture was patriarchal. Men controlled and owned women as property. For a man to assume the role of a woman was to abdicate his role of authority in the community. For a man to treat another man as if he were a woman was a great offense and a violation of community. According to Leviticus 20:13, these behaviors were so objectionable that they warranted death for both parties.

Today, these proscriptions have nothing to do with gay, lesbian, and bisexual persons in loving, caring same-gender sexual relations. They are relics of a fight that no longer needs to be waged, vestiges of a time that no longer exists. Gay people need not abstain from sexual expressions of love because of ancient strategies for ethnic and cultural purity and national survival. There is no justification for maintaining a patriarchal cultural norm that, by rigidly defining gender roles, imposes a hierarchical social order that puts men above women and denies people the freedom to love and bond without regard to gender.

The passages from the Holiness Code found in Leviticus are echoed in the Apostle Paul's letter to the Romans, written to a Jewish community living in a gentile world. His first chapter is most often cited as conclusive evidence of the condemnation of homosexuality in Christian scripture. In this chapter, Paul's specific concern is with the idolatry of the gentiles. But his overarching concern is what he perceives to be the universal human condition, "since all have sinned and fall short of the glory of God" (3:23).

Paul identifies the sin of the gentiles, or "Greeks," as their rebellion against "God's truth" and their practice of idolatry: "they exchanged the truth about God for a lie and worshipped and served the creature rather than the Creator" (1:25). Paul then describes what he believes is one consequence of the gentiles' worship of "lies and creatures" (other words for idols): "For this reason God gave them up to dishonorable passions. Their women exchanged natural relations for unnatural, and the men likewise gave up natural relations with women and were consumed with passion for one another, men committing shameless acts with men" (1:26–27).

Paul says same-gender sexual conduct is a consequence of the sin, not the sin itself. Furthermore, it is only one of the consequences. He lists many others in a diatribe that labels as morally corrupt all who practice non-Jewish and non-Christian religions: "And since they did not see fit to acknowledge God, God gave them up to a base mind and to improper conduct. They were filled with all manner of wickedness, evil, covetousness, malice. Full of envy, murder, strife, deceit, malignity, they are gossips, slanderers, haters of God, insolent, haughty, boastful, inventors of evil, disobedient to parents, foolish, faithless, heartless, ruthless. Though they know God's decree that those who do such things deserve to die, they not only do them but even approve those others who practice them" (1:28–32).

For Paul, a "base mind" and "improper conduct" emanate from idolatry and rebellion against the truth of God.

As a devout Jew and rabbinical student, Paul knew well the long struggle of the Jews to resist the fertility religions in their homeland. He knew the Levitical Holiness Code and its prohibition against sexual behavior between men and its relationship to pagan worship. But, Paul had no understanding of sexual orientation, so he could not attribute same-gender sexual conduct to it. As a man shaped by the Jewish patriarchal culture of the first century BCE, he understood men and women to have specific and distinct social and political roles. Neither sex, he believed, should assume the role of the other. Like the writers of Leviticus, Paul assumed that same-gender sexual activity turns the world upside down and is "unnatural," his term for what is contrary to convention. To worship the creature instead of the creator is equally "unnatural" to his Jewish mind.

While there was no public tolerance of same-gender sexual conduct among the Jews, there was such tolerance in the gentile world. The most prevalent form of same-gender sexual conduct of which Paul would have been aware was pederasty, a common practice in the Greek world since as early as the seventh century BCE. This was a social arrangement in which an adult male acted as mentor to an adolescent boy in exchange for sexual gratification. This practice was not limited or defined by the sexual orientation of either the man or the boy. It was generally practiced by wealthy men, who were usually married with children, and the young boys did not become homosexuals because of this experience. In ancient Greece, the practice of pederasty had strict guidelines to protect young boys from exploitation and abuse. However, the Roman world of Paul's day lacked the social controls and public respectability of ancient Greece, and young boys were often exploited and abused by older men who preyed on them sexually. Paul was not the only critic of pederasty. Many of the pagan philosophers and moralists of his day also condemned it.

The publicly recognized same-gender sexual activity that Paul would have known was that related to idolatry and pederasty. Paul understood the first as rebellion against the creator and the worship of idols; he understood the second to be abusive and exploitative. Neither can be compared to or equated with loving, caring, and committed same-gender relationships.

The sexual orientation and behavior of gay, lesbian, and bisexual people are not consequences of their rebellion against God. From its beginning, the Christian church has been served by God-loving, faithful, and dedicated lesbian, gay, and bisexual members, most anonymous but some well known. The Apostle Paul's conclusion that same-gender sexual behavior was a consequence of "ungodliness and wicked suppression of the truth" is dispelled by the existence of these gay believers whose Christian devotion and faithful discipleship is undeniable.

Two other passages commonly considered to condemn homosexuality, I Corinthians 6:1–10 and I Timothy 1:8–10, have significant linguistic problems and should be eliminated from the list of citations used to denounce it. In both passages, Paul condemns a list of vices, including one he names *arsenokoitai,* a Greek word whose meaning is now unknown. The various English translations are not only inaccurate but unfortunate. *Malakoi,* which means soft, is combined with *arsenokoitai* in the I Corinthians passage and translated in the King James Version as "effeminate, abusers of themselves with mankind." *Arsenokoitai* is used alone in I Timothy and is translated in the same version as "them that defile themselves with mankind." The 1952 Revised Standard Version translates these words as *homosexuals* in I Corinthians and *sodomites* in I Timothy. As noted earlier, there was no Greek word for *homosexual,* and *sodomite* was invented in the Middle Ages with no Greek precursor. While the 1971 Revised Standard Version replaces *homosexuals* with the more comprehensive term *sexual perverts,* which has no reference to gender or sexual orientation, the 1989 New Revised Standard Version uses *sodomites* in both I Corinthians and I Timothy.

Because Paul is the first to use *arsenokoitai* in the Bible, it has no literary history from which its meaning can be determined. Furthermore, no one in the early Christian church after Paul used *malakoi* and *arsenokoitai* when talking about same-gender sexual activity. Many of the early church leaders discuss same-gender sexual activity, but they ignore I Corinthians and I Timothy. Eusebius (a theologian of the fourth century CE) interpreted *malakoi* and *arsenokoitai* to refer to a male prostitute for women. John Chrysostom (a preacher who was Eusebius's contemporary), who strongly condemned same-gender sexual activity and wrote commentaries on both I Corinthians and I Timothy, did not see any references to same-gender sexual activity in these passages. Peter Cantor (a twelfth-century theologian) made a list of all passages in the Bible that he believed referred to same-gender sexual activity and did not include these two. It was not until the thirteenth century that Thomas Aquinas (1224–74) associated *arsenokoitai* and *malakoi* with same-gender sexual activity. From then on, the conventional interpretation was that these two words, used separately or together, mean a "man who has sex with a man."[6]

While careful study redeems these two passages of any condemnation of loving same-gender sexual intimacy, the problem remains that many of the most-read translations use the words *homosexuals* and *sodomites*, reinforcing the bigotry and supporting the persecution of gays. This makes it extremely difficult, if not impossible, to help people understand that the Bible doesn't talk about homosexuality, much less condemn it.

I was once challenged by Leona Green, a church member in her nineties. "Jimmy," she said, "don't you know the Bible says homosexuals can't enter the kingdom of God?" She handed me her Bible, the 1952 Revised Standard Version, and asked me to read I Corinthians 6:9 to her. I read the verse aloud and then explained how the Greek words used in this passage were not understood and how the translators simply read homosexuality into the text because of a long history of hostility toward it. I read the same passage to Leona from *The New Testament and Psalms: An Inclusive Version*,[7] my preferred translation, which uses the words *male prostitutes* instead of *homosexuals*. Leona sat patiently and smiled, waiting for me to finish. "Jimmy, I don't know about all of that, but I do know what my Bible says," she told me. "I know that it says homosexuals can't go to heaven. I don't have anything against homosexuals. I don't think what they do is right, but I don't judge them. Only God can do that. But I want you to think about what you're doing and tell me how you can say God loves homosexuals when Paul says they can't go to heaven." I was no match for her conviction. My explanation sounded to her like double talk and nonsense. The word *homosexual* was printed in the book. Not just in any old book, mind you — *the* book, *her* Bible! What injustice translators have done — what a major obstacle to understanding and acceptance they've created!

The way the Bible has been used against gay people is not unique. It has been misused in similar ways to support other cultural prejudices, practices, and institutions, such as slavery, racism, anti-Semitism, sexism, wars, inquisitions, colonialism, and classism. Such misuse does not serve the biblical understanding of God, Christ, or the church. Each misuse, along with the bigotry against gay, lesbian, and bisexual people, is an offense against God, assaults the souls of God's children, and compromises the ability of the church to be a faithful witness to Jesus Christ. Any use of God's name to condemn the essential humanity of people is blasphemous.

My search for what the Bible says about homosexuality provided no basis for the claim that it is a sin. Same-gender sexual behavior simply is not an issue in the Bible.

Furthermore, there is no condemnation of same-gender sexual relations between two people who are in a mutually loving, nurturing, caring, and supportive relationship. While it emphatically condemns same-gender sexual violence, just as it condemns other-gender sexual violence, the Bible is silent about same-gender sexual love. It's not surprising that same-gender love would not be understood and affirmed in an ancient, prescientific, patriarchal culture, but that's no reason to reject and condemn it today.

So if the Bible was not the source of Christian antipathy toward same-gender sexual loving, where did that hostility come from? Further research revealed its origins to be in the medieval Roman Catholic Church.

Jesus's teachings and way of life radically challenged the political, social, and religious orders of his day. In no way did he teach anything that was not already part of the Jewish tradition, but what he brought that was new was a spirituality emphasizing God's immanence and intimacy with the world and elevating mercy over law, compassion over piety, and inherent human dignity over social status. Jesus taught and practiced compassion and forgiveness. He taught that God's realm of love is immanent, "in your midst," not something distant in time or space. He challenged the arrogance of the powerful, the indifference of the rich, and the hypocrisy of the pious. He welcomed and honored the outcast and the sinner (a term referring not to immoral behavior, but to cultic impurity), the poor, the sick, and the despised, such as tax collectors, Samaritans, and gentiles. His disciples included women as well as men. There was a strong tradition of Jewish asceticism—the denial of sensual needs and pleasures—in Jesus's day, exemplified by John the Baptist. But Jesus was no ascetic, an aspect of his life ignored by the early church fathers (it was an exclusive, all-male club). Rather, he behaved in a way that led critics of his day to accuse him of being a drunkard and glutton, and to castigate him for associating with foreigners, women, and harlots.

The Christian movement that emerged in the years immediately following the death of Jesus continued to be Jewish in its basic theology, ethics, and culture. The early Christian church understood the human person to be a unity of body and spirit, created and declared to be good by God. The purpose of sexual activity was both lovemaking and procreation. It was unitive, both emotionally and legally. In biblical times it was the act of sexual intercourse, not a religious ritual or civil ceremony, that consummated marriage, when—as the common expression has it—"two became one" (Gospel of Matthew 19:5). In *Law, Sex, and Christian Society in Medieval Europe*, James Brundage writes: "While Jesus did not reject traditional Jewish beliefs about marriage and the family, he differed from most traditional teachers in the emphasis that he placed upon love as a paramount element in marriage. Both Jesus and his early followers anticipated that Christian married couples would live within the context of traditional Jewish culture, but encouraged them to pattern their personal relationships upon the mutual self-giving that lay at the heart of the notion of *agape* [a Greek word for self-giving or sacrificial love] among his early followers."[8]

When the Christian movement expanded from its Jewish context into the Greek world, it encountered and began to adopt elements of a culture that had an entirely different perspective on the body, spirit, and sexuality. While the earlier culture of Classical Greece (fourth and fifth centuries BCE) celebrated and honored the human body and sexuality, certain elements of the Greco-Roman culture of the Early Church period did not. The Greek philosophies of Stoicism, Gnosticism, and Manichaeism defined reality as a dualism of the physical and the spiritual. The physical realm was corrupt and evil; the spiritual, good and godly. Consequently, the human body was understood to be evil and corrupt, and sensual pleasure was considered immoral. To attain the spiritual, one must denounce and deprive the physical.

When Emperor Constantine I of Rome officially ended the persecution of the Christian church with the Edict of Milan (313 CE) and gave Christianity favored status, the church fathers began putting together the first systematic Christian theology. They were obsessed with sexuality. They abandoned the Jewish view that God's creation—the earth and all that dwells upon it—was good; that a human being is a unity of body and spirit; and that sexuality is a blessed gift for lovemaking, shared pleasure, and the creation of children. Marriage was disparaged; virginity and chastity were honored. Because many of the early church fathers were monks or hermits, at one time or another in their careers, their views of sex were dominated by ascetic values. Asceticism became the preferred way to commune with God. Because they believed a human being was a spirit trapped in a body, the preeminent challenge for Christians seeking eternal salvation was to deprive and conquer the physical appetites, especially the erotic.

The mix of patriarchy with a dualistic worldview of the spiritual or good versus the physical or evil produced misogyny, causing great harm to women as well as gay people because of the resulting rigid gender roles and fear of the feminine. The church father whose views on sexuality most influenced the early church's teachings was Augustine of Hippo (354–430 CE). Brundage writes:

> Sexual desire, Augustine believed, was the most foul and unclean of human wickednesses, the most pervasive manifestation of man's disobedience to God's designs. Other bodily desires and pleasures, Augustine felt, did not overwhelm reason and disarm the will: one can be sensible while enjoying a good meal, one can discuss matters reasonably over a bottle of wine. But sex, Augustine argued, was more powerful than other sensual attractions; it could overcome reason and free will altogether. Married people, who ought to have sex only in order to beget children, can be overwhelmed by lubricious desires that blot out reason and restraint; they tumble into bed together simply in order to enjoy the pleasure of each other's body. This, Augustine thought, was not only irrational but sinful. Augustine's underlying belief in the intrinsic sinfulness of carnal desire and the sensual delight that accompanied sexual union became

a standard premise of Western beliefs about sexuality during the Middle Ages and beyond.[9]

A consequence of Augustine's teaching is the separation of spirituality and sexuality. When spirituality is understood as our capacity to love the Holy, our neighbor, and the natural world, and sexuality is understood as the way we embody ourselves in the world, then spirituality and sexuality are inseparable and interdependent. Sexuality is the embodiment of our connection with realities beyond our individual selves: our spirituality. Spirituality determines the character and values of our embodiment: our sexuality. When the unity of sexuality and spirituality was denied, spirituality became disembodied and sexuality was reduced to a physical appetite narrowly defined as lust. Sexual intimacy, consequently, was separated from love and approved only as a necessary evil for the sole purpose of procreation. Brundage explains: "Writers [i.e., medieval Christian theologians] who place primary emphasis on sex as reproduction, therefore, condemn homosexual relations as well as heterosexual oral and anal sex practices and often maintain that even the postures used in marital sex are morally good or bad depending on whether they hinder or promote conception. Those who consider reproduction the primary criterion of sexual morality usually deny any positive value to sexual pleasure . . . Hence they minimize the value of sexual satisfaction as a binding mechanism in marriage."[10]

This view laid the foundation for the writings of Aquinas, whose impact on biblical interpretation was noted earlier. Aquinas has an especially prominent role in the history of the persecution of gay people. In *Sex in History*, Reay Tannahill observes:

If any one man was responsible for the hardening of the church's attitude toward homosexuals, it was the great philosopher and theologian of the thirteenth century, St. Thomas Aquinas. Just as Augustine . . . had given a rationale to the Church Fathers' distaste for the heterosexual act and rendered it acceptable only in terms of procreation, so Thomas Aquinas consolidated traditional fears of homosexuality as the crime that had brought down fire and brimstone on Sodom and Gomorrah, by "proving" what every heterosexual male had always believed—that it was as unnatural in the sight of God as of man. It was not difficult to prove, especially as he started from Augustine's proposition that the

sexual organs had been designed by the Creator specifically for reproduction, and could only be legitimately used in ways that did not exclude
the possibility of it. Homosexuality was thus, by definition, a deviation
from the natural order laid down by God (as, of course, were heterosexual anal and oral intercourse, and, obviously, zoophilia), and a deviation that was not only unnatural but, by the same Augustinian token,
lustful and heretical . . . From the fourteenth century on, homosexuals as
a group were to find neither refuge nor tolerance anywhere in the Western Church or state.[11]

Not only were church laws enacted that condemned same-gender sexual
intimacy, but civil laws calling for the violent execution of people caught
in or believed to be guilty of it became widespread. Ironically, one of the
precipitating reasons was the all-male priesthood and the sexual segregation of religious orders. Once celibacy was required,[12] the popular suspicion
intensified that same-gender sexual activity was prevalent among the all-
male clergy and the religious orders of monks and nuns. In addition, same-
gender sexual activity became associated, if not synonymous, with heresy,
an opinion or teaching at odds with official doctrine.

The appalling truth is that the dominant expression of Christian sexual
morality that shaped Western culture over the last two millennia, affecting
both intimate relationships and social institutions, was formulated during
the historical period known as the Dark Ages by celibate men who believed
the physical world to be evil, held women in contempt, considered pleasure a vice, and equated sex with sin. They could not have taken us further
from Jesus. The course they established led tragically in the wrong direction for the spiritual evolution of humanity. In spite of our vastly superior
knowledge of human sexuality, we continue to be victims of their medieval
ignorance, fear, and prejudice, which are still embedded in the teachings of
the Christian church and in archaic civil laws. More tragic than the exter-
nal violence done to bisexual, gay, and lesbian people is the fact that they
have been taught by the Christian church and the society that it has shaped
for centuries to hate themselves and believe themselves to be rejected by
and separated from God because of their sexuality, because of who they are
and whom they love. The Christian antipathy toward same-gender sexual
loving comes from the fear of sexuality, not from the Bible. Because of this
fear, gay, lesbian, and bisexual people have been oppressed, persecuted, and

killed in the name of God and in defense of society. It's a scandalous and shameful history.

When I studied the policies and teachings of The United Methodist Church to understand its position on homosexuality, I learned that my church first formally addressed the subject at the 1972 United Methodist General Conference meeting in Atlanta, Georgia. There the delegates adopted the church's newly composed Social Principles.[13] Under a section addressing human sexuality was the following statement: "Homosexuals no less than heterosexuals are persons of sacred worth who need the ministry and guidance of the church in their struggles for human fulfillment, as well as the spiritual and emotional care of a fellowship which enables reconciling relationships with God, with others and with self. Further, we insist that all persons are entitled to have their human and civil rights ensured." Near the end of the General Conference, an amendment was adopted to the Social Principles to add the sentence: "We do not condone the practice of homosexuality and consider this practice to be incompatible with Christian teaching."[14] These words laid the foundation for an evolving process to officially exclude lesbians, gay men, and bisexual people and their allies from The United Methodist Church.

Following the 1972 General Conference, the Good News movement, an evangelical caucus organized in 1967 by the Reverend Charles W. Keysor, became obsessed with denying lesbian and gay men ordination to the ministry within The United Methodist Church, as well as denying them other rights of church membership. That summer, Keysor published an article in the *Good News* magazine claiming that the 1972 General Conference was "dominated by a coalition of special interest groups . . . which showed great political skill . . . [in] promoting such issues as free-choice abortion, approval of the homosexual life style, and condemnation of the US for its role in Viet Nam."[15] In reality, there was no organized homosexual caucus, as Keysor claimed. The first such caucus was organized three years later, in 1975. Nonetheless, Keysor alleged that homosexuals had great power within The United Methodist Church and even suggested that those who supported the inclusion and acceptance of gay people in the church were themselves homosexual. With this article, Keysor inaugurated the Good News's antigay campaign that eventually came to dominate The United Methodist Church's policies.

At the 1976 General Conference in Portland, Oregon, a proposed churchwide study of human sexuality was defeated. In addition, a new policy was added to *The Book of Discipline* that forbade national United Methodist Church funds to be given to any gay organization or used to "promote the acceptance of homosexuality." Keysor and his Good News movement had been successful.

Even though the theology and social policy agenda of the evangelical caucus was to the right of the majority of United Methodists, the fear of homosexuality and the imagined harm that would result from the full acceptance of homosexuals into the life of the church prevailed even among self-described liberals. The Good News movement succeeded by harping on the possibilities that a congregation would have to accept a "practicing homosexual" as its pastor, that church funds, given in good faith by loyal Bible-believing members, could be used to promote homosexuality, and on the characterization of lesbian and gay people as "sex perverts" and "sinners." Of course, the Good News movement had an ally in the culturally conditioned fear and contempt of gay people. Among even the most sincere United Methodist Christians, the gospel message encouraging "love of neighbor" did not extend to "homosexuals," "queers," and "dykes."

In 1977, during a conference titled "Homosexuality and the Church," held at Washington Square United Methodist Church in New York City, the host pastor, the Reverend Paul Abels, publicly announced that he was gay. The Good News movement castigated New York Bishop Ralph Ward for allowing Abels to continue serving Washington Square United Methodist Church after coming out.

This controversy was eclipsed in 1981, when Bishop Melvin Wheatley appointed Julian Rush, an openly gay man, to be the pastor of St. Paul's United Methodist Church in Denver, Colorado. James V. Heidinger II, the new editor of *Good News* magazine, jumped on the antigay vendetta with gusto. In "Looking for Bold Leadership," Heidinger stated that Bishop Wheatley had acted in "clear violation" of *The Discipline* and that, if left unchallenged, his action "would become, *de facto*, the position of the church on this issue."[16]

A judicial complaint filed against Bishop Wheatley for appointing Julian Rush was dismissed as without merit, and The United Methodist Church's Judicial Council, its highest court, later affirmed his action as legally correct. But the appointment of Rush and the exoneration of Bishop Wheatley set the stage for the passage at the 1984 General Conference of legislation prohibiting the ordination and appointment of "self-avowed practicing homosexuals." This action fully institutionalized antigay bigotry within The United Methodist Church. It was this General Conference action that drove Adam to come out to me and leave The United Methodist Church.

Adam had motivated me to pursue my research about homosexuality, the Bible, and the church. Because of what I learned, I no longer had reason to believe that being lesbian, gay, or bisexual was anything other than normal and natural. The intellectual and theological barriers had fallen. But another more persistent barrier remained — the emotional resistance of my culturally conditioned assumptions about healthy sexuality, assumptions shaped more by fear and misinformation than by knowledge and understanding. Deep within my psyche, fighting against my new knowledge, was an irrational revulsion to the idea of men having sex with men. All of the old negative messages about sex being dirty and disgusting surfaced when I thought about it. But I was willing to allow myself to be vulnerable to the truth of what I now knew I shouldn't fear. It would take much more time and work before this barrier would fall, too. That would happen because of the humanity, dignity, and integrity of people like Adam whom I would get to know. Books changed my mind. These people changed my heart.

Chapter 4   **STEPPING OFF THE CURB**

In June 1987, I moved from Warsaw to Raleigh, North Carolina, to be the pastor of Fairmont United Methodist Church. While I'd enjoyed my six years at Warsaw United Methodist Church, I was ready for new challenges and had requested the move. I was glad to return to Raleigh, which had been my home from 1970 to 1973, when I was an associate pastor at Edenton Street United Methodist Church following my graduation from Duke Divinity School. The Fairmont Church, a congregation of about seven hundred members located just two blocks from the campus of North Carolina State University, offered exciting opportunities and challenges for ministry.

My enthusiasm for this change was tempered, however, by the stress and grief I felt because my marriage was failing. Merle Smith and I had married in 1967, a month after I graduated from the University of North Carolina, Chapel Hill. We'd met while working with the youth program at University Methodist Church. In 1972, we had a son, Kennedy Patrick-Jubal. I still call him Patrick, his childhood name, but as a professional musician, he now goes by Jubal, a name mentioned once in the Bible as "the father of all who play the lyre and pipe" (Genesis 4:21).

In the week before Christmas 1986, just seven months before my move from Warsaw, Merle told me that she was no longer committed to our marriage and that she didn't know if she would be going with me. There had been signs of trouble for years, signs I had ignored or dismissed. I believed that our conflicts and disagreements were typical of any normal relationship and had to be tolerated. She and I weren't good at working things out together; we didn't know how to be open or honest about our feelings.

Nonetheless, I wasn't prepared for her announcement. I was devastated. The one thing that I had been surest of was that Merle and I would be together for the rest of our lives. I could not imagine life without her. I loved her dearly.

I fell into a deep despair, unable to eat and sleep. My whole body was numb, my mind dazed. Somehow, I made it through the Christmas celebrations at the church. Friends and church members commented on my weight loss and red eyes. They told me I was working too hard and should ease up. I told no one the truth.

It's hard to say just how close I came to ending my life. I can only say that I wanted to and became obsessed with how and when I would do it. I often drove thirty-four miles from Warsaw to Goldsboro for meetings. Along the way, the highway goes over a railroad track. The unusually high overpass amazingly had no guard rails along the sides of its steep banks. My plan was to drive off the overpass just at the top and crash onto the steel tracks and stone bed below.

Each time I drove to or from Goldsboro and approached the crest of the overpass, I would speed up, my hands tightly gripping the wheel, my eyes fixed on the oncoming outside corner of the bridge, and I would see myself flying off into the open air to end the pain. But I couldn't let myself do it. There were always things I needed to do, parishioners I needed to visit, a wedding to prepare for, a death and funeral that got in the way. Most of all, I couldn't bear not seeing Patrick one more time. My love for my son and my sense of obligation to the church kept me alive.

In April, still hurting and depressed, I went to Duke University to hear a lecture by Gustavo Gutiérrez, a renowned theologian from Peru. I had read his *Theology of Liberation*[1] and found his writing to be refreshing and exciting, stating in new ways old truths about God and the life of faith. I was prepared for a scholarly presentation, and Gutiérrez didn't disappoint me. But he was also pastoral. In his lecture, he said something that shook me from my despair: "What makes life meaningful is not what you get out of it, but what you give to it."

There was nothing exceptional about his words. I'm sure I'd said them and heard them said many times before in various ways. It's a simple truth that we all know. But on that day, this truth filled the emptiness of my soul. It was as if he had thrown me a life preserver while I was drowning in depression, and I clung to it for rescue. I realized how selfish I had been. While

Gutiérrez counseled not to measure the meaning of your life by what you get out of it, I was measuring the value of my life on the basis of what I was losing—that's pretty much the same thing, really. My loss and pain were not to be trivialized, but at the same time they were not the whole of who I was. I realized that my individual reality had no value in isolation; it was only in my giving to my community—as a father, son, brother, neighbor, citizen, and fellow human being—that my individual qualities and abilities had value. I don't remember much else from the lecture. Gutiérrez needed to say nothing more that day to set me free, to save me. Even as a pastor, he was a practitioner of liberation theology.

I didn't recover overnight; it took me months to feel healthy again. But that day the process began, and I already felt different as I left Durham to drive home. My body felt lighter, freer. The knot in my stomach started to relax. I could sleep and eat again. I stopped thinking of dying and started thinking of what I had to offer to Patrick, the church, society, and the world. Because I couldn't imagine ever hurting so badly again, I felt fearless. I was wounded and scarred, but I believed that if I could survive this pain, I could survive anything. It was a personal resurrection. My pain had been caused by the death of my living passionately with Merle, not by the death of all passion. And if I had something to give, I had reason to live.

Soon after I learned of my appointment to Fairmont United Methodist Church, Merle was offered a new job in Raleigh. I invited her to live with Patrick and me at the parsonage until she could afford to move out on her own. I hurt because she no longer loved me, but I still loved her and wanted her to be safe and secure. For the next three years, we lived in the same house although we were estranged, with separate bedrooms, meals, and daily schedules. We had little interaction except when Patrick was involved.

The congregation of Fairmont Church graciously welcomed me as its pastor, and I immediately felt at home. The church had a full-time staff of three in addition to me, plus a part-time organist and choir director. The Reverend Bill Sharpe, director of the Raleigh Wesley Foundation—the United Methodist ministry to students at the six colleges and universities in Raleigh—had his office at Fairmont and was considered an adjunct member of the staff. I enjoyed preaching in the spacious sanctuary. Each Sunday, a large number of college students attended worship, and I found their energy and openness to be stimulating. Beyond the congregation, I became active in community efforts to end homelessness and to oppose the U.S.-sponsored Contras in the war in Nicaragua. The first year at Fairmont went smoothly with lots of support from the congregation. I couldn't have been happier in my ministry.

Since Adam had awakened me to the church's persecution of lesbian, gay, and bisexual people three years earlier, I had come to understand and accept sexual orientation as an essential, normal, and natural aspect of the human personality, regardless of whether its orientation was other-, both-, or same-gender. I believed The United Methodist Church's policies and teachings about homosexuality were expressions of bigotry, comparable to racism.

In September of my first year at Fairmont, I accepted an invitation from Nancy Keppel to attend a meeting of clergy who wanted to discuss what could be done to end the mistreatment of gay people, especially by churches. I'd met Nancy, a lay minister in the United Church of Christ, as we stood together outside of U.S. Representative David Price's office during a protest against the war in Nicaragua. She explained that Raleigh's Human Resources and Human Rights Commission earlier in the summer had sponsored a public hearing regarding the discrimination and violence that gay people experienced in Raleigh. At the hearing, lesbians and gay men spoke bravely about being fired from jobs, denied apartments, harassed on the street, and physically attacked. Almost every testimony included an experience of being rejected by a church. Nancy's meeting was in response to the stories about the abuse inflicted by clergy and congregations.

It took several meetings and lots of discussion about what to do and how to do it, but ultimately we created the Raleigh Religious Network for Gay and Lesbian Equality (RRNGLE), originally composed of about fifteen pastors and lay persons from Episcopal, Roman Catholic, Lutheran, Presbyterian, Unitarian Universalist, United Church of Christ, Baptist, Metropolitan Community, and United Methodist churches, along with the rabbi of Raleigh's reform Jewish congregation. Our goal was to do educational work in the religious communities and in secular settings. We were committed to bearing public witness against discrimination, believing there was no integrity in offering support to gay people in the privacy of our offices but not in public arenas. In early 1988, I was chosen to be the convener of RRNGLE, a position I would hold for the next two years.

The 1988 North Carolina Gay Pride Weekend was scheduled to take place in Raleigh in June, and RRNGLE was concerned that clergy in local churches might use the event as an opportunity for gay bashing. In the hope of preventing that, we sent a letter to all clergy in the county, urging them to be sensitive to the fact that every congregation has members who are gay and members who are parents or siblings of gays. Since this was our first official correspondence, we created a letterhead with the names of all RRNGLE members printed down the left side of the page. As the convener, I signed the letter and used the Fairmont Church address and telephone number on the letterhead in case anyone wanted to respond.

A small RRNGLE delegation was to walk in the Pride March, one of the Gay Pride Weekend events. On Friday evening, the day before the march, Sarah Hitchcock, chairperson of Fairmont's Pastor-Parish Relations Committee,[2] called to tell me that a copy of RRNGLE's letter to the area's clergy had been sent to Fairmont's Wesley Bible Class — a Sunday school class for older men — by a local United Methodist minister, and that for the last two or three Sundays the letter had been the main topic of discussion. Sarah told me that the class was preparing a resolution condemning the practice of homosexuality and anyone supporting homosexuals, which would be presented to me before worship on Sunday morning.

"Are you going to be in the gay pride march tomorrow?" Sarah asked. "Yes," I answered, "I will be walking with RRNGLE." While she assured me that she supported what I was doing, she wanted me to understand that others did not. Sarah's call alarmed me, and for the first time, I felt anxious about how my work with RRNGLE might adversely affect my relationship with the Fairmont congregation. I had known this time would ultimately come because of the controversy over homosexuality in the church. I also knew that the emancipation of gay people from discrimination and violence was a just and necessary cause, and that no social change happens without resistance and conflict. So, though I was worried that night, I was determined to follow through with the march and with my work with RRNGLE.

The next day, I stood at the curb on Hillsborough Street with the Reverend Jim Lewis, director of Christian Social Ministries for the North Carolina Episcopal Diocese, and the Reverend Mahan Siler, pastor of Pullen Memorial Baptist Church, holding our new RRNGLE banner. It was a gorgeous June morning. The sun was unusually hot for so early in the day, and the sky was a bold Carolina blue with a few scattered, fluffy clouds. Already the atmosphere was exuberant. Lesbians and gay men, bisexual and transgender people, and their friends and families were all in a festive mood. Laughter and loud, cheerful voices filled the air.

As I watched the parade forming and moving along the street, a shiver of dread passed over me, like the shadow of a cloud riding a summer breeze. I knew that walking in the march would be an irreversible act, and my life wouldn't be the same afterward. Not by chance, Charles Holland drove by in his red pickup truck. Our eyes met, and he quickly looked away. He was the scout for the Wesley Bible Class, come to confirm their suspicions about my actions.

My stomach churned as apprehension contended with compulsion, but I finally stepped off the curb to join the march. I was quickly swept up by the festivity, and my dread was dissolved by the energy of the crowd. Pink and lavender balloons filled the air. People carried banners and placards and wore T-shirts, buttons, and sashes with slogans proclaiming gay pride. The rainbow symbol was everywhere, affirming diversity and unity. Male couples and female couples walked together, unashamedly holding hands and occasionally kissing. A lesbian marching band somewhere up ahead established the rhythm and tempo for us to follow.

The march stretched for blocks. On the crests of the hills, I strained to see its beginning and end, but both were too far away. The estimated number of participants—from three to five thousand—was, for North Carolina in 1988, an amazingly large gathering for a gay pride march.

Walking immediately ahead of us was the Raleigh chapter of PFLAG. Thinking this must be a Polish gay rights organization, I asked one of the people holding the PFLAG banner about the group. She explained that the acronym stood for Parents, Families, and Friends of Lesbians and Gays, a proud group of mothers and fathers, sisters and brothers, sons and daughters, grandparents, aunts and uncles. I was moved by their courageous public display of unconditional love and acceptance of the gay people in their lives, in spite of the hostile climate in Raleigh.

Just behind us, members of St. John's Metropolitan Community Church pulled a little red wagon carrying a boom box playing familiar hymns— "Jesus Loves Me, This I Know," "Blessed Assurance, Jesus Is Mine," and "Just as I Am, without One Plea." They sang as they walked, transforming the hymns from songs of private piety into profound public affirmations of a faith in God's radically unconditional love and acceptance. These lesbian, gay, transgender, and bisexual people had every reason to turn their backs on the church because they had been condemned, rejected, and vilified in the name of God and Jesus. But they were not just singing, they were testifying:

Just as I am, without one plea,
But that thy blood was shed for me,
And that thou bidst me come to thee,
O Lamb of God, I come, I come!
Just as I am, though tossed about,
With many a conflict, many a doubt,
Fightings and fears within, without,
O Lamb of God, I come, I come![3]

What I heard in these brave voices was a refusal to identify the rejection by the Christian church with the heart and mind of God. I heard them claim that they, too, were children of a loving God who had blessed them with innate dignity and integrity. The traditional church might have cast them out, but these faithful people knew that God had not and would not.

As we walked down Hillsborough Street toward downtown Raleigh, we passed several churches, their doors locked and windows dark. There was no acknowledgment of the march by the people who would gather in those churches the next morning.

Two young men followed beside us on the sidewalk, both dressed in white shirts and black slacks. One carried on his shoulder a large wooden cross with small wheels on the long end, allowing it to roll while creating the illusion that he bore a great burden. The other man, shaking a large floppy black leather Bible above his head, harangued us, spitting out: "Homosexuality is an abomination! Repent or be damned to the eternal fires of hell!"

On that Saturday morning, God was not in the hateful words of the men with the cross and Bible or in the empty churches. God was in the mass of proud and beautiful people on Hillsborough Street. God was the pride, dignity, and integrity that were being celebrated. God was the unconditional love that empowered the courage of PFLAG and the members of St. John's Metropolitan Community Church.

Walking in the 1988 Gay Pride March was no big deal in many respects. Yet it profoundly affected and defined the rest of my life. The intellectual inquiry into issues affecting gay people that Adam had started me on in Warsaw became that day walking down Raleigh's Hillsborough Street an existential passion for me. God's spirit—free from the small, cramped boxes of petty theological and cultural convention—was leading and moving within this flow of humanity, breathing life, energy, and hope into its shared vision for a just world in which freedom, equality, and peace for all people are real.

The next morning, just before the eleven o'clock worship, as Sarah Hitchcock had warned me, I was handed the resolution from the Wesley Bible Class. It read: "The class members believe that in His Scriptures God has made it clear that homosexuality is an abomination in His sight. The class members believe for Fairmont, or any of its members, or leaders, or any other church to embrace homosexuality, or those who practice it, is an insult to God, that should be strictly avoided, even the appearance of it. Homosexual persons may have equal rights under man's law as it applies to any human being, but God himself made it clear where they stand in relationship to Him. The Wesley Bible Class wants to clearly uphold the position of the God they worship."

During worship, I acknowledged to the congregation that some members had objected to my involvement with RRNGLE and my participation in the previous day's Pride March, and I invited anyone interested to meet with me that evening for an open discussion about their concerns. About twenty-five parishioners showed up. While most disapproved of my actions, there was nonetheless a respectful and civil discussion. I was asked a broad range of questions about the march, RRNGLE, The United Methodist Church's teachings about homosexuality, and my theological perspective on homosexuality. I answered the questions as well as I could, explaining my journey in coming to understand sexual orientation and the role the Christian church has played in the persecution of lesbian and gay persons. When the evening ended, I felt good about the discussion.

My optimism was unfounded. During the following week, members of the Pastor-Parish Relations Committee received many calls from irate parishioners who accused me of violating *The Book of Discipline* and demanded that I be removed as the pastor. Sarah asked me to meet with the committee to discuss the controversy and review the duties of a pastor to the congregation and the community outlined in *The Book of Discipline*. After our meeting, the nine committee members concluded that I had done nothing wrong or inappropriate. On the contrary, they agreed I was fulfilling my responsibilities faithfully, and they sent a letter explaining their conclusion to all members of the congregation. The letter was a strong and unambiguous endorsement of my ministry. I felt enormous encouragement and was sure we were making progress.

The day after the meeting, I traveled to Nicaragua to spend two weeks with a Witness for Peace delegation protesting the U.S.-sponsored war there. When I returned to Raleigh, I learned that the committee's letter had not convinced the congregation. During my absence, a petition demanding my immediate removal had been circulated among the members. The petition, with seventy-nine signatures, was sent to the Raleigh district superintendent, Dr. Joseph Bethea. At his direction, Sarah scheduled an open meeting for all church members to air their opinions about my leadership at Fairmont.

The meeting, moderated by Dr. Bethea, took place on Monday night, August 22, 1988, and the crowd packed the main floor and balcony of Fairmont's sanctuary. The nine members of the Pastor-Parish Relations Committee sat together at a table in front of the gathering. Forbidden to attend, I sat at home, three blocks from the church, anxiously wondering what was happening and waiting to hear the outcome. I prepared myself to be removed from Fairmont.

It was a long and contentious meeting, I was told later, with speakers equally divided between supporting and opposing me. After the open meeting, the committee met in private to review what they'd heard and decide my fate. Sarah called just before midnight to tell me the vote was six to two to keep me as the church's pastor. I was relieved and elated by the vote, as well as optimistic that positive change was happening within the congregation.

Some days after the meeting, Steve Churchill came to my office to tell me he was gay. A native of Raleigh and a student at North Carolina State University, he attended worship at Fairmont regularly and was active in the Raleigh Wesley Foundation. He'd never told anyone before he was gay, he said. He'd known he was gay as long as he could remember, but he had been taught and believed that homosexuality was a sin. Shame and fear locked him tightly in the closet.

But as he had watched me walk in the Pride March from a safe place hidden in the crowd along Hillsborough Street, and as he heard the anger of church members at the recent meeting, he began to rethink his beliefs about his sexuality and about hiding it. If I could accept and affirm gay people, including him, he could accept himself as a gay man. And he felt that he shouldn't let me take the heat alone, standing up for him and other gays. He'd decided he would come out of the closet, declare who he really was, and stand with me.

One afternoon, Steve brought his parents to my office to tell them he was gay. I assured them that being gay was healthy, normal, and natural for Steve. It was who he was, and neither he nor they should feel shame because of it.

His parents were in shock. Steve tried hard to help them understand that he'd accepted his sexuality as a part of who he was. He talked about what it had been like to live with the shame and hide the truth about himself for so long. I encouraged Steve's parents to talk with other parents of lesbian and gay children and offered contact information for PFLAG. As is often the case, they weren't ready to have anyone know their son was gay, not even other parents of gay children. It would take a while before they were ready.

Steve grew more and more comfortable about his sexuality and was fully out to everyone. He lived at home, and his openness created more conflict with his parents, as well as with his older brother, who refused to believe Steve was gay. Steve and his family's honest but painful effort to talk and listen to each other gave them an opportunity for real understanding that hadn't existed before, and, finally, for his parents' full acceptance of Steve's sexuality.

During the months that followed the big meeting of church members, there were several attempts to discredit and intimidate me. Rumors circulated that I'd given the keys of the church to gays so that they could have sex in the sanctuary at night, and that I had misused church funds. A photo of me with members of the youth group on one of the bulletin boards was vandalized, with my face cut out. On separate occasions, two unsigned notes were slipped under my office door, both written by the same hand. One read: "We hope you are satisfied with what you did to Fairmont Methodist Church. Thanks to you, it's been anything but united!" The other read: "Calling all queers! Calling all gays! There will be a meeting at Creech homosexual church (formerly Fairmont United Methodist Church) at 7:30 on September 12, 1988. All weirdos invited!"

Those wanting me removed persistently contacted the district superintendent and the bishop, demanding I be ousted. Two other adult Sunday school classes, along with the Wesley Bible Class, became the crucibles of opposition where discussions, planning, and networking took place. Those who objected to my ministry wouldn't talk to me. Each Sunday morning, as I stood at the main entrance of the Sunday school, they either refused to shake my hand or avoided me by entering through other doors.

There were exceptions to this pattern. Lonnie and Polly Thompson, adamantly opposed to my ministry at Fairmont, continued to attend worship. I admired them for that. Polly was quiet and rarely voiced her opinion, but Lonnie was blunt. One Sunday morning, as I greeted him at the door, he said to me: "You're doing the work of the devil! I think the bishop sent you here to run off all the old folks and make this a church for young people and homosexuals." He then walked into the sanctuary for worship. It was the sort of encounter to which I'd become accustomed.

Tom and Louise Byrum were avid choir members. When my work on gay rights became an issue for the congregation, Tom and Louise continued singing in the choir but would not speak to me. They were kind people, and I believed they'd understand my ministry if we could talk. So I went to their home one afternoon to visit with them. It was clear that they were very upset. They explained that when they found Fairmont, they expected it to be their church until their deaths. But now, they said, I had "taken their church away from them" by creating this controversy. They felt grief more than anger.

Among the members angriest with me was a couple whose son was gay. He had come out to them years before, and they had tried to convince him that his "lifestyle" was sinful. The father compared welcoming gays into the church with the welcoming of black people in the 1960s. He said both were wrong because they caused conflict and disruption within the congregation. Despite being charter members of Fairmont for over fifty years, they transferred their membership to Raleigh's First Presbyterian Church, after conferring with its pastor to be sure his position on homosexuality was the same as theirs.

In spite of the opposition, there was a lot of commitment and positive energy among the active church leaders and members, and I began 1989 with much hope and enthusiasm. While I expected difficulty keeping the ministry and programs going, I was eager to take the work on, sure that we could make a go of things. But my hope and enthusiasm quickly deflated. By late February, Fairmont was facing a desperate financial crisis. The church was receiving only two-thirds of the contributions we needed, and I feared that we would soon be unable to keep the church doors open.

I called a few close RRNGLE friends and asked them to meet me for breakfast. I was distraught and needed their counsel. I explained the crippling financial crisis and told them that I didn't want Fairmont to be irreparably harmed. I said the only way to avoid this was for me to leave.

"Don't leave," they pleaded. "Give the situation more time to turn around." What was happening at Fairmont, they said, was not merely an internal private congregational matter, but a witness for the larger Raleigh community, as well as for the whole country. My leaving would mean that those who wanted to keep the church closed to lesbian and gay members had prevailed, and such an outcome would only discourage other churches from taking a stand against discrimination in the future. My friends promised that I wouldn't have to bear this burden alone, that RRNGLE would raise funds for Fairmont. These clergy and lay people had modest incomes and were already heavily committed financially to their own congregations, but they pledged financial support to a church that was not even of their own denomination. Each month thereafter, the treasurer of Fairmont received checks in the mail from a Roman Catholic priest, a rabbi, and Presbyterian, Unitarian Universalist, Episcopalian, Lutheran, United Church of Christ, and Baptist clergy and laity.

The leadership and many members of Fairmont were encouraged by this outpouring of support from the community. It gave us new resolve to not only survive but prevail. We tightened our collective financial belt, cutting back on program expenses by planning low- and no-cost activities. The church school teachers created their own lessons and materials, instead of purchasing expensive curriculum materials from The United Methodist Publishing House. Recycled computer paper was used for children's artwork. Members brought old but usable pencils and crayons from home. Potluck suppers replaced catered events. Because Fairmont was receiving only about two-thirds of its monthly budget, I instructed the church treasurer to pay me only two-thirds of my salary to help meet the expenses for the rest of the year. The financial crisis was averted.

My work with RRNGLE continued uninterrupted, with cautious support from Fairmont's leadership. RRNGLE planned a conference to be held in March titled "Homophobia: Breaking the Silence, Facing the Fears, Finding the Truth," with the Reverend Dr. Carter Heyward[4] the featured speaker. In an effort to encourage greater participation by clergy, we solicited support from various denominational leaders. Bishop Robert W. Estill of the

Episcopal Diocese of North Carolina and the Reverend Rollin O. Russell, conference minister of the Southern Conference of the United Church of Christ, were early endorsers. I approached C. P. Minnick Jr., bishop of the North Carolina Annual Conference of The United Methodist Church, for his endorsement. Without hesitation, he said no. Several weeks later, however, he called me at home late one night. "Jimmy," he said, "I've decided to give my endorsement to the RRNGLE conference. I've just returned from a very disturbing and painful meeting at a church where the music director was fired because he's gay. This sort of thing has got to stop. I'll prepare a letter and send it out to the clergy in the conference, and you can use my name in your brochure." I could hardly believe it. I was ecstatic! With all the controversy that my involvement with RRNGLE had generated, this was a bold and courageous thing for him to do. He certainly knew his decision would be controversial.

Bishop Minnick came to North Carolina with the reputation of being liberal on racial and women's issues in the church. He had also been a strong voice opposing the U.S. sponsored war in Nicaragua and had coauthored a statement in support of nuclear disarmament on behalf of the United Methodist Council of Bishops. But, until now, he'd been silent about gay issues.

In his letter to United Methodist clergy, Bishop Minnick wrote:

> On March 10–11, the Raleigh Religious Network for Gay and Lesbian Equality will sponsor a conference in Raleigh at Pullen Memorial Baptist Church. This conference is designed to equip us as pastors to minister more effectively and more meaningfully to gay men and lesbians and their families in our congregations and in the larger community. The topic for this conference will be "Homophobia in the Religious Community." This letter is my endorsement of this event and my encouragement to you to avail yourselves of this opportunity to enhance your understanding of the fears, the hate, and the hostility toward homosexual persons and their families. These emotions are expressed in so many painful and destructive ways in our churches and society. Homophobia is an urgent pastoral care issue which we need to address.

Reaction was swift and relentless. Many people thought Bishop Minnick's endorsement was scandalous. Copies of his letter circulated in many venues as evidence that the leadership of The United Methodist Church was promoting homosexuality. He became a target for scathing criticism. Not only had he refused to remove me from Fairmont because of my work with RRNGLE, he now had endorsed a RRNGLE conference. People who believed same-gender sexual relations to be sinful could not understand his view that "homophobia is an urgent pastoral care issue," nor could they see the church's exclusion of gays as an expression of "the fears, the hate, and the hostility toward homosexual persons and their families."

Since the churchwide meeting back in September, some Fairmont members refused to allow me to visit them in the hospital or in their homes. When several members died, their families told me that my involvement was not wanted, and they invited pastors of other churches to conduct the funeral services at funeral homes instead of at Fairmont. This was especially difficult for me as a pastor. Since they could not persuade the bishop to remove me as their pastor, they removed themselves from my pastoral care.

Two longtime members of Fairmont died in the spring of 1989. Horace Springer had been hospitalized for several weeks. He and his wife, Helen, had welcomed my visits. Horace was always pleasant. Although he disagreed with me, perhaps even disapproved of me, he was incapable of being unkind. During my visits, we never talked about what was happening at the church or about my civil and human rights advocacy for gay people. There were many other things we did talk about, mostly stories about his life — such as the time he spilled the offering plate in the church balcony during worship. Horace was deaf and, consequently, unaware of how loudly he spoke. When the dimes, nickels, and quarters hit the hardwood floor, bouncing and rolling about, Horace shouted, "Damn it!" "Everybody in the sanctuary heard me," he'd say, chuckling, as if proud of himself for his lapse of discretion.

One day, I found his hospital room empty and was told he'd died earlier in the day. I went immediately to see Helen. She thanked me for my frequent hospital visits with Horace but said his service would be held at a funeral home, and she didn't want me involved with it. Most of Helen's church friends wanted me gone. She had to make a choice between them and allowing me to conduct Horace's funeral. She chose her friends. I understood, but her decision hurt deeply.

Raymond Talton also died that spring. He was a quintessential Southern gentleman with impeccable manners and a friendly disposition. Like

Horace, Raymond could not be unkind. When he was hospitalized, I was told by one of his friends that Raymond didn't want me to visit him. Denied the opportunity to visit, but wanting to connect with Raymond in some way, I wrote him a note saying I would honor his desire that I not visit him but would keep him in my prayers. A few days later, I received a telephone call from Raymond's wife, Beuna. She told me I had been misinformed about Raymond's wishes; on the contrary, she said, he would like me to visit. I went to see him right away.

Raymond was weak and wasting away rapidly. His face, arms, and hands were little more than skin and bones. Nonetheless, he greeted me with a smile when I entered his hospital room. I offered to pray with him, and he nodded his permission. As I prepared to leave, he asked me to come back soon. I visited twice a day thereafter until his death.

During my next to last visit, Raymond beckoned me to come close so I could hear him speak. There was urgency in his gesture. I knelt by his side, took his left hand, and leaned toward him, looking into his pale blue eyes. Lifting his other hand from his chest and pointing his finger at me, he said: "You are a preacher . . . God called you to be a preacher . . . you have to do what God calls you to do, what you know is right . . . you can't worry about pleasing everybody . . . don't ever forget that."

I was moved deeply by his words, not expecting this from him, one of the teachers of the Wesley Bible Class and the principal author of its resolution condemning me back in 1988. No bishop's hand or ecclesial endorsement could have confirmed my calling to ministry more, or been more compelling, than what he said to me.

When I last visited Raymond, he was unconscious, his struggle to live nearing its end. I prayed with him a final time in his dying. Although she knew it displeased many of her church friends, Beuna asked me to conduct Raymond's funeral in Fairmont's sanctuary.

In July 1989, I received a letter inviting me to show support for the AIDS Service Agency (ASA) of Wake County by attending one of its Board of Directors meetings. This was a newly formed group of professional service providers and volunteers who worked with people living with HIV/AIDS.

When I arrived at the August ASA board meeting, I introduced myself to the president, Beth McAlister, and explained that I was there to show support. She began the meeting by introducing me and, to my surprise, moving that I be made a member of the board. There were no clergy on the ASA board, she explained, and she thought it would help improve community relations to include a minister.

Immediately, a woman sitting to Beth's left objected, calmly explaining that the bylaws of the ASA limited the board's membership to twenty-one, and there were no vacancies. She pointed out that only half of the current board members were active and suggested that inactive members be contacted to determine their interest and commitment. Rather than increasing the number of the board, board members who no longer wanted to serve should be removed to make room for truly interested and committed new members. She suggested that the board really didn't know me or what my commitment was to the ASA's mission, and people shouldn't be added just because they happen to show up at a meeting.

She further argued that the board needed to carefully consider what categories of people were not represented on it before replacing old members with new members. She pointed out that there were currently no people living with HIV/AIDS, no family members of people living with HIV/AIDS, and no people of color on the board. She argued that these categories should take priority over other categories of people, such as clergy.

Finally, she noted that even if the group wanted to add me to the current membership, it would require changing the bylaws to increase the number of members allowed. Such a vote, she reminded the group, could not happen without a thirty-day notice to all board members.

Beth listened patiently, a strained smile on her face and annoyance in her eyes. When the woman finished what I thought was a compelling argument against making me a board member, Beth turned to the other members and said, "All in favor of making Reverend Creech a member of the board, raise your hand." All hands but one went up. "All opposed, raise your hand," Beth said. Only the woman who had been outspoken against electing me raised her hand. I was impressed.

At the conclusion of the meeting, I wanted to speak to the woman who had voted against my joining the board, but she left too quickly. When I inquired about her, I learned her name was Chris Weedy and that she was one of the creators of the ASA and its vice president. She worked at Duke Medical Center as the senior clinical social worker in the Pediatric Infectious Disease Clinic. Her clients were children and their mothers with HIV/AIDS.

While I was strongly committed to the mission of the ASA, I had an additional motive to be an active member of the board. I knew that I had to earn Chris Weedy's respect and confidence. I left the meeting not only determined to help end the AIDS epidemic, but also to meet and get to know this extraordinary woman.

It would be nearly two months before I had a conversation with Chris Weedy. It seemed we always sat at opposite sides of the room at meetings. When we did interact, she always was cordial and professional. And because I had been concealing my true situation with Merle for two years at this point, I did not want to reveal my attraction to Chris and treated her with indifference.

One night in October, I spoke at an AIDS rally in front of the Old North Carolina State Capitol in Raleigh. Chris arrived pushing a wheelchair carrying a thin, frail, obviously very sick man. They were accompanied by several other men carrying hand-painted signs with messages like "Fight AIDS, Not People With AIDS," and "Fund Education, Not Fear." The men, I learned later, were members of the Raleigh HIV/AIDS Support Group that Chris had started and led since 1987 — the first HIV/AIDS support group in North Carolina. She pushed the wheelchair to the front of the crowd so that her friend could see the stage. As I spoke to the crowd, I watched her out of the corner of my eye.

A few days later, Chris called and asked if I would be willing to host the World AIDS Day observance at Fairmont on December 1. She explained that for the past couple of years, the event had taken place at various sites, none of which had been churches. She said it would be great to have it in a church, although she knew that the fear of AIDS and the controversy surrounding it made it difficult for churches to open their doors to such an event. I happily agreed to host the event.

Soon after our first planning meeting for the World AIDS Day event, Chris called again. Michael, the man in the wheelchair at the AIDS rally, had died. She told me his only real family was the support group. He had asked Chris to plan his memorial service and told her it was his wish to be cremated. She asked me if I would be willing to help her prepare the service and conduct it at her apartment one afternoon in the coming week. Many people in the support group had been badly abused and wounded by churches in the past, and her home, where the support group regularly met, was a safe haven for them to gather for Michael's service.

I arrived for the service and found about a dozen men sitting in Chris's living room. I spoke to each of them, introducing myself and learning their names. Then I sat off to the side as we waited for a few others to arrive. As I waited, I watched Chris console the men. She spoke to each one softly, hugging them, holding and caressing their hands, and gently stroking their heads. I had seen her strength and courage on display at my first ASA meeting. Now I was witnessing her tenderness and compassion. I had never been touched like that. My body ached with envy.

World AIDS Day was on Friday that year. The theme was "A Celebration of Hope." We planned an all-day prayer vigil that began at seven thirty in the morning. The sanctuary was open so people could come at any time during the day to pray or meditate or light a candle in memory or honor of someone who had died because of AIDS or who was living with HIV/AIDS.

At five thirty that evening, we held an ecumenical service of worship. The sanctuary was nearly full. There were people living with HIV/AIDS, some by themselves and others with family, lovers, friends, or caregivers. There were doctors, nurses, and social workers, all working on the front lines against the AIDS epidemic. The service was simple, with readings and prayers, times to speak about loved ones living and dead, and a time to light candles in their names. The media provided excellent coverage of the service. TV crews were careful to film from the back to protect the anonymity of those who were afraid to have their faces seen on the late-night news. Consequently, Fairmont United Methodist Church was publicly identified as a sanctuary for people living with and suffering from HIV/AIDS.

Later in December, Chris and her daughter, Natalia, were to travel to Chile for two weeks. In 1978, Chris had gone to Chile with the Peace Corps as a health educator to work in rural hospitals and remote outposts. There she met and fell in love with Jorge, a physician's assistant. Chris didn't want to marry. She would tell me much later in our relationship that she'd never seen a good marriage, so she didn't believe in the institution. But she did want a child, and she believed that Jorge would be a good partner in parenting their child.

As soon as Chris became pregnant, however, Jorge began to ignore her and pursue other women. Disillusioned and hurt, Chris ended the relationship. Wanting better hospital care than what was available in Chile, she returned to the United States and moved in with her brother, Mark, a few months before Natalia was born, on June 29, 1981. Chris believed it was time for Natalia, now eight years old, to meet her father and paternal grandparents for the first time.

Soon after Michael's memorial service, Chris had invited me to one of the support group meetings. The guys wanted me to talk about religion, the Bible, and homosexuality. They felt comfortable with me. Before Chris left for Chile, they asked if it would be okay with her if I served as the group's facilitator while she was away. Thus began my relationship with the Raleigh HIV/AIDS Support Group. When Chris returned from Chile, she made me her permanent co-leader. And in January, the ASA board elected Chris its president and me its vice president for the new year. I'd been on the board for only four months, but I was delighted to accept the responsibility of the position and, of course, to work more closely with Chris.

This involvement with the ASA introduced me to men and women living with AIDS who were desperately sick, some of whom died in the last months of 1989 and early in 1990. I made it a practice during worship at Fairmont to announce the names of those I knew who had died, even though they were not Fairmont members. I'd call out their first names and say something about them, such as "she was six years old, and her foster parents loved her dearly" or "he was his mother's only son and a dedicated lawyer" or "he was seventy-seven and enjoyed his garden." For most church members, this was the closest they came to knowing about a real person who had died of AIDS. At that time, the media was regularly reporting statistics about the AIDS epidemic, but little about the people who were infected. And obituary pages never attributed HIV/AIDS as the cause of death. My ritual of remembering those who died helped to personalize the epidemic for members at Fairmont, making it about real people.

For one of Fairmont's newsletters, I wrote a short article about AIDS in which I said: "You can't catch AIDS by hugging, shaking hands, or simply being near a person who is infected with the virus." Not long after the newsletter was mailed out to the congregation, a church member came to my office door with a brown paper bag. "People don't like the way you touch the bread when you serve communion," he explained. "They don't want to catch AIDS. If you're going to handle the bread with your hands, use these," he said, thrusting the bag at me. Inside were latex gloves. My article hadn't eased some people's fear but instead had inflamed it. For many Fairmont members, AIDS was a reality distant from them in terms of space, culture, and class. It was also an ominous mix of mystery, morals, and mortality. My frequent reference to people who had died brought the epidemic fearfully close for some members of the congregation.

Others responded with compassion and courage. They feared the disease no less than the others, but their compassion was stronger. They understood that the effects of this deadly virus were not just physical devastation and death, but also ostracism and isolation. They knew that while they could not cure the disease, they could help cure the loneliness. These members became involved in activities and programs that provided support to people with AIDS, such as helping to renovate a house in Raleigh that became a group home for people too sick with AIDS to live alone, volunteering to care for an infected three-year-old on weekends so his mother, who also had AIDS, could have some time for herself, and volunteering with a buddy program to give companionship to someone living with AIDS.

My involvement with people living with HIV/AIDS became widely known in the community and around The United Methodist Church in North Carolina. One night, I received a telephone call from a colleague, the pastor of a large downtown United Methodist church in Fayetteville, North Carolina. He said he had a church member at Raleigh Community Hospital who had AIDS and asked if I would visit the young man, Ron. The pastor explained that although Ron was still a member of the church, he had been estranged from it for several years. When it became public that he was gay, Ron was shunned and told he was no longer welcome at the church. His family continued to be members and didn't have a relationship with him, either. My colleague said that I was the only person he knew whom he could ask to visit his parishioner.

When I introduced myself to Ron, he was surprised that I'd come to visit him. He knew who I was, but he had no interest in a visit from a minister. I told him about his pastor's telephone call. Ron said that his pastor had been friendly in private but couldn't be openly supportive of him because of "church politics." So, Ron explained, he'd left the church and never intended to go back. He was hurt. He spoke with sarcastic and irreverent humor about the church, his family, society, himself, AIDS — everything. It was his way of dealing with his anger, as well as his longing and grief, his love and loss.

Two friends were visiting Ron when I arrived and, to give him a change of scenery, the three of us took him for a walk around the hospital in his wheelchair. It was the first time I'd hung out with a group of gay men. To my consternation, they brazenly flirted with every male we passed, loudly whispering comments about the physical attributes of each — or lack thereof — without regard to anyone's reaction or opinion. It seemed as if they wanted to scandalize people, to offend them. I'd never been with a group of non-gay guys who were as conspicuously lusty in their comments about women as these guys were about men. I was embarrassed. But I understood their public disdain for decorum in the shadow of homophobia and AIDS to be a way of fighting back, a way of taunting bigotry and death. Their behavior protested the socially imposed shame and denial that they experienced.

Because I was with them, I knew that the people we encountered on our walk around the hospital would think I was gay. I was uncomfortable. I felt fear tugging at me to distance myself from Ron and his friends, to walk away or to announce to everyone that I was not gay. But I couldn't reject and affirm these gay men at the same time. When I stepped off the curb to join the Pride March in the summer of 1988, I stepped into their world and would be identified with it forever — the good as well as the bad. I didn't intend for that to happen, but it did and I accepted it. I would not use my heterosexuality as a privilege and protection from the social scorn and discrimination that gay people experience. It became my personal policy not to identify my sexual orientation unless I was asked to do so.

As his health deteriorated, Ron moved to a hospital in Fayetteville to be closer to his family who, because he was dying, embraced him once again. There was no similar reconciliation with his church.

The Raleigh HIV/AIDS Support Group became a small, intimate family for me. They taught me not only what life is like for people living with HIV/AIDS, but what it's like for gay people to live in a hostile society. Until this time, my contact with lesbian, gay, bisexual, and transgender people had been limited to discussions about issues such as discrimination and violence, the legal problems they had to deal with, religious bigotry, and rejection by family and friends. Beneath the surface of these issues, my knowledge of what life was really like for someone who is gay had been minimal. I didn't really comprehend the existential consequences. Over time, the support group members trusted me with their dreams, fears, longings, pains, passions, and loves, the truly human dimension beyond the issues. They gave me an understanding of their world that comes only from sharing life with others.

One night, just after a group meeting ended, Thomas approached me and, with a flush of embarrassment on his face, said, "Jimmy, I need to apologize to you."

"Why, Thomas?" I asked.

"I didn't know you're not gay," he explained. "I was making passes at you all during the meeting." We'd met for the first time that night. Thomas was in his early twenties and had an outgoing cheerful personality.

"That's okay, Thomas," I said. "I didn't know you were making passes at me. And I'm flattered that you would."

Then his mood became somber, almost angry. "I also didn't know you're a minister," he continued. "I want to tell you that I've known I was queer since I was a kid, and there's nothing I can do to change that. I also know that God hates me because I'm queer. I know I'm going to hell. I know that because I learned it at my church and that's what I believe. I want you to know that there is nothing you can say to me to make me believe any different. I don't want you to ever talk to me about God, the Bible, and religion."

His words were uncompromising, like a shield thrown up before him. He'd been wounded so much and so badly by religion that he wanted no words about it from me, not even the assurance that God loved him. To unlearn what he'd so painfully learned and internalized was a challenge he was unwilling to meet. He didn't come to many group meetings after that night. I couldn't help but think he wanted to avoid me. Some months later, we learned that Thomas had died. He died believing that God hated him and he was going to hell. Just as the virus had destroyed his body, the church had destroyed his spirit.

Another member of the support group, a young man named Peter, began attending worship at Fairmont every other week. One Sunday, as he left worship, he asked if we could meet for lunch the next day. Peter was a quiet, gentle person in his late twenties, polite and neatly dressed. He was a lawyer who worked in the North Carolina attorney general's office, in downtown Raleigh. He was devoted to his mother and visited her every other weekend in the small eastern North Carolina town where she lived and he had grown up. He explained that he'd been active in his hometown United Methodist church since he was a child.

Peter told me his mother didn't know that he was gay and had AIDS. Although they were close and he knew she loved him dearly, he feared that her heart would break if she knew the truth about him. He also feared that if the members of his church found out, neither he nor his mother would be welcome there any longer. He was sure that she'd have no support and would be isolated. He knew and understood Southern small-town culture, and how it can drive away what is unfamiliar or threatening.

Peter had been diagnosed with AIDS over a year before. When he first was hospitalized with *Pneumocystis carinii*, a strain of pneumonia that can be deadly for people with AIDS, he told his mother that he was being treated for ulcers. He had covered subsequent episodes of his AIDS-related illnesses by saying he had flu or sinus infections—anything to hide the truth.

He'd recently been at Duke Medical Center with another bout of pneumonia. He was growing weaker; he'd lost his appetite and was missing more and more days of work. He knew that his time was short and that he could not keep the truth from his mother much longer. Besides, he really wanted her to know all about him before his death. I encouraged him to trust his mother's love and offered to talk with her after he'd told her. He was going home the following weekend and planned to tell her then.

Peter's mother, Ruth, called me that Sunday afternoon. She was heartsick and frightened. She'd just discovered that her only child—the diligent and bright student, the pride of her life, the caring, dependable, devoted son—was gay. Adding horror to shock, she'd learned that he was dying of AIDS. She didn't really know what she wanted to ask or say to me, but she was in no hurry to hang up the phone. Her words, choked with tears, were punctuated with long pauses. I told her that no mother could ask for a finer son, that Peter was a person of dignity and integrity of whom she could always be proud. I assured her that God loved Peter unconditionally. After a long pause, she thanked me and said good-bye.

When Peter's health began a rapid decline, Ruth moved to Raleigh to take care of him. The day after she arrived, she called and asked to see me. That afternoon she greeted me with a warm but weary smile and invited me to sit in Peter's living room. She needed to tell me a story. One Sunday morning, months before, when Peter was visiting her, they were sitting together reading the Raleigh *News & Observer*. There was an article on the controversy about me and my ministry with gay people and people with AIDS. "I just can't understand how a minister could associate with that kind of people," Ruth said she told Peter. Her church and culture had taught her that "that kind of people" was undesirable and should be shunned. Peter didn't respond, she said. He didn't even look up from the newspaper, but just sat quietly, reading. They never discussed the article or her comment.

When Peter told her that he was gay and had AIDS, she immediately remembered her comment to him that Sunday. She apologized to me for saying it and thanked me for supporting Peter. But what really broke her heart, what she could not forgive herself for, was that she'd said what she had to Peter, her precious son, only later to learn that he was "that kind of people." She blamed herself for giving Peter reason to fear she would reject him, reason to conceal the truth from her for so long. "If only he had told me, could have told me," she grieved, "I could have taken care of him, could have been with him and helped him during all this time he's been sick."

"Help me," she pleaded, putting her face in her hands and crying. I knelt beside her, took her hands, and spoke to her about her love for Peter and his for her, about putting the past behind her and giving him the love and care she could now, during his dying. I assured her that God was with her and Peter, that they would not be alone.

I went with Ruth to Peter's bedroom to visit with him for a few minutes before leaving. We held hands and prayed. My spoken prayer was for Peter, for his comfort and peace. My silent prayer was for Ruth, who believed she'd betrayed the person she loved most in the world. Peter was loved, and he knew it. He no longer feared being rejected and abandoned by his mother. Medications had taken away his pain. He was comfortable and prepared to die. Death was no longer an enemy, but a friend that would set him free from the awful scourge of AIDS. But Ruth would live with a pain that she could not escape, a pain that no drug could numb or cure. She needed prayer that day for the days to come without Peter, the days of remembering how long he had suffered without her knowledge and support.

There were twenty-nine members in the Raleigh HIV/AIDS Support Group when I joined Chris Weedy as her co-leader. None are alive today. Since then, many others have been members of the group and have died. All of them—those who have died and those who are still with us—have been my mentors, giving me an understanding that comes only from being with, living with, and sharing with someone. That understanding is a big part of the reason why I am who I am, and why I feel and act the way I do. Their humanity—including their integrity, dignity, weakness, strength, fears, hopes, love, passion, joy, courage, and determination to survive and thrive—has inspired me profoundly. In many ways, the story I'm telling would not have happened, or at the least would have happened in a much different way, had it not been for the members of the support group.

Every fall, each United Methodist church holds a Charge or All Church Conference when officers are elected and the budget is approved for the coming year. Among the most important officers elected are the members of the Pastor-Parish Relations Committee. I had received the support of the majority of the nine committee members for the two previous years at Fairmont. However, three of the four new members elected to the committee in the fall of 1989 were people I knew would not support my ministry. Their commitment to Fairmont was strong. They never withdrew their financial support or active participation, but I knew they didn't want me at Fairmont. I knew I'd be forced to leave at the end of the Annual Conference meeting in June 1990.

Soon after, Alma Blount asked if I would agree to be interviewed by *The Independent*, a weekly alternative newspaper known for solid, in-depth investigative reporting and widely distributed throughout the Triangle area of Raleigh, Durham, and Chapel Hill. She said the paper wanted to do an article about the controversy at Fairmont. Alma was a dear friend with whom I'd worked opposing U.S. foreign policy in Central America; she was also one of the founders of *The Independent*. My initial impulse was to decline her request. I knew the article would make public what was essentially a family secret. Any public exposure of the crisis within Fairmont and the reason for it would only intensify the controversy and the anger directed at me by some members of the church. It would be easier for me to lick my wounds and keep quiet during what little time I had left at the church. The more I considered what to do, however, the more clearly I saw that I had a responsibility to do the interview in spite of the risk. What was happening at Fairmont was not a unique or isolated incident. Rather, the controversy reflected what was happening all over the country in regard to gay people, the church, and society. Silence makes injustice possible. While *The Independent*'s article would focus on my ministry at Fairmont, it would reveal larger social and theological issues that needed to be addressed. I decided it would be wrong and self-serving of me to avoid this opportunity for a public discussion of these issues that could help change hearts and minds. I was convinced that making the story public was the only way positive change could come out of all that had happened at Fairmont. The boil of bigotry had to be opened before healing could happen. My hope was that the story would help not only Fairmont in its struggle with this insidious conflict, but all who would read it. So, with a deep sigh of apprehension for what surely was to come, but also with a firm purpose in mind, I agreed to the interview.

Melinda Ruley was assigned to write the story. During November and December, she interviewed me several times, as well as members of the congregation, members of RRNGLE, biblical scholars, and church leaders.

On Friday, January 19, 1990, *The Independent* hit the streets with a full-page photo of me on the front and a feature article five tabloid pages long titled "Ministering to Our Fears." The text continued: "Jimmy Creech offered the grace of God—and was met with empty pews, whispered rumors and a fight over his future."

Melinda told the story well, placing it in the larger context of religion-based fears about sexuality in general, and homosexuality in particular. She condensed what had been a whirlwind of controversy and conflict into a concise and understandable story about the resistance to changing attitudes about homosexuality:

> So part of Fairmont's reaction to Jimmy Creech—part of what makes up homophobia—is a fear of confronting sexuality itself, everything from the societal norm of patriarchy to the individual sexual politics of the missionary position. Homosexuality calls on people to think about their sexuality in the same way a sudden catastrophe makes us consider our mortality. Gay men and lesbians are forced, in a way straight people aren't, to deal with their sexuality. "Coming out means saying, 'I'm a sexual being,'" one gay man told me. "It means saying it's part of my identity, part of the way God made me. I feel like God is part of my relationship with my lover, and knowing that has put me sort of newly in awe of sex—my sexuality." . . .
>
> "At Fairmont, the prejudice, the silence, comes from lack of understanding," says Willie Pilkington, co-chair of the Southeastern Conference for Lesbians and Gay Men. "These are not mean or hateful people." . . .
>
> If you weren't brought up to believe in the authority of religious doctrine, it's difficult to understand how painful the church's rejection is to gay men and lesbians who grew up thinking God speaks through that institution's traditions and doctrines. What's taught by soft-spoken ministers on Sunday mornings is for many gay men and lesbians more

devastating than the jeers and bawdy jokes heard at their schools and jobs . . .

It's when you listen to the men and women who have struggled with — and stayed within — their churches that you realize how important some- one like Jimmy Creech is . . . Homophobia isn't just gay people being hated by straight people. It's gay people hating themselves — a transferral of emotions that's intensified when the victim is unable to distinguish be- tween rejection by the church and rejection by God . . .

What are the proper channels of affection and eroticism — and why do we allow them to be dictated to us? What makes Jimmy Creech's mes- sage so difficult is that it asks that question and others, breaks down old boundaries based on outdated or wrong thinking — and explores instead what's possible and healthy for us as sexual beings. That's scary, Creech says, but it can only make us happier with ourselves and our God.

As I sat in my office reading the article for the first time, the telephone rang. The church secretary was at lunch, so I answered. "What time is your worship service on Sunday?" an unidentified voice asked. "I've just read the article in *The Independent*, and I want to come to show my support."

The sanctuary was packed with visitors on the following Sunday morn- ing. A mother and father with two adolescent children traveled from Chapel Hill to be there. They explained that they wanted their children to be part of a church that was open to all people. Many lesbian and gay individuals and couples filled the pews. It had been months since the sanctuary had been full. The Fairmont members were surprised and excited by this outpouring of community support.

Soon after Melinda's article appeared in *The Independent*, the *News & Ob- server*, Raleigh's newspaper with statewide circulation, published a similar article that was picked up by the Associated Press and reprinted in news- papers all over the state and across the country. Before long, a horde of newspaper reporters descended upon Fairmont from cities like Atlanta, Philadelphia, and Detroit. The controversy at Fairmont had become a na- tional story.

The media coverage gave me a larger audience for the message about God's love for and acceptance of lesbian, gay, and bisexual people. Many who read the articles felt affirmed by the message and felt they were re- ceiving acceptance and respect from a minister for the first time in their lives. I began to get letters from all across the country. Each told a story of rejection and suffering because of religion, family, or—most often—both. Each told of a struggle for self-acceptance, a healthy love of self. The letters were both painful and inspiring to read. I was grateful that a message of hope and love had been conveyed to so many. There were letters like this one:

Dear Reverend Creech,

To tell you the truth, I don't think there are words to express how I feel about your sacrifice. I sometimes feel the pressure of the mix of intolerance, misunderstanding, and outright hatred, and that darkness can be pretty depressing. One comes to expect it and maybe that's the internalized homophobia Ruley [who wrote *The Independent* article] hints at.

Anyway, your gesture, your campaign, your truth, your friendship will serve so many people. Thank you. People like me will read the article and feel encouraged. If a prominent Methodist minister can be tolerant of us and recognize that God made us, too, then surely others can. The hand you extend to my community and the enlightenment you offer us all will be worth it. Thank you so much.

Love,
Allison

Some letters revealed long-held secrets:

Dear Jimmy,

I was 10 or 11 years old when you came to Edenton Street Church. I remember you as being a very warm and caring person. Little did I realize then that we would be marching in the same gay pride march some 18 years later. I can't thank you enough for standing up for gay rights as you have done. You have put your job on the line to support what is often a very unpopular cause. Believe me when I say that we in the [gay] community appreciate your effort and are praying for you. We know we are right! God bless you.

Sincerely,
Jesse

Just as Jesse had done in his letter, in the years to come, many high school and university classmates and teachers, colleagues, parishioners, and friends whom I'd known well would disclose to me what I'd never suspected, that they were lesbian or gay. I had entered their world, and they could now trust me with the whole truth about themselves.

It was not long after the explosion of publicity that the Pastor-Parish Relations Committee held its first meeting in 1990. The committee focused on the financial stress that the church was experiencing, and the continuing loss or inactivity of longtime members. The impact of those who withheld funds had been severe, and it was too early to appreciate the impact of the new community support inspired by the publicity. Even members of the committee who had previously been resolute in their support of me now wanted me to leave.

At the Administrative Board meeting in March, the committee announced its decision to ask Bishop Minnick for a new pastor. Because I didn't want a divisive fight between those who supported me and those who didn't, I chose not to contest their decision. After the board meeting, I returned to my office, closed the door, and began to weep uncontrollably. I was emotionally exhausted and felt defeated. The stress of the past two years and the finality of the committee's decision had sapped my strength. I stood at my desk sobbing, my body shaking.

The church telephone rang. No one answered it. It rang and rang. I finally composed myself enough to pick up the phone. A woman's soft voice said, "I was just in worship at the Unitarian Universalist Fellowship here in Raleigh, and learned about what you have been doing for the lesbian and gay community. I'm Roman Catholic, and my daughter is lesbian. She's been badly hurt by my church, and will no longer have anything to do with it. I want you to know how much what you've done means to me and to her. I called just to say 'Thank you!'" I swallowed the lump in my throat and managed to whisper, "Thank you." In the midst of my pain, this grateful mother touched me with grace, assuring me that my ministry had not been in vain.

During my remaining few months at Fairmont, support from the larger community remained strong. Sunday worship services were well attended by visitors, bringing new energy to the congregation. While I was excited by this, I also grieved, knowing that I'd be leaving in June. The members who had been supportive were grieving, too. We had been through a tough struggle. Some threatened to leave after I was gone. I worked hard to convince them that their continued faithfulness and commitment to Fairmont was crucial if my departure was not to be a defeat. I reminded them that their commitment was not to me, but to helping the church be faithful, inclusive, compassionate, and just.

Even as my time at Fairmont grew shorter, the opportunities to address the pastoral issues related to lesbian and gay people increased. Encouraged by the public exposure of the internal controversy at Fairmont, Robert Bryant came to me for guidance and support in coming out. Tall, handsome, and gregarious, Robert was active at Fairmont and a popular leader of the Raleigh Wesley Foundation Campus Ministry, always ready to extend a helping hand and say a kind word. One Sunday evening, in the living room of the parsonage, Robert told me he was gay. He said he'd been rehearsing how to tell me as he drove that afternoon from his hometown in northeastern North Carolina back to Raleigh. He said that, after years of hiding in the closet, he'd finally decided to come out to everyone. He wanted his mother, father, and sister to know the truth. He wanted his friends to know, and all of his relatives. We talked about ways he could do this, and he carefully made his plan. He would compose a "coming out" letter that he would send first to his parents, and then to his other relatives and friends. After much thoughtful work, his beautifully written letter was just the way he wanted it to be:

March 17, 1990

This letter I'm writing to you is a gift from me. It is the biggest and most dear gift I've ever given you. It comes from deep down and with much love, because I do care even though my answers to your personal questions over the years have been short and brief or at least not too deep.

For the past two years I have been working on a lot of personal issues . . . It has been really hard. It's kinda like finally stopping the games, hiding and running and sitting down and looking face to face with who you really are. When you do this, it is like opening your personal closet of issues, fears, habits, problems, etc. that you've only opened before to quickly throw something in, slam it shut and seal it. When you open it, a lifetime of garbage, with a few jewels mixed in, falls out. I say garbage and jewels because there is a lot of stuff you will sort out, work through and THROW AWAY!! But, yes, there are things you find that you'll want to treasure like jewels. You'll even want to polish them and let them shine, to share with others.

Well, needless to say, being the silent type, I had filled my closet to the max. While sorting through all the garbage I found one very important jewel I would like to share with you my family. The jewel I found was my sexuality. I am homosexual. Yes, I'm sure. There is no doubt . . . I know some of you may have had some suspicions, because I have dropped some clues over the past year. Whether you knew or not, I'm sure having it confirmed in black and white must be rather shocking and upsetting. So, why wouldn't I carry such a thing to the grave? (The first 24 years of my life, I promised myself I would. Yes, I have felt this way since the first memory I have. I've always been attracted to men.) Because I'm choosing to share my life with the people I love, instead of growing further and further apart until there was nothing there.

My being gay is special and means a lot to me. Yes, I've had to work hard to have such a *healthy* view of my sexual orientation. Sometimes it has been pure Hell and still is and unfortunately will be always to some degree because of our society and its prejudiced, bigoted views. The deep inner peace I have attained from working and being more open and honest about my feelings and who I am is like life's breath itself, so refreshing and renewing, like the exhilarating smell of a crisp spring breeze that awakens our nose and lungs with sweet aromas of nature and what is natural. I am very happy now as a gay man. I have established a good network of friends in the gay community. I go to Integrity (Episcopalians for Gay and Lesbian concerns) twice a month . . . [I]t has affirmed me as a homosexual and a Christian. The two are very much a part of each other; they can't be separated . . .

Of course, I've drawn great strength from Jimmy Creech, my minister at Fairmont United Methodist Church who has gone out on a limb for gay rights. He is a warm beautiful person and lives the Christian life out as I've never seen before. Really saying and doing what it means to be Christian. Not hesitating to back up his words, beliefs with *action*. I'm sorry for the "Jimmy for President" speech, but his support has meant a lot to me . . .

Well, I think that should be enough to overload you for a while . . . I would like a response when you're ready but I know it will take time and that's okay. Hey, it took me over two years to be able to tell you, so I understand. When it's right, it'll happen. One thing that will not change for me, no matter what decisions or choices you make, most importantly

I will always love each and every one of you and in some way you will always be a part of me no matter where we go or where we end up . . .

With more love than you've ever gotten before,
Robert

Robert's letter was courageous, caring, and insightful. The very public discussion in the media of the controversy at Fairmont gave Robert a safe context and encouraged him to take this step of coming out to his family and friends, all of whom responded with loving acceptance.[5]

There were others who trusted me with the truth of their sexuality because of the publicity. Two United Methodist clergy colleagues I'd known for years came out to me separately and in confidence. One was married and a chaplain at one of the state hospitals. The other served a local church. Both were afraid of exposure in general, and of losing their ministries because they were gay. Yet they were desperate to share and talk about the truth they hid with someone they trusted. The isolation and hypocrisy with which they lived was a daily denial of their humanity. They wanted my acceptance and affirmation. Throughout that spring, we met just to talk. One decided he wanted to keep his ministry so much that he chose to keep his sexuality secret and remain in a marriage that was unsatisfying to both him and his wife. The other chose to end his ministry in the church because he met and fell in love with a man.

Boo Tyson, whose father was a prominent United Methodist pastor in North Carolina, called and asked to meet with me. Now in her early twenties, she'd left the church some years before. Over lunch, Boo explained why—she was lesbian. Her faith in God was strong and sure, but she couldn't accept the church's teachings about homosexuality. After reading *The Independent* article, she reconsidered her relationship with the church and the importance of helping it change. Boo and I talked often after that day. Together with Robert Bryant, we started a North Carolina chapter of Affirmation: United Methodists for Lesbian, Gay, Bisexual and Transgender Concerns. We had success for about a year, but couldn't keep the group going. Boo confided that, like her grandfather, father, and five uncles who were ministers, she too wanted to serve the church but didn't know how. The United Methodist Church was not an option because she intended to be open about her sexuality. Although Boo did attend seminary later on, she found her calling outside the church with nonprofit organizations that served the homeless and victims of domestic abuse and advocated for civil rights.

That spring, James and Timothy asked if I would conduct a holy union ceremony for them. They had begun attending worship at Fairmont soon after *The Independent* article. They had been life partners for several years and owned a home together. James worked for the State of North Carolina, and Timothy had his own business as a landscape architect. The public celebration of their commitment to each other would be in the backyard garden that Timothy had planted and tended. I said I'd be honored to help them.

While conducting a holy union ceremony for two men was a new experience for me, I didn't think of it as controversial. In fact, it was a rather traditional Christian thing to do. How could I recognize and affirm gay people without recognizing, affirming, and supporting their loving, committed relationships? Civil and religious authorities may deny them recognition, but no one can invalidate a relationship grounded in love and integrity. Such grounding is the very reality of God, the ultimate authority and blessing. James and Timothy's holy union ceremony, using the traditional United Methodist marriage liturgy with the Eucharist, was the first of many that I would conduct over the remaining years of my ministry.

Now that it was definite I would be leaving Fairmont and Raleigh, Merle found an apartment and moved out of the parsonage. Patrick remained with me at the parsonage. Scheduled to graduate from high school in June, he had no college plans and would go with me to my new appointment, wherever it was. No one at Fairmont knew about the disintegration of my marriage to Merle. In fact, because she had not been involved at the church over the past three years, few members had met her, and her departure from the parsonage wasn't noticed. As painful as it was to deal with the conflict at the church, going home to cold, stressful silence for three years had been more painful. Her finally leaving brought me welcome but sad relief.

The process of appointing a pastor in The United Methodist Church is tedious, usually beginning in March and concluding in late May. Belton Joyner was then superintendent of the Raleigh District, and he told me that my move from Fairmont would be to one or two smaller churches and would have a much lower salary because of the controversy around my ministry at Fairmont. He said the bishop and his cabinet[6] were having difficulty agreeing on where they were willing to put me.

Finally, after weeks of waiting, Belton informed me that I would be appointed to two small churches in rural Vance County—Rehobeth United Methodist Church and Harris Chapel United Methodist Church—located north of Raleigh, near the Virginia border. In late May, Wallace Kirby, who would be my new district superintendent, drove me to meet the churches' joint Pastor-Parish Relations Committee. On the way, he stressed that the cabinet had worked hard to make this appointment, and that it was the last possible option for me. He said my problem was not that I had advocated for gay rights, but that I had done so publicly. If I had been quiet about it, he said, I wouldn't have had such a problem getting another appointment. He said I should be grateful to Bishop Minnick and the cabinet, given the circumstances that had prompted my leaving Fairmont.

The meeting with the committee members was amicable. Because the controversy at Fairmont had been reported in all the newspapers around the state, I assumed the members were well aware of my history. Yet I sensed no hostility or resistance from them. No one asked about the controversy, and no one appeared to be uncomfortable. We ended the meeting with cordial farewells and handshakes.

Wallace took me to see the parsonage where Patrick and I were soon to make our home. As we rode through the countryside, the prospect of living and working in this rural setting, far from the stress I'd known for the past two years, became surprisingly seductive. The landscape was quiet, healing, and beautiful. The pain of leaving Fairmont began to ease as I looked forward to the new life for which I was now preparing.

When the 1990 North Carolina Annual Conference of The United Methodist Church ended on Saturday, June 16, my appointment to the two Vance County churches was official. However, the next day Wallace Kirby telephoned me: "We have some problems with your appointment. I want you to meet me at Wendy's tomorrow at 3:00." Belton Joyner would be there, too, he said.

That Monday afternoon I sat with Wallace and Belton at a Wendy's restaurant on Highway 70 between Raleigh and Durham. I don't recall Belton saying anything the whole time. He was conspicuously uncomfortable. Wallace, on the other hand, had the brutal directness of an executioner. "Jimmy," he said, "a member of the Pastor-Parish Relations Committee called me Saturday night and said that if the bishop insists on sending you to the Vance County churches, the members won't attend worship and won't send money to the Annual Conference. So I told him I'd cancel your appointment and send someone else to be their pastor. I called Bishop Minnick, and he supports my decision. We've already appointed a student pastor in your place." Wallace coldly added: "Jimmy, you've got ten days to move out of the Fairmont parsonage and find someplace else to live, and you'll need to find a job. You're on your own now. The Annual Conference is over, and all the appointments are made. We don't have a place for you."

I was stunned. Already emotionally drained from the stress of the past two years, the end of my marriage, and the grief of leaving Fairmont, I now was being cut off by the church that had nurtured me into adulthood, the church that I was committed to serve and had served for twenty years. I had broken no church laws. I had simply taken a public stand in support of lesbian, gay, bisexual, and transgender persons. The church leaders were fearful of controversy and did not know how to use it for education and growth, nor did they want to lose money and members. As a result, I was being abandoned. The key players in this decision were people I respected, trusted, and considered my friends. How I got myself back home from Wendy's I don't know. I was physically sick with anger, hurt, disbelief, and grief.

I learned more than a decade later that the resistance to my appointment had been festering for some time at the Rehobeth and Harris Chapel churches. At that time, I was the guest preacher at St. Mark's United Methodist Church in Atlanta. After worship, a young man introduced himself and told me he'd grown up in the Harris Chapel Church. He'd attended a meeting there with his parents to talk about my coming to be its pastor. He told me that somebody at Fairmont had sent a packet of newspaper articles about me to a member of the Harris Chapel congregation. He'd never before heard the leaders of the church use the hateful language that he heard that night. Everyone was angry with the bishop, and no one wanted me to come. The vicious words weren't directed only at me, but at those "disgusting homosexual perverts" as well. The young man silently suffered through the meeting, he said, fearful those "good people" would discover that he was gay.

On my final Sunday at Fairmont, I was overcome with emotion. It was the last time I would be with the people who had been supportive and faithful, people for whom I cared so deeply. I preached about the Christian mandate to love and accept everyone without condition. As I celebrated the Eucharist with these people whom I knew and loved dearly, giving each the bread and cup as they came forward, a steady stream of tears ran down my cheeks.

After the final hymn, I asked the congregation to be seated. "I need to let you know my appointment to the Rehobeth and Harris Chapel churches has been taken away," I explained. "The people there don't want me. The bishop has appointed someone else. I don't know what I'll be doing. But I want you to know that I'll be okay." I then prayed my final blessing on the people of Fairmont.

As I walked away from the chancel area and down the center aisle, the congregation stood and applauded me. Chuck Herrin, a United Methodist minister who had assisted in worship that morning, was walking next to me and sensed that I was about to collapse. He put his arm around my shoulders and carried me out at his side. He wouldn't let me go, wouldn't let me falter. As the choir sang its closing response to the last prayer, I gathered my composure as best I could to say good-bye for the last time to the members as they departed.

The news about my being without a church, home, and job was quickly broadcast around the state on the Sunday evening television news and in Monday's newspapers. Friends and strangers called to offer sympathy and encouragement. One of the first was Fred Herzog, my teacher and friend at the Duke Divinity School. "Remember the Easter laughter," he said, referring to the resurrection. He knew this was not the end for me, but the beginning of something as yet undisclosed. He didn't discount the pain, uncertainty, and difficulty of my situation, but he was confident that, as life laughs at death in Easter, life would laugh at the church's effort to bury and silence me.

Unwilling to give up on being a pastor, I requested a meeting with Bishop Minnick and his cabinet to discuss an idea I had. When we met a month later, I told them about the many people I'd met over the past three years who were committed to social justice and peace, who were hungry for a spiritual home, but who felt alienated by the institutional church. I explained to the bishop and cabinet that I wanted their permission to start a new church in the Triangle area, a congregation dedicated to a social justice ministry. I didn't want money from the Annual Conference, I explained — nothing for salary or expenses. All I wanted was their blessing. I would find a job to support myself and get the new church going on my own.

Bishop Minnick and the cabinet asked me to leave the room so they could discuss the proposal among themselves. After a brief wait, I was invited back in and told they would not give their permission. After twenty years of ministry, I was no longer welcome in The United Methodist Church in North Carolina. They couldn't legally remove me because I was an ordained elder in good standing and had broken no church law. However, my advocacy for human and civil rights for gay people made me a pariah among my colleagues, especially the bishop and district superintendents, who had the power to deny me an appointment as a pastor in a local church.

Some days later, one of the superintendents told me that the cabinet and bishop thought my idea for a new congregation was great for someone else to start, but not me. The idea was vetoed by a superintendent who feared that under my leadership, it would become a gay United Methodist church. He didn't want that, nor did the others.

At Nancy Keppel's insistence, Patrick and I moved into her guest room and stored our few belongings in her basement. We stayed with her for about a month, until my cousins Susan and Doug Hammer offered us an apartment they owned that was being vacated. They said we could stay there for free, as long as we needed.

I had no savings and only enough money to get through the first month after leaving Fairmont. I'd been a pastor for twenty years and didn't know how or where to start, but I urgently needed to find a job. Mahan Siler, good pastor that he was, helped me understand just how fragile my mind and spirit were. I was operating on my last reserve of emotional energy. Once it was gone, Mahan warned, I might have a complete breakdown. Then my recovery would be longer and more difficult. He convinced me to not start a job right away and to focus on recovering from the stress of the past two years. He assured me that somehow Patrick and I would be taken care of financially.

For the next six months, we survived solely on the grace and generosity of many friends and supporters, both known and unknown to me. Every day, there would be at least one check or some cash in the mail from someone I did not know. Along with the gift would be a note thanking me for my ministry and wishing me well. I expected the generosity to wane as the months passed and I was forgotten, but that never happened. We always had just enough money to meet our needs.

I had been cast out by The United Methodist Church and taken under the protective wing of a diverse community, largely composed of gay, lesbian, bisexual, and transgender people. Abused and wounded by religious teachings and practices themselves, they offered the grace that made it possible for me to survive the wilderness that lay between my past life in the church and the unknown future.

While I was supported financially by many people I didn't know, the one person I knew best was my soul support. The qualities that had first attracted me to Chris Weedy—her courage, strength, tenderness, and compassion—fed my exhausted spirit and nursed me toward wholeness. Although she was angry at the church for abandoning me, she never felt sorry for me or treated me like a victim. She helped me believe that I had control of my future and would be able to create a new life I could believe in. Although she didn't tell me so until much later, she loved me in a way I had not known before. And I realized that I loved her although I had thought I would never love again.

As fall approached, I learned that the North Carolina Council of Churches was accepting applications for a part-time program associate position. Created in 1935, the council was dedicated to the goals of racial justice, world peace, and collective bargaining for factory workers. Its social justice advocacy had expanded these goals to include gender equality, children's rights, protection of migrant farmworkers, abolition of capital punishment, and other issues. Its membership was composed of mainline Protestant denominations and the Roman Catholic Church in North Carolina.[7] It was a prophetic and progressive Christian voice, unafraid of controversy. I had great respect for the council's executive director, the Reverend Collins Kilburn. In the early years of his ministry in the late 1950s and early 1960s, Collins had been one of Raleigh's key church leaders in the civil rights movement while serving as pastor of the Community United Church of Christ. He was a passionate preacher of the Christian gospel and advocate for the disenfranchised and oppressed. While I hadn't abandoned my dream of being a pastor again, I decided to apply for the part-time position. I was invited for an interview and offered the job.

The Right Reverend Robert Estill, bishop of the North Carolina Diocese of the Episcopal Church, was serving as the president of the council at the time. When he welcomed me to the staff at the December Executive Committee meeting, he suggested that one of my first tasks should be drafting a public policy statement for the council dealing with homosexuality. The council hadn't addressed this issue, and hiring me made it an appropriate time to do so.

I officially began work on January 1, 1991, and immediately began drafting "A Policy Statement Regarding Violence, Harassment, and Discrimination against Gay Men and Lesbians." It reported national and North Carolina statistics on antigay hate crimes and recognized that "certain religious teachings have labeled gay men and lesbians as persons worthy of contempt and punishment. Gay men and lesbians are perceived by some religious communities as threats to the moral structure of society, and attacks against them are viewed as moral and righteous." The statement said: "The North Carolina Council of Churches rejects the fear, prejudice, and hatred that foster societal and religious attitudes which either encourage, condone, or ignore violence and discrimination against gay men and lesbians. The Council stands with gay men and lesbians in their struggle to achieve equal human and civil rights under the laws of North Carolina and of the United States. The Council recognizes that this struggle is not only for the freedom and equality of gay men and lesbians, but is also for the emancipation of the whole society from the destructive, emotionally crippling effects of fear and hatred."

The policy statement was adopted by the council's Executive Committee on December 4, 1991, the anniversary of my being hired. Included in the statement were resolutions that urged all religious communities to study their teachings and practices with an eye toward how they might contribute to the mistreatment of lesbians and gay men, called on the State of North Carolina and all its municipalities to add "sexual orientation" to existing nondiscrimination policies, and called on the North Carolina General Assembly to abolish the state's Crimes Against Nature (or Sodomy) law.[8] These resolutions shaped a significant part of my advocacy work for the council over the years that followed and contributed to an increasing tension between the council and The United Methodist Church in North Carolina. Because I actively lobbied the North Carolina General Assembly on behalf of the council for the repeal of the Crimes Against Nature Law, the council took on a very public and controversial role in support of equal rights for gay people, a role that many United Methodists could neither understand nor accept.

The resolution that had the most significant impact on the council and its relationship with The United Methodist Church was one that initially seemed the least controversial. It stated: "The North Carolina Council of Churches . . . confesses the complicity of our churches in the suffering of gay men and lesbians and seeks all appropriate means of dialogue with them and with church bodies such as the Metropolitan Community Churches in North Carolina, believing that understanding and respect come out of sharing in community and being in dialogue."

Soon after the policy statement was adopted by the council, I called the Reverend Wayne Lindsey, pastor of St. John's Metropolitan Community Church in Raleigh, and suggested that the Universal Fellowship of Metropolitan Community Churches (UFMCC) apply for membership in the North Carolina Council of Churches. Wayne was interested and said he would talk with the district coordinator of the UFMCC, the Reverend Jay Neely. The UFMCC had been trying for years to become a member of the National Council of Churches without success. And no statewide ecumenical agency in the nation had ever before voted the UFMCC into membership. Its ministry was primarily to lesbian, gay, bisexual, and transgender people, and as a result, many church bodies and leaders did not consider it a legitimate denomination. Some even considered it to be an apostasy.

When the application for membership from the UFMCC was received by the council, the council leadership knew the procedure for approval would not be simple. In the past, when church bodies applied for membership in the council, there had been little need for investigation or debate. Membership applications were routinely approved by a vote of the House of Delegates, on recommendation by the Executive Committee. The only membership requirements were that the applying body be Christian and that it be committed to the goals of the North Carolina Council of Churches. On the basis of these requirements, there should have been no obstacles for approving the UFMCC application. But the council leadership had to consider political issues — would admitting the UFMCC alienate other members of the council? The members of the Executive Committee were nervous. We had been warned that some church bodies might withdraw from membership or terminate their financial support of the council if the UFMCC was made a member. Nonetheless, after a careful study of the UFMCC's theological statement, constitution, and polity, Father Joe Vetter, a Roman Catholic priest, moved to recommend the UFMCC for membership, and the motion was approved by the committee. While this vote was a political risk, the council's leaders were undaunted.

The next hurdle was the House of Delegates, the legislative body of the North Carolina Council of Churches. It was composed of delegates from all member bodies and had the final vote on membership applications. The House of Delegates met at the Trinity African Methodist Episcopal Zion Church in Greensboro on May 5, 1993. The sanctuary was packed, and the air was electric with excitement. Supporters and opponents alike wanted to be part of this history-making event.

In his annual report to the House of Delegates, Collins Kilburn said the right thing for the delegates to do that day was approve the membership application. "The UFMCC is an authentic Christian church with an important ministry," he said. If the delegates voted to approve its application, he said he would welcome it into the ecumenical family. However, he cautioned that there might be repercussions that could endanger the very existence of the council and admitted that "he was wary of any action which might strain or break the ties of the council to member bodies."[9] This caution was underscored by his report that "1992 and this year [1993] are the most difficult financial years that I have seen as Executive Director of the council."[10] He pointed out that 1992 had ended with a $7,000 shortfall in income, and that the $10,000 emergency reserve fund had been exhausted. Collins wanted everyone to understand the potential cost of granting the UFMCC membership, even if it was the right thing to do.

When the floor was opened for discussion and debate, only a few people spoke in opposition to the membership application. Some of them questioned the morality of same-gender sexual activity, and others questioned whether the UFMCC was truly a "church." Still others were opposed because they wanted to protect the council from backlash. A substitute motion, referring the membership application back to the Executive Committee for further study, was defeated by a vote of thirty-nine to thirty.

Those who objected to the UFMCC's application were not right-wing religious fanatics. They were people who had fought many battles for justice, people who would be labeled liberals or moderates on most social issues. They were people of integrity and courage. Yet, for them, homosexuality was an emotional issue they were not yet prepared to deal with, or a cause they did not yet find compelling enough to risk the council's survival.

An overwhelming number of people spoke in support of granting the UFMCC membership. For them, approving the application was a simple matter of doing the right thing, of being faithful to Christ's call for unity, compassion, and justice. It was a matter of being led by faith, rather than driven by fear.

After two hours of discussion, a standing vote was taken. The count was fifty in favor and fifteen against, with seven abstentions. It was a 70 percent vote in favor of membership for the UFMCC. Even most of those who had urged that the vote be delayed, out of concern for negative repercussions, had voted to approve the application. When the results were announced, joyous applause and shouting erupted. Tears flowed as delegates hugged one another. May 5, 1993, was a historic day!

Two months later, the 1993 North Carolina Annual Conference of The United Methodist Church voted to discontinue its annual contribution ($18,000) to the North Carolina Council of Churches until the council reversed its decision and expelled the UFMCC. This was a significant re-duction in income for the council, approximately 10 percent of its annual budget. This action by the United Methodists was disappointing in light of the denomination's historical relationship with the North Carolina Coun-cil of Churches. From the council's earliest days, strong leadership for it had come from the Methodists. On the day that the council's House of Delegates approved the UFMCC's membership application, twenty United Methodist delegates were present, and many of them were vocal advocates for UFMCC membership. Most of them also were serving in key leadership positions on the council's Executive Committee and its other committees. The North Carolina Annual Conference did not want to end this histori-cal relationship by withdrawing from membership in the council. Instead, it wanted to use its financial leverage to force the Universal Fellowship of Metropolitan Community Churches out of the council.[11]

Throughout its history, the North Carolina Council of Churches had championed many unpopular causes. It was the first church body in North Carolina to hold racially integrated meetings. It supported organized labor and collective bargaining in a state that had one of the bloodiest union-busting episodes in U.S. history.[12] In the 1960s, it pushed for alternatives to tobacco farming, the most controversial action taken by the council prior to the UFMCC vote. The council publicly opposed the Gulf War in 1991. While these and other actions brought the council criticism from its mem-ber church bodies, never before had a member voted to cut off funding in reaction to a position or action taken by the council. Neither advocacy for racial justice, antiwar demonstrations, support for labor unions, nor challenging the tobacco-based economy of North Carolina touched the fear and prejudice of the North Carolina Annual Conference of The United Methodist Church like the council's vote to welcome the UFMCC into membership.

A good bit of conversation took place among the council's officers and staff about the possibility that other denominational members would follow the lead of the United Methodists. Yet no one suggested that the UFMCC be removed from membership. The council's leaders believed in their decision, knew it was just and right, and had no intention of being financially manipulated.

As news of the United Methodists' decision to withhold financial support spread around the state, contributions to the council from individuals increased in number and amount. After only a few months, the financial deficit created by the United Methodists was erased.

In mid-March 1996, I received a telephone call from the Reverend Susan Davies, superintendent of the Omaha District of The United Methodist Church in Nebraska. She asked if I would consider an appointment to be the senior pastor of a church in Omaha. "First United Methodist Church is not your typical church," she explained. The 1,900-member congregation was "the flagship of the Nebraska Annual Conference." When I asked Susan why she had called me in North Carolina about serving a church in Omaha, Nebraska, she explained that the Staff-Parish Relations Committee of First Church included in its wish list of qualities it wanted in a senior pastor an openness and sensitivity to lesbian and gay people, and a willingness to be in ministry to and with gay and lesbian persons. She told me that she had conducted a national search to find just the right pastor for this appointment. My history was the reason she wanted to talk with me. She said Bishop Joel Martinez of the Nebraska Annual Conference already had talked with Bishop Minnick of the North Carolina Annual Conference about my ministry in North Carolina and asked permission to talk with me. Susan assured me that she and the Nebraska bishop were aware of my history, as well as my skills and commitments as a pastor.

After the call, I sat at my desk for a long time in disbelief, wondering if I'd just imagined this conversation or if it had actually happened. After more than six years, I had resigned myself to the fact I'd never be a pastor again. Could this invitation be real?

Life was good for me. I enjoyed my work with the council, and I especially liked and respected the people with whom I worked. Nebraska was an unknown quantity. I'd never been there and knew nothing about it except its association with corn, Mutual of Omaha, Omaha Steaks, and football. I knew it was in the Midwest, somewhere out there with Kansas and the Dakotas. I had lived my entire life in North Carolina, where my sense of place was bounded by the Blue Ridge Mountains and the Atlantic Ocean. Time for me was measured by the glorious beauty of Carolina springs and autumns, sultry summers, and mild winters. I'd never wanted to live anywhere else.

Chris Weedy and I had married in 1992. Our work together with the Raleigh HIV/AIDS Support Group since the fall of 1989 had nurtured our friendship and love for one another. During my ordeal of leaving Fairmont and pastoral ministry, being alone and unemployed, and starting a new ministry with the North Carolina Council of Churches, Chris had been my constant companion and support. After two and a half years of working together and dating, we had decided to marry.

Chris and I were living in the first house either of us had been able to call our own, a two-story structure built in 1908, located in one of Raleigh's historic districts. We had had our wedding celebration in its backyard, so we had a strong emotional attachment to it. Although Patrick, now twenty, was on his own, pursuing a career in music, Chris's daughter Natalia was fifteen and in her first year at Enloe High School, rated one of the best schools in the nation. She and her friends had been classmates since kindergarten. Chris's work at Duke University Medical Center was on the cutting edge of HIV/AIDS research and treatment. She had worked there for over eight years, developing the center's psychological and social program for children with HIV/AIDS and their parents, and she was recognized nationally among her peers as a pioneer in her field. She also received statewide recognition. In January 1996, she had been honored by the Raleigh *News & Observer* as "Tar Heel of the Week" (Tar Heel being the traditional nickname for residents of North Carolina) for her work. In a major article about her, the newspaper noted that in 1994 she had "convinced state legislators that foster and adoptive families needed higher monthly subsidies to take care of children with AIDS." One of Chris's accomplishments mentioned in the article was a bill that she wrote and that State Representative Howard Hunter Jr. successfully sponsored, which increased monthly subsidies for children with AIDS from $265 to as much as $1,600. "If it wasn't for Chris, children with AIDS would not be getting the attention they are getting," Hunter said in the article. "There ain't no noise about Chris. She's into this because she cares about those children and their families."[13]

Her work with and advocacy for children with HIV/AIDS had drawn the attention of North Carolina's governor Jim Hunt, who awarded her the Order of the Long Leaf Pine, the highest civilian honor given by the State of North Carolina. Chris loved her work and was dedicated and exceptionally good at it. Leaving it would be hard for her.

My gravest concern about being a pastor again was that Chris and Natalia had never had the experience of being a minister's family. I knew and understood the pressures involved in the life of a pastor—how unpleasant it can be, and how conspicuous it makes you. There were many good reasons to dismiss the opportunity. Yet my longing to be a pastor again—to serve a congregation, to preach and teach, to baptize and marry, to care for the dying and the grieving, to empower and lead—was irresistible.

I put together a packet of information about my ministry in North Carolina and sent it off to Susan Davies. The packet included *The Independent* and other newspaper articles about my time at Fairmont United Methodist Church and with the North Carolina Council of Churches, public policy statements I'd written for the council, and a copy of Keith Hartman's newly published book, *Congregations in Conflict: The Battle over Homosexuality*, which included the story of my ministry at Fairmont. I wanted no surprises, misunderstanding, or misrepresentation about who I was or the ministry I would pursue in Nebraska. In my cover letter, I said: "I am perhaps giving you more information than you may want, but I want you to know my history. I'd rather you have more than you want than to not know."

A few days later, a packet of material about First United Methodist Church arrived from Susan, including pictures of the facilities; the church's mission statement, annual budget, and worship bulletins; and a pictorial directory of the membership. I spread everything out on the kitchen counter for Chris and Natalia to see.

"Hell no, I won't go!" was Chris's first reaction when I told her about Susan's telephone call. She had moved from Ohio to North Carolina in 1984 to get away from bleak, frigid winters as much as to get her master's degree in social work at the University of North Carolina, Chapel Hill. She had no desire to return to the Midwest.

But when she looked at the information and saw my excitement, she opened up to the possibility. She knew that I respected the work I was doing at the council, but she understood that my head was in it more than my heart was, and that being a pastor was my dream. Chris decided that going to Omaha was just too important to me for us to pass it up, in spite of the sacrifices that she and Natalia would have to make.

Susan Davies invited us to come out to Nebraska the week following Easter for an interview and to see First Church. On the first night of our visit, I met with Bishop Martínez and his cabinet at a downtown restaurant in Lincoln, Nebraska. When I explained what had happened at Fairmont United Methodist Church and how I came to be without an appointment, the cabinet members seemed genuinely distressed for me. They assured me that what had happened to me in North Carolina never would have happened in Nebraska. They were certain that I would have received support from the clergy of the Nebraska Annual Conference.

The district superintendents asked questions about my priorities as a pastor, my experience working with a staff, and other issues. At the end of our conversation, Bishop Martínez explained that he would be attending the 1996 General Conference of The United Methodist Church, which was meeting in Denver, during the following two weeks. After that, he and the cabinet would meet again to evaluate me for the appointment at First Church. He stressed that he felt no urgency in making this appointment because it was such an important one, and he wanted to make the best choice. If finding the right person meant delaying the decision, that's what he would do.

The next day, Susan took Chris, Natalia, and me to see First United Methodist Church. The sandstone structure stretches across a grassy hilltop in the heart of Omaha. The sanctuary breaks the horizontal spread of the building, rising high into the air and crowned with an elegant, slender steeple visible from miles around the city. We toured the church's halls, classrooms, meeting rooms, offices, fellowship hall with basketball court and stage, and the small chapel. The large sanctuary, with its high ceiling and seating capacity of a thousand or more, was the most impressive part of the facilities. The tall windows were made of gorgeous stained glass, and the pulpit, lectern, and pews of handsome sculptured wood. A massive white marble communion table sat against the front wall, over which hung a large golden sunburst. Colorful antiphonal organ pipes covered the back wall in the balcony area. Natalia, Chris, and I were dazzled. Once again, I felt certain I was dreaming, and this couldn't be real.

After returning to Raleigh, I was preoccupied with the thought of being the pastor of First United Methodist Church in Omaha, but I was used to disappointments and wouldn't allow myself to expect the invitation. I could tell that Chris and Natalia were less eager to move to Nebraska after our visit. Their losses in leaving were more than any apparent gains that they could see in the new situation. I was the only one struggling not to be too excited.

Early news from the 1996 General Conference meeting in Denver was encouraging. There was hope that it would reverse the movement of The United Methodist Church toward the increasing exclusion and persecution of lesbian, gay, and bisexual people. Petitions had been submitted calling for the removal of the "incompatibility statement" in the Social Principles, and for the end to the prohibition of ordaining "self-avowed, practicing homosexuals." The Reconciling Congregation Program[14] conducted a campaign called Open the Doors for the General Conference, advocating the elimination of the antigay language and policies in *The Book of Discipline.*

On the eve of the General Conference, something unprecedented happened. Fifteen United Methodist bishops[15] issued a simple statement about the church's position regarding lesbians and gay men. The statement read: "We the undersigned bishops wish to affirm the commitment made at our consecration to the vows to uphold the *Discipline* of the church. However, we must confess the pain we feel over our personal convictions that are contradicted by the proscriptions in the *Discipline* against gay and lesbian persons within our church and within our ordained and diaconal ministers . . . We believe it is time to break the silence and state where we are on this issue that is hurting and silencing countless faithful Christians. We will continue our responsibility to the order and discipline of the church but urge our United Methodist churches to open the doors in gracious hospitality to all our brothers and sisters in the faith."

The action of the Denver 15, as they became known, was considered a breach of covenant with the other 109 bishops. In reaction, a closed session of the Council of Bishops was held, and the Denver 15 were admonished for releasing the statement without the approval of the entire council. As a group, the Denver 15 was never to be heard from again. Individually, however, most of the Denver 15 continued to oppose publicly the antigay policies and discriminatory language of the church and to advocate for change.

As legislation reached the floor of the General Conference and was acted upon, it became clear with each passing day that the early optimism had been unfounded. All petitions to remove the antigay language were defeated decisively. On the final day of the General Conference, legislation was adopted amending the Social Principles by adding the sentence: "Ceremonies that celebrate homosexual unions shall not be conducted by our ministers and shall not be conducted in our churches."[16]

Since James and Timothy's ceremony in the spring of 1990, I had conducted at least a dozen holy unions for gay and lesbian couples. The marks of these unions were "love, mutual support, personal commitment and shared fidelity," part of *The Book of Discipline*'s definition of marriage. The United Methodist Church had earlier defined lesbian, gay, and bisexual people as spiritually inferior to nongays through the incompatibility statement in the Social Principles. It had proclaimed them unfit to serve as ordained clergy. Now the church was denying same-gender couples the opportunity to celebrate their love publicly as a gift from God and to make life commitments in the context of their faith communities. The General Conference did this by forbidding its pastors to be in full ministry to lesbian, gay, and bisexual members.

I knew I could not and would not honor this prohibition. To do so would be a repudiation of the integrity of the lesbian and gay couples whose unions I had been honored to celebrate. This prohibition was not only a restriction of pastoral ministry, it was also an attack on the essential human dignity of lesbian, gay, and bisexual people by discounting their loving relationships.

On the Monday night after the General Conference, Susan Davies called to tell me that Bishop Martínez had decided to appoint me as the senior pastor of First United Methodist Church in Omaha. I told her I would like to accept the appointment, but there was one thing that she should know first: I disagreed with the General Conference's recent action prohibiting clergy from celebrating unions for gay and lesbian couples. I told her that if a gay couple asked me to conduct a union ceremony for them, I would do so in spite of the prohibition. If this made a difference in the decision to offer me the position, I assured her that I would understand. Her response was: "We'll walk that road together when the time comes."

District superintendents are the eyes and ears of the bishop, and as Susan had called me on behalf of Bishop Martínez, I understood that I was speaking to her as his proxy. I accepted her response as his response. With this assurance from Susan, I accepted the invitation to be appointed the senior pastor at First United Methodist Church in Omaha.

I was confident that I had been clear with Susan about my position, and that there was no reason for misunderstanding in regard to my not obeying the prohibition. The last thing I wanted to happen was to move my family from our home in Raleigh to Omaha, and then find out that my ministry would not be supported. I did not want what happened at Fairmont United Methodist Church to happen at First United Methodist Church in Omaha. I wanted there to be no surprises and no misunderstandings. I wanted the bishop and the congregation to want me with a full and clear understanding of my priorities and commitments for ministry. I did not want the appointment badly enough to be deceptive or evasive about my intentions. If I was to be rejected, I preferred that to happen before we left Raleigh, rather than after.

I returned to Nebraska twice in preparation for moving there, once in May to meet the church staff and the Staff-Parish Relations Committee. When I met with the Reverends Don Bredthauer and Susan Mullins, the associate pastors at First Church with whom I would be working, they were helpful and gracious in talking about the ministry and programs of the church. Bishop Martínez had confided to me in our early conversation that Don badly wanted the appointment as senior pastor, and he might be difficult to work with because he didn't get it. Don was among the most respected clergy in the Nebraska Annual Conference and had been the associate pastor at First Church for the past ten years. Prior to that, he had served as the Omaha district superintendent. However, Don was open with me about his disappointment in not getting the appointment and pledged me his full support. He was proud of the progressive ministry and programs that First Church had developed during his time there and I sensed his apprehension that I might bring changes he would not welcome. Susan Mullins, who had been at First Church only one year, felt she was still learning her role there. A change of senior pastors at this time was a bit unsettling for her, and she wondered if her role would change. I assured Don and Susan that my intention was for us to work as a team to build on what First Church was doing already and on the energy and vision of the congregation as we moved forward together. The other sixteen staff members were pleasant but reserved, clearly unsure what to make of me. I realized that I was an unknown and that there would be a good bit of curiosity and anxiety regarding what my style of leadership and priorities in ministry would be. Their caution was understandable.

The Staff-Parish Relations Committee members and their spouses graciously welcomed me at a dinner at the home of Joan Byerhof, the chairperson of the committee, and her husband, Lloyd. These were the first members of First Church that I had the opportunity to meet. Susan Davies had informed them a week or so earlier that I had been selected to be their new senior pastor. She assured me that she had told the committee all about my history in North Carolina in regard to my advocacy for gay rights and other social justice issues. She said the committee members had no concerns then, and they asked no questions about it when I met with them in May.

In the first week of June, I returned to Nebraska to attend the Annual Conference meeting in Lincoln. On the first day of the four-day meeting, my transfer from the North Carolina Annual Conference to the Nebraska Annual Conference was made official; on the last day, I was appointed to First United Methodist Church in Omaha, Nebraska. My ministry there was to begin on July 1.

I was ecstatic. In a sense, I had been holding my breath since that first telephone call from Susan Davies, fearing that there might be a change of mind about my appointment. After my experience at Fairmont United Methodist Church and with Bishop C. P. Minnick, skepticism had a strong hold on me. Emotionally, I expected the appointment not to happen. Finally, I could exhale. The appointment had been made. I was the senior pastor at First United Methodist Church. Drunk with euphoria, I finally allowed myself to believe it was true. My chest felt as if it might explode. I was a pastor again!

"A North Carolina pastor and social activist will be taking over the pulpit of First United Methodist Church in Omaha on July 1," read the opening sentence of an article announcing my appointment by Julia McCord, religion editor of the *Omaha World-Herald*. The article continued: "For the last five years he has lobbied the North Carolina General Assembly on behalf of the North Carolina Council of Churches, tackling such issues as welfare reform, criminal justice and matters affecting farmworkers, health care, and children. Creech also is an outspoken opponent of the death penalty and has served as pastor to death-row inmates. 'Jimmy's not been a stranger to controversy,' said his boss, Collins Kilburn, the council's executive secretary. 'He's used to saying pretty much what he thinks, even when that's not popular . . .' Creech said he is looking forward to his move to Nebraska. He said his first priority is getting acquainted with the congregation and Omaha. Political activism, however, will continue to be a part of his ministry, he said."[1]

Ms. McCord's introduction wasn't incorrect, but it did define me narrowly. I didn't think of myself as an activist. I understood myself to be a pastor, concerned with nurturing people's relationships with God and with others. To me, this meant helping to change not only the interior realities, but the social and cultural realities in which people live.

In my first sermon, I shared with my new congregation my belief that the church is called not just to compassion and charity, but to set people free from whatever cripples their lives, whatever is dehumanizing and demeaning, whatever destroys relationships within the community of humankind. As the Hebrews called to God for deliverance from Egyptian slavery, "the homeless, the hungry, those who suffer domestic abuse and violence, lesbian, gay, bisexual, and transgender persons, people living with AIDS, people living in countries where there is war, people whose streets are not safe . . . call out to us, as God's representatives, saying, 'set us free.'" Jesus's ministry was to restore to their community those who had been cast out, who were deemed undesirable by the pious, wealthy, and powerful, and our ministry is the same.

The congregation's response to my first sermon was overwhelmingly positive, but my second one got a different reaction. Soon after I arrived in Omaha, I learned that the State of Nebraska was preparing to execute John Joubert who had been convicted in 1984 of brutally murdering two young boys in the Omaha area. The death penalty, I was convinced, was incompatible with the Christian gospel, and I believed that it would be irresponsible for me, as the pastor of First Church, to ignore Joubert's pending execution. I had worked hard to abolish capital punishment in North Carolina and had been pastor to several men on death row while working with the North Carolina Council of Churches. I witnessed the execution in North Carolina's gas chamber of David Lawson, a man who had become my friend and whom I'd baptized and served the Eucharist to just hours before his death. On my second Sunday in Omaha, I told the congregation of First Church that capital punishment was un-Christian, and that we who execute killers are no less killers than Joubert.

Although the negative reactions to my sermon were few, they were strong and angry. One parishioner who described himself as a liberal Democrat angrily denounced me and the sermon as he left at the end of the service, saying I had insulted the people of Nebraska by calling them "killers." An anonymous letter I received soon afterward stated:

> After your sermon on July 14 . . . , you can pack your bags to go back to North Carolina. By your overwhelming support of convicted killers, you have demonstrated no compassion whatsoever for the victims . . . How can a Minister of the Gospel not be more concerned with the victims of this tragic event rather than support the cold blooded murderer? You have a distorted mind. If Christ had not been executed, we would not have salvation for our sins. I know you are not following the teaching of the Bible, but pursuing your own personal belief . . . Is this what you are all about, promoting deviant causes . . . ? Maybe you need to concen-

trate your energy to the declining membership of First United Methodist Church. Your stand on the death penalty will certainly do nothing to increase attendance. If you keep this up my family and a few others I know will be looking for a new church.

Most First Church members, however, expressed appreciation for my sermon. Some agreed with what I said, and others said the sermon changed their minds about supporting capital punishment.

First Church, in its early days, had been a "country club" church of the Establishment, home to the political and business leaders of Omaha. But its pastoral leaders in the previous two decades had been theologically liberal and had worked to diversify the congregation in terms of race and class. Omaha was growing westward, with many affluent neighborhoods cropping up and new churches being started. A slow exodus of members had taken place not only because of this expansion, but because of the internal changes at First Church. Some members had moved to other churches that identified more with the status quo and evangelical Christian theology. The church's membership had dropped from over 3,000 at its peak to 1,900 by the time I arrived. Still, First Church was considered to be the flagship United Methodist church in Nebraska because of its progressive involvement with social justice issues, mission programs, and outreach to the Omaha community.

I immediately felt at home at First Church and relished once again the routine of pastoral ministry. With the associate pastors, Don Bredthauer and Susan Mullins, I took turns making the rounds to visit members who were at the three hospitals in Omaha. Each weeknight I had a committee meeting to attend or a program to lead. Sermon preparation, staff supervision, counseling, administrative work, and planning and conducting baptisms, weddings, and funerals kept me busy beyond my expectation. But I was a pastor again and loving every minute of it.

In the spring of 1996, just prior to my arrival, First Church initiated a discernment process, to develop a mission statement intended to lead the congregation into the next decade. Input about values and priorities for ministry was gathered from as many members of the congregation as possible through small group meetings over several months. The process was well under way when I arrived, and I immediately became an active participant. The mission statement, which we called our Vision Focus, was to be presented for adoption at the congregation's All Church Conference in December 1996.

The process was a meticulous one that looked at every facet of the church's life and ministry. Some members' perspective was informed by what First Church had been in the past. Others focused on what was currently happening in Omaha and emerging cultural and community issues, one of which was the greater diversity of the population and the need for First Church to actively and intentionally include people of diverse backgrounds and situations in regard to race, ethnicity, language, class, marital status, and sexual orientation. Out of this discussion of diversity emerged an interest in First Church's becoming a Reconciling Congregation—a congregation that publicly welcomes and affirms lesbian, gay, bisexual, and transgender persons. First Church had a history of providing meeting space for the Omaha chapter of PFLAG and for Proud Horizons, a support group for lesbian, gay, bisexual, and transgender youth, and those who were questioning their sexual orientation. Yet, like most congregations, First Church still did not have a truly welcoming atmosphere for gay, bisexual, lesbian, and transgender people. The national civil rights movement for gay people moved many in the congregation to want to change that and end the anti-gay policies and practices of The United Methodist Church.

As conversation about becoming a Reconciling Congregation increased, opposition began to be voiced. "Since there's no other Reconciling United Methodist Church in Nebraska," one member asked, "why should we be the first?" Another said: "We already welcome everyone, so why do we need to call ourselves 'Reconciling'?" Both claimed not to be against gay people's presence at First Church, just against taking a public stance in the community that might hurt membership growth and financial support.

Although much of the early opposition to the idea of becoming a Reconciling Congregation proved intractable, some was transformed into support. Carol LaCroix, a medical doctor who had grown up in South Korea as the daughter of Methodist missionaries, wrote a note to me that said: "I do not feel that homosexuals, as individuals, should be banned or ostracized from the church, but I do believe that homosexuality is wrong by Scriptural standards. I have been a Methodist all my life (42 years), but it has dismayed me to watch this denomination water things down in an effort to be 'everything to everybody.' We need to teach right and wrong as well as loving everybody."

I asked Carol if I might meet with her and her husband, Michael, and she invited me to their home one Sunday after worship. I found them to be open to discussion, in no way defensive or hostile. I shared a little of my experience with them and discussed how the church historically had fostered prejudice against gay, lesbian, and bisexual people. I explained that, while my hope was that First Church would one day become a Reconciling Congregation, there was no intention to make that part of the Vision Focus.

We didn't attempt to reach agreement but simply tried to hear and understand one another. Before leaving, I offered Carol and Michael my worn and ragged copy of *Is the Homosexual My Neighbor? Another Christian View*, by Letha Scanzoni and Virginia Ramey Mollenkott, a book I'd found to be helpful to people with questions about religion and homosexuality. A few weeks later, Carol returned it, along with a brand-new copy as a gift. She included a note saying that she had also purchased a copy for herself, and that the book had helped her and Michael to think differently about the church's teachings about homosexuality. Over the next year, Carol would become a key advocate for the church's recognizing the committed relationships of lesbian and gay couples.

The congregation's self-study process was completed in the fall of 1996, and the resulting Vision Focus was adopted in early December at the All Church Conference, the church's annual business meeting attended by all members. No dissent was voiced, and only one vote was cast against adopting the Vision Focus. We didn't intend the document to be a creed, but rather a statement of discipleship, a vision of how we were to embody the Christian gospel in the context of our life together. Its preamble read: "We are the body of Christ. As such: we welcome and celebrate the diversity of God's children; we are a healing and caring community where all people can seek to become whole persons in Christ; we are a vital center of spiritual growth; and, we are in ministry to and with the community of Omaha and the world."

The preamble was followed by six paragraphs that indicated how the Vision Focus would be supported through worship, spiritual growth, community action, children and youth ministries, and resources such as facilities, staff, and money. The paragraph that proved to be the basis for great controversy, as well as profound transformation, at First Church in the year to come was called "Welcoming, Acceptance, and Togetherness." It read: "We are welcoming, accepting, and encouraging of involvement for all who wish to join in the worship and service of God. We are inclusive of those associated with all economic levels, races, ethnicities, sexual orientations, marital states, abilities, and age levels. We are a place where people feel comfortable and want to be. An integral aspect of our congregation is the mutual respect we have for one another in our diversity. All intentionally reach out to build new relationships and strengthen existing relationships especially during difficult times."

The Vision Focus belonged to the congregation, created out of its Christian values and hope for a just and peaceful world. Don Bredthauer, Susan Mullins, and I gave pastoral guidance and encouragement, but we were only facilitators. The vision belonged to the members, and its adoption was a historical moment in the life of First United Methodist Church.

Not long after the All Church Conference, another statement became public that would contribute to the debate over homosexuality within The United Methodist Church. On New Year's Day, 1997, a group of fifteen clergy[2] from around the United States issued a manifesto of sorts titled "In All Things Charity." It was a challenge to The United Methodist Church's antigay policies, especially the prohibition of "homosexual unions." The Reverend Susan Davies, superintendent of the Omaha District, and the Reverend Gregory Dell, pastor of Broadway United Methodist Church in Chicago were the principal authors of this statement. Described by its signers as "a statement of conscience and commitment," the manifesto declared that "the practice of homosexuality" was not "incompatible with Christian teaching" and affirmed the appropriateness of "liturgical support for all covenantal commitments between same-gendered couples. To withhold rituals of support and accountability for committed relationships," it said, "is unconscionable."

After its publication, other clergy were invited to add their signatures to the manifesto. I was excited about its potential to help reverse the church's discrimination against gay people and immediately sent my name to be added to the statement. I wrote Bishop Martínez to inform him that I'd signed the statement, emphasizing that this meant I would conduct same-gender unions if requested to do so. My colleagues Don Bredthauer and Susan Mullins added their names, also, and we informed the congregation about our action in the January 15 issue of *Bread*, First Church's weekly newspaper. By April of that year, more than 1,300 United Methodist clergy had signed "In All Things Charity."

Sunday, January 19, 1997, was Human Relations Day in The United Methodist Church, an annual occasion to focus on the diversity of the human family and the call of Christ to overcome destructive divisions. The theme that year was "We Are All God's Children." I had yet to preach at First Church about the need to overcome the religious prejudice against gay, lesbian, bisexual, and transgender people, and I felt that this was the opportune time to do so.

Because racial divisions and discrimination within society had been the traditional focus of Human Relations Day, I began my sermon by reflecting on my experience growing up in the racist Southern culture. I told how prejudice against black Americans was taught to me by my parents, teachers, and civic leaders, people I loved and respected. I told how I internalized without critical reflection the message implicit in segregated movie theaters, doctors' offices, restaurants, bus terminals, schools, and neighborhoods — a message of moral, intellectual, and cultural inequality. These messages gave me a false sense of superiority to black people, a false sense of righteousness and entitlement.

This stratified social order of black and white was ordained by preachers and Sunday school teachers as "God's will," I explained. "It's in the Bible," they claimed. "Colored people aren't civilized; they're morally inferior to whites," they argued; "We can love them and treat them well as long as they stay in their place." The claim of white superiority and black inferiority relied on biblical references to racial and tribal separation and slavery, conventional morality, and Southern custom.

"These lessons helped prepare me to recognize another structure of prejudice and discrimination in our society," I said. Then I told the story of Adam and how he made me aware of the oppression and persecution that lesbian, gay, and bisexual people experience from the Christian church and society. I said:

I have come to understand how the church's teachings and practices have incited, encouraged, and supported the discrimination and violence gay people experience in our society. And it is clear to me now that there is no biblical or ethical justification for the condemnation that the church has perpetrated against gay men and lesbians, just as there is none to support racism. The parallel of antigay bigotry with racism is for me a perfect one. The Christian gospel compels us to identify and challenge prejudice, because prejudice provides the basis for the unjust treatment of people considered to be different from the majority of society. Any social structure that dehumanizes and oppresses people, that withholds freedom and denies justice, that assaults their spirit and integrity, is evil and must be broken down.

I closed the sermon by commending the congregation for recently adopting the Vision Focus in which we committed ourselves to include all people without regard to sexual orientation.

Response to the sermon was mostly positive. But, not surprisingly, I received negative letters like this one, signed only by "A Group of Members that are interested in the Welfare of the Church":

Dear Reverend Creech,

A group of us are extremely disappointed that you are putting your own selfish desires above the welfare of the church. The homosexual issue is quite simple, God made man and God made woman and they fit together, anything else is deviant, you are deviant for even suggesting alternative lifestyles. If it weren't for heterogeneous groupings we wouldn't have a society. YOU are advocating a sick society, and promoting the work of the devil. We don't want to be hit upon in our rest rooms for sex, like happens in many public places. Last summer a Preacher was arrested for having sex with another man in one of our parks. Dozens of other men were arrested for the same reason. Apparently you think this is perfectly normal behavior . . .

Many Ministers in our city are calling homosexual activity a sin, but you are promoting it, and you call yourself a minister? Why do you think homosexuals are called "queer"? The reasoning you presented in your sermon is shallow and is totally without merit. If you feel so strongly about this issue, why don't you leave and start your own church for gays and lesbians?

Some of us think that "aids" [sic] was a message sent to earth by God to bring his children back into the fold, but people such as you, are ignoring the message. We are totally frustrated. We thought you would want to unify and build the church rather than insult the integrity of its members. We have a few options — contacting the Staff Perish [sic] committee, contacting the Bishop, or just plain leaving the church. The last option seems to be the easiest, but we wonder why we have to leave when we have been their [sic] so long. The decision will be left up to you.

Next time you are preaching a sermon and you look out at the sanctuary and see about 200 people (or less) in a facility that will hold 1,000, you might ask the Lord, "What am I doing wrong?"

Other letters were painfully poignant. A couple with a young son wrote: "This is a letter that we write with a very sad heart . . . We have decided to find another church to attend." They wanted to protect their child from something they did not understand. Church as a context for confronting ethical, justice, and political issues was alien to them. They wanted First Church to be a safe, predictable haven of support for their beliefs, and I had taken that away from them.

In these and similar letters were echoes of the complaints, objections, and condemnations that I had heard at Fairmont. I felt the familiar knot and nausea in my stomach, the stress of causing others' unhappiness and anger, as well as the dread that the world would come crashing down around me as had happened in Raleigh. But I knew that there was significant support for gay people at First Church as well as for me. The Vision Focus was evidence of that. So I tried to reassure myself and ignore my anxiety.

On the Tuesday after Human Relations Day, Robert Howell, a retired insurance company executive; his sister Helen; and his daughter Diane West met with me to discuss Sunday's sermon. They were outraged. What had angered them most was my statement that "I have come to understand that sexual orientation is predetermined and that being gay is just as natural, normal, and healthy as being nongay." They called homosexuality abnormal, perverse, and immoral. They left my office saying they weren't sure if they could continue attending worship at First Church.

A week later, I received the following letter from the Howells as a follow-up to our meeting. They had sent copies to Bishop Martínez, District Superintendent Susan Davies, members of the Staff-Parish Relations Committee, and Bob Peirce, treasurer of First Church.

January 27, 1997
Dear Reverend Creech:
    Your continued focus on gays and lesbians has caused us to consider attending church elsewhere as many other dedicated members are doing.

Being what we believe to be a fairly conservative church, your views on homosexuals and the death penalty are not accepted in the way you might like. Church has been a place for teaching lessons from the Bible. It appears, however, that your approach is to change our way of thinking to your deeply-held political/social convictions.

Comments during your January 19th sermon caused three of us (Elizabeth and Jeff couldn't attend) to meet with you Tuesday to see where our beliefs differed. With grave concern, we learned that you:

1. Find it acceptable for homosexuals committed to each other to engage in sexual activities. Find that homosexual activities are not sinful or against the beliefs of Christianity.
2. Say adultery is not involved when a divorced person is remarried.
3. Believe that under certain circumstances, it is acceptable for an unmarried heterosexual couple to have sex prior to marriage . . .

Our concern does not come from homosexuals attending church and taking part in activities. There is no way, however, that we could accept practicing homosexuals in leadership positions — especially as teachers or ministers where children can be taught something other than moral, decent behavior.

Until our pastoral staff and The Methodist Church returns to traditional stands, Jeff and Diane's family and Robert and Elizabeth are canceling their pledges (which were reduced from last year in response to our mounting displeasure) . . . [O]ur hope is that others who find your various positions unacceptable will do the same.

The Howells were longtime members of First Church, but their activity had declined after Robert's retirement years earlier. Their primary involvement was now in a church school class of older members. Diane West and her husband, Jeff, centered their church involvement around their young son's activities in the children's program. Helen Howell, Robert's sister, a retired professor at the University of Nebraska, Omaha, was the most active of the Howells at the church. Just one month before, at my recommendation, she had been elected to a three-year term on the Staff-Parish Relations Committee. The Howells would become the principal leaders in the organized opposition to the Vision Focus and my ministry.

Because he was a member of the Staff-Parish Relations Committee, Bob Dorr received a copy of the Howells' letter. A senior writer for the *Omaha*

World-Herald, Bob was recognized in the church as an open-minded and fair person who could offer wise counsel on just about every matter. Betty, Bob's wife, was a leader in the Omaha chapter of PFLAG, which held its monthly meetings at First Church. The Dorrs responded to the Howells' letter:

January 29, 1997
Dear Robert and Elizabeth,

Betty and I are writing this letter as individual members of the church. How many people would share our views, we have no idea. That doesn't matter.

We are heartbroken by your letter to Reverend Jimmy Creech. We always have greatly valued your friendship. We hope you will remain our friends after we tell you about our families.

I have one sibling, my brother. We were raised as close to the same as any two brothers could be raised. He is gay. I am straight. Betty has one sibling, her brother. They were raised the same. He is gay. Betty is straight.

With homosexuality in both our families, we wondered how our three sons would turn out. However, we dismissed that from our minds. We raised our three sons the same. We hope and believe we raised them in a loving, Christian family. Dave and Rick are straight. Mike is gay. We love them equally. The idea many people have that choice is involved in a person's basic sexual inclination is one of the great hoaxes in America today. I can no more imagine myself being gay than my brother can imagine himself being straight.

We never asked Mike whether he was gay. At age 27, he came to us and told us that he couldn't any longer masquerade as a straight person. He had wrestled long and hard with the question of whether to openly admit he is gay before deciding to do so. We told him we loved him. He said he knew that was what we would say.

We have a very close family, a very traditional family . . . Unfortunately, what we have learned the last few years is that our loving family is in the minority among families that have gay or lesbian sons and daughters. Betty and I have become active in an organization of parents of gay and lesbian children. It is a support group for parents.

Betty has spent hundreds of hours helping to staff a telephone line, a hotline, for parents and for their gay and lesbian children who are in distress. It is common, not just an occasional event, for parents to throw a gay son or a lesbian daughter out of their house and never want to see them again upon hearing that their offspring is gay or lesbian. Thankfully, most young people are old enough to take care of themselves once they are thrown out. The suicide rate for gay and lesbian teenagers is several times the suicide rate for all teens.

We would love to sit down with you some time as friends and tell you the heartache that Betty has heard over the phone.

You say in your letter, referring in part to your point on homosexuality: "By accepting lower morals and standards, we continue to add to the deterioration of society in religious beliefs just as we have done in every aspect of life." It's the words, "lower morals and standards," that are painful. Those words don't apply to my brother, who has had a productive career and who, incidentally, still bears the scar on his face from a gay-bashing many years ago. Those words don't apply to Betty's brother, who has had a distinguished teaching career. And they certainly don't apply to our son, Mike.

Thank God, the overriding message of our faith is one of love. We could barely keep the tears from flowing down our faces when we heard Reverend Creech's sermon recently. Betty didn't even make a good try to hold back the tears. Our church, our minister, was actually affirming the love that we long have felt, and that we believe is the heart of Christ's message to us, for our family members, our brothers and our son.

With love,
Bob and Betty Dorr

The Dorrs' hope that their friendship with the Howells would continue would be painfully disappointed in the months to come.

Another emerging leader in the effort to halt the inclusive direction of the church and to remove me was Mel Semrad, a gas and electric corporate executive. Mel had just completed his tenure as chairperson of the church's Finance Committee at the end of December. I had worked closely with him to develop the 1997 church budget. He had been present at the All Church Conference when the Vision Focus was adopted and had not opposed it.

I had noticed that Mel and his wife, Virginia, were not in worship during the early part of 1997. Thinking that they were vacationing in a warmer climate for the winter, a common practice for Omahans, I didn't give their absence much thought. However, I learned in a roundabout way that Mel was unhappy with what was happening at the church. I called him to make an appointment to see him, and we met on the Monday following Easter.

Mel said he didn't like my preaching about capital punishment or my public advocacy for lesbian and gay people. My Human Relations Day sermon had been especially disturbing to him. He advised me to leave the social and political issues alone and preach "the saving gospel of Jesus Christ." If I continued to "push" the idea of becoming a Reconciling Congregation, he promised he'd "push" the Confessing Movement at First Church. The Reverend Ira Gallaway, associate director of the Confessing Movement, was a personal friend, Mel claimed, warning me that he would call on Gallaway for resources and support.

The Confessing Movement had grown out of a 1994 gathering of leaders—clergy and lay people—in the Good News movement, an evangelical caucus within The United Methodist Church. For more than thirty years, the Good News movement had condemned what it called the liberal bias of the church. While the Methodist movement, which began in the late 1700s, was never focused on a religious creed, the Good News movement insisted on strict and rigid orthodoxy of belief and practice.

Following the 1994 gathering, the nascent Confessing Movement issued a manifesto called "An Invitation to the Church," distributed throughout The United Methodist Church. The manifesto declared that there was a "crisis" in the church because of its "abandonment of the truth of the gospel of Jesus Christ as revealed in Scripture and asserted in the classic Christian tradition and historic ecumenical creeds." This crisis, according to the manifesto, "extends beyond our denomination," with "similar strains and struggles among our sisters and brothers in all the churches of the West." The document was an appeal to evangelicals to rescue The United Methodist Church from "the peril of abandoning the Christian faith."

The Confessing Movement was fully birthed at a follow-up conference in Atlanta, Georgia, in April 1995. Those present at the conference adopted "A Confessional Statement," which addressed specific social and cultural issues that it claimed threatened to "undermine or deny" the lordship of Jesus. The statement read: "We repudiate teachings and practices that misuse principles of inclusiveness and tolerance to distort the doctrine and discipline of the church. We deny the claim that the individual is free to decide what is true and what is false, what is good and what is evil. We reject widespread and often unchallenged practices in and by the church that rebel against the Lordship of Jesus Christ. For example: experimenting with pagan ritual and practice . . . ; accommodating the prevailing patterns of sexual promiscuity, serial marriage and divorce, condoning homosexual practice."

The Confessing Movement is part of the global emergence of militant religious fundamentalism that seeks to hold onto archaic cultural structures of power. Power shifts in Western culture brought about by the human and civil rights movements for women, African Americans, and gay people have threatened the traditional culture of male domination that maintains rigid, hierarchical gender roles. The Confessing Movement is intent on protecting and enforcing an endangered patriarchal understanding of God and the resulting social order within and through The United Methodist Church.

As he prepared to leave our meeting, Mel told me he had a check in his pocket made payable to First Church, which he'd been carrying around since January. It was for the money he had pledged to the church budget, which ironically he had helped develop and promote the previous year. He didn't think he could honor this pledge, he said, because of the direction the church was going—unless I promised him I would leave these divisive issues alone and get back to preaching about Jesus Christ. When I assured Mel that I was preaching and acting on the gospel of Jesus Christ as I understood and believed it, that the issues that troubled him so much were issues of justice and compassion that this Christian gospel compelled me to address, and that I was excited about where First Church was going, he was not convinced.

That day, I sensed a contest for the mind and soul of First Church had begun, not as an isolated internal affair, but as part of the larger political and theological struggle taking place within The United Methodist Church. It was fortuitous that Mel and I met the day after Easter, which marks the mythic victory of God's new order of life and freedom over the old order of oppression and death. It was a bit scary to sense that a monumental confrontation lay ahead. But the Easter faith comforted and strengthened me. I knew that something new was happening at First Church, and I was convinced that it came from God. I trusted that what was just and compassionate would ultimately prevail in some Easter-like surprise, and that my only duty was to be faithful.

Two couples who had attended worship for the first time that Easter morning were to have significant roles in the future of First Church. Roy and J Wright had heard that we had adopted what they called a "pro-gay" statement, our Vision Focus, and that I was supportive of the gay community. Following worship, they waited until almost everyone else had left the sanctuary before introducing themselves to me. Roy, a black man, sparkled with joyous energy. His voice and laughter were full and loud; his manner, assertive and engaging. J, his partner, was a reserved and reflective white man. They wanted to know if they would be welcome as out gay men and as a couple. I assured them that their presence at First Church would be a gift to us, helping us to realize our vision of being truly diverse and inclusive.

Chris, standing next to me at the door, asked Roy and J if they'd be interested in attending a Sunday school class. When they said they would, she recommended the Pathfinders Class, which seemed a perfect fit. The group studied a variety of subjects, all relevant to the interests of couples in their twenties and early thirties, including parenting and keeping marriages strong.

The next Sunday, Roy and J attended the class, introducing themselves, of course, as a couple. Afterward, they passed by my office on their way to worship and were ecstatic. They had felt genuinely welcomed by the class members and enjoyed the class discussion. It seemed to be an auspicious beginning of a new and very special era for First Church.

Following worship, however, I found George and Kristen Barben, the teachers of the Pathfinders Class, waiting in my office. They were distressed. They assured me that they had no problems with Roy and J's presence in the class and that they wanted them to be welcome, but they were concerned. From its beginning, the class had struggled to keep going, and it remained pretty fragile—a state that was typical of young adult classes everywhere. A few members were committed to making the class work, but the commitment of the others was tenuous. George and Kristen had worked hard to keep the class members interested, and they feared that the presence of Roy and J would cause some to stay away. Some people had felt uncomfortable hearing Roy and J talk about their intimate marriage issues. In addition, most of the couples in the class had children, and the discussion often focused on parenting issues. The class members didn't feel that Roy and J had much in common with them. "Couldn't I recommend another class to Roy and J? Or help form a class for gay couples where they would have more in common?" they asked me.

George and Kristen had just experienced a cultural earthquake, where the not-so-solid ground beneath their feet had shifted, and they were unsettled. They and the other members of the class weren't prepared for Roy and J attending as just another couple. I encouraged George and Kristen to see their role as one of helping to make First Church truly inclusive. They might lose class members, I told them, but they had the chance to do something very important. I assured them of my full support and said I'd be glad to meet with the class to talk about any issues and concerns. I explained that all other parts and programs of the church should be open to Roy and J as well, and that they should be welcomed fully, with respect. It would be wrong to create a class just for gays, I said, because the result of that would be to marginalize them within the church.

At Kristen and George's invitation, I met with the class to discuss the struggle they were having. The class members were uncomfortable with Roy and J's being there for the discussion, but I felt it would be inappropriate to tell them not to attend because we were going to "talk about them." That happens to lesbian, gay, bisexual, and transgender people all the time, and decisions and assumptions are made about them without their input. I wasn't going to let this happen.

Some members intentionally stayed away from the class that morning. At one point, one of the women yelled, "What about the kids? What about the kids? How do we explain you to our kids?" Roy replied simply, "Just tell them we're two people who love each other." Others said nothing. Nonetheless, the discussion was significant. I knew it would not be enough to end the struggle, but I believed it would be a positive contribution toward understanding and change.

In the course of the discussion, someone suggested that the class embark on a study about what the Bible says about homosexuality. I answered that the Bible is the least helpful resource in understanding homosexuality. I explained that our cultural prejudice against gays has influenced how we read the Bible, so that we read our beliefs into it instead of finding helpful information there. In fact, I said, the Bible contains no understanding of homosexuality. I suggested that the class do a study on human sexuality first. My suggestion shocked some in the class, who thought I had dismissed the Bible as irrelevant or unimportant. Ultimately, the subject of human sexuality was much too uncomfortable for the class, and the whole idea was dropped.

For Roy and J, the class discussion was painful. What was said and how it was said made it clear they were not welcome. I encouraged them to understand that for any out gay individual or couple to be truly welcome at First Church, this kind of struggle was required. They didn't want it or choose it, but it was a necessary part of the transformation we hoped for in the Vision Focus. Ultimately, they decided to continue and give the class, as well as the Vision Focus, a chance to work.

I knew that this was a lonely and stressful time for them. They were new to the church, wanting only to be accepted, not to cause conflict. It was hard to watch Roy and J go through this ordeal. I could have encouraged them to leave and find another more welcoming church, but I didn't want them to be demoralized by giving up and leaving any more than I wanted First Church let off the hook. There was no avoiding conflict, however, if they chose to stay, and somebody had to be the first to break down the congregation's resistance to truly becoming inclusive.

Over the next several months, the dynamics within the class were volatile. Roy and J attended regularly, even as the atmosphere grew chilly. Class members made subtle and not-so-subtle comments to them that were judgmental and disrespectful. One Sunday, in the hall just outside the classroom, Roy and J kissed in the full view of some children. Some members stopped attending the Pathfinders Class. Some came to talk with me, recognizing the moral conflict they felt between their Christian conscience and the emotionally conditioned cultural prejudice that made it difficult to accept Roy and J. Some said they resented what they felt was the use of the class as a laboratory or test case for changing attitudes about gay people. One member expressed the feelings of many others when she wrote to me: "All of a sudden, out of the blue, we had a gay couple visit our class. We had no warning and no preparation for this happening. You're probably thinking, 'Why should we treat this couple any differently from any other couple joining the class?' Well, it's because they are different from the persons in our class. Every couple in that class is heterosexual and I can tell you that no one was prepared for what happened." Word about what was happening in the Pathfinders Class spread through the congregation, increasing the concerns that some people had about my ministry at First Church.

George and Kristen were overwhelmed. There were Sunday mornings when the only class members in attendance were Roy and J and the two of them. Eventually, George and Kristen decided they'd given it all that they could and resigned as teachers of the Pathfinders. The class ceased to exist. They had done their best. Roy and J, too, had tried hard to make the class work. I was terribly disappointed and felt that I had failed them by not knowing how to overcome the class's resistance to their presence. I also felt deep regret because most of the class members left First Church, with unresolved issues about sexuality and theology. At least we had given them a unique chance to confront their beliefs and feelings about these issues. The class members who remained at First Church became active supporters of our inclusive vision.

In April 1997, at my request, Bishop Martínez and I had lunch together to discuss some administrative matters at First Church. When our conversation drew to a close, as if as an afterthought, the bishop brought up the letter I had sent to him in January regarding my signing "In All Things Charity" and my commitment to conduct holy unions for same-gender couples. He apologized for not responding, saying that he really didn't know what he would do if I conducted a union ceremony for a same-gender couple. He explained that a little over a year earlier, before the General Conference adopted the "homosexual union" prohibition in 1996, a United Methodist pastor in Lincoln had celebrated a ceremony for two men. The bishop said he was upset that he had known nothing about the ceremony beforehand, learning about it only after the fact from a newspaper report. He said he'd felt ambushed because the publicity created a lot of controversy, for which he had been unprepared. He felt compelled as bishop to take some kind of action, so he had forbidden the pastor from conducting another such ceremony. Yet Bishop Martínez said all he asked of me was that I inform him in advance if I agreed to celebrate a same-gender union. I promised that I would.

I left the meeting that day feeling good about our conversation. I was encouraged not so much by what the bishop had said as by what he hadn't said. He hadn't told me not to conduct holy union ceremonies, nor had he told me to stop including references to gay people in my sermons. He hadn't even brought up the letter that he had received from Robert Howell. He gave me no reason to believe that he would be anything but supportive of me and my ministry at First Church.

The invitation to celebrate a same-gender union was not long in coming. In late May, I spoke to the Omaha chapter of PFLAG. During the question-and-answer session, a young woman asked if I would be willing to conduct a commitment or covenant ceremony for a gay or lesbian couple. I explained that I had conducted same-gender unions since 1990 and said that I would continue to celebrate them.

At the end of the meeting, two women approached me and introduced themselves as Mary and Martha. I had seen them at worship over the past couple of months. They had come for the first time on Easter Sunday and were the second new couple present that day, along with Roy and J Wright, who would play an important role at First Church and in my ministry. Mary and Martha explained that they were drawn to First Church because, like Roy and J, they had heard of our Vision Focus that specifically included lesbian and gay people in the life and ministry of our church.

While they talked with me, their faces beamed with joy and excitement. They had been together for over a year, they said, and wanted to have a covenant ceremony to celebrate their commitment to each other. They wanted to have their ceremony in the sanctuary, if I was willing to conduct it for them. I told them I would be honored to do so. I explained that I was preparing to be away from Omaha for a week of Annual Conference and a month of vacation, and I asked them to make an appointment with the pastors' secretary to meet with me following worship on my first Sunday back. I wanted to get to know them, talk about what this commitment meant to them, and discuss the particulars of the ceremony. Mary and Martha agreed, and a noon meeting was scheduled for July 13.

Chris and Natalia were spending that summer on Ocracoke Island, part of the Outer Banks of North Carolina. Chris had gone ahead in early May and was staying in the old Soundfront Inn — the home of our friend Maggie Boos, who had died the previous fall. Ocracoke is remote, accessible only by ferry, sail or motor boat, and small plane. I had been the pastor of its United Methodist church from 1973 to 1981. I knew and loved its people like family. It had become a spiritual home for Chris and me, and we returned at every opportunity. My plan was to join her there for my vacation.

We spent lots of time walking and sitting on the beach, soaking up as much sun and salt air as possible, watching the sometimes turbulent, sometimes gentle waves, and thinking. I reflected on the past twelve months and all that had happened in Omaha. It had been a good first year, I thought. I knew that some members of the congregation were not happy with the direction First Church was going, but that often happens with a new pastor, especially one who clearly defines priorities for ministry. Not everyone will be supportive. Some people will resist. Some will leave because of the priorities chosen, while others will come because of them. It's an adjustment process, a transition.

The lay leadership at First Church was competent and strong, with more than three hundred members serving on twenty-three active committees. Together, we had worked hard at discerning what God was calling us to be and do as First United Methodist Church, and the Vision Focus articulated the priorities of this calling. However, there had been contention about our vision of being welcoming and accepting of lesbian, gay, and bisexual people. Mel Semrad's threat of bringing the Confessing Movement into the struggle remained a concern, even though I had not heard from him since our meeting at the end of March. Whether or not it was an empty threat, I was aware of the harm that the Confessing Movement was doing nationally, and I was sure that First Church would be affected by it sooner or later. I realized that, once I was back in Omaha, I would need to prepare the church leadership for that likelihood.

Chris and I talked about Mary and Martha's request for me to conduct their covenant ceremony. We knew that it could cause problems, potentially very serious ones, because of the prohibition enacted by the 1996 General Conference. Since I was committed to conducting union ceremonies for same-gender couples, we knew it was inevitable that someday I would have to deal with the church's prohibition.

Chris's support was unwavering. We talked about the new home we had bought in March. It had taken nine months of apartment living to find this charming little Cape Cod–style house, located in one of Omaha's older neighborhoods. What the house on Jackson Street meant in emotional terms was that we had finally unpacked our bags. We were there to stay. Omaha was now our home.

When my vacation on Ocracoke ended, I was physically and spiritually refreshed, ready to return to my ministry. A year earlier, I had made the drive from North Carolina to Nebraska with eager anticipation, like an explorer entering an unknown land. I was just as eager—if not more so—this year, because I knew the landscape now, knew the people and their vision, knew the resistance and the promise.

Mary, Martha, and I met as planned on July 13, my first Sunday back from vacation. They bubbled with excitement as we talked about their relationship and the ceremony they wanted to have. At the same time, they were concerned about possible repercussions I might face. Someone had told them the bishop might remove me from First Church if I conducted their ceremony. They said they would understand if I chose not to do it. I thanked them for their concern but told them that it was not only my honor to conduct their covenant ceremony, it was also my responsibility as their pastor. I would deal with any reactions or fallout later and would not let fear of the consequences deter me.

They chose the date of September 22, 1997, for the ceremony. I explained that they needed to talk with Roberta Coss, the pastors' secretary, to reserve the sanctuary on that date and to complete a form required of all couples when scheduling a wedding. After they left my office, I wrote Bishop Martínez to let him know about the ceremony, just as I had promised back in April. I sent a copy of the letter to District Superintendent Susan Davies.

When Martha called the next day, Roberta was wonderful. I had not prepared her for the conversation. Nonetheless, without a trace of surprise, she graciously took the necessary information from Martha, put the date on the calendar, and asked the question she always asks when weddings are scheduled: "Would you and Mary like to have a reception at the church after the ceremony?" Surprised by the offer, Martha stammered with delight, "Yes!" Roberta had given the most accepting welcome possible. She treated Mary and Martha's covenant ceremony just like any other wedding she had scheduled.

A few weeks later, Martha called me to explain that a conflict had developed with the September 22 date, so we rescheduled the ceremony for Saturday, September 13. I wrote Bishop Martínez to let him know of the date change, again copying Susan Davies. The next morning, before I had a chance to tell Roberta about the new date for the ceremony, Martha called me back to ask if we could reschedule the ceremony for Sunday, the fourteenth, instead of Saturday, the thirteenth. So, Roberta rescheduled their ceremony for Sunday, September 14. The ceremony was never written on the church calendar for the thirteenth. No one at the church other than Mary, Martha, and me knew that the first proposed date for rescheduling was September 13. Only the bishop and Susan Davies were given the date of the thirteenth. I didn't bother to write the bishop a third time, giving him the date of the fourteenth, since I had heard nothing from him in response to my first letter and this latest change involved only one day. This little dance with the calendar would prove to be significant in the mysterious way in which the ceremony would become public knowledge.

At their August meetings, I informed the Staff-Parish Relations Committee and the Board of Trustees about Mary and Martha's ceremony. My decision to conduct it was a pastoral decision, which I had full and complete authority to make without asking anyone's approval. Don Bredthauer, Susan Mullins, and I did not routinely inform these two bodies about the weddings we scheduled. However, because of the prohibition of "homosexual unions" in The United Methodist Church's Social Principles, I felt these groups deserved to be aware of this ceremony and prepared for any repercussions. The trustees simply accepted the information without discussion. All members of the Staff-Parish Relations Committee, except one, voiced support for my conducting the ceremony.

On Saturday morning, August 30, the telephone call that I had been expecting since mid-July finally came. After he greeted me, Bishop Martínez said: "Jimmy, I of course got your letters about the holy union you've agreed to do for the two women in your church. District Superintendent Davies tells me you're committed to doing it. Tell me why."

"Mary and Martha are members of First United Methodist Church," I said, "and I am their pastor. They love each other and are committed to their relationship. They want to publicly recognize their love and commitment, and the church is where they want to do it. They have a right to the same affirmation and support that other couples receive when they marry.

Because they are two women does not matter." Since conducting James and Timothy's holy union ceremony back in 1989, I had conducted more than twelve covenant ceremonies for same-gender couples. I wasn't willing to repudiate the unions of these couples by suddenly deciding that Mary and Martha shouldn't have their opportunity for a holy union.

If I refused to perform a ceremony for Mary and Martha, I explained to Bishop Martínez, I would be forfeiting my call to ministry. I told him I believed that it was my pastoral responsibility to conduct such ceremonies, that The United Methodist Church was guilty of bigotry toward gay people, and that I felt morally compelled not to cooperate with that prejudice. He seemed to understand my position and be somewhat sympathetic. But he was concerned about the media and the effect that publicity about the ceremony would have on First Church and on the Nebraska Annual Conference.

Finally, he said: "I know you're going to do it, but I have to tell you not to. I believe such ceremonies conflicted with the *Discipline* even before the prohibition was added last year. But since you're going to do it anyway, I would like to request that you ask the women if they would reschedule the ceremony. I'm going to be out of the country on the thirteenth, and I'd like to be here when it happens so I can deal with it if it gets in the media." He explained that he would be in Spain on study leave. "If it can't be worked out," he said, "I'll draft some press releases and give them to Dick Turner in case they're needed." Dick was the bishop's assistant.

I told him the ceremony would actually be on September 14 instead of the thirteenth. With the ceremony just two weeks away, and considering that the women had worked hard to choose a date when all their family and friends could attend, I doubted that they could or would want to change the date. But I agreed to ask them. The bishop thanked me, and I wished him well on his trip to Spain. He had been pastoral and collegial. He had respected my position and decision, even while telling me not to conduct the ceremony.

When I contacted Mary and Martha about the bishop's request to reschedule the ceremony, they were incredulous. They had been making preparations for their ceremony since July, the invitations had been sent out, and family members had made plans for travel and accommodations. It would be not only impossible to start over, but disrespectful to everyone planning to attend. I passed their response on to Bishop Martínez.

Julia McCord, the religion editor for the *Omaha World-Herald*, telephoned me on Tuesday afternoon, September 9. She had received an anonymous note informing her that I would be conducting a covenant ceremony for two women on Saturday, September 13. I told her the information was true except for the date — which was, along with the names of the women, confidential. I explained that, even though he'd instructed me not to do it, Bishop Martínez knew that I was going to conduct the ceremony. Julia said she was writing an article for the Wednesday afternoon edition of the newspaper, and I agreed to meet with her early the next morning to discuss the ceremony more fully.

Establishing a positive relationship with Julia and any other media representatives who might contact me was crucial. I had learned from my experience at Fairmont United Methodist Church to consider the media as an ally. Reporters might not always present a story in the way I would prefer, but the media was an important way to speak to the public. Being available to reporters as a trustworthy source of information was the best way to establish a good relationship with them.

I wondered who had sent the anonymous note to Julia. My first thought was that it had come from someone at First Church. A number of members would be prime suspects, especially with the growing opposition to my ministry and the inclusivity of the Vision Focus. I had informed the Board of Trustees and the Staff-Parish Relations Committee about the ceremony, so it was not secret, and the church calendar was always available for anyone in the congregation to see. Then I realized the note couldn't have come from someone at First Church. The date given in the note, September 13, was never on the church calendar, and no one at the church other than me knew it had ever been considered. Only Bishop Martínez and Susan Davies had been informed that the date would be the thirteenth. I concluded that the information about the ceremony and the date had come from either the bishop's or the district superintendent's office. I later learned from Julia that the note had been postmarked in Lincoln, where Bishop Martínez had his office.

Julia and I met for about an hour. She questioned me about my communication with Bishop Martínez, about support and lack of support at First Church, and about my history in North Carolina. She had a late-morning deadline for that afternoon's edition of the paper, so we ended the visit with my promise to inform her after the covenant ceremony had happened.

After I left Julia's office, I met Dene and Joan Pruett for lunch. Both were leaders at First Church, and my friends. But they weren't happy about the ceremony and said they had heard similar reactions from other members. Dene's concern focused on my defiance of the bishop: "In the military, if you disobey an order, you're history." He said that people who had served in the military wouldn't understand how I could disobey my "commanding officer," regardless of whether I agreed with him or not. I said that I felt a moral responsibility to do what is right, regardless of what the bishop and the law of the church might say. Joan had a different concern: "If you are going to do it, don't do it in the sanctuary. Do it at your home or in a garden some place." She said performing the ceremony in church would be sacrilegious, and people would never feel the same about the sanctuary if the ceremony happened there. I explained that the sanctuary was where Mary and Martha worshiped, and like other members of the congregation, they had a right to celebrate their love and commitment there. To deny them that opportunity would be to say that their love and commitment was not worthy of God's blessing and that their church membership was second class.

Dene and Joan were candid and forceful in their comments to me, but also respectful. I've always found it harder to differ with and resist the counsel of friends and supporters than to withstand the attacks of opponents. While Dene and Joan strongly opposed the covenant ceremony, their greatest concern was to protect me from what they were sure would be a whole lot of problems ahead. They didn't change their minds, but they promised to support First Church and me whatever I decided, a promise that they would more than honor in the months and years ahead.

Later that afternoon, Julia's article appeared on the front page of the *Omaha World-Herald* with the headline "Pastor Says He'll Unite Two Lesbians" and the following text: "Methodist clergyman says he will perform a ceremony despite a warning from his bishop."[1] As soon as the newspaper was out, TV stations in both Omaha and Lincoln started calling me. By late afternoon, I was standing in front of a bank of TV cameras, with the church in the background, doing live interviews. The story headlined the six o'clock news on all the local TV channels and was repeated on the late-night broadcasts.

The next morning's edition of the *Omaha World-Herald* carried another article by Julia, which reported: "Joan Byerhof, head of the church council, and Bob Maline, chairman of the board of trustees, said that under the

Methodist system, the Reverend Jimmy Creech has the right to determine what goes on in the church sanctuary. 'It's a pastoral act.' Joan Zetterman, chairwoman of the staff parish relations committee, said it also is the right thing to do. 'Jesus' message is peace, love and justice for all,' she said. 'To deny people because of their sexual orientation the opportunity to commit themselves to one another in the context of their faith is going against those Christian principles.'"[2]

I knew that Julia had planned to interview the three people quoted for a follow-up article—I'd given her their names and telephone numbers. But I had had no idea what they would say to her. When I read the article I exploded with gratitude. The three of them had taken a stand that was faithful to our Vision Focus and that made it possible for First Church to unite and prevail in the long journey ahead. Had they opposed my action or simply refused to take a stand, saying the matter was between me and the bishop, they would have made it difficult for First Church to have a united front. They had acted just the way leaders should.

On Sunday, as soon as everyone had left the sanctuary after the last service of worship, Steve Nehrig, the building manager, began setting up for Mary and Martha's ceremony scheduled for two in the afternoon. I went to my office to be quiet and prepare for the ceremony. I thought about Mary and Martha and their courage, integrity, and love. I thought about the congregation and its vision of a truly inclusive church. It was a peaceful interlude, yet one pregnant with profound grace. I was never more convinced that what I was about to do was right, that what I was about to be a part of was holy, part of life's sacred mystery moving toward what Jesus called the realm of God.

Soon after one o'clock, the wedding party began to arrive, and I went to the entrance to greet them. The air became electric, a mixture of solemnity and gaiety. Mary and Martha, like most couples in the hour before their wedding, were nervous about whether everyone would show up on time, about when to walk in and where to stand, about correctly following the order of the ceremony. Wedding photos were taken: the couple alone, the couple with the wedding party, the flowers, the couple with guests. Twenty minutes before two, Mary and Martha met with me in my study for a quiet moment to center ourselves. I urged them to forget about the mechanics of the ceremony, assuring them that I would make certain everything went as planned. They needed only to think about each other, the promises they were making, and the union they were creating.

As we left my study to walk to the sanctuary, a sudden rush of anxiety hit me and I stopped, my head throbbing and my heart pounding. I had felt this way once before, in 1988 when I prepared to step off the curb to join the Gay Pride March. I realized that now, just like then, everything—Mary and Martha, First Church, my family, me, and more that I could not yet know—was about to change. There would be no going back. We were seizing the status quo and shaking it up. We were stepping into the future, innocently yet knowingly. I took a deep breath, put out of my mind the larger consequences of what we were about to do, focused myself again solely on Mary and Martha, their love and commitment, and walked briskly through the hall to the sanctuary. The anxiety passed; my head cleared and my pulse eased.

The ceremony was attended by fifty or more of the couple's friends, along with church members and staff. Mary's young daughter and a close friend stood by her, and Martha's daughter and two sons stood beside her. They had chosen to use The United Methodist Service of Christian Marriage, speaking vows to each other and exchanging rings. I announced that Mary and Martha were now joined in covenant together as life partners, and I prayed for God's blessing on their union. It was a holy moment.

The reception that followed was graciously hosted by members of the United Methodist Women of First Church. Mary, Martha, and their friends were deeply touched by this rare opportunity to be their true selves and welcomed within the walls of a church. Throughout the afternoon, tears often ran down people's cheeks.

Mary and Martha had each taken difficult and painful journeys that had led them to this joyous moment. Martha grew up a Roman Catholic. Her earliest memories were of doing "boy" things, always wanting to play with the boys and their toys. She was fascinated with insects, and her brothers boasted to their friends that their sister "wasn't like other girls because she wasn't afraid of bugs." When she was old enough to pick out her own clothes, she chose to dress like a boy. Her masculinity was a problem when, as an adult, she went to work for a large corporation. Because she "walked like a truck driver," she got coaching to walk "like a woman." She regularly sought other women's advice when picking out clothes. By taking careful note of her female colleagues' offices, she learned to decorate her office with pastels and soft colors.

Martha had learned at an early age at home and at church that her attraction to girls and women was a sin, unnatural and obscene. Martha didn't know anything about lesbians, didn't even know they existed. She just knew her feelings didn't match what was expected of her—to marry a man and have children—and she decided she would just have to get over what she felt and do what she was taught she should do.

She married her brother's best friend. They bought a large house in one of Omaha's suburbs and had three children. On the surface, it appeared that their life was good and she was happy. But the truth inside of Martha, although long denied, was restless. All the years of pretending had not changed it. It became impossible for her to continue performing what was for her an unnatural role. She talked with her best friend—her husband—and told him about the conflict she felt inside and her lifelong effort to suppress her attraction to women. He was shocked but understanding and supportive, and he encouraged her to seek help.

Martha found a support group for people coming to terms with their sexuality. There she met and became friends with William, a United Methodist minister from Iowa. They would go out for coffee after the meetings and talk about things they couldn't share with the group. They cried a lot together and laughed a lot together. They found that, wherever their conversation might begin, they would always end up talking about their spouses, about how much they loved them and how painful it was to hurt them in this pursuit of honesty and integrity. One night, it occurred to them that they should introduce their spouses, believing them to be a perfect match. They were right. After both Martha and William came out and began new lives, their spouses dated and married each other. Martha and her former husband, who had been married for twenty-five years, remained the best of friends. For years after their divorce, he and his new family went to Martha's each Thanksgiving and Christmas for dinner.

Martha was a deeply spiritual person. Unfortunately, she knew a divorced open lesbian could not be active in the Roman Catholic Church without being constantly reminded that she was living in sin. In her search for a church where she could be accepted and respected, she found the Metropolitan Community Church of Omaha.

Mary grew up in a devout Mormon home in Salt Lake City. She loved her family, friends, and church, and there was nothing she wanted more than their love and approval. However, at an early age, she discovered she had a strong attraction to women. Her religion taught that it was offensive to God for a woman to love a woman. She felt absolutely alone with her secret. The inner conflict was excruciating. Believing God knew her secret, Mary believed herself condemned to hell. She was angry with God for making her who she was. Still she wanted God's love, in the same way that an abused child often seeks the love of an abusive parent. She believed that if she tried really hard, she could overcome her attraction for women and God would love her again.

Mary married a man in the Mormon Temple in Salt Lake City, usually a moment of great privilege for a Mormon girl. But she found no joy in it. A few years after her marriage, she gave birth to a daughter who brought her joy, but not enough to soothe her agony. As her inner conflict raged, her husband added to the hell she was living by becoming abusive. Depression consumed her. When her inner and outer conflicts became unbearable, she tried to kill herself. Her failed attempt convinced her that she had to tell her husband and family the truth, and her worst fears were realized. They all renounced her. She didn't try to return to her Mormon church. She knew she would be excommunicated "out of love," as they like to say. When her husband divorced her, he did everything he could to deny Mary all rights as the mother of her daughter, even the right to visit her.

Being true to herself cost Mary her family, her church, and, she was convinced, even God. It was necessary, she believed, to turn away from God in order to accept herself. The pain of leaving the Mormon Church made her want to have nothing to do with organized religion.

Mary found her way to Omaha, where she met new friends who introduced her to the Metropolitan Community Church. There she found lesbian, gay, bisexual, and transgender Christians and learned about God's unconditional love for everyone. She discovered that it wasn't really God she had left in order to live, but only a distorted notion of God. It was at the Metropolitan Community Church that Mary and Martha met and grew to love each other.

After a few years, although indebted to the Metropolitan Community Church for giving them a spiritual home, they began to look for a church with a more diverse membership. When they discovered First United Methodist Church, they knew they had found what they were looking for.

When, on September 14, 1997, in the sanctuary of First United Methodist Church in Omaha, they pledged their love and faith to one another, becoming one family, Mary and Martha recognized not only their love for each other, but the end of painful separate journeys in pursuit of self-acceptance, love, and respect.

The covenant ceremony had been simple and sacred. Time seemed suspended. For the few remaining hours of that day, I savored the beauty and grace of the ceremony, not suspecting the outrage that this extraordinary expression of love would ignite.

After Mary and Martha's reception, I called Julia McCord to tell her the ceremony had happened that afternoon, and she put a brief article about it in the next morning's *Omaha World-Herald*. Almost immediately, formal complaints against me began to pour into the bishop's office, and First Church was swamped with telephone calls and letters from angry, outraged church members and nonmembers. I had prayed God's blessing upon Mary and Martha's union on Sunday, and on Monday all hell broke loose within The United Methodist Church:

> How dare you place your own selfish, sinful, personal beliefs above the welfare of the church! This is not the act of a minister, but merely that of a troublemaker. The Devil can be real proud to have you in his camp. YOU need to resign immediately before the church is entirely split. YOU ARE ONE SICK SOUL! RESIGN! RESIGN! RESIGN! so that we can return to the fundamental teachings of Jesus and God.
> — A former Worshiper at First Church

> Prior to this week, I should have recognized you, without even knowing you, as my colleague and brother. I do neither today! Nor shall my opinion of you alter until you repent before God and apologize to the church for the damage you have done it. I suspect the day you do either will be the proverbial "cold day in Hell!" . . . Shame on you for shaming us so!
> — A retired pastor from Cantonment, Florida

> Where will you stop? Where will you draw the line? Man-boy marriages? What if someone wants a "commitment ceremony" with his cocker spaniel? Or an oak tree? It is such a shame, with so many devoted, loving

and Godly pastors laboring away in obscurity, that a man like you can make front page news by pridefully riding into town with the single-minded agenda of perverting one of the few remaining sacraments that this society still observes . . . [I]f you, Pastor Creech, want to defy the bishop and ignore *The Book of Discipline* then you are jolly-well invited to start your own church, preach your own misbegotten version of the Gospel and perform any sort of "sacrament" you choose . . .

—a United Methodist pastor in Omaha

Other angry letters and phone calls repeated this refrain. Some people told me face to face about their anger and embarrassment. One day soon after the ceremony, I went to Methodist Hospital to visit a longtime church member, a widow in her eighties, who was recovering from serious surgery. When she saw me enter the room, she scowled. Even though she was in physical pain, her first impulse was to scold me severely for getting "First Church in the paper about sex." Once she had expressed her feelings, however, she was able to tell me about her surgery and how she was feeling. She asked me to pray with her.

While expressions of anger garnered the most attention and energy from the staff and me, expressions of support for my conducting the ceremony nearly equaled their number, if not their intensity. One was especially poignant:

I am a 53-year-old man from Omaha. My parents were married at First Church. I was born into and baptized at First Church. I went through classes and was accepted into the membership of First Church (all of these events took place at the original First United Methodist Church at 20th and Capitol). I was married at First Church. My daughter was baptized at First Church. I was on the Administrative Board, chaired the Children's Council and taught Sunday school at First Church.

Nearly 20 years ago I got honest with myself, my God, and my family and came out. All of a sudden my rich life at First Church came to an end because I chose to no longer hide. I was approached by clergy and urged to leave. Hearing the events of the last several weeks has given me the encouragement to consider "coming home" again. I appreciate your efforts at promoting tolerance within the Omaha community and commend you for taking a difficult stand. God bless! and Thank you!

—former First Church member

The call that moved me most was from Shellie Coffey, a schoolteacher in her mid-twenties. She and her husband had had their first baby, Mason, just weeks before. "Jimmy," she said, "thank you for what you did. I think the church should be open to everyone. If Mason should discover he's gay when he grows up, I hope my church will welcome and accept him, and assure him that God loves him." I was accustomed to parents' denying or refusing to entertain the possibility that their children could be lesbian, gay, or bisexual, but Shellie was open to that possibility without fear or shame, certain that she would love her son no less, and expecting, if not demanding, her church to do the same.

Mike McClellan, a member of First Church and an attorney, called after reading about the complaints in Wednesday's *Omaha World-Herald*: "We need to get together and talk about your defense. Do you have a *Book of Discipline* I can borrow, or know where I can get one?"

I was touched by Mike's generosity and deeply grateful to him. I had not thought about a defense, or about having to go through a judicial process. Church trials are rare, and I didn't know anything about how they were conducted. The issue was simple and clear in my mind: I had no doubt that what I'd done was right, and I was just as certain that The United Methodist Church was guilty of bigotry and injustice.

Beginning just days before the covenant ceremony, the *Omaha World-Herald* carried almost daily articles related to the ceremony and the negative reaction to it. The local television stations also had regular reports on the story. The covenant ceremony itself and the fact that I, a United Methodist pastor, had conducted what was a forbidden ceremony became an enormous sensation. It continued to command media attention not only because it involved two women, raising the issue of full civil rights for gay people, but because of the ecclesiastical drama it provided: the confrontation between a bishop and a pastor, between institutional authority and individual conscience. The formal complaints filed against me and the opposition within First Church kept the story alive.

I believed the covenant ceremony, in the midst of intense public reaction and constant media attention, presented First Church with an extraordinary opportunity. In the next issue of *Bread*, I wrote: "This covenant of love, in all of its simplicity, has presented us as a congregation a challenge to delve more deeply into what it means to be the Body of Christ, a means of God's grace and justice for the world, and what it means to be truly open to all persons. It is my hope that we will accept this challenge. It is my hope that by committing ourselves to listen to one another and to share from our hearts, we can hear God speaking in and from our midst, and that we can grow into deeper faithfulness as sisters and brothers of Christ. I pray my blessing on you. May we all be filled with God's grace and peace."

Bishop Martínez returned from Spain three weeks earlier than scheduled, and I met with him soon after he got back. Because he had interrupted his study leave in order to deal with the growing controversy, I expected him to be annoyed, perhaps even hostile. But he was neither. He was calm and relaxed, even pastoral in his concern for me and my family. He carefully reviewed with me the judicial process that would be followed because of the more than 150 complaints filed against me. Because they were virtually identical, he'd chosen one that he thought was well written to represent them all.

The bishop said that, in addition to the complaints, he had been overwhelmed with letters and phone calls from United Methodists from all over Nebraska and the nation supporting me.

A new handbook for the United Methodist judicial process had just been published. Bishop Martínez gave me a copy and advised me to study it carefully. He explained that I would have an opportunity to talk with the person who filed the complaint, to see if we might be reconciled. If we couldn't, the complaint would be turned over to a church counsel, who would act as the prosecutor. The judicial process would be pretty much like a civil proceeding. I would need a defense counsel to represent me, and a committee on investigation would hold a hearing, like a grand jury, to determine if the complaint had merit. If the committee determined it did, the complaint would then become a charge against me, and I would be put on trial.

As our meeting drew to a close, Bishop Martínez told me that he would not be making any public comments about the judicial process because he considered it an internal personnel matter, and he didn't want me to talk to the media either. I told him I couldn't agree because I believed this was more than a personnel issue. It had to do with an injustice perpetrated by The United Methodist Church, and I believed it was important to be open and candid with the media about it. He wasn't happy with my response, but he didn't argue with me.

Because he had brought up the media, I explained that Julia McCord had received an anonymous note, postmarked in Lincoln, informing her about the covenant ceremony. I told him that the note gave September 13 as the date for the ceremony, and I explained how only he and Susan Davies could have known about that date. When he realized that his office was the source of the leak, he was furious. He explained that he had shared my letters with some of the district superintendents. The leak could have come from one of them, or someone else they might have told in spite of his instructions not to talk about the ceremony. The bishop's secretary was also a suspect. It's ironic that the bishop had unwittingly become the cause of the publicity that he had feared.

I left the meeting a bit overwhelmed by the judicial process. Mike McClellan had volunteered to work with me and could serve as my assistant counsel, but I also needed a member of the clergy to represent me, and I had no idea whom to ask. I had been in Nebraska only a little over a year. I wanted someone who was known and respected by the clergy in the conference, someone who was intelligent and articulate, and someone who would be committed both to me and to the cause of justice for lesbian, gay, bisexual, and transgender people. Whoever accepted this role would be taking a great risk, perhaps putting his or her career in the conference in jeopardy.

I asked Don Bredthauer about Nebraska clergy who might serve as my defense counsel, and his suggestions included the Reverend Dr. Doug Williamson, the Mattingly Assistant Professor of Theology and Religion at Nebraska Wesleyan University, in Lincoln. But Williamson was a native of Boston, Massachusetts. If he represented me, we would be two outsiders going up against the Nebraska Annual Conference. On the other hand, Doug's strengths were enormous. He taught United Methodist history and doctrine, as well as theology and ethics. He was bright, articulate, and highly respected by the progressive clergy in the conference. And, to top all of this, he was the very successful women's soccer coach at Nebraska Wesleyan University, which meant he was a strong competitor. He was ideal. Yet one question remained: Would he really care about my case? The answer came unsolicited in the mail.

Soon after talking with Don, I received a letter from Doug in which he referred to my "pastoral faithfulness in performing the service of union/covenant for the two women in your Church." He said: "Please know that you have my respect, admiration, and support in what you have done and are doing . . . Please know, Jimmy, that you are regularly in my thoughts and prayers. If I can be supportive in more tangible and/or specific ways, please call me and let me know."

I called Doug right away and asked if he'd be willing to be my defense counsel. When a reporter for *The Cornerstone*, the Nebraska Wesleyan University student newspaper, asked Doug later about his decision, Doug said "I hesitated for about twenty seconds" before agreeing to my request. Doug was not naive about the risk he was taking. "Williams accepted this responsibility," the article in *The Cornerstone* noted, "knowing full well that it could not only mean the destruction of Creech's clergy career, but of his own as well. He took the position 'knowing the way our (the UMC) system works, our Bishop would probably be unwilling to appoint me as a pastor to a church if I ever decided to leave Wesleyan.'"[1]

Now that I had found someone capable and willing to serve as my counsel, I wanted to reach out across the church for insight about the judicial process. An Internet discussion list called CORNET (Celebrating Our Relationships Network), composed of people committed to ending The United Methodist Church's oppression of lesbian, gay, bisexual, and transgender people, had been created in July. The Methodist Federation for Social Action (MFSA) also had an Internet discussion list, which included most of the progressive members of The United Methodist Church. Without a true community of colleagues in Nebraska, I decided to send an e-mail to each of these lists asking for advice and suggestions of people who might guide me through the judicial process. The online conversations that resulted were stimulating and helpful. Through these two discussion groups, I met people who became loyal friends throughout the succeeding years, some of whom I have yet to meet face to face. The groups provided me a community, very real even if it was virtual.

I knew I was a part of a movement much bigger than myself. I could not see their faces, shake hands with them, hear their words, or hug them, but from this point on, I knew that hundreds of colleagues were with me. I never felt alone. The Internet was a lifeline for me, as well as a tool to broaden the accountability of The United Methodist Church.

Among the many e-mails I received was this one from Russ Hawkins, pastor of Kairos United Methodist Church in Kansas City, Missouri. Russ wrote in late October that he was reveling in the Internet dialogue:

> Would you believe it? I can't wait each morning to pour my cup of coffee and get to my computer. Every morning now there are e-mails galore from many of you sharing some very inspiring witnesses about the issues

facing us as we reflect on who we are as members of The United Methodist Church and as Christians. I am proud to be part of this movement . . .

What makes your action so remarkable to me, Jimmy, is . . . that even
if those words in the *Discipline* were placed in the appropriate legal place,
you would still have performed that service . . . I believe you would still
have stood firm, for the bottom line has to do with who we want to be
as the church of Jesus Christ — inclusive, loving, life-affirming. In a news
release you are quoted as saying, "For me, gay or lesbian people who are
saying, 'we have a right to be here,' are challenging us to a broader and
deeper understanding of what it means to be the church . . . the body of
Christ in ministry to all people." Isn't that what continues to compel us
to move forward no matter what?

We are dealing with fundamental, basic issues of our faith, it seems to
me. Jimmy, you have called us to take the high ground, and I for one hope
we will never let such things as "order and discipline" and any institution
pull us down from that high calling. Pardon my hearkening again to years
gone by, but an old song comes to mind . . . "The answer, my friend, is
blowing in the wind."

As responses to my requests for help to the CORNET and MFSA discussion lists came in, Jerry, a pastor in California, was mentioned frequently as
someone with extensive experience with the judicial process of The United
Methodist Church. So, I e-mailed Jerry, asking for guidance, and he replied:

From what I've read, I suspect you wanted to make this holy union you
performed a test case. From a very technical standpoint within the devel-
opment of the polity, I personally wish a test case could have waited, for
there is much movement of subterranean feelings going on within the
denomination on this issue, among the Poo Bahs [*sic*] who are nomi
nally "the leadership." What it boils down to is that the Judicial Council
has already said in writing (and one member told me, unofficially,) that
they don't want to touch this issue with a ten foot pole. The bishops, and
I suspect this includes Joel Martínez, don't want to do anything about this
because of the great ambiguities involved. But now that you have done
this, you have forced Bishop Martínez to file, or at least to entertain, complaints against you lest he have complaints filed against "him" for failure
to perform the work of the ministry. My hunch is that now everyone has

gotten backed into a corner, the very best thing which could happen is to find a face-saving way for everyone to back down gracefully, without officially doing anything to your orders or conference relationship, without the bishop having to say he's in favor of same-sex unions, and most importantly of all, not setting any church law precedent we might regret at some future point.

I say this last provision with a great deal of thought and care, Jimmy. Right now, the provision against holy unions is only in the Social Principles, where what it means is quite ambiguous. The General Conference rather decisively voted NOT to make the prohibition against doing holy unions an operational rule. Ditto against making it a chargeable offense in and of itself. And think about this: I don't think you could find one United Methodist clergy (or bishop) who could affirm that s/he agrees with every provision of the Social Principles. The precedent which could break the church would be to have it declared that the Social Principles constitute operational rules. And yet there are those on the right wing of the church who, not having thought through all the implications of such an act, would like to do that very thing. The last thing in the world we want to do is to create a milieu where the Judicial Council gets backed into stating that the Social Principles are operational rules. Or to state that they are NOT operational rules, which would make them nothing more than a joke. Likewise, we don't want to hand the 2000 General Conference an excuse to make forbidding of the conduct of holy unions an operational rule in and of itself. Then we'd all lose on what we'd like to see happen.

So in a sense, your act of ministry can do one of two things: it can lead us into a polity crisis in which our goal of ultimately allowing the regular conduct of same-sex unions as a ministry of the church could be jeopardized; or we can find a way in which everyone can back down gracefully without looking like they are capitulating on principle. I think this can be done, if you are willing to look at that option. Think about it, pray about it, and call me . . . and we'll talk.

My prayers are with you.

I found Jerry's observations insightful and sobering. He seemed to have clearheaded, objective guidance to offer. However, he sent a second e-mail soon after with very specific advice:

The problem in this case was the publicity. Our denomination hates negative and/or controversial publicity with a passion (as do most institutions other than Political Parties!). Once the publicity got out, and given the fact that you are in the South Central Jurisdiction, the bishop I am sure got lots of pressure to "do something" to you . . . So, I'd like you to think about, and pray about, finding a gracious way to let him "do something" to you in the nature of a slap on the wrist, the details of which can be kept confidential, so that you won't have your orders subject to review and/ or removal (or a church trial), and your bishop can go out with a straight face and say he disciplined you.

What I have in mind is that you personally apologize to him for creating adverse publicity (watch the words here) regarding a worship service you performed; and to affirm to him that if you ever feel constrained to have a similar worship service (we are trying to avoid the words "same-sex union"), you will be sure that it is held away from premises owned by The United Methodist Church. We would then ask him to agree that you have been "disciplined," the details of which would be mandatorily confidential (so he can't tell the conservatives what happened but he can tell them he disciplined you!), and determine that the matter has been satisfactorily resolved. The key word here is resolved, as in "supervisory resolution."

Suffice it to say that if the bishop does not allow the matter to be "resolved" at the supervisory level, not only does he lose control of the situation, but it gets thrown into your conference which is split 45–45–10, left, right, and center. That's too narrow a spread to go into the Committee on Investigation with any level of comfort. Get it resolved at this level, and you and your bishop can find a way to help each other get out of the corners you've each backed each other into. Remember, the goal is to allow you to remain a clergyman so you can do similar services in the future: to do so in a way which won't f**k [sic] up my right (and that of other clergy who agree with us) to do similar kinds of services in the future, and to pull all of this off in a way which won't completely destroy your church, nor the denomination. I think it's do-able.

I was disturbed by the second e-mail, so I called Jerry. He was cordial, but there was a discernible edge to his voice. He told me that he was something of an expert on United Methodist law and was sometimes called upon by the Judicial Council to write legal briefs. He said he was willing to offer advice and guidance along the way to me, my counsel, and assistant counsel.

We talked about the ceremony. I was somewhat offended by his suggestion that I had conducted it in order to create a test case for the legality of the prohibition. He urged me, as he had in his e-mail, to negotiate with Bishop Martínez to see if I could prevent the judicial process from moving forward. He suggested that I promise to never again conduct a same-gender union service, and perhaps suggest to the bishop that I be briefly suspended—anything to keep this case from going to trial and setting a precedent.

Then Jerry angrily began to lecture me. He told me that I had made a major mistake by informing Bishop Martínez about the ceremony beforehand. He said that he and others had had ministries to gay people for a long time but kept it secret so as not to attract the attention and incite the wrath of the right wing of the church. Although the teachings and policies of The United Methodist Church clearly discriminated against lesbian, gay, and bisexual people, he said, he could live with that fact and work around it. What he most feared was an extreme reaction to my conducting the ceremony that would result in more discriminatory and restrictive church laws. I had made a mess of things for him and other clergy operating in the closet by allowing the complaint to be processed. What bishops and other church leaders most disliked and feared, he said, was publicity, because it exposed them to public scrutiny and required them to take a public stand. They hate accountability, he said. If I had only kept quiet and the ceremony had not been reported in the media, everything would have been okay, and those clergy who ministered to the gay community could have gone on doing so for years.

I was caught off guard by Jerry's anger, and I disagreed with his advice in my case. I was quite clear about my values and priorities, about my decision to conduct the ceremony and the risk involved. But my conversation with Jerry raised a whole other concern that I had not thought about: how might what I had done affect other clergy? The possibility that my action might harm the movement for gay equality had never occurred to me. How could my performing the ceremony cause harm? How can resisting evil do harm? What was I missing? I believed that the route Jerry insisted I take had no integrity; it was a cop-out that only made the bigotry more oppressive.

To get a larger perspective on this point, I posted the following letter to the CORNET and MFSA Internet discussion groups:

I have been encouraged to try to negotiate with Bishop Martínez for a resolution of the complaint against me so that the complaint process will not go beyond the supervisory response. The concern is that should the process proceed to the Investigating Committee, it will be out of the hands/control of the bishop and annual conference and there will be no turning back.

I have been advised that the Judicial Council does not want to deal with the question of whether or not the Social Principles can be used as the basis of a chargeable offense. The result of the Judicial Council dealing with the question may be to treat the Social Principles as coercive, rather than as persuasive.

My questions to you are: What do you think is at stake here for us? Do we challenge the Judicial Council to deal with this issue or not? I realize the risk. But, do we allow The United Methodist Church to continue with the lack of integrity we now have in order to avoid the risk, or do we challenge the church to self-examination and give it the chance to struggle through to greater integrity? On the other hand, should I press on, will the cost to other clergy be too great (as in stricter application of the Social Principles)?

I have been told that my "sin" was informing the bishop which resulted in the publicity. Had I done the covenant ceremony in silence, I have been told, it would have been ignored. I accept that. But, we know what silence has done to us and to gay people. It has cost us a great deal. Is it not time to be open? Is seeing the judicial process through not the right thing to do now? Is there not a great deal to gain by doing so? Or, are the risks too great for The United Methodist Church?

Responses came quickly:

I only want to say that surely silence was not the best way. It speaks of "don't ask, don't tell" which doesn't solve anything, it seems to me. I continue to appreciate your courage and your ministry to the two women. I hope that brothers and sisters in this list group will help you in the decision making and bring you through to a sense of peace in that decision. —Alice

We think you are asking the right question about the effect this push would have on other clergy but you must also consider your own life, would this result in your being located?[2] Are you willing to take that risk?
— Deana and Kenneth

I'll be honest with you I think this one should go to the Judicial Council. First, it is the perfect case (not a fly-by-night but rooted in pastoral ministry and the local church). Second, I do not think the JC [Judicial Council] will move toward a coercive understanding of the Social Principles. To make the content of this book binding would set the stage for charges and counter charges until the Last Day. Such a decision of the JC would only intensify the progressive-conservative split. Third, Alice is surely right about the history of silence and sweeping everything under the rug . . . In sum, my advice, if you feel up to it, is to go the full course. But if you decide to negotiate I will hold you in no less esteem than I do now.
— Art

Jimmy, you have made it clear from the start that you respond to a gay or lesbian couple in the same loving and caring way in which you respond to any couple who approaches you to participate in a union service. If the Judicial Council finds that, because these words were placed in the Social Principles, that they have no legal authority, then at the next General Conference a move will be made to place them in the "correct" place, thus giving them full "coercive" status as legally binding legislation. If I am hearing you correctly, it will have no effect on your decision to disobey that legislation. Wherever it is placed, it is unjust . . . What we are about, it seems to me, is disobedience of a "law" that, as Bishop White and others have said, is demonic. Do I read you wrong on this point, Jimmy?

I wonder where the line is for those who are complying with this "legislation" simply because it is part of the *Discipline* and thus their duty. How far will the institution be allowed to go before people in high places and throughout the denomination say "No?"

Surely they have been allowed to go way too far already. I for one, believe we should not rest until all such hateful language concerning the GLBT community is stricken from the *Discipline*. I am grateful that you have simply continued to do what you have obviously always done in your ministry: Put people, all people, and their needs before the dictates of the institution. I think we have mighty good precedence for such an approach to ministry from our true "Discipline." Thank you for who you are and what you are doing.

—Russ

Jeremy Vetter, son of a United Methodist minister in Lincoln, Nebraska, provided valuable insight into the process that took place at the 1996 General Conference when the prohibition was debated and adopted:

I am a 22-year-old student just beginning graduate work at Oxford University in England. I have been an active member of the Nebraska Conference of The United Methodist Church since I was a freshman in high school, and I was lay delegate to General Conference in 1996. In fact, I was Nebraska's representative on the Church and Society committee when the language in the Social Principles under which a complaint has been filed was enacted. The discussion among sub-committee members indicated they did not understand the language to be binding or coercive because of its location within the Social Principles rather than elsewhere in the *Discipline*. There was explicit discussion of whether the Social Principles could be binding on pastors, and my impression was that most delegates voting on the same-sex union prohibition did not think they could be. So it is disturbing to me that it is now being manipulated and used in order to charge pastors. In response to your queries about whether or not to seek a compromise with the bishop, I personally believe that this issue must be dealt with openly and honestly. Thus I would be inclined to see the issue taken forward. I can't imagine that the Judicial Council could possibly start ruling that pastors can be disciplined under the Social Principles. I am also concerned that I don't want to see your own conscience compromised with the bishop in negotiations that lead to some kind of agreement that you not perform same-sex unions or that they be performed covertly. Although I've heard others say that you should have kept quiet about the whole thing, I believe your act was a courageous one that is worthy of great commendation for its openness and honesty. Not many pastors who perform same-sex unions would be so willing to risk themselves personally in so obvious a way for the issue. If our church really is an unjust church, then I want to know that it is an unjust church. I think it could be pivotal for many young people like myself who want to see where The United Methodist Church really stands—on the side of human beings wanting to commit their lives to each other, or on the side of intolerance and oppression of gays and lesbians. Please take heart, and know that there are many of us out there who admire what you are doing.

—Jeremy

There were other e-mails like this that encouraged me to stay the course.

On Wednesday, October 8, I drove to the Cornhusker Quality Inn in Lincoln to meet with Bishop Martínez and the yet-to-be-identified person who filed the complaint against me. The bishop instructed me to tell no one where I was going or why. He didn't even tell his secretary where he was going, not wanting to take a chance on alerting the media.

The bishop was waiting in the lobby for me when I arrived, and he ushered me downstairs to a conference room. A banquet table was set up for the meeting, with a bowl of hard candy and bananas that Bishop Martínez had brought and placed in the center, along with a pitcher of ice water, three glasses, and a copy of *The Book of Discipline of The United Methodist Church*. The bishop gave me a copy of the official complaint filed against me, which I had not yet seen. He said that the person who filed the complaint was in another room and that I would meet with him after I had had time to read the complaint. Then the bishop left the room. The complaint read:

First United Methodist Church
Ogallala, Nebraska

Greetings,

I write this letter to file a complaint against Reverend James Creech of The Nebraska Annual Conference.

This letter comes with a heavy heart. I know that I am going to be disagreeing with several people I consider friends and colleagues.

The actions of Rev. James Creech presents [sic] a lot of questions.

It is the right of every United Methodist to bring up issues for discussion and change.

The position of the church on homosexuality has been questioned every four years for several quadrenniums now. The stance of the church remains unchanged. Even though some delegates choose to come home every year and report that they are getting closer to having the church's present position overturned, the facts from General Conference do not support that.

The church's position on the union of homosexuals is stated in *The 1996 Book of Discipline* in paragraph 65, pages 87 and 89.

My greatest question does not have to do with his [Creech's] disagreement with General Conference, but with what he chose to do with that disagreement in the total disregard of his ordination vows.

Rev. Creech is in direct conflict with Paragraph 2624 part 1, sub-parts (b), (e), and (f) of the 1996 *Discipline*.

It is his right to continue the effort to overturn the conviction of the mainstream United Methodist Church. There is a way to do that. However, what Rev. Creech is saying by his actions is that the church may speak and that is supposed to be official, but that does not matter. "My conscience supersedes all church conscience. I will do what I want to do."

Many United Methodists have chosen to throw out the authority of Scripture. If you add to that total disregard for *The Book of Discipline*, my question is, "What do we base our ministry on?"

Is every pastor an authority unto himself?

Sincerely,
Glenn W. Loy, Pastor

I'd never met Glenn Loy. It was clear that the issues of homosexuality and obedience to church law were important to him, making my so-called disobedience a particular concern for him. He mischaracterized my act of conscience as an act of self-serving defiance in disregard of the church, forgetting that conscience is shaped and informed by the community to which one belongs. It was the community of The United Methodist Church that taught me the stories of Jesus, the prophets, and other heroes of faith, with their lessons about integrity, justice, and ethical responsibility, about standing against wrong and doing what is right regardless of the cost.

I read the complaint carefully several times. But something was not quite right about it. Something was missing.

The door opened, and Bishop Martínez escorted Glenn Loy to the table. Glenn sat down across from me. The bishop sat at the end of the table between us. Tall and lanky, Glenn was dressed in a black suit, black tie, black shoes, and white shirt, looking like a country preacher from an earlier era. His stern, no-nonsense expression told me not to expect casual, convivial conversation. During our meeting, he never once smiled or showed warmth. He appeared uncomfortable in his role of accuser, but the controlled anger in his words revealed that this was a serious matter for him. He identified himself as an evangelical, though he was careful to say that he did not belong to the "fundamentalist fringe." He argued that if church laws are not binding, they are worthless, and that anyone who breaks a church law should be punished. There is no "order and discipline" in the church if the laws are not enforced, he insisted.

I argued that this so-called law was unjust and that all United Methodist clergy were morally obligated to defy it. I described the prohibition of "homosexual unions" as an act of bigotry by The United Methodist Church. I compared my disobedience to that of civil disobedience to unjust laws, a morally responsible act that the church has long supported. Glenn acknowledged the parallel but reminded me that engaging in civil disobedience meant accepting the consequences. I told him I understood that and was prepared to accept the consequences. But, I said, while I may be punished, I will use the opportunity to argue that the church is in error, and that conducting a union ceremony for two people who love and are committed to one another was a far more faithful act than cooperating with the church's bigotry.

After more than an hour of conversation, the bishop ended the meeting. He told Glenn to call him the next morning to let him know whether or not anything I had said had given him reason to drop the complaint. He then invited us to pray.

But while I was talking with Glenn, I had realized what was missing from his letter. "Excuse me, Bishop," I interrupted, "would you read Glenn's complaint again? Something important is missing. Glenn doesn't say what I did to disobey *The Book of Discipline*. There's no mention of the covenant ceremony."

I knew that *The United Methodist Administrative and Judicial Procedures Handbook* stated: "As much as possible, an initial complaint should be written with specifications containing as many facts as are available, such as date, place, and specific events alleged to have occurred." While Glenn may not have been aware of this, the bishop had to be. He was the one who gave me a copy of the handbook, so I would be informed about the process. Surely this letter of complaint could not possibly be the best written of the more than 150 filed against me. Why, I wondered, did the bishop choose this particular letter of complaint or this particular person to be the complainant? Could it have anything to do with Glenn's being from rural Ogallala, in the westernmost part of Nebraska — or with the fact that he was part of the evangelical caucus in the Nebraska Annual Conference? Was his selection an effort to appease the right wing?

The bishop and Glenn quickly reread the complaint. The covenant ceremony was public knowledge, but Glenn's letter made no direct reference to it. My offense was so obvious to him and the bishop, it seems, that they had felt no need to mention it or provide details about it. Rather sheepishly, the bishop said he would make sure that this oversight was remedied. Then he prayed and we departed.

The next morning Bishop Martínez called to tell me that Glenn Loy would not drop his complaint. I wasn't surprised. Two days later, the bishop called to tell me that he had appointed the Reverend Lauren Ekdahl to be the church counsel. Lauren would redraft Glenn's complaint, with all the details about the "chargeable offense" I was accused of committing, and refer it to the Committee on Investigation for a hearing. Our conversation was brief, but I could hear stress in the bishop's voice. While he was typically calm and deliberate, his voice was a bit husky and strained, and he sighed deeply.

"Bishop, I know this is difficult for you," I said. "Are you doing okay?"

"Oh, I'm okay, I guess," he answered. "I'm not sleeping well. What really worries me is what this is going to do to me in 2000." With these words, Bishop Martínez revealed what he perceived to be his personal stake in how the controversy and judicial process would be resolved. He would be completing his second four-year term as bishop of the Nebraska Annual Conference in 2000. After eight years in one annual conference, it was customary for a bishop to be transferred to another annual conference, and Bishop Martínez hoped to be assigned to the Rio Grande Annual Conference in southwest Texas, where his hometown was located. He worried, he admitted, how my case would affect his career and his chance to go back home.

Lauren Ekdahl was an active member of the Nebraska chapter of the Methodist Federation for Social Action and considered to be among the more liberal members of the Nebraska Annual Conference. I liked him and respected his persistent public effort to abolish capital punishment in Nebraska. In this church drama that would now be played out on a very public stage, I considered him to be more of a colleague than an adversary.

I was curious why Lauren had accepted this appointment as church counsel. As I came to understand it, Lauren held the Social Principles to be almost as inviolable as Holy Writ. I believe he accepted this appointment as a way to uphold not just the one sentence about "homosexual unions" but the whole of the principles. Whether by design or accident, the two theological wings of the Nebraska Annual Conference were now poised against me: Glenn Loy, the complainant, coming from the evangelical right of the church; and, Lauren Ekdahl, the prosecuting church counsel, from the liberal left.

On October 28, 1997, Lauren sent the following letter to the Reverend David Lux, chairperson of the Nebraska Conference Committee on Investigation:

Dear David,

It is my sad but solemn duty to communicate to the Committee on Investigation of the Nebraska Conference Board of Ordained Ministry, a complaint, in accordance with Paragraph #2624 1.(e) of *The 1996 Book of Discipline*, against Rev. Jimmy Creech currently serving as Senior Pastor of First United Methodist Church at Omaha, Nebraska.

On Sunday, September 14, 1997, in First United Methodist Church, Omaha, Nebraska, Reverend Jimmy Creech, a minister of The United Methodist Church, performed a "covenanting ceremony" that celebrated a homosexual union between two women.

Performance of a covenanting ceremony places Rev. Creech in "disobedience to the Order and Discipline of The United Methodist Church" [Paragraph #2624 1.(e)] in the following manner:

It places him in conflict with *The Social Principles Paragraph #65C of The 1996 Book of Discipline of The United Methodist Church* especially with the wording added by the 1996 General Conference which states: "Ceremonies that celebrate homosexual unions shall not be conducted by our ministers and shall not be conducted in our churches."

Additional conflict exists where, *The Book of Discipline* authorizes the General Conference in Article IV to "provide and revise the hymnal and ritual of the Church and to regulate all matters relating to the form and mode of worship . . ." (15.6). Since the ritual of The United Methodist

Church makes no provision for same-sex covenanting ceremonies, Rev. Creech exceeded the bounds set by General Conference by proceeding to conduct one.

Sincerely,
Rev. Lauren D. Ekdahl
Counsel for the Church

Unlike Glenn Loy's letter, Lauren's carefully referred to the specific act alleged to be my crime. While there was no question that I had conducted the covenant ceremony, there was a question about whether doing so meant that I had broken a church law. If I had, then I had disobeyed the Order and Discipline of the church. If I had not broken a law, I had not disobeyed. "Disobedience" was a chargeable offense; conducting the ceremony was not.

Lauren's letter revealed a curious wrinkle in regard to the complaint against me. After Bishop Martínez's call on Saturday, August 30, when he instructed me not to conduct the covenant ceremony, he had followed up our conversation with a letter that outlined what he considered to be the basis for a potential complaint against me. The last two paragraphs of his letter to me were nearly identical to the last two paragraphs of Lauren's letter.

Even though the envelope and letter that the bishop had sent me were both prominently marked "Confidential," the bishop had obviously shared his letter with Lauren to help him draft the official complaint to be filed with the committee. Not only had Lauren used the bishop's letter to construct his own, but he also sent a copy of the bishop's original letter along with his own official letter of complaint to the Committee on Investigation. Consequently, the committee knew that the bishop was not neutral and that he believed I was guilty of disobedience.

Soon after I received a copy of Lauren's letter, David Lux wrote to inform me I had thirty days to submit a written response, laying out my case for the committee. I thought that I could write a succinct response of two to three pages, and I began to compose it in my mind. But with the programs and ministries at First Church in full swing, it was difficult to find the time to sit down and write it. I kept putting it off. It would be an easy task, I thought, once I got around to it.

The national furor over Mary and Martha's covenant ceremony continued to rage, especially within the evangelical Good News movement. The November–December issue of *Good News: The Bimonthly Magazine for United Methodists*[3] included two articles about the covenant ceremony, written by the movement's president and magazine's publisher, James V. Heidinger II. He wrote: "Jimmy Creech is doing irreparable damage to First United Methodist Church in Omaha, just as he did to Fairmont United Methodist Church in Raleigh seven years ago . . . He admits he broke church law. Now we will see if our church system will hold him accountable."[4] And, "If United Methodism is serious about halting its plummeting membership and being faithful to biblical truth, it must come to grips with its 'church-busters.' These are the pastors and leaders who are doing irreparable harm to local United Methodist churches by pushing upon them the pro-homosexual agenda. They do so in direct violation of our denominational standards on homosexual practice."[5]

Within the Nebraska Annual Conference, Maurie Johnson sent letters to churches and clergy advocating open rebellion:

> We urge you and every church in the Nebraska Conference to withhold any further payment of the "Leadership Ministries" and "Structural Ministries" portions of your Conference apportionments . . .[6] We should inform the conference office that these will continue to be withheld until Jimmy Creech and Susan Davies (she sought Jimmy Creech out after he was removed from the ministry in North Carolina) are removed from the Nebraska Conference as ministers and Donald Bredthauer and Susan Mullins informed that they likewise will be removed if they carry out their intention of performing such ceremonies or in any other way sanctioning homosexual behavior.
>
> It's up to us, folks. We can either ignore this movement until most committed Christians leave The United Methodist Churches or we can stop it and preserve the church we love and support.

A little more than a month after Mary and Martha's covenant ceremony, Julia McCord had a long, front-page article in the Saturday Living section of the *Omaha World-Herald*, explaining the significance of the judicial complaint against me in regard to the national debate about homosexuality being waged within The United Methodist Church. She wrote:

> Creech's action was the first public challenge to a 1996 church ban on such ceremonies. It has galvanized Methodists locally, statewide and nationally.

The outcome of the Creech case could shape the direction of the church on the divisive issue of homosexuality. It also could have an impact on the fortunes of the national groups themselves . . .

National church caucuses, smelling a precedent-setting case, have responded with a flurry of editorials, mailings and e-mail messages. "It's an important test case," said the Reverend James V. Heidinger II, president and publisher of the conservative Good News, an evangelical renewal group based in Wilmore, Kentucky. "It's an opportunity to see if a church can discipline a pastor."

"It raised the question about how one interprets Scripture and the legal standing of the Social Principles," said the Reverend George McClain, executive director of the liberal Methodist Federation for Social Action in Staten Island, New York. "It also has raised the question about what our responsibility is to a portion of our church."[7]

My conducting Mary and Martha's covenant ceremony had provoked strong responses, both positive and negative, whose reverberations intensified during the weeks and months that followed. Throughout The United Methodist Church, it was called both an act of Christian conscience for compassion and justice, and mutiny or apostasy. In the first weeks after the ceremony, however, my concern was not the national furor raging outside of First Church, but the conflict that had erupted within the congregation.

Just weeks before the covenant ceremony, I had learned that Mel and Virginia Semrad and Robert and Elizabeth Howell were holding secret meetings in church members' homes, organizing to have me removed as senior pastor and wrest control of First Church from the current lay leadership. Terry Klipsch, a First Church member who had attended one of the meetings, came to my office to tell me that the Semrads and Howells had distributed a collection of newspaper articles related to my ministry in North Carolina and at First Church as evidence of my "gay agenda." She said that there was talk of a suspected conspiracy between Bishop Martínez and Susan Davies in bringing me to First Church to make it a Reconciling Congregation, that the members of the congregation who attended the meeting were encouraged to withhold their financial support from First Church to help force my removal, and that the Confessing Movement was promoted as the preferred alternative to the direction in which First Church was currently headed.

Contributing to the conspiracy talk was the fact that District Superintendent Susan Davies had not informed the Staff-Parish Relations Committee about my ministry in North Carolina prior to my appointment in 1996. People like the Semrads and the Howells believed that Susan and the bishop had deliberately kept this information from the congregation.

In my initial conversations with Susan Davies about First Church, she described the congregation as one moving toward being an inclusive church, specifically of gay and lesbian people. Consequently, I was confident that a lot of conversation about gay issues had already taken place at First Church.

The eruption of criticism and controversy following the covenant ceremony revealed that Susan had misled me. Part of what she told me was true; the other part was embellished.

For example, when Susan highlighted the fact that PFLAG and Proud Horizons—a support group for lesbian, gay, bisexual, transgender, and questioning youth—were meeting at First Church, she implied that this was evidence the congregation was progressive and open to diversity. In reality, most parishioners were unaware that these groups met at the church, much less what the groups were. Several community groups met at the church, such as Alcoholics Anonymous, classes in English as a second language, and square dance groups. PFLAG and Proud Horizons were just two among a cluster of community groups that met at First Church.

Susan had also praised First Church to me for doing the Study on Homosexuality, which the 1988 General Conference had mandated for all United Methodist churches. I learned later that it had been attended by between thirty-five and fifty parishioners, a small percentage of the more than 1,900 members. The study presented both sides of the debate over homosexuality without taking a position. "It was not a momentous event that brought a change," Bob Dorr told me. Susan Davies, however, had given me the impression that the study was a major step for First Church toward becoming an inclusive community.

The most significant misinformation Susan gave me had to do with her conversations with the Staff-Parish Relations Committee in the spring of 1996 during the search for a new senior pastor. She told me the committee had identified someone willing to be in ministry to and with gay people as a top priority in the selection of the new senior pastor. Committee members told me later that there had been no such discussion. It simply was not a priority of the Staff-Parish Relations Committee, as Susan had led me to believe.

In early May 1996, I had flown to Omaha to meet with the Staff-Parish Relations Committee prior to my appointment. Before the meeting, I had asked Susan if she had told the committee all about my ministry in North Carolina. I wanted there to be no misunderstanding or secrets. My ministry in North Carolina had been controversial, and First Church deserved to know about it before accepting me. I had sent lots of information about myself to Susan, and I expected her to share it with everyone concerned—the bishop, the cabinet, and the congregation. Susan assured me that she had told the committee everything and that I didn't need to go over it all again. All I needed to do was meet the committee members and answer whatever questions they might have.

But, Susan had not told the committee everything. She had told them nothing about what had happened at Fairmont United Methodist Church, or about my advocacy for gay, lesbian, bisexual, and transgender people with the North Carolina Council of Churches. Bob Dorr, who was on the committee, told me later that Susan "didn't volunteer any information at all to link you to the gay and lesbian issue. I have a very clear memory that the issue did not come up. We questioned her about your previous church. But it wasn't explained that you had anything to do with the gay and lesbian issue."

I went to First Church believing that the congregation knew everything of significance about me, and that its welcome meant acceptance not only of me but of my priorities in ministry. I would not have gone to Omaha if I had not believed that to be the case. I had been completely open with Susan, the bishop, and the cabinet about my ministry in North Carolina and trusted them to be equally open with this information with the leadership of First Church. Not informing its leadership helped to make conditions ripe at First Church for controversy and claims of conspiracy. Withholding this information betrayed the congregation, my family, and me.

Because the Semrads and the Howells had carefully and quietly built a base of opposition, they were prepared to exploit the controversy ignited by the covenant ceremony. Immediately after the ceremony, the opposition initiated a churchwide campaign to solicit signatures on a petition denouncing me. Within two weeks, 342 people had signed it and a copy was mailed to the entire congregation, along with a letter urging others to sign and to write the bishop in support of the petition. There were a few surprises among the signers, such as a couple who had spoken to me privately about their gay son, whom they dearly loved, and two retired educators who had visited me soon after my arrival at First Church, urging me to be bold and take charge in leading the congregation. There were some names on the petition that shouldn't have been there: Dick Smith had died two months before the ceremony, and three other signers were not members of the congregation. There were also names of people who had not given permission to be listed. One woman told me that she had found a message on her answering machine saying: "If you don't want your name included, call me back. Otherwise, I'll add your name." Her name was put on the petition that was sent to the bishop before she could get back to the caller. Another woman signed the petition in the Anchor Sunday School Class, thinking she was signing up to bring a dish to a potluck dinner.

Who was not on the petition was more important than who was. With the exception of Jim Morgan and Helen Howell, both members of the Staff-Parish Relations Committee, none of the elected leaders of First Church had signed it. While 340 or so members are a significant part of the congregation, the great majority of the more than 1,900 members had not signed the petition.

The opposition's petition campaign caught most of the congregation by surprise. It was only when they received a copy of the document in the mail that many people realized the magnitude of unhappiness at First Church. The church leadership believed the stealth organizing of Mel Semrad and Robert Howell had limited support within the congregation. After all, the fall activities and programs were under way, with most members busily involved at the church. The seven choirs were in rehearsal, the Christian education programs filled Sundays and weekdays with classes of all types, the weekday preschool program was in full gear, special events and mission programs were being organized and conducted almost every week, and the United Methodist Women had resumed their monthly meetings. Fourteen church committees were meeting regularly at least once each month. Renovation of the parlor had begun with the completion scheduled for November — the first phase of a major renovation that would include the sanctuary and foyer. Every night, one or more community groups, such as Alcoholics Anonymous, the River City Chorus, PFLAG, and community college GED classes, met at First Church. And the annual stewardship campaign was under way. We were soliciting pledges for the following year's operating budget, projected to be more than $1.2 million. On top of that, there was a new three-year Landmark Capital Campaign to support the renovation program, whose goal was an additional $1.25 million.

In late September, however, the impact of the opposition's financial boycott began to be felt. Since we normally experienced a drop in revenue in the summer, we didn't appreciate the seriousness of the shortfall until it was almost too late. The usual seasonal recovery wasn't happening, and we faced a major deficit. In addition, the capital campaign was in danger of failing because, after the covenant ceremony, some major donors who had pledged

1988 Gay Pride March, Raleigh, North Carolina. Carrying the Raleigh Religious Network for Gay and Lesbian Equality banner. Left to right: Jimmy, pastor of Fairmont United Methodist Church; the Reverend Mahan Siler, pastor of Pullen Memorial Baptist Church; and the Reverend Jim Lewis, director of Christian Social Ministries, North Carolina Episcopal Diocese. (Reprinted with permission from *The Front Page*)

Chris Weedy painting yellow parking lines at First United Methodist Church, Omaha, Nebraska, July 1996. (Photo by Linda Story/First United Methodist Church, Omaha)

Jimmy in the sanctuary of First United Methodist Church, Omaha, July 1996. (Photo by Chris Weedy)

Some of the defense witnesses at the trial in Kearney, Nebraska, March 1998. Left to right: Joanie Zetterman, Roy Wright, Jimmy, Joan Byerhof, Bill Jenks, the Reverend Don Bredthauer, and the Reverend Dr. Roy Reed. (Photo by Linda Story/First United Methodist Church, Omaha)

The Reverend Cecil Williams introduces Jimmy to an enthusiastically supportive congregation at Glide Memorial United Methodist Church, San Francisco, February 1998. (Photo from author's personal collection)

Members of First United Methodist Church, Omaha, attending the trial in Kearney, March 1998. Left to right, kneeling: Lara Hicks-Tack and Coyner Smith. Front row: Marj Phillips, Marjorie Limprecht, Deb Keeney, Phyllis Burroughs, JoAnn Dickerson, Donna Smith, and Maggie Roe (a supporter from Denver, Colorado). Back row: Bill Jenks, Patrice Lockhart, Mike Herrington, Leigh Ann Scharp, Jimmy, Ivan Richardson, Chris Weedy, J Wright, Roy Wright, Dick Burroughs, Charles Dickerson, Dave England, Kathy England, and Linda Story. (Photo from author's personal collection)

Jimmy speaking to the media and supporters following his acquittal, at First United Methodist Church, Kearney, March 1998. (Photo from author's personal collection)

After his acquittal, March 1998. Left to right: Mike McClellan, assistant defense counsel; the Reverend
Dr. Doug Williamson, defense counsel; and Jimmy. (Photo by Linda Story/First United Methodist
Church, Omaha)

Jimmy with Chris, Natalia, and their cat, George, after returning to their home in Raleigh, North Carolina,
September 1998. (Photo from author's personal collection)

Jimmy with the Reverend Gregory Dell at his church trial in Downers Grove, Illinois, March 1999.

Jimmy with Larry Ellis (left) and Jim Raymer (right) at their marriage ceremony in Chapel Hill, North Carolina, April 1999. (Photo by Cliff Haac)

Press conference at the Anti-Violence Conference, Thomas Road Baptist Church, Lynchburg, Virginia, October 1999. Left to right: the Reverend Jerry Falwell, pastor of Thomas Road Baptist Church; the Reverend Dr. Mel White, founder and executive director of Soulforce; Mary Lou Wallner, founder and executive director of TEACH (To Educate about the Consequences of Homophobia) Ministries; and Jimmy. During the press conference, Jimmy called Jerry Falwell's antigay rhetoric "spiritual violence." "Stop spiritual violence" subsequently became a central demand in the work of Soulforce. (Photo from Soulforce archives)

Soulforce volunteers, including clergy from Nebraska, lock arms to block the entrance to Trinity United Methodist Church in Grand Island, Nebraska, in an attempt to stop Jimmy's second trial, in November 1999. Bill Jenks, center, locks arms with his children, Dexter and Eliza. The Reverend Ken Martin of Austin, Texas, is at the left, and Betty Dorr is at the right. (Photo by Jeffrey Z. Carney; reprinted with permission from the *Omaha World-Herald*)

Soulforce kept vigil on the steps of Trinity United Methodist Church throughout Jimmy's second trial. (Photo from Soulforce archives)

Speaking to media and supporters immediately following the guilty verdict and withdrawal of his credentials of ordination at the trial at Trinity United Methodist Church. (Photo from Soulforce archives)

Soulforce civil disobedience, blocking the parking deck exit at the Cleveland Convention Center, site of the 2000 General Conference of The United Methodist Church, May 2000. The first of the 191 Soulforce volunteers to be arrested were in the front row. Left to right: Rodney Powell, a civil rights leader from the 1960s; Jimmy; the Reverend James Lawson, another civil rights leader and a mentor of the Reverend Dr. Martin Luther King Jr.; Arun Gandhi, grandson of Mohandas Karamchand Gandhi; the Reverend Phil Lawson, James's brother; United Methodist Bishop Joseph Sprague; the Reverend Gregory Dell; and Soulforce volunteer Saundra Farmer-Wiley, holding a sign that reads "No Exit without Justice." (Photo by Chuck Phelan)

Being arrested with Judy Osborne (to Jimmy's left) for civil disobedience as part of a Soulforce protest at the Southern Baptist Convention in New Orleans, June 2001. (Photo from Soulforce archives)

part of the initial $345,000 said that they would not honor their commitments unless I resigned or was removed by the bishop.

Disheartened by the opposition's petition, Bob and Betty Dorr decided to try to talk to the Semrads. They believed that if they could just sit down and talk with them, Mel and Virginia would understand and perhaps change their minds about my ministry and the Vision Focus of First Church. Bob and Betty invited the Semrads to their home for coffee and dessert, but the Semrads insisted that Bob and Betty come to their home instead.

The meeting lasted two and a half hours and was cordial, the Dorrs told me later. Mel and Virginia patiently listened as Bob and Betty talked about their gay brothers and son, and about how much they wanted them to be welcomed and treated fairly by the church. When Mel responded, he talked about his belief that the Bible said homosexuality was a sin and that prayer had the power to change people's sexual behavior.

"If you really knew how to pray and had your heart in the right place," Virginia said, "you could have changed your gay family members."

Burning with indignation, Betty responded: "I'm sorry you feel that way, Virginia, but this is a time we're going to have to disagree because I love my gay family members and I'm really proud of who they are."

Even after the meeting, Bob and Betty were undaunted. They knew most of the people who had signed the petition. Surely some of them, they thought, would respond differently than the Semrads. So they sent a letter to everyone who had signed the document, inviting them to their home for coffee, cake, and conversation about the controversy. Not one person accepted their invitation. Betty spent nearly three hours talking with Robert Howell on the phone one day. He was upset not only with my stand on gay rights, but also with my stands on the death penalty and abortion. And he told Betty that I was a sinner because I had been married and divorced before marrying again. He told Betty that "you're only allowed to be married once." He also commented that "Marylin Stewart should not be a lay leader because women do not belong in positions of leadership in the church." Robert Howell acknowledged he had a gay nephew but said: "Arizona is where he lives and that's where he stays, and he's not allowed back in the State of Nebraska." Betty confessed to me: "At that point, I thought, 'There's no hope!'"

The Dorrs also experienced rejection face to face. Betty was shocked when she learned that one of her longtime friends had signed the petition.

When Betty questioned her about it, her friend replied: "Your son Mike lives in Chicago. As long as he stays there, that's okay. But don't ever bring him to church."

In late September, Don Bredthauer asked Mike McClellan; his wife, Carol; and Deb Keeney, a volunteer youth leader at First Church and a skilled organizer, to meet with him in his office. "We need to do something," Don told them. "Jimmy's not doing enough to defend himself." He talked with them about the need to identify and organize support for me, as well as for the Vision Focus, which also was under attack.

Deb, Mike, and Carol agreed to see what they could do. They set up a meeting for the night of October 9 and advertised it throughout the church. They had no idea who or how many would come. Seventy-five members of the congregation attended that meeting. "It was amazing," Mike said. "You just can't look at people and predict whether or not they'll be supportive. We handed out invitations to people we didn't think would be, but they showed up." The room had been set up for a smaller number, and extra chairs had to be brought in.

The meeting ran late into the night. Those present volunteered to undertake various tasks to support me and defend the Vision Focus, such as creating a database of all church members and developing committees to write letters and make phone calls. They decided that fundraising had to be an important part of their effort because of the deficit created by the opposition. To get started, slips of paper were passed out and everyone was asked to write down how much they would add to their pledge for 1997 to help overcome the deficit. The seventy-five members at the meeting pledged an additional $41,000 to keep First Church moving forward. This was more than a boost to the church's finances. It was a measure of the group's commitment and a sign of hope.

Out of this gathering, "Supporting the Vision" was born, without question the most significant step taken to preserve the integrity and future of First United Methodist Church in Omaha. From that night on, this group met every week throughout the crisis, with small task groups and committees meeting more often, to build support for the pastors and for the vision. The number involved grew and grew, until meetings of the entire group had to be held in Cary Hall, the church's gymnasium. While the opposition was empowered by its early and apparent success, it had underestimated the commitment of the members who had brought the Vision Focus into being.

The vision might be under siege, but its defenders were passionately faithful members of First Church, and now they had organized.

When Chris first learned that the Howells and Semrads were organizing to remove me from First Church, her reaction was: "Nobody's going to run us out of town!" It was quite a contrast from her initial reaction to the possibility of moving to Omaha: "Hell no, I won't go!" She felt close to the people at the church and believed in their vision for the congregation; even more important, she wasn't about to let the opposition force us out without a fight. Supporting the vision gave her a way to fight, and she became one of its primary organizers.

In early October, Bishop Martínez asked me how Chris was handling the stress of the controversy. When I told her about the bishop's concern, Chris wrote him:

Dear Bishop Martínez:
    Jimmy told me you were concerned about me, so I thought I would write you and share a few things about me and where I am. First I'd like to tell you about my feelings, and then share with you my thoughts

    I came to Nebraska because Jimmy was offered the job at First Church. I did not want to come. I gave up an exciting career, close friends, a paid-for college education for my daughter, access to the beach and the Carolina mountains, and life in the historic home Jimmy and I were married in. Every day, I am painfully aware of the losses I've suffered in coming to Nebraska, including memories of 3, 8, and 10-year-old clients I miss dearly, and HIV support group members whom I've known seven years or more who are now traveling the journey alone.

    Since coming to Omaha I have gotten quite involved with the church and the community. As you know, I am teaching Social Work full-time now at the University of Nebraska at Omaha, after having started there part-time last semester. I have been volunteering at La Casa del Pueblo [a United Methodist storefront ministry to Latinos in South Omaha]. I have started a [nonprofit organization] in Omaha to help congregations become involved with people with AIDS. I drive the church van once a month to pick up parishioners. I have painted the curbs and parking spaces in the church parking lot. I am providing support to Latinos with HIV/AIDS through the Charles Drew Health Center. I am clearly invested in this church and community.

Bishop, I was baptized in the Methodist church soon after I was born. However, soon thereafter, my parents left the Methodist Church because it wasn't conservative enough. They began a local church of the Christian and Missionary Alliance, which I attended three times a week until I left home to go to college. I could quote you more scripture than I care to admit. I got all kinds of awards for attendance, recognition, and debating (scripture quiz teams). I served as president of the Alliance Youth Fellowship. In the summers I worked at our church camp on Lake Erie. So, you see, I "grew up in the church." I know the church. I concluded from my lengthy experience that most of the folks I met in church were not "Christ-like," nor were *striving* to be "Christ-like." What I "know" is that a lot of church people behave like the reported 400 people who sent you the letter last week. When I finally had a choice, I left the church.

Which is why eight years ago when I met Jimmy I ruled out a relationship with him based on the fact that he was a minister. I had had my fill! Nonetheless, Jimmy and I continued to work together on an AIDS service agency board, and I grew to know Jimmy *as a person*, not just a minister.

I came to Nebraska last summer because Jimmy loves the parish. I couldn't deny him the opportunity to be back in a parish, despite my own experience, feelings, and losses. Being in the parish again has made him very happy. I remember the first night he came home from an emergency room visit where one of his parishioners died. He was happy to be there for the family. He was back doing what he loves most. Funerals, baptisms, weddings, all make his heart sing. Being in the parish gives him something I cannot. My current involvement with the church is based on the fact that I'm married to Jimmy and want to be supportive of him and his work and out of my own commitment to make this world a better place.

That's how I feel, now this is what I think.

You are being called upon to show special leadership at this time on this issue. What other bishop *in the country* is in the position you are in to really act as a leader on this issue? What other social issue is more important in this day and time in The United Methodist Church in the United States than how we are treating gays and lesbians? What other contemporary issue presses the boundaries more than this? I can think of none.

So your challenge, whether you relish it or not, is to respond to the call for leadership in such a way that the church *grows* and doesn't go backwards. Growth really needs to be the focus, otherwise we are all doomed.

I see your position and pray that you will have the strength and insight you need. Some of the traps I see are:

- Buying into the myth that Jimmy *created* this situation or that Jimmy has an "agenda." Neither is true.
- Buying into the myth that *you* created this problem. First of all, it's not true, and second of all, you will get sucked into the "rescuer" role by way of guilt. They (we) need you to act as a bishop, not as a rescuer. Your role needs to be one of moral and ethical leadership, *not* personal involvement. Don't rescue First Church from this problem. By doing so, you'll create a worse problem, and the church will turn to you again and again, and never learn they can solve their own problems.
- Buying into the myth that Jimmy *needs to go* in order for the church to "recover." There's a lot to be gained for the church, *if* the wrong lessons are not learned.

Jimmy, Natalia, and I came to Nebraska with the understanding that people here knew Jimmy's position on gays and lesbians, capital punishment, etc. We were led to believe this was a progressive congregation. We would NOT have come if we had known that there would be the backlash that has occurred. Our relationship and our family do not need the stress that this situation has caused. We were *not* looking for another battleground. Normally, I'd be tempted to ask you to resolve this issue as rapidly as possible; however, I feel that time is needed to talk things out, time for the pastor and the church to work things out. Time is what is needed to heal, instead of focusing on my selfishness.

Sincerely,
Chris Weedy

With her letter, Chris included a copy of an article by Richard Taylor titled "With All Due Respect: An Historical Perspective on Civil Disobedience,"[1] and a copy of the Reverend Dr. Martin Luther King's "Letter from Birmingham Jail." Bishop Martínez's reply gave no sign that he acknowledged or even understood the challenge Chris had extended to him.

When I first met with Bishop Martínez after the covenant ceremony, one of the things he told me was that I must try to resolve the internal conflict at First Church. He was aware that opposition to my ministry had been festering since the beginning of the year and had exploded since the ceremony. He believed that it was imperative for me to exercise strong leadership in establishing ways to communicate with the opposition. He acknowledged that it would be impossible for me to accomplish this by myself. I couldn't change who I was or my priorities in ministry, and the opposition wouldn't change its mind about me. All of the staff and lay leadership would need to be involved for any reconciliation to occur.

I called together the key church leaders, creating an ad hoc emergency executive committee, and gave them the responsibility of leading the church through the crisis. At its first meeting, the committee decided to hold two congregational forums, on October 12 and 16, as opportunities for sharing information about and discussing the covenant ceremony. With the assistance of the bishop's office, we engaged Dr. Kathy Russell, a licensed clinical social worker with a Ph.D. in conflict resolution and a specialist in church conflict, to work with us. When the forums were announced, the opposition immediately denounced them as efforts by the bishop, Susan Davies, the pastors, and the church leadership to force the congregation to agree with me. The word was that these meetings would neither provide full disclosure nor allow free discussion.

Nonetheless, the forums were packed. Lay Leader Bruce Deines began both sessions by explaining that the forums were designed to "separate fact from rumor, to build bridges, and to come together as a church community."[2] The forums were divided into two parts: a plenary session for information sharing and small groups for discussion. Unfortunately, the opposition didn't like or trust this format, and Kathy Russell had a difficult time controlling speakers from the floor. At one point during the first forum, Mel Semrad snatched the microphone from her hand and refused to relinquish it until the format was changed. He charged that the "process [was intended] to control open dialogue, . . . protested what he called 'steamrolled, funnel-feeding of information,'" and said the purpose of the small groups was to "divide and conquer" those who were upset about the covenant ceremony. Mel demanded that the large group stay intact throughout the forum, and that people be allowed to state their grievances. "We need open dialogue to hold our pastors and our bishop accountable," he argued.[3] Russell was able to retrieve the microphone from Mel only after giving in to his demand that members be allowed to vent their grievances during the plenary. When the raucous plenary sessions finally broke into small groups, the conversations were no less heated.

In one small group, Coyner Smith witnessed a man verbally attack Betty

Dorr. In a loud and angry voice, the man told Betty that she was wrong to accept gay people, that they were evil sinners, and that they had to change before they could be welcomed and included in the church. Coyner was surprised by the hate and hostility directed at Betty because of her support for her son, brother, and brother-in-law. The irrational bigotry he observed in both the plenary session and small group surprised and shocked him.

Coyner and Donna Smith were close friends of the Dorrs, but they had no desire to get involved with this controversy. They felt no personal connection to it, having no family members or friends who were gay. Soon after the controversy erupted, Coyner had told Bob and Betty, "I know this means a lot to you, but it's not our fight."

The Smiths came to worship regularly and sometimes attended the Galilean Class, but they were not active in other ways. As the son of a United Methodist minister, Coyner had seen many church fights and preferred keeping as far away from them as possible. He also had become disillusioned with conventional Christian teaching because of what he perceived to be its elevation of blind faith over reason. The denial of reason seemed to him to deny a basic God-given gift and foster uncritical obedience to institutional claims and loyalties. He also felt that it did not contribute to a mature relationship with God. Consequently, church had become for him little more than a social activity.

Coyner and Donna attended the forum because they wanted to better understand what the controversy was all about, not to get involved. However, the forum made them realize that this controversy was not just another petty church squabble to be avoided. It was a contest over the essential mission of the church. It was exclusion versus welcome, hatred versus love, fear versus reason — and too important to ignore. In addition, they refused to tolerate attacks on their friends. So they attended the next Supporting the Vision meeting, took on tasks, increased their financial support of the congregation, and quickly assumed prominent leadership roles in what had earlier not been their fight.

We had hoped the forums would bring some reconciliation within the congregation. Rather than bring the polarized groups together, however, the forums more clearly defined the gulf between them. Afterward, the opposition was even more determined to remove Don, Susan, and me, revise the Vision Focus, and take over the leadership of First Church. The forums had shown the members of Supporting the Vision how formidable and obstinate the opposition was, and how urgently they needed to do whatever it would take to preserve the Vision Focus and to keep the church leadership and the pastors.

On October 22, a week after the second forum I received Kathy Russell's written assessment of the conflict within First Church and her recommendations for corrective action. Her five-page report included these observations:

> I believe that the level of conflict at First United Methodist Church is at least a Level IV (Fight or Flight) or a Level V (Intractable Situation). Members of the congregation are polarized around an issue and anything less than the removal of the senior pastor will not satisfy the angriest members . . .
>
> The underlying issue that confronts this church, inclusiveness for gays and lesbians, is under discussion in all mainline churches in America. This denomination's Social Principles are not subject to revision for another 3 years. The presenting problem involves differences in values and beliefs about the nature of humankind, the church, and the ministry of Jesus Christ. Therefore, it is unlikely that the presenting problem can be solved to the satisfaction of all or most of the members of the congregation . . .
>
> The Conference judicial process has been initiated and will require at least 120 days to complete. The only possible change in the 120 days is that the bishop might exercise his option to suspend the senior pastor for up to 60 days . . . Whether or not the senior pastor remains in his position, the new vision statement for the congregation must be revisited. It is clear that it has implications for some that are not universally held. Any ambiguity about the meaning and values in the vision statement will feed distrust.

Kathy Russell's analysis was ominous. It read like the diagnosis of a fatal illness, if not the autopsy of a tragic and untimely death. And I was the culprit. My initial reading of the report seduced me into taking full responsibility for the conflict and pain of the church. I felt accused and convicted of a horrendous crime. I felt awful. But although Russell described realities that could not be denied, her analysis did not correlate with what I understood to be happening at First Church. I read her report again, and then again and again, trying to put my finger on what was wrong with it.

Finally, I realized that the assumptions about conflict that Russell brought with her had shaped her analysis, rather than the realities at play at First Church. She had brought particular assumptions from another context and imposed them on First Church, as if one size would fit all. She was accustomed to working with congregations that had experienced some form of professional misconduct by clergy: sexual misconduct, abuse of power, or malfeasance, for example. Her work focused on deep hurt and grief within a congregation. The model with which she worked treated the congregation as victim and the pastor as villain. The consequences were losses and grief. She assumed that recovery or healing was the priority for First Church. This meant repairing what was broken, reestablishing what had existed before, and restoring unity within the congregation. These, she assumed, were the goals of the process she was contracted to facilitate at First Church.

Consequently, Kathy Russell did not address the conflict at First Church as the kind of struggle inherent in a social change movement or, in our case, a theological or spiritual change movement for justice. Such an approach would have recognized that the conflict or heat at First Church had been caused by the movement and friction between an old culture and a new one, between a romanticized past and a prophetic vision of the future. She did acknowledge that the "underlying issue that confronts this church, inclusiveness for gays and lesbians . . . involves differences in values and beliefs about the nature of humankind, the church, and the ministry of Jesus Christ." But after recognizing this source of the seismic conflict, she then dismissed that point as essentially unresolvable and not the immediate priority of recovery: "Therefore, it is unlikely that the presenting problem can be solved to the satisfaction of all or most of the members of the congregation."

Kathy Russell failed to deal with the fact that First Church had evolved over a significant period of time into a theologically, socially, and politically different congregation than the one the opposition claimed it to be, beginning long before my arrival in Omaha. Her priorities and operating assumptions caused her to treat the congregation as a static entity that had had the misfortune of becoming destabilized, when in truth First Church was a dynamic congregation evolving toward a prophetic vision.

The leadership, staff, and most active members were following a paradigm different from that of fifteen to twenty years before. Because of the size of the congregation, not everyone was fully aware of this paradigm shift, let alone had completely understood and accepted it. Many members had not been paying attention or simply didn't take the language of the Vision Focus seriously. The fact that part of the congregation was now opposing the Vision Focus and the way I embodied it in my ministry was evidence of this. But there was no way to return to the earlier era of a conventional, if not conservative, congregation. Removing me as pastor wouldn't do the trick. Nor would removing all of the pastors and staff. The only way to do it would be to remove the majority of the members and the lay leadership — in other words, exchange the minority (the opposition) for the majority (the supporters of the vision).

I wondered how Kathy Russell's assumptions about conflict would be applied to the civil rights movement of the 1950s and 1960s. Should the priority then have been recovery and healing? Should the "angriest" white people have been given priority over those challenging the status quo? Should the goal have been the restoration of order and a return to the way things had been? Was my comparison far-fetched? Granted, there are differences. But I think the comparison is on target because the dynamics that operated in the civil rights movement, as well as in other historic social justice movements, were also operating at First Church: contending beliefs about what it means to be human, to be free, to have dignity, and to be children of God; a new vision challenging old assumptions about how life was to be lived, about what is God's will, about who is included in the community, about justice.

I don't think Kathy Russell intended to misinterpret the conflict at First Church. I think she didn't fully comprehend what was happening there and relied on old models of church conflict in her analysis and recommendations. She had experience helping congregations that had been victimized, often split, by pastors who had abused power or were guilty of sexual misconduct or some other transgression or malfeasance. The First Church opposition presented itself as the injured party, and consequently the healing and recovery in the model of conflict resolution that she employed seemed most necessary for them. The time-honored practice for resolving conflict in a church is to remove the pastor, and then to try to get the opposing factions to sit down together and pretend to be a happy family. For this reason, she assumed that I was history and that the Vision Focus would leave with me. She was wrong.

Among the recommendations that Kathy Russell proposed in her report was the creation of a committee that would address concerns held in common by the opposition and by Supporting the Vision and that would help lead First Church to recovery. The committee was to be composed of six people from each side of the conflict. The criteria for membership on the committee included active membership and current financial support. The committee never materialized because the opposition could not find six people who met the criteria, since nearly all of them had long before become inactive and had stopped giving financial support to the church. They also had a fundamental distrust of this process, fearing that the committee would co-opt their representatives into unwittingly supporting the First Church leadership. Cooperation with the committee would encourage the belief that some consensus or compromise was possible. That perception would work against the opposition. They wanted to subvert and obstruct the leadership in order to take control of First Church, not work with the leadership. Not cooperating, from their perspective, was the best strategy to get rid of me and take over the church. They believed that if they exacerbated the conflict and financial crisis, the bishop would have no choice but to remove me. Consequently, none of what Kathy Russell recommended ever happened. The elected leadership remained at the helm of the church, and the opposition continued its subversive attempt to sink it.

Bishop Martínez called me early on the morning of Thursday, October 30. Apologizing for the late notice, he said he needed to meet with me for dinner in Omaha later that evening. I told him I had a Nominations Committee meeting at seven in the evening, but could meet him at five or five thirty. We agreed to meet at a restaurant near the church.

Because it was early in the dinner hour, the restaurant was almost empty. We ordered, and our food arrived quickly. As usual, the bishop was cordial, asking how things were with Chris and Natalia. Then he dropped his bombshell: "Jimmy, I'm going to suspend you for sixty days."

"Why?" I demanded.

"Jimmy, you've made no progress in reaching out and reconciling with the opposition. Attendance and giving continue to be down. The annual conference is in an uproar over the covenant ceremony. I'm getting angry letters from all over the country. And you've not told me you won't celebrate another covenant ceremony if asked to by a gay couple." He said he hadn't yet had a chance to read Kathy Russell's report but had been informed about her analysis and recommendations. He mentioned that he understood that she had put the conflict at First Church at the highest level, "intractable." He said he had no confidence that I could do anything to improve the situation.

When the bishop finally finished his monologue, allowing me only a few minutes to respond before we both had to leave, I had so much I wanted to say that I didn't know where to begin. I told him that I strongly disagreed with his decision and that it would be detrimental to First Church for me to be suspended. I said I agreed with him that I was not the one to reconcile the opposition, but suspending me would make them only more determined and bold in their effort to take over First Church. I told him that he was sending a message to lesbian, gay, bisexual, and transgender people that he was willing to use his power to discourage clergy from offering them full membership in The United Methodist Church. I said he was supporting the injustice and bigotry of the church.

He bristled. His genteel facade slipped, and with restrained but visible anger he said: "Jimmy, do you know how long Hispanics and blacks had to wait to gain acceptance and equality in the church?"

"Yes," I responded, "a long time."

"That's right, and gay people are going to have to wait, too."

In his early years as a minister, Joel Martínez, who knew prejudice and injustice firsthand as a Mexican American, had been a champion of justice for people on the margins of American society, both within the church and in the larger society. He had been an advocate for people of color, for women, and for others ignored, exploited, and neglected by the people and institutions of power in the United States. When he was on the outside of the dominant culture, he challenged it. Now, having gained a position in that culture, Bishop Martínez was speaking the language of dominance and using his power to maintain the oppression of gay people.

I was astounded. The bishop's words exposed in a profoundly personal way the church's institutional bigotry against gay, bisexual, transgender, and lesbian people. He could talk about having compassion and understanding for them, condemn violence against them, and even support their civil rights. However, when it came to changing the teachings and policies of the church and sharing equal status and power in the church, they had to wait. I had heard these words before.

Over and over in the 1950s and 1960s, I had heard people—often those considered liberal—say: "Colored people have to wait until attitudes change. They have to be patient. They can't expect us to change overnight." For Bishop Martínez, gay rights was not a justice issue, but an issue of political expediency. Justice didn't matter. Not only was he saying that gay people would have to wait their turn, he was saying that justice, integrity, and decency had to wait until the people in power were willing to end the oppression and persecution of gay people. Injustice could and would be tolerated in deference to the political realities and dynamics of The United Methodist Church.

"Jimmy," he said as he stood to leave, "I'm instructing you to tell no one about the suspension until I've informed the Staff-Parish Relations Committee. I'll be calling Joanie Zetterman tomorrow to set up a meeting for Monday night. I'll fax her a letter to read to the committee." He paid for my salad and we left.

On my way back to the church that night, I stopped by Methodist Hospital to visit Marjorie Limprecht, a member of First Church for over fifty years who had knee-replacement surgery earlier that day. I found her back in her room, not long out of the recovery room. As always, she smiled and greeted me warmly. I asked how she was feeling, and she said, "Not too good." She was nauseated and hurting from the surgery. She asked how I was, and if I had any news. "I'm fine," I lied. "No news." It hurt. I knew I couldn't keep up this deceit. I had been instructed just minutes before to be complicit in the culture of secrecy that pervades the clergy of The United Methodist Church, and already I felt like I was suffocating.

Suddenly, Marge's eyes widened in panic. "Hand me that bowl, I feel sick," she blurted. I came to her side with the small plastic bowl that hospitals put by your bed, a bowl just big enough to spit in. Vomit spewed out of Marge, filling the bowl and covering the front of my suit, tie, and shirt. Serves me right for spewing lies out on her, I thought.

I wet a cloth and washed her face. She was clammy. I rinsed the cloth and put it on her forehead as she laid back and closed her eyes. I wiped off my suit as best I could. Then I went for the nurse. Marge was feeling terrible, but she still worried about my clothes and was quite embarrassed that she "threw up on my minister." She apologized profusely to me and had to tell the nurse all about it. Later, when she found out that I had learned of my suspension right before I had come to see her, she felt even worse about what had happened. Somehow, it seemed to me an appropriate part of that night.

Why now, seven weeks after Mary and Martha's ceremony, would Bishop Martínez suspend me? Certainly, pressure on him to punish me was intense. The opposition within First Church was increasingly angry as the days passed, demanding that he do something. The growing national significance of my action put his reaction to it under close scrutiny by the entire United Methodist Church, as well as the whole country. What I had done was clear. People were now impatient to see what he was going to do. In the media and the minds of many people, my conducting the covenant ceremony was more about my defiance of him than about the church's injustice against gay people. Some argued that I had disregarded and disrespected his authority, and the judicial process was irrelevant. They felt that there was no question of my guilt. I didn't deserve due process. I should be punished immediately, without waiting for a jury to confirm the obvious in a trial. The bishop was perceived as indecisive and weak. Some people even considered him to be complicit because he'd brought me to First Church, and because he hadn't suspended me when I informed him I planned to conduct the ceremony. People were demanding that he demonstrate his authority, to show that he was in charge.

This was a reaction that completely overlooked the moral and theological implications of the church's prohibition of homosexual unions and the responsibility of pastors to conscientiously stand against injustice and bigotry, even if the church is the perpetrator. The bishop and I understood from the beginning that we had a difference of opinion. He knew my history in North Carolina and knew that I would continue to act consistently with it. He had told me that he respected my integrity as a pastor even as he forbade me to perform the ceremony; and I had told him that I respected him and the office of bishop. In the beginning, there was no personal contest between us, no animosity or hostility. He was acting as he thought a bishop should, upholding what he thought to be a law of the church. It was this law that I was defying, not him. We both understood that. We also understood that the difference he and I had would have to be resolved in the larger venue of The United Methodist Church. Bishop Martínez could have spoken publicly about this and made it clear that ours was an honest disagreement reflecting the painful division within the whole church. By so doing, he would have upheld the integrity of his own office, along with the judicial process as an appropriate forum to address the controversy. Instead, he succumbed to pressure and suspended me.

Kathy Russell's report, suggesting that my removal be considered as one of the remedial actions to placate the "angriest" and supposedly disenfranchised members of the congregation, helped to legitimize his decision. To suspend me seven weeks after the covenant ceremony accomplished nothing for First Church. And the bishop suspended me without consulting the Staff-Parish Relations Committee. If he had consulted the committee, as he had promised to do, the members would have told him they didn't want and wouldn't support the suspension, believing it would only add to the congregation's difficulties and exacerbate the conflict. After this, the bishop was no longer trusted by the elected leadership of First Church. The Staff-Parish Relations Committee, as well as the entire church leadership, perceived itself to be in an adversarial relationship with Bishop Martínez, as if it had been censured along with me. The committee and the church leadership felt betrayed and abandoned by the bishop, and isolated within the Nebraska Annual Conference. In his effort to regain the confidence of his critics and appease the opposition, Bishop Martínez had lost the trust of the rest of First Church.

On the following Monday night, Joanie Zetterman read to the Staff-Parish Relations Committee the bishop's letter, announcing that I would be suspended effective Monday, November 10, and that Don Bredthauer would be acting senior pastor. By then almost all of the committee's members had already heard about the suspension. The atmosphere was somber. We discussed what I could and could not do while on suspension. I explained that I had been instructed not to perform weddings or visit members of the congregation who were in the hospital. I could not come on church property unless it was to attend a Staff-Parish Relations Committee meeting at the invitation of the bishop.[4] I could not use my office. I was not to work with committees, participate in planning, or have any input regarding the church budget or other financial concerns. I was not to initiate contact with staff or church members for any reason. They, however, were free to contact me.

Sunday, November 9, was my last opportunity to preach at First Church before the suspension began. Monday morning's *Omaha World-Herald* carried this report by Cindy Gonzalez:

The Reverend Jimmy Creech bid a reluctant farewell to his divided congregation Sunday but did not back down on his support of homosexual unions—a stand that led to his job suspension and a public uproar at Omaha's First United Methodist Church.

In his last sermon before his 60-day job suspension took effect, Creech told members of the 1,900-member church that he, like the slain civil rights leader Dr. Martin Luther King, Jr., has a dream. "It is my dream," the 53-year-old senior pastor said, "that one day we will be a community that can celebrate freely and completely the love between two people, regardless of their gender."

He said his hope was to lead a congregation that would not judge anyone on the basis of color, whether they're gay or straight, rich or poor, married or divorced, strong or weak, young or old—"but simply welcomes them because they are children of God . . ."

Most of the more than 200 people who attended the 10:45 a.m. service clapped and jumped to their feet after Creech finished his sermon. Many hugged Creech and his wife, Chris Weedy, as they left the sanctuary at 7020 Cass Street. Even as some cried and told Creech they looked forward to his return to the pulpit, others lamented what had happened to their congregation over the past several months.

A 22-year church member, who spoke on the condition of anonymity, called Creech a fantastic minister. "But I don't go along with this 'new age' thing. It's just too bad. A lot of the congregation is hurting."

Ray Bordeaux, who attended his first service at First United Methodist on Sunday, said he was both surprised and inspired by Creech's words. "I thought it was absolutely wonderful. It's history," said Bordeaux, an Omaha native who just moved back from Los Angeles. "He's definitely out there on a limb and didn't back down at all."

Creech says he intends to return to his duties as senior pastor in two months. Creech told audiences Sunday that he was sorry about one thing—that his suspension prohibits him from being in constant touch with the congregation as it works through the conflict. "I'm very disappointed," he said. "It's going to be very hard and difficult to be separated from you."

Creech said afterward that a suspension was not a healthy way to resolve the conflict. "I don't see how people can reconcile differences when they're not talking together," he said. "Taking me out of the situation makes it impossible to talk."

Creech asked church members to let love be the force that guides them at this crossroads. Throughout Sunday's service, Creech emphasized the Christian principle of loving others, including those who are different. At one point, he called all children to the front of the church and told them to sit in a circle. So that no one had to sit behind or outside the circle, Creech asked the children to make the circle larger. "Go out those doors, and you're going to see lots of people, lots of faces," Creech said. "And the Bible is telling us if you want to love God, we have to love all the people we see. If we love each other, then God, whom we can't see, lives in us."

Creech told his audience that the direction he favors for the church is a "challenging vision" that requires fears and stereotypes to be set aside. "This is a growth experience," he said. "Growth creates conflict—for it is change, and change is difficult."[5]

Susan Merrick who was among those attending First Church for the first time that Sunday morning, wrote to Bishop Martínez about how the worship affected her and about her spiritual journey through the pain of being rejected by the church into self-acceptance, wholeness, and hope. She was a staff member of the Nebraska AIDS Project, a nonprofit organization giving support and services to people living with AIDS. Her letter tells a story common to many lesbian, gay, bisexual, and transgender people who have had to find their spiritual wholeness outside of the church.

Dear Bishop Martínez:

I am writing today because of the dynamics at First United Methodist Church in reaction to the commitment ceremony performed for a lesbian couple by Reverend Jimmy Creech. I feared that my support, at best, would not help Reverend Creech, and at worst, might just add fuel to the fires of the opposition. After hearing Reverend Creech's sermon on Sunday, I can no longer remain silent.

I attended the service this past Sunday because it was important to me, to my community, and because I try to support people who have the courage to do the RIGHT thing. I did not expect to be so moved by the gentle passion of Reverend Creech's words that I sat crying throughout his sermon. What struck me was that for so long I have just accepted that "the church" rejects me because I am gay and I have made the choice to stay away. Sunday, I suddenly felt the pain this rejection causes me. A part of me awakened to the truth that this attitude is no longer OK with me and shouldn't be for the millions of gay people world wide who have either been rejected by the church or who are uncomfortably "tolerated" by the church. I have spent more than half my life disconnected from a spiritual community. My solitary spiritual practice has sustained me well, but I desperately miss the ritual, the music, the social action and the community that a church SHOULD provide for ALL people.

As a social worker and psychotherapist I have worked with many gay and lesbian clients who feel there is no safe place to have a spiritual life, which is difficult enough on a day-to-day basis, but many of these clients who are dealing with terminal illness not only need to feel accepted by their concept of God, but especially need the support a church community should provide . . .

I am an out lesbian and very proud of who I am. Being gay is not a choice and it is not an illness. I spent years severely depressed because I was trying to fit into the dominant culture. Fortunately, I reevaluated my life and found my true self. It was then and only then, that I began growing into the more content, loving, very spiritual productive member of society that I am today. I know I would not be where I am today had I remained "in the closet" to myself and the world around me.

Bishop Martínez, I am as much a human being, and a person of God, as you are, or as are any of the parishioners who maintain their homophobic stance against Reverend Creech's brave actions. I am perplexed that you, a person from a minority community, have not been more vocal about how wrong this oppression and hatred of an entire group of human beings is — just because we are different. Your silence tells me that perhaps you hold the belief that gays and lesbians are not people of God, that we are sick and perverted and sinners. If that is the case, it profoundly saddens me — profoundly.

It seems to me that "the church" has lost touch with who Christ was — that he brought forth radical ideas because it was time for change. I am saddened by the stagnation and lack of vision of the church with respect to acceptance of gays and lesbians and the unwillingness to recognize and bless their unions of love and commitment to each other . . . Instead of just saying that what Reverend Creech did was against the rules and choosing to punish him for it, can't we look at this as an opportunity to review the validity and appropriateness of this rule? Creech's actions in this case were actually something I can imagine Christ doing—to challenge a rule that no longer fits the needs of a community wanting to be people of God in today's world . . .

Nothing would make me happier than to have my assumptions about "the church" finally challenged through a sign of true compassion and understanding at both the conference level and from the group that so vehemently opposes Reverend Creech's actions. Wouldn't it be wonderful if First United Methodist and the United Methodist Conference, here in the Midwest, could stand as a leader for change long past due? It is my firm belief that removing Reverend Creech from his post at First United Methodist would truly be a tragic mistake.

With my prayers for your wisdom and the wisdom and compassion of those in decision-making positions around this issue,
Susan B. Merrick, LCSW [6]

The first Sunday morning of my suspension, I assumed that Chris and I would stay home, have breakfast in bed, read the paper together, and try to ignore the fact that I should be at the church. Instead, Chris got up and dressed just as she always did, except earlier than usual.

"Where are you going?" I asked.

"I'm going to church. I'm going to all three services," she said. "I'm not going to let them forget that you're still the senior pastor at First Church. Since you can't be there, I'm going to be there for you. Until your suspension is over, I'm going to stand at the door to greet people as they arrive and tell them good-bye when they leave. They're going to have to see me and deal with me. And I want to let your supporters know that you're still here for them."

When she left home to go to college, Chris had also left the church. As she had written Bishop Martínez, she had grown up in a strict Christian fundamentalist environment that she felt was oppressive. She decided as a youth to leave it behind the first chance she had. Going away to college was that opportunity. When we met, Chris was clear with me about how she felt about organized religion. She said she'd seen and experienced more pain than good coming from it. She went with me to worship but never expressed interest in getting involved with a church.

When we came to Omaha, she remained faithful to her own values and spirit. Nonetheless, before she found a job, Chris looked around for something to do at First Church, some way to make a contribution that didn't have anything to do with "religious" things. She noticed that the yellow lines throughout the parking lot were faded and, in some cases, nearly scraped away by winter snowplows. So she went to the nearby Sears store, bought bright yellow industrial paint and a wide brush, and went to work painting the lines and curbs.

The First Church property is about seven acres, and the parking area covered the back part of it. When Chris began, she expected to finish the job within a week. However, it took two and a half months and thirteen gallons of paint. From July into September, in the intense Nebraska heat, First Church members saw Chris on her knees painting yellow lines and curbs in First Church's parking lot, and they loved her for it.

It was my habit throughout my ministry to stand at one of the entrance doors to the sanctuary at the beginning of each worship service to welcome people as they entered, and at the end to say good-bye. Chris usually attended one of the Sunday morning services and joined me in this ritual. Now that I was not allowed to be there, she intended to take my place and stand where I always stood to touch, greet, and briefly visit with the members as they entered and left at all three of the services. She would be my proxy.

That first Sunday of my suspension, I was already fighting to control my emotions. When Chris explained why she was dressing for church, I could hardly speak. I knew it was a struggle for her to be comfortable with the talk about God and Jesus, with a lot of what happens in worship, and that she would much rather be at home than at church on Sunday morning. But she felt compelled to represent me at First Church. She would not let the opposition have the satisfaction of my absence. And she would be there to support the leadership of the church. Throughout my suspension, not only did she attend each of the three services of worship on Sunday mornings, but all the important church meetings that took place as well. The opposition avoided her by using side doors, refused to speak when they approached her, or made comments to let her know they didn't want her there. None of this fazed her. Her presence was a symbol of undaunted resolve and courage for those determined to preserve the Vision Focus.

In the first days of my suspension, I wasn't sure what to do with myself. Chris was gone during the day, teaching in the Department of Social Work at the University of Nebraska at Omaha. The house was empty and quiet.

Soon, however, my days filled up. Church members and staff came for visits. Don Bredthauer stayed in close touch. Roberta Coss, the pastors' secretary, faxed me reports on all aspects of the church's life, including information about members who were in the hospital or experiencing some other crisis. Coyner and Donna Smith hosted a luncheon for Chris and me at a nearby restaurant every Tuesday throughout the suspension. Each week they invited a different group of twelve or so church members and staff to join us, graciously picking up the tab for everyone. Dene Pruett dropped by from time to time to show me the latest architectural drawings for the renovation of the sanctuary. One Thursday night, the chancel choir came by after rehearsal, filled our front lawn, and sang to Chris and me.

The Supporting the Vision leadership invited me to attend their planning sessions at their regular meeting place, Espresso Mary's, a nearby coffee shop. Most Saturday mornings, they pulled the couches and big padded chairs at Mary's into a circle and held a strategy session for two or three hours, while their children played on the floor.

Of course, I also had to write my response to the judicial complaint filed against me. I had to deliver it to the Committee on Investigation by December 5. I had made a start on it before my suspension, but only a feeble one because I was then so busy at the church. Now I could devote all of my time to writing it, without interruption or distraction. Doug, Mike, and I also had a lot to do to prepare for the committee's hearing and a possible trial. Unwittingly, the bishop had given me the time to get ready for the judicial process.

When Supporting the Vision had organized in early October, it faced a monstrous uphill battle to overcome the opposition's months-long head start. In an effort to catch up, Supporting the Vision sent a letter, followed up by a telephone call, to all members of First Church in early November urging them to make a pledge to the 1998 budget and the Landmark Capital Campaign, and to "give an additional donation for the last two months of 1997." Their effort produced more than $28,000, the largest weekly income of the year. While this reduced the deficit a bit, much more had to be done.

Convinced there were United Methodists throughout the state who would support First Church, Supporting the Vision sent a letter to the clergy and lay leaders in the Nebraska Annual Conference asking for financial support. Since the media had made it appear that I stood alone against the entire congregation, as well as against the bishop, the letter stated the leadership's solidarity with me and identified the covenant ceremony as an act of ministry consistent with our Vision Focus, a copy of which accompanied the letter. The hoped-for support didn't come. "All we got were angry responses," Mike said. "There wasn't one United Methodist Church in Nebraska that said, 'We stand with you.' We did have some individual clergy who signed on, but they were few and far between. It was overwhelming when it was clear how many were against us. I was stunned."

But Supporting the Vision was undaunted. No matter what was the case in Nebraska, they said, there must be United Methodists and other church people around the country who would be supportive. So the group mailed a nationwide appeal for financial support.

In addition to its attack on the church's finances, the opposition was organizing to take control of First Church at the 1997 All Church Conference on December 2. This annual meeting is when the congregation's members elect the lay leadership, establish the church budget, and approve the priorities for ministry for the coming year. The opposition's objectives were to elect their people to the church leadership and change the Vision Focus to make it conform to *The Book of Discipline*, especially in regard to the proscriptions against gay people. Fully aware of the opposition's intention, Supporting the Vision began organizing, too. They knew if the Vision Focus was to be reaffirmed, the programs and ministry sustained, and the current lay leadership continued, they had to get their supporters to the All Church Conference. The conflict was approaching a climax. On December 2, the direction of the church and who controlled it would be decided.

Supporting the Vision approached the conference with dread, not only because they were late in organizing for it, but because of a change in the district superintendent's office. On November 10, the day my suspension began, Bishop Martínez announced that the Reverend Marv Koelling, superintendent of the Northeast District, would share the supervision of First Church with Susan Davies. The relationship was not equal, however, and Susan was little more than Marv's shadow. This was another concession to the opposition. They blamed Susan for bringing me to First Church and wanted her gone as much as they wanted me gone. The opposition was delighted with Marv and regularly consulted with him. Because he was the bishop's choice and seemed sympathetic to the opposition, the church leadership didn't trust him, causing them to feel even more alienated from the bishop. Bishop Martínez assigned Marv Koelling to preside at the All Church Conference, the pivotal meeting that would determine the future of First Church.

At seven o'clock in the evening on Tuesday, December 2, Marv called the 1997 All Church Conference to order in the sanctuary, with more than five hundred people attending.[7] As it had for the forums back in October, the opposition brought in a large number of inactive members sympathetic to their cause. Supporting the Vision had telephoned and written to all active members, urging them to attend.

The first two items of business were resolutions sponsored by the church council proposing a churchwide study of *The Book of Discipline* and reaffirming the Vision Focus, described in the resolutions as two documents "guiding" the ministry of First Church. On behalf of the opposition, former U.S. Senator David Karnes moved to amend each resolution by adding language stipulating that First Church would comply with all of the "rules and procedures" of *The Book of Discipline*. Had it not been for The United Methodist Church's restrictive policies and teachings about homosexuality, the proposed amendments would have been innocuous. Because First Church had gone through a long process of study and discernment that led it to open its doors to all people, however, the amendment struck at the essence of the Vision Focus. The leaders of the church wanted to be loyal to The United Methodist Church, but they were not about to comply with its exclusion and oppression of gay people.

Twenty-eight people spoke against the opposition's amendments. Roy Wright stood up and said:

> I've just come up to say I'm in favor of reaffirming the Vision Focus. Not only do I speak to this as a black man, but I speak to this as a gay man as well. When I heard about the Vision Focus of this church that was passed at last year's conference, I thought I had a church home I can go to now where I can be fully accepted as a child of God, and have a church family that will accept me. The recent events over the past few months have kind of gotten me a little scared, because I don't know whether I'll be accepted as a human being and a child of God, or if I'll be run out of the church. I'd like to say that I've been run out of a lot of churches before because of my orientation alone. What bothers me is that no one got to know me as a human being and as a child of God. That's why I stand before you and

ask that I still be accepted into this body, because this is my church home, too, and that you reaffirm the Vision Focus.

Roy embodied what was at stake in the votes being taken that night. For him, there was nothing abstract or academic about them. They had to do with his life and spirit, his relationship with a church community, his relationship with God. He had come to First Church because it offered the church home he had longed for all his life. Now that home was about to be taken from him. Roy's words were calm and measured, but his voice made clear his grief and apprehension, like those of a lover pleading for love about to be withdrawn.

When he finished speaking, Roy was greeted with appreciative applause, but not from the opposition. For them, who Roy was and what he wanted was what they most feared: a gay man in the church openly honoring his relationship with another gay man. Marv Koelling called the body to order, reminding everyone such outbursts would not be tolerated.

Others who spoke against the opposition's proposed amendments pointed out that the Social Principles of The United Methodist Church addressed many issues about which there was a diversity of opinion, and that compliance with all of them would be difficult. When Mike McClellan pointedly stated that many of Senator Karnes's political positions had not been consistent with the Social Principles, he was loudly booed by the audience. Although Marv Koelling had called the applause for Roy Wright out of order, he said nothing to quiet the angry reaction to Mike.

Jann Dappen spoke in support of leaving the Vision Focus unaltered. She identified herself as a high school teacher committed to teaching acceptance of all people and said that she had taught her two daughters to honor the love between two people of the same gender. When Jann returned to her seat, a man sitting behind her grabbed her arm and angrily shouted, "You are wrong to be teaching your kids that, and you're wrong to teach that in school!" Jann had to pull away to free herself. Pregnant with her third child, Jann was attending her first All Church Conference. "It was scary to see that much hate," she recalled.

The controversy over the past three months had brought First Church families with gay members out of hiding into open solidarity. They called themselves 100 Good Families. Joy Johnson, the mother of a lesbian daughter, spoke on their behalf:

We are the mothers and fathers, sisters and brothers of beloved family members who are homosexual. We, the 100 Families, recognize that beneath the anger and even the hate lies fear. We want you to know that you do not need to fear our daughters and sons, our sisters and brothers. They are good, hardworking people. They have loving, committed, responsible relationships. We believe that biblical statements about homosexuality have been misinterpreted. We believe our children and siblings are held in the grace of God as much as anyone in this room. We believe our daughters and sons, sisters and brothers receive the unconditional boundless love of the living Christ, as does everyone in this room. We, the 100 Families, ask that this body of Christ accept our loved ones and us into the full ministry, the full sacraments of this church as stated by our Vision Focus.

Only eight members spoke in favor of the opposition's amendments. One said that the Vision Focus was a nice statement, but the amendments were necessary because the senior pastor had defied the bishop and *The Book of Discipline*. Another said that the amendments only recognized that every one has rules to follow, and that if you break them you'll be punished. A third said: "I want to say to the gentleman who considers himself black and gay that I think the belief that the people who disagree with the marriage that took place in this church, or commitment ceremony, do not recognize gay people as children of God is not correct. We do recognize them as children of God the same way we recognize a person that has committed another sin, such as alcoholism or abuse of a child. They are no less a child of God. We have not tried to keep them from coming to our church, in fact we welcome them. I know personally, I've sat by them for many, many years, and it hasn't bothered me a bit."

The opposition's amendments passed, each time by a vote of 260 for and 225 against. The amended version of the Vision Focus was then approved. The opposition had shown its strength. The thirty-five-vote advantage foretold ultimate victory for the opposition in the more important business to come. Supporting the Vision and the church leadership didn't have the votes to stop them.

The Vision Focus had been compromised, but not revoked. If the current church leadership prevailed, the vision still could lead First Church toward true inclusiveness and hospitality. Should the opposition take over, however, the amended Vision Focus would merely camouflage conformity and bigotry.

The All Church Conference was now in its third hour. For those supportive of the Vision Focus, time moved slowly toward inevitable disaster. The rest of the evening would be nothing more than a formal confirmation of the opposition's coup. The contest for the soul of First Church was virtually decided.

The election of officers for 1998, the most crucial business of the conference, was next on the agenda. Printed ballots, which included the Nomination Committee's official slate of nominees for church officers, were distributed. Marv Koelling then explained that additional nominations could be made from the floor and written on the ballots.

The lay leaders, Bruce Deines and Marylin Stewart, had been elected in prior All Church Conferences to terms of three years and did not need to be voted on. Consequently, their names were not on the ballot. However, Bob Lueder, speaking for the opposition, moved that they be added so that alternate nominations for their positions could be made. Bill Jenks objected, saying the motion was out of order, since it would nullify the action of the previous All Church Conference. Marv Koelling disagreed and ruled Bob's motion to be in order.

"I've belonged here for sixty-two years, and I feel very sincerely that the present group of officers has been voting against the opinion of the majority of the members of the church. We're only going to ask you to vote for one new lay leader," Bob explained, "and you're free to keep one of the others. That's our intention. To simplify things, I've got a list of nominations I'm going to present."

Mike McClellan turned and whispered to his wife, Carol: "Do you hear what he's saying? We can't let him say that. Somebody's got to stand up there."

"I can't get up there," Carol protested.

"Yeah, you've got to get up there," Mike insisted. The last time Mike spoke, he had been booed, so he knew he couldn't do it.

Carol went to the microphone and said: "Mr. Lueder, you said the current leadership is stacked or loaded against your group. My question is, where was your group when we elected this leadership?"

Bob responded: "I have been very happy within this church for sixty-one years of my life, give or take a half a year. I have not been happy recently."

His voice was tired and sad as he continued: "I would say we've been very guilty of letting people do things. We know we've already lost a lot of our good members. This church is never going to be the same. I'd like to get it back to the way it was."

Carol persisted: "But now it's time to leave the process we've established for years, deviate from that and do something new because your group doesn't like the leadership we have in place?"

"We plan to nominate a few people for a few spots," Bob responded. "Now, some of them are up for reelection, anyway. But the lay leaders weren't mentioned here, and I noticed it right away. Where were they?"

"They're not on the ballot because their terms don't expire until the end of '98 and '99," Carol explained. "We don't need to vote on them tonight. They're already in place."

"But the process allows us to and we want to," Bob retorted.

"You want to remove two people who this body elected before?" Carol asked.

"We want to remove one of them," Bob admitted.

"And which one is that?" Carol demanded.

"We will tell you," Bob shot back.

Marylin Stewart went to the microphone and said: "It's pretty obvious that I'm the target." Embarrassed sarcastic laughter came from the opposition.

This debate ended when Rowen Zetterman moved to table Bob's motion to put the lay leaders on the ballot. A standing vote was taken, and the motion to table passed. Many of the older members recruited by the opposition didn't understand what this was all about, or why some people didn't like Marylin. President of the United Methodist Women as well as one of the lay leaders, Marylin was held in high esteem by most members.

Marv Koelling proceeded with a call for nominations from the floor for each office, one at a time, and Bob Lueder responded with sixty-one nominees chosen by the opposition. Marv patiently guided Bob through the tedious process. It was well past eleven at night when the vote finally was taken. The tellers collected the ballots and went to another room to begin the arduous task of counting, while the meeting continued.

The last business for the night had to do with finances. Del Bowden, chairperson of the Finance Committee, reported that First Church would finish 1997 with all its obligations paid. The stewardship campaign for 1998, however, was approximately $300,000 behind its goal of $1.2 million. Ninety pledge cards had been returned indicating that no pledge would be made as long as the current ministers remained. Another hundred pledge cards had not been returned.

Del moved that the ministers' salaries remain at the current level for the next year. Immediately, Warren DeGoler stood and shouted: "The ministerial staff is responsible for our current financial crisis . . . We could make our budget by asking for a voluntary resignation at this time of the entire ministerial staff. Save us the hardship. Resign! The people of this congregation do have a vote on what goes on at this church, and they are voting with their pocketbooks right now, saying, 'Change what's going on.' Or, they'll change with their feet before long . . ."

"I would suggest that it is not the pastoral staff that has created this rift," Phyllis Burroughs retorted. "It is the people who are so sanctimonious and have decided that they have . . . the more proper Christian attitude than a person who is reaching out in love to people who care for one another and want to have a relationship blessed. This is not a matter of the ministers' failing. It is a matter of this congregation failing."

Joan Byerhof said: "I sense a new understanding of the word 'cleansing.' People are cleansing in Bosnia; people are cleansing in Croatia and Serbia. I sense that there's an ideological cleansing in this sanctuary tonight."

A vote was taken, and the ministers' salaries were approved at the current level.

There had been significant attrition since the ballots were cast for church officers. Most who remained were from Supporting the Vision and the church leadership, with only a few members of the opposition. A somber silence settled over those waiting for the election results. The mood was heavy with hopelessness, as if someone was dying in the next room and everyone else was waiting to hear it was over. After half an hour, word came from the tellers that counting the votes would take much longer than expected because of all the write-ins. Someone moved to adjourn. The results of the election would be announced the next day. The meeting ended. Don Bredthauer stood at the front of the sanctuary, holding Susan Mullins as she openly wept, devastated by the hurtful words she had heard spoken and by her apprehension about what was to come. It was well past midnight.

I was home, anxiously waiting to learn the outcome of the meeting. Chris left the meeting shortly before it adjourned and told me what had happened. I was numb.

We had invited Supporting the Vision and the church leadership to come by our home for refreshments after the All Church Conference. Since it was so late, we didn't expect anyone to come, but they began to arrive before one in the morning, and our home quickly filled. Even though physically and emotionally exhausted, they wanted to be together, having become like family over the past two months. They were desperate for a reason to hope, for something to comfort them. Their grief was palpable. Eyes welled with tears, and jaws clenched. Some people broke down and wept. Others cursed in anger. Only occasionally did laughter vainly try to mask the anguish.

What had just happened at the church was rehearsed over and over. It had been acrimonious and hurtful. The overwhelming defeats on the resolutions, the large number of inactive members who showed up, the manipulation of the opposition and its slate of nominees, and the poor, seemingly biased leadership of Marv Koelling were lamented and denounced. First Church had been taken over by the opposition; the Vision Focus was dead. People occasionally suggested that they should leave First Church and go to another church or start a new church. But this was grief and anger working through the group, not reason. No one really wanted to leave First Church or make any decisions about the future that night.

Although a few people left, the living room, dining room, and kitchen were still full when the telephone rang about two thirty in the morning. Someone near the phone answered and then shouted: "Joanie Zetterman's at the church and she says the votes are all counted. We won!"

I hurried to the phone. "Jimmy," Joanie shouted, "our candidates won all the elections except for just a few. Our only major loss was the chair of the Church Council. Frank Rathbun won and Joan Byerhof lost. But all the others were elected." "Are you sure?" I asked. "Yes," she assured me. Although everyone else except the tellers had left the church when the conference was adjourned, Joanie had remained, sitting alone in the hallway outside the room where the votes were being counted, patiently waiting until the outcome was determined. When she learned the news, she had to tell me.

Everyone waited in silent disbelief. When I gave the mourning crowd Joanie's report, they erupted into a delirious celebration. How could this be? We didn't yet know all the details about vote totals and margins, about the few exceptions, but our apparent defeat had turned to victory. That night, we had experienced both Good Friday and Easter: "There's been a resurrection!" I told the gathering. "The vision appeared dead, but God's spirit prevailed. The vision is alive! This is what Easter is all about!" The euphoric celebration continued on into the morning. Our last guest didn't leave until after four in the morning.

The winners that night weren't the supporters of the Vision Focus. They didn't have the votes. The Vision Focus won. Something happened in the midst of the meeting to make the elections turn out differently than the votes on the resolutions. The character and motives of those leading the opposition had been exposed, and what was revealed was distasteful even to some of the people they had recruited to attend the conference. This was especially true in the opposition's attempt to remove Marylin Stewart, a ruthless arrogance that many people believed changed the meeting's outcome. The ugliness of the opposition's behavior and rhetoric sharply contrasted with what those supporting the Vision Focus said and did. Passing the resolutions satisfied the desire of some people to protest the covenant ceremony, and that was all they had come to do that night. To them, letting the opposition lead First Church was unthinkable.

The official report on the election was incredible. Only twelve of the opposition's sixty-one nominees were elected. None were elected to the Staff-Parish Relations Committee, making it stronger than ever in support of the Vision Focus and the church staff. The opposition's only significant success was the election of Frank Rathbun as chairperson of the Church Council, and he had defeated Joan Byerhof by only eighteen votes. The opposition couldn't believe they had lost and called for a recount the next day. The result was the same.

Just as the All Church Conference tempered First Church's internal crisis, its sense of isolation also began to abate. In response to the letter Supporting the Vision had sent out in November, a torrent of mail poured in from individuals and churches of various denominational and religious affiliations all over the nation. The moral support and solidarity this demonstrated was most encouraging. At its December meeting, the Finance Committee recognized the extraordinary work of Supporting the Vision in overcoming the congregation's desperate financial deficit. Because of its efforts, First Church members contributed $100,000 more than their pledges in the last two months of 1997. In addition, individuals from around the country added $12,750. Three congregations—Pullen Memorial Baptist Church in Raleigh, Bering Memorial United Methodist Church in Houston, and Broadway United Methodist Church in Chicago—sent a combined total of $7,035.

Supporting the Vision had broken the opposition's financial siege and won the fight for the heart and soul of First United Methodist Church in Omaha. The Vision Focus, though modified, had been reaffirmed, and the progressive leadership of the church maintained. There were lingering wounds and more pain still to come, but the victory had been won. The vision had prevailed.

The judicial complaint against me was now in the hands of the Committee on Investigation of the Nebraska Annual Conference. The Reverend David Lux, pastor of the First United Methodist Church in North Platte, Nebraska, was the chairperson of the committee, which included six other clergy and two lay observers. I had met some of the committee members, but I didn't really know any of them. The committee functioned like a grand jury. According to *The Book of Discipline*, it was to conduct an investigation and hold a hearing in order to determine whether or not I should be put on trial.

Soon after my suspension began, Doug Williamson, my defense counsel, came to Omaha from Lincoln to meet with Mike McClellan, my assistant defense counsel, and me at my home to begin preparation for the hearing. It was the first time they had met, and they immediately developed a rapport. Doug trusted Mike's legal knowledge and insights about how to develop the defense. Mike, in turn, respected Doug's knowledge of United Methodist history and theology, as well as his understanding of the current political dynamics within the Nebraska Annual Conference.

In early December, ahead of the deadline, we mailed a packet of documents to David Lux outlining our defense, including my written response to the complaint. Although the fundamental issue for me was the unjust policy of The United Methodist Church that caused harm to lesbian, gay, and bisexual people and their families, the heart of our defense was to challenge the legal status of the prohibition against homosexual unions in the Social Principles.

With the exception of their appalling stand on homosexuality, The Social

Principles are a compendium of liberal moral theology that includes stands against capital punishment and war and stands for legalized abortion, divorce, labor unions, and affirmative action, all anathema to the very people who wanted me prosecuted for violating one of the principles. No one in the history of The United Methodist Church had been prosecuted for acting in conflict with the Social Principles. While many clergy and lay people disagreed with the social principle supporting legal abortions and actively tried to stop abortions, no one had been prosecuted for such actions. Although the principles declare war to be "incompatible with the gospel and spirit of Christ,"[1] no United Methodist had ever been prosecuted for fighting in a war.

Incredibly, it was the conservative evangelical element of The United Methodist Church that was arguing for the Social Principles to be treated as church law, at least in my case. The other side of this debate, representing the liberal tradition of the church from which the principles came, argued that they were not binding as law. These people considered the principles to be enlightened guides for responsible conduct in today's world, with the glaring exception of the statement regarding homosexuality.

On December 16, at Trinity United Methodist Church in Grand Island, Nebraska, the Committee on Investigation held a preliminary meeting to establish the procedures and ground rules we would use during the course of the hearing. Lauren Ekdahl, the church counsel, brought with him his assistant counsel, Warren Urbom, who was a federal district court judge and a prominent layperson in the Nebraska Annual Conference who had been a delegate to the 1996 General Conference. Glenn Loy, the complainant, was also there, along with Doug, Mike, and me. The two-hour meeting covered a range of matters, including setting the date for the hearing for nine in the morning on January 23, 1998, at Trinity United Methodist Church.

Just as we were about to adjourn, Lauren Ekdahl reminded the committee that they had the prerogative to recommend that my sixty-day suspension be extended. Noting that my suspension was to end on January 9, 1998, before the hearing we had just scheduled, Lauren urged the committee to take this opportunity to make such a recommendation for the convenience of the bishop.

Doug, Mike, and I were caught off guard. Doug warned that such an extension would be detrimental to First Church and contrary to the desire of the congregation. He insisted that members of First Church be consulted before the committee took any such action, pointing out that the Staff-Parish Relations Committee had already requested that I be reinstated. When Mike McClellan tried to speak, not as my assistant counsel but as a First Church member, David Lux interrupted him and ended the discussion. The issue was left hanging in the air, and the meeting was adjourned.

On Christmas Eve, I received a letter from David Lux informing me that the committee had voted to recommend to Bishop Martínez that my "suspension from pastoral duties be continued, pending the outcome of the judicial process. This recommendation is advisory only, and gives the Bishop latitude to do what he thinks best."

I called David for an explanation. He said the committee didn't intend to endorse an extension but had acted on the understanding that if they had not voted to recommend one at the meeting, the bishop wouldn't be able to extend the suspension if he wanted to. David assured me the committee's vote was a matter of opportunity and convenience, not one of conviction.

The day after Christmas, I wrote to the bishop, imploring him to consult with the Staff-Parish Relations Committee and me before deciding to extend the suspension. I concluded with a concession that I hoped would persuade him to let me return to First Church. "When you met with me on October 30 to inform me of your decision to put me on suspension, one of the concerns you expressed had to do with my celebrating another covenant ceremony. I have given a great deal of thought to this since then. As you know, I believe the language in the Social Principles (re. the prohibition of 'homosexual unions') to be unjust and discriminatory. I cannot and will not abide by it in good faith. However, in deference to you, to First Church, and to the Nebraska Conference, I will not celebrate a covenant ceremony until the Committee on Investigation has completed its work and, should it be necessary, a church trial has taken place."

As the New Year began, I prepared to return to First Church. I felt as if I were getting ready for a feast at the end of a long fast. Because I had heard nothing from the bishop, I was confident that the suspension would not be extended. I was scheduled to preach on my first Sunday back, so on Monday, January 5, I sent the scripture references and my sermon title to Roberta Coss, the pastors' secretary, to put in Sunday's bulletin.

The next day, however, my excitement was dampened by a fax from Bishop Martínez: "Susan Davies, Marv Koelling, and I would like to meet with you on Friday, January 9, 1998, at 8:00 a.m. for breakfast." Apparently not wanting to give advance notice to anyone who might want to stage a public demonstration,[2] he concluded: "We will call you on Thursday night to identify the location for the meeting."

The night before our meeting, the bishop met with the Staff-Parish Relations Committee and told them he was considering extending my suspension. The committee strongly advised against it, saying that continuing my absence would be detrimental to First Church.

As promised, Susan Davies called that night to tell me that the meeting would be at the Holiday Inn on 72nd Street in Omaha. I awoke Friday morning to find heavy snow falling. Knowing I would have to make my way through unplowed streets, I left home early to be sure that I would get to the Holiday Inn on time. Rather than meet in the restaurant, which would be public, the bishop wanted us to meet in his hotel room. He had ordered Danish pastries and coffee for all of us. I wasn't hungry.

Bishop Martínez explained that he was trying to decide whether or not to end my suspension. He acknowledged my promise not to conduct a covenant ceremony until the judicial process had concluded and said that he appreciated the progress that had been made at the church. However, he stressed that the controversy had engulfed the entire Nebraska Annual Conference, and he had to consider more than just the interests of First Church. He promised he would let me know as soon as he made his decision. The meeting was brief.

Friday afternoon's edition of the *Omaha World-Herald* carried a brief article with the headline, "Suspension Has Ended for Methodist Pastor." It said I would be back in the pulpit at First Church on Sunday and that the Bishop was "unavailable for comment," but would be releasing a statement "later Friday."[3]

And he did:

A STATEMENT FROM BISHOP JOEL N. MARTÍNEZ
REGARDING SUSPENSION OF JIMMY CREECH

Upon recommendation of the Committee on Investigation of the Nebraska Annual Conference, I have determined to extend the suspension of the Reverend Jimmy Creech from all clergy duties at First United Methodist Church in Omaha.

While progress has been made at First United Methodist Church in working through some of the divisiveness in the congregation, more work needs to be done. The widespread concern among laity and clergy in the Nebraska Annual Conference continues and is another primary consideration in making my decision. It is my best judgment that additional time will serve the best interests of all, considering the continuing volatility of the climate both at First United Methodist Church and in the Nebraska Annual Conference.

I have consulted with the conference Cabinet, the First United Methodist Church Staff-Parish Relations Committee, and Reverend Creech, before making this decision.

The Judicial process continues to move forward in an orderly and deliberate fashion. I have every expectation that a fair resolution of the complaint regarding Reverend Creech will be made as early as possibly practical by those charged with this responsibility.

I will continue to be in close and continuing conversation with the pastoral leadership at First United Methodist Church, the Staff-Parish Relations Committee and with Reverend Creech, as this extended period of suspension begins.

On the Sunday morning I should have been back in the pulpit, Bill Jenks read to the congregation a letter from Bishop Martínez explaining his decision. His letter made these claims: "My decision to continue Reverend Jimmy Creech on suspension was not easily arrived at. I had extensive consultation with the conference Cabinet and with Reverend Jimmy Creech prior to making this determination. I recognize that some progress has been made at the church. At the same time, I believe more work needs to be done in the congregation through the efforts already under way. I will review and monitor progress through continuing consultation with the Staff-Parish Relations Committee during the coming weeks. Reverend Creech and I will meet in the coming days as part of my continuing effort to explore resolution even as the judicial process continues."

Bishop Martínez was disingenuous in both the press release and letter to the congregation. The first sentence of his press release was carefully crafted to put responsibility for the extension on the Committee on Investigation, as if he were following its advice. He also said he would "continue to be in close and continuing conversation with the pastoral leadership at First United Methodist Church, the Staff-Parish Relations Committee and with Reverend Creech," as if he had been doing so all along. And he said in his letter to the congregation that he had had "extensive consultation" with me prior to his decision. Both claims were false. The Staff-Parish Relations Committee had long complained of the difficulty it experienced in communicating with the bishop. He hadn't consulted with them until the day before he announced his decision, and then he ignored their advice. The only conversation he had had with me about the extension was the brief meeting in his hotel room on the day he announced his decision. The bishop was sensitive about the criticism directed at him for his lack of communication, and his public pretensions to the contrary were purely fictional and defensive.

The bishop's decision to extend my suspension created a stressful situation for the First Church staff, especially Don and Susan. Susan had announced to the congregation just one week earlier that she would be taking a four-month-long spiritual growth leave, beginning January 21. The situation at First Church had "taken a toll on my spiritual and physical health," she explained, and she said that she needed "to take some time apart for healing and to discern the continuing direction of my ministry."

Susan's decision was based on the expectation that I would be back before her leave began. The bishop knew the demands and pressures that Susan and Don had experienced in my absence had been enormous, and he knew Susan would be on leave. Yet he was willing to continue my suspension at the expense of the ministry and well-being of the church staff.

Early on the morning of January 23, Mike and I picked up Doug in Lincoln, and we drove together to Grand Island for the hearing of the Committee on Investigation. It was a typically frigid January day in Nebraska, with the temperature in the teens. When we arrived, the Trinity United Methodist Church parking lot was covered with snow and ice. We walked cautiously from the car to the church, waddling slowly like penguins as we followed hand-lettered signs directing us to the side entrance.

Promptly at nine the hearing began. David Lux reminded everyone present that the committee was "to conduct an investigation in order to determine whether there is reasonable ground for charges, and if so, to sign and certify the charges as proper for trial."[4] The standard, he emphasized, was "reasonable grounds."

Glenn Loy testified first, asking if everyone had a copy of his written complaint and Lauren's official letter of complaint. Then he said: "I don't have a thing to add to that at all." When asked, "In what way do you understand

Jimmy to have violated the Order and Discipline of the Church?" Glenn answered: "I believe *The Book of Discipline* to be the guideline for the Church and that the ordained ministry holds people accountable to that. If we're all free to say our conscience is our guide and we can go against it [*The Book of Discipline*], then I'm not sure what foundational documents to work from." When asked, "That includes the Social Principles?" he muttered: "Uh-huh." There were no other questions for Glenn.

Lauren Ekdahl came next. "There is a collegiality that undergirds the authority of *The Book of Discipline* where United Methodist clergy, through ordination, promise to support the Order and Discipline of The United Methodist Church," he said. "The complaint lodged against Reverend Jimmy Creech is . . . recognition of his breaking of the covenant he embraced through his ordination and his denial of the authority of *The Discipline* to define rite and ritual in The United Methodist Church, according to a consistent and democratically-determined process." He went on to argue that the language in the Social Principles prohibiting clergy from conducting "homosexual unions" was binding, and that by adapting the official marriage ceremony for the covenant ceremony, I had "knowingly and willfully made a decision about rite and ritual that is relegated solely to the General Conference. By engaging in this act, Reverend Jimmy Creech exceeded the bounds of his pastoral authority and placed himself in a state of 'disobedience to the Order and Discipline of The United Methodist Church.'" David Lux asked if the committee members had any questions for Lauren, and nobody did.

It was then my turn to address the committee:

I want to emphasize that my decision was one that I made carefully, with a great deal of prayer and thought over a period of a number of years . . . I consider myself to be a very loyal United Methodist. I do not consider what I have done to be an act of disobedience. I think, first of all, as ordained clergy and as baptized Christians, we are committed to hold up the gospel of Jesus Christ as that which ultimately guides us. I do not think that any promise or pledge or covenant with the institution of the church supersedes that. I think if we should ever claim that, that that would be a form of idolatry . . . I certainly stand in judgment by the church and I accept that . . . I do not claim to be above the church. But I am first accountable to God who called me into ministry and I must be faithful to God, even if it means standing in conflict with the church. I consider it to be a part of my calling and my way of serving the church to take such a stand . . . It is my belief that I acted in faithfulness to the gospel of Jesus Christ.

Doug spoke next, repeating our argument that the church has the burden to prove that there was a law that applied to the complaint against me: "General Conference has passed no law prohibiting United Methodist clergy from officiating at a covenant service. That means the church cannot meet its burden in this issue."

Doug refuted the allegation that I had violated the church's constitution by adapting the official marriage ceremony. He observed that clergy have historically created and improvised liturgy for special occasions. He insisted that I had acted faithfully in my role as pastor, especially in the context of First United Methodist Church, Omaha, which had adopted a policy of inclusiveness. In conclusion, Doug said:

Beyond all of the arguments based on ecclesiastical law stand important theological considerations related to the matter at hand. For Jesus, compassion was the central quality of God and the central moral quality of a life centered in God. Jesus's ethic of compassion brought him into conflict on a regular basis with the ideology of the dominant elitists of his time and an ideology grounded in the ethic of purity.

Jesus challenged over and over again those who would draw boundaries based on purity to keep out of the community of faith those determined to be unclean. We are at a crossroads in the life of the church. With regard to gay and lesbian persons, we must choose to treat them with an ethic of compassion or an ethic of purity. Jimmy Creech has, in my opinion, acted with the same ethic of compassion modeled by Jesus, reaching out to marginalized people, rather than excluding them from the ministry of the church . . .

I struggled mightily with the burden of responsibility attendant upon my role as Jimmy's counsel. It is a weight made even heavier by the clamoring of those within our denomination who would deny Jimmy the fair process guaranteed to him by our Discipline, by those who glibly assert that the Social Principles of United Methodism have the force of coercive law, even though they can cite no historical or church judicial precedence to support such a contention.

The burden to which I have referred is made yet heavier by Bishop Martínez's comment to Jimmy that moderate and progressive pastors in the conference have called him in support of Jimmy's suspension, stating that because Jimmy had been in our conference for only fourteen months, he did not have the standing or the prerogative to officiate at a covenant service that had the potential to stir up so much conflict. We all ought to be ashamed of ourselves if we are to begin judging the justice and/or the propriety of a pastor's actions by how long they have been in our midst.

The weight I feel has been made almost unbearable by a conversation I had with a pastor who is a friend of several members of this committee, and he said that a couple of you folks have told him that you are afraid that if the committee does not find Jimmy to have committed a chargeable offense, your careers in this conference may be damaged. I know that fear myself. Being in this position has made me afraid for my future role in this conference should I ever, as I believe I will, desire to return to local church ministry.

Shame on us if our system intimidates us into a course of action contrary to acting justly, loving tenderly, and walking humbly with our God. Shame on us if our fears cause us to treat a colleague unjustly.

When Doug finished, David invited the committee members to ask him questions. But no one did. Either the committee members were convinced, or they were simply dismissing everything he had said. They sat in unresponsive silence.

I felt the committee's "investigation" was a ruse, and the hearing, a charade. The committee was to investigate whether or not there were reasonable grounds to believe I had committed a "chargeable offense" against the church, but there was no investigation. There was no examination of the legal status of the Social Principles to determine if in fact a law existed to apply to the complaint against me. No witnesses testified, and no material evidence was presented. There was no probing into church history or judicial rulings. The committee simply met for two hours, heard our statements, and asked a few superficial questions.

The next morning, David Lux faxed the following statement to Bishop Martínez: "The Committee on Investigation has conducted its investigation and with a vote of 6 for to 1 against find [sic] there is [sic] reasonable grounds for the charge and specifications against Reverend Jimmy Creech set forth in the October 28, 1997, letter submitted by Reverend Lauren D. Ekdahl as counsel for the Nebraska Annual Conference of The United Methodist Church as proper for trial."

While the committee's vote didn't surprise us, it was disappointing and discouraging. It meant that our well-reasoned defense had been ignored, and that we now had to prepare for a trial. It also meant that I would not be returning to First Church. With the performance of the Committee on Investigation as a preview of how a trial would turn out, the die seemed cast: my exile would be permanent.

In my mind, the committee's decision put The United Methodist Church on trial, not me, exposing the bigotry and hypocrisy of the church in a very public way. Just how far would the church go to enforce its oppressive treatment of gay people? Would it really prosecute a pastor for blessing the loving commitment of two people? An open, public trial would let the world know, putting The United Methodist Church's policies and teachings about homosexuality on a national stage and making the church—along with most other Christian denominations—accountable for its bigotry.

The Committee on Investigation's decision essentially presented me with a calling to a new way of serving The United Methodist Church. I saw myself as neither defendant nor victim. I had no illusion that it would be fun and painless. Doubtless, I would be hurt. It could end my ministry as a pastor. But helping to purge The United Methodist Church of the poison of fear, prejudice, and injustice was of far greater importance than whatever a trial might cost me.

Bishop Martínez had wanted to make the judicial process an internal matter hidden from public view, one that could be easily managed and controlled. However, I believed that what was at stake was far too important for the wider church and society. The trial wasn't about me; it was about The United Methodist Church and the pervasive, religion-based antigay prejudice in it and in society at large. I believed that it was crucial to make my case against the church's oppression of gay people as public as possible. I decided to do this by publishing and circulating my fourteen-page single-spaced written response to the complaint, which best articulated the case I wanted to make.

In my response, I described Mary and Martha's covenant ceremony and explained my reason for conducting it in spite of the prohibition in the Social Principles and Bishop Martínez's instruction not to do so. I told about Adam's visit to my office in 1984 and the discoveries I had made in my subsequent study of the Bible, church history, and sexuality, which I had undertaken so that I could understand the church's treatment of gay people. I described the suffering of gay people I had witnessed, as well as the devoted loving relationships of gay and lesbian couples I knew. I explained how my experience growing up in a racist culture helped me understand the prejudice against gay people and the primary role of religion in justifying and sustaining it. I discussed the references in *The Book of Discipline* that relate to homosexuality and explained why they were not only wrong, but evil. I said:

> It is my belief that the position taken by The United Methodist Church regarding same-gender unions, as well as that regarding "the practice" of homosexuality, is wrong, unjust, discriminatory and inconsistent with the spirit of Christ and our Wesleyan and Methodist traditions . . .
>
> Sexual orientation is not a moral issue; it is morally neutral. Sexual ethics are simple: sexual relationships should be mutual, non-exploitative, nurturing and loving. What is immoral are unequal, exploitative, abusive and unloving sexual acts toward another person. This is true regardless of the orientation of the persons involved. I believe that sexual activity which is considered moral when practiced by two people of different genders, is no less moral when practiced by two people of the same gender. The crucial test is whether the activity is mutual, non-exploitative, nurturing and loving . . .
>
> I believe that the sin of heterosexism is no less a sin than that of racism. While some of the dynamics may be different, they are fundamentally identical in nature as an expression of a dominant culture over another.
>
> Just as it was the church in the South that perpetuated racism so that slavery and white supremacy could have legitimacy, the Christian church has been responsible, more than any other institution, for perpetuating the sin of heterosexism as a form of control over what is feared within all of us: the mystery of human sexuality and intimacy (sexual or nonsexual) with persons of the same gender.
>
> Because of the heterosexism taught and practiced by the institution of the Christian church, countless young people have committed suicide, adults have lived lifetimes of lies, families have been destroyed, gay men

and lesbians have been cruelly treated and murdered, the spirit and lives of millions of gay people have been crippled, and they have been told that the love of God is denied to them because of who they are, and will continue to be unless they become other than who they are . . .

Just as The United Methodist Church renounces racism, so, too, should it renounce heterosexism. Both bear the fruits of prejudice, bigotry, discrimination, and dehumanization. Both are value systems contrary to the Christian gospel because they deny integrity, dignity, and wholeness to persons who are children of God created in God's image. People of faith and conscience must address both for what they are: evil. The United Methodist Church must no longer be allowed to continue its destructive positions regarding homosexuality. Good people can no longer passively support and condone this evil through silence. If there is any hope for us being saved from our egregious error, it is for us to speak and act against the evil of heterosexism, just as we must against racism, within The United Methodist Church as well as within society.

With all that I came to understand from reflections upon the dynamics I witnessed growing up in a racist society, along with my study of sexual orientation and my firsthand observations about the experiences of gay men and lesbians in society and in the church, it was no longer possible for me to be quiet about the injustices perpetuated against lesbians and gay men. Once there is understanding, behavior has to change or there is no faithfulness, no integrity. It does not serve God to uphold injustice for the sake of preserving an unhealthy and destructive peace. To be faithful to my calling as a Christian, to my calling as an ordained United Methodist pastor, I could not but agree to offer God's blessing upon Mary and Martha as they committed themselves to each other . . .

I consider the following language in the Social Principles to be an expression of evil: "Although we do not condone the practice of homosexuality and consider this practice incompatible with Christian teaching . . ." It is on the basis of this language that the prohibition against the ordination of "self-avowed practicing homosexuals" and the advice against United Methodist clergy conducting ceremonies that celebrate "homosexual unions" are justified. This value judgment is institutionalized prejudice and bigotry, classifying as sin sexual acts of intimacy and love, expressions of "God's good gift to all persons." On this basis, the right of a couple to conscientiously covenant together in the context of their faith community and in witness to their faith in Jesus Christ is denied. Pastors and congregations are restricted from giving support to gay couples who intend to live in a committed relationship as a family . . .

I acted out of loyalty to The United Methodist Church. I am devoted to it. I came to awareness of God and Jesus Christ as a child growing up in it. It nurtured me in my faith journey through Sunday school, worship, Bible School, Methodist Youth Fellowship into young adulthood. I have served The United Methodist Church in ordained ministry for twenty-seven years. I remain United Methodist because I love The United Methodist Church, even though I am in strong disagreement with its position regarding lesbians and gay men. Had I not this love for The United Methodist Church, it would have been easy and convenient to leave when I began to understand its sin. My hope is, by being faithful to the liberating gospel of Jesus Christ, I can serve The United Methodist Church by calling it to turn away from the sin of heterosexism and to faithfulness.

While a charge has been brought against me, I believe that in this case it is The United Methodist Church that is being placed on trial. Does the church really want to judge me wrong for praying God's blessing upon Mary and Martha in their commitment to each other? Would such a judgment bear witness to the love of God in Christ Jesus for all the world to see?

Supporting the Vision sent copies to all members of First Church and to the local and national media. The Nebraska chapter of the Methodist Federation for Social Action sent copies to all clergy and lay leaders in the Nebraska Annual Conference. In a short time, my response was being circulated around the country.

In January, the Staff-Parish Relations Committee voted to request the reappointment of Don Bredthauer, Susan Mullins, and me to First Church for another year. In his letter reporting the committee's decision to Bishop Martínez, Bill Jenks, just beginning his tenure as chairperson, wrote:

The consensus of the committee is that we currently have the strongest pastoral team in memory in this church. We feel this is true in every category of pastoral responsibility: spiritual leadership, administrative skill and effectiveness, sensitivity and attention to the needs of diverse groups and individuals within the church, and understanding of and commitment to our shared vision . . .

We feel that we are more vital as a spiritual community than we have ever been, and we attribute that directly to the inspiring leadership of our pastoral team. We hope and pray that you will recommend their continued service with us.

During our meeting, the committee also passed a motion directing me to urge you, in the strongest possible terms, to end Jimmy Creech's suspension and let him return to his congregation as soon as possible . . . The uncertainty inherent in a continuing, open-ended suspension wears heavily on our ability to continue effectively the diverse activities and missions of the church . . . There is much to be done here, and it can be done most effectively if Jimmy Creech is allowed to return to his place with us. I can't vouch for how much longer we can hold things together in his absence.

The Staff-Parish Relations Committee also directed me to request that you meet with us at your earliest possible convenience if your decision is to continue Jimmy's suspension.

Bill's past efforts to communicate with the bishop had been futile. His letters, faxes, and phone calls to the bishop had gone unanswered. This time, however, Bishop Martínez responded and agreed to a private meeting with Bill and a later, separate meeting with the Staff-Parish Relations Committee.

Bill and Bishop Martínez met at Mahoney State Park restaurant, midway between Omaha and Lincoln. Bill told me:

The bishop was very defensive. I couldn't pin him down on anything. He would only keep talking about "my responsibility is to the whole conference, not just to First Church, blah, blah, blah." He told me the only reason to suspend a pastor is if it's in the pastor's best interest or the best interest of the parish. I said: "Well, in what way is this in the best interest of Jimmy Creech or First Church? All you've told us is that it's in the best interest of the conference, that it's upsetting to other churches. We need Jimmy at our church." I said: "It's not in our best interest to have him gone." The bishop couldn't answer that. I left there thinking there was no substance to what the bishop said. I didn't feel that he was looking out for the best interest of First Church. It seemed he was thinking first of his own skin and second about the squeaky wheels in western Nebraska and the opposition in First Church. Meeting with him accomplished nothing.

The bishop's subsequent three-hour meeting with the Staff-Parish Relations Committee was much the same, with one significant exception. He repeated his reasons for extending the suspension and then answered questions from the committee members about the upcoming trial. Someone asked: "Frankly, it looks as if Jimmy will be found guilty. But, just suppose, for argument's sake, hypothetically, if Jimmy's found not guilty, will you lift the suspension immediately, and will you reappoint him to First Church in June?"

"Well, of course, the suspension will end," the bishop replied, "and there will be no reason not to reappoint him because the process will have run its course, the court will have spoken. If the verdict's not guilty, that's it. Of course I'll reappoint him."

The secular media had taken some interest in the covenant ceremony and the complaint filed against me but had treated both as local news until the Committee on Investigation referred the complaint to trial. Then the case became a national story. Gustav Niebuhr, a religion reporter for the *New York Times*, came to Omaha at the end of January to do research for a story about my upcoming trial. Published on Sunday, February 15, his article told about the covenant ceremony and the reaction to it, both inside and outside of First Church. The pending trial, Niebuhr wrote, "will highlight a divisive pattern emerging within Protestantism, where the consensus against homosexuality has been eroding, as it has elsewhere in American society."[5] The *Times* article was reprinted in other papers around the country.

In a similar way, United Methodists treated the judicial process as a Nebraska matter until the trial was announced. I think there was both an assumption and a hope that the complaint would be resolved without a trial, making all the controversy just a localized hiccup within The United Methodist Church. After all, no one had ever been tried for violating one of the Social Principles, and it didn't make any sense that this case should be the exception. But it became the exception and had an impact on the whole church. Reactionaries in the church feared that I would find some loophole (for instance, that the principles are not legally binding) and be acquitted. Progressives in the church believed that trying a pastor for not obeying one of the principles was appalling and incredible.

When Bishop Martínez announced that the trial would be on March 11–13, 1998, at First United Methodist Church in Kearney, Nebraska—189 miles west of Omaha, almost exactly in the middle of the state—and that Bishop Leroy Hodapp, a retired bishop from Evansville, Indiana, would be the presiding officer (the judge), support immediately began pouring in from around the country. The Reverend George McClain, executive director of the Methodist Federation for Social Action (MFSA), issued a national "Emergency Bulletin," announcing the place and dates of the trial, with these observations and requests:

> The Issues at Stake: Can the church of Jesus Christ extend love and justice to lesbians and gay men? Can United Methodist clergy celebrate covenant services between United Methodists of the same sex? Jimmy Creech is going on trial for celebrating a covenant service between two women members of First United Methodist Church, Omaha, where he is a pastor. But much more than Jimmy, The United Methodist Church is on trial. What kind of church are we? Whom do we serve—the God who is love? Or some other god? Are we willing to *be* the church, even if there's some risk? Do we mean what we say in the Social Principles, that "Homosexual persons no less than heterosexual persons are individuals of sacred worth?" We are each, in fact, on trial. Our personal witness is now critical. Therefore I am rushing this invitation to you by first-class mail in order for you to receive this invitation in as timely a manner as possible. PLEASE COME TO KEARNEY—ONE WAY OR ANOTHER!

George hired Laura Montgomery Rutt to be the national coordinator of MFSA's presence at the trial. George and Laura organized a national letter writing campaign they called "Proclaiming the Vision," which encouraged MFSA members to write to their local newspapers in my support. They also set up a fund to cover the defense expenses in the upcoming trial.

Support came not only from religious groups. Nancy McDonald, the national president of Parents, Families, and Friends of Lesbians and Gays (PFLAG), for example, issued a press release with this appeal: "On behalf of PFLAG's 70,000 households, I strongly urge all fair-minded people to show support for Reverend Jimmy Creech."

Now that we knew when and where the trial would be, and who would be the presiding officer, Doug, Mike, and I intensified our preparations. I sent out an e-mail to the MFSA listserv, asking for background information on Bishop Hodapp. The feedback I got was cause for concern.

In 1992, just before Bishop Hodapp retired, a holy union for two gay men was conducted at Broadway United Methodist Church in Indianapolis. When he learned of it, the bishop sent a letter to all clergy under his supervision that said in part: "Both biblical tradition and our United Methodist *Discipline* are very clear that the marriage ceremony is to be performed 'between a man and a woman' and that 'sexual relations are only clearly affirmed in the marriage bond.' We admonish United Methodist clergy in Indiana to refrain from officiating, or from permitting their church facilities to be used, in any ceremony for homosexual persons which resembles the rite of marriage. This would include ceremonies or celebrations which involve the exchange of vows or rings, or incorporate any of the elements of the traditional marriage ritual."

Bishop Martínez had carefully chosen as the presiding officer someone who agreed with his own position that *The Book of Discipline*, even prior to the 1996 prohibition, included an implicit ban on same-gender ceremonies of holy union. If Bishop Hodapp were somehow to impose this opinion on the trial proceedings, our argument that the Social Principles are not legally binding would be irrelevant.

While this was disturbing news, other feedback touted Bishop Hodapp as a fair and compassionate person, one who "always does his homework," "knows his polity," and "is friendly with good folk on the Judicial Council." One response said that the bishop had "worked around some rather nasty conference members to keep from removing the credentials of gay clergy." But then, from an astute observer of the church, I got this message: "Be prepared. From the site chosen for the trial and the bishop chosen to preside, it appears that someone has begun thinking through clearly how to put Jimmy and his defense in the most difficult position possible."

On February 26, Doug, Mike, and I, along with the prosecution team of Lauren Ekdahl and Warren Urbom, met with Bishop Hodapp for a preliminary hearing in preparation for the trial. The bishop was tall and imposing, but his manner was gentle and gracious. He was relaxed and informal, yet there was no doubt that he understood and adhered to church law.

During the hearing, Doug argued that the prohibition of "homosexual unions" was not law because it was located in the Social Principles and that, therefore, I could not be prosecuted for violating it. Bishop Hodapp surprised us by acknowledging that the presumed coercive power of the prohibition was questionable, and that if the prohibition was not church law, the charge against me could not stand and there should be no trial. He said it would be in the best interest of The United Methodist Church and me if the legal ambiguity of the prohibition could be resolved before the trial. The only way for that to happen would be to put the trial on hold, contingent on a declaratory ruling on the legal status of the prohibition by the United Methodist Judicial Council, scheduled to meet April 22–25 in Hershey, Pennsylvania. Bishop Hodapp asked if we would be willing for him to explore the possibility of getting this on the Judicial Council's April agenda, thereby postponing the trial.

Lauren Ekdahl and Warren Urbom were confident that the Judicial Council would support their argument and recognized that a ruling to that effect would strengthen their case against me, and essentially nullify my defense in a trial. Doug, Mike, and I were just as certain that the Judicial Council would rule in our favor, invalidating the charge and making a trial unnecessary. Everyone believed, though for conflicting reasons, that we had much to gain by delaying the trial until a Judicial Council ruling was made. Everyone except me.

My suspension from First Church had to be lifted, I insisted, as a condition for waiting for a ruling on the prohibition from the Judicial Council. Since I was the accused, I had the right to have the charge resolved by trial, or the suspension lifted if there was delay. While the Judicial Council was to meet in April, the council's members could take longer to decide, even postponing a decision until their fall meeting. Should they rule in April that the prohibition was church law, restarting the trial process would take another month or more, making it more probable that Bishop Martínez would permanently remove me from First Church. If I was to have a chance to return to First Church, it had to be now, or we needed to proceed with the trial as scheduled. Everyone agreed that the suspension should be lifted if the Judicial Council agreed to consider the legal status of the prohibition.

Bishop Hodapp called Tom Methany, president of the Judicial Council, who agreed to add the prohibition to the agenda for the upcoming meeting. Getting Bishop Martínez's cooperation was not so easy. When Bishop Hodapp called him and explained our desire to delay the trial to allow the

Judicial Council to rule on the prohibition, with the condition that my suspension be ended immediately, Bishop Martínez refused to make a decision. He said he needed to think it over and would give us an answer by the following morning, a Friday.

The next morning, the bishop hadn't made a decision and insisted on meeting with me, along with Marv Koelling and Susan Davies, later that afternoon. I explained that I was to fly to the West Coast that morning and offered to meet with him after I returned. Chris, Natalia, and I were going to San Francisco as guests of Metropolitan Community Church in the Castro. After the *New York Times* article appeared, I had been contacted by the pastor and invited to preach there on that coming Sunday. Consequently, the status of the trial was left in limbo for the weekend.

On Saturday morning, Metropolitan held a press conference that proved to be significant. It began with the church's pastor, the Reverend Jim Mitulski, welcoming us. The Reverend Karen Oliveto, pastor of Bethany United Methodist Church, a Reconciling Congregation, also spoke, saying that holy union ceremonies had been conducted at her church for several decades. The Reverend Thomas Kimball, superintendent of the Golden Gate District, gave unqualified support to Karen and Bethany's commitment to provide the ceremonies to same-gender couples. He said the cabinet of the California-Nevada United Methodist Annual Conference, headed by Bishop Melvin G. Talbert, was "'unequivocal' in supporting 'the right of our pastors' to be pastors in the local settings. Kimball said the cabinet 'affirmed' Bethany's decision to 'provide opportunity and space for celebration of holy unions between loving, committed life partners.'"[6]

Because the women of Metropolitan were away on a weekend retreat, I was scheduled to preach Sunday evening after the retreat was over. So, Chris, Natalia, and I went to Glide Memorial United Methodist Church for morning worship. Cecil Williams, its charismatic pastor, is legendary in San Francisco and in The United Methodist Church as a prophet who embodies God's grace and dismantles all kinds of barriers for those on the margins of society. The three morning services at Glide are attended by people from diverse backgrounds and situations — rich and poor, powerful and powerless, believers and doubters. All are welcome without regard to status or condition. People stand in line to get in and if you don't arrive early, you don't get a seat. Cecil had reserved space on a second row pew for us so we'd be sure to have a place to sit when we arrived. During the service, he invited us to join him in the chancel area to introduce and welcome us. He explained to the congregation about the covenant ceremony and the pending trial. He prayed a blessing on us and the congregation applauded wildly. The support was tremendous.

Sunday evening, the Metropolitan sanctuary was packed. When the pews filled to capacity, people sat on the floor in front of the raised chancel area and stood in the side aisles, behind the back pews, and in the foyer. The windows were opened so the people who couldn't get in could stand outside and listen to the service. Invited clergy from various denominations in the Bay Area sat with us on stage in the chancel.

The worship service had the spirit and energy of a revival meeting. The music and singing rocked. Each of the guest clergy spoke briefly. The Reverend Bruce McSpadden, United Methodist superintendent of the Bay View District, said: "It is not the Omaha pastor who is on trial, but the denomination. I am here to stand in repentance because of the church's 'sin' against sexual minorities." He declared his hope that the final result of the matter might be that "every church and United Methodist institution might be transformed to be open to all persons."[7]

District Superintendent Thomas Kimball announced to me for everyone to hear: "If Nebraska kicks you out, we'll find a place for you."[8] The congregation roared approval.

Finally, I spoke, telling about Adam, the Raleigh Religious Network for Gay and Lesbian Equality, Mary and Martha, and the coming trial. The congregation was tremendously supportive and affirming. The spirit of God was palpable in the gathering, dissolving the many of us into one.

It was no secret that The United Methodist Church was divided on the question of whether it should accept lesbian, gay, bisexual, and transgender people. But never before had the leadership of an annual conference spoken so boldly about its unconditional acceptance of gay people, doing so as a direct challenge to another annual conference and to the denomination as a whole. This public differing with the Nebraska Annual Conference exposed the unevenness of how *The Book of Discipline* was interpreted and applied, and the geographic and cultural differences within The United Methodist Church. I was being prosecuted in the Nebraska Annual Conference for having performed a covenant ceremony, but I would not have been in the California-Nevada Annual Conference.

It was bold and courageous for the bishop and cabinet of the California-Nevada Annual Conference to go public about their position. They understood that this trial wasn't really about me but was about how the church's exclusion and abuse of lesbian, gay, bisexual, and transgender people had compromised its ministry. The California-Nevada Annual Conference leadership had offered, in effect, the first defense and verdict on my behalf, even before a Judicial Council ruling or the convening of a trial court. Everyone across the country now knew that The United Methodist Church was not of one mind on the issue of homosexuality, nor on the reading of the Social Principles. If the prohibition was not legally binding in California, how could it be in Nebraska?

Additional evidence of the inconsistency within The United Methodist Church regarding homosexuality came to us in an extraordinary and unexpected letter from United Methodist Bishop Susan M. Morrison and the cabinet of the Troy Annual Conference (consisting of Vermont and northeastern New York State). Acknowledging "over 20 years of opposition to the official position of The United Methodist Church on the practice of homosexuality," the letter stated: "We also support Reverend James Creech's decision to respond to the pastoral needs of members of his congregation by performing a service of Holy Union." Mike, Doug, and I were ecstatic. The California-Nevada and the Troy Annual Conferences had provided proof that The United Methodist Church's leadership was not unanimous on this issue. This made nonsense of the charge that I had been disobedient to The United Methodist Church.

On my return from San Francisco, I met with Marv Koelling, Susan Davies, and Bishop Martínez at his office in Lincoln. I had been told to come alone. The bishop and the two district superintendents had prepared what they called a "Tentative Agreement on Suspension" that they wanted me to sign. It was a list of conditions, including reaffirming my promise not to conduct a same-gender covenant ceremony during the judicial process, making reconciliation and healing within the congregation my priority, "minimizing" my contact with the media, and focusing on Lenten and Easter themes in my preaching and teaching.

The four of us spent two and a half hours talking about what this agreement meant, what the real issues were, and how the agreement would be monitored. My first impulse was to sign it. I wanted to trust them and be cooperative. More important, I wanted to return to First Church. But I had learned the hard way that my desire to cooperate often put me in a vulnerable and compromised position. So I asked questions and pushed for clarification of several issues.

Returning to First Church with restrictions was troubling. I felt that the agreement was vague and set me up for other charges of misconduct. I would refrain from conducting a covenant ceremony, and of course I would work at reconciliation with the opposition in the congregation, but tying my hands in the pulpit and with the media was not acceptable to me. By having me focus on Lenten and Easter themes in preaching, the bishop and the two superintendents wanted me to avoid controversial subjects in my sermons, subjects such as the death penalty and the full inclusion of gay people in the life of the church. I said this was unacceptable: how could I preach about the crucifixion and the resurrection without relating them to the realities of our day? And I insisted that I had a responsibility to be available and open to the media. After much discussion, they accepted my positions, allowing for appropriate references to controversial issues in sermons and for candor with the media. But they wanted to leave the wording of the agreement unchanged. I was not prepared to sign. Something didn't feel right. The written agreement—not the negotiated interpretation of it reached privately in the bishop's office—would be the basis of any criticized or contested behavior on my part. Most of all, I had learned not to trust Bishop Martínez. He was essentially putting me on probation, and he could use any appearance of my breaking the written agreement as justification to remove me from First Church. I said I would need to think about the agreement overnight, and that I would let them know my decision the next morning. We parted, understanding that if I should sign the agreement, my suspension would be lifted immediately and the trial would be put on hold.

My gut feeling was not to sign, even though that almost certainly meant I would never return to First Church. I conferred with Chris and Mike McClellan, and they agreed with me, both saying that if I signed, I would be setting myself up to be removed without due process. That night, I called the bishop, Marv, and Susan to tell them that I would not sign the agreement. "I am an elder in The United Methodist Church serving under the guidance and authority of *The Book of Discipline*, to which I am accountable," I said. "That's a sufficient basis to evaluate my ministry. I expect to be treated like all other clergy. The suspension must end without conditions."

My position was unacceptable to Bishop Martínez, and the suspension remained in effect. Consequently, the request for a Judicial Council ruling was withdrawn and preparations for the trial proceeded. It was, as Mike McClellan said, "an opportunity lost." The United Methodist Church had lost the opportunity to avoid a trial and allow the Judicial Council to make a ruling. And I had lost the opportunity to return to First Church.

The eight days left before the trial were packed with things to do. Since the Committee on Investigation announced its decision in January, Supporting the Vision had been organizing for the trial and was now in a frenzy of preparation. Supporters from all over the country were coming to Kearney to observe the trial and give us support. The vision group organized to provide housing, transportation, and entertainment for them. The Regency Inn was designated as our headquarters.

While attention and energy were intensely focused on the trial, the leadership within First Church had not forgotten its Vision Focus and future. On Tuesday, March 3, the Missions and Social Action Commission, undaunted by potential fallout from the trial, voted to recommend to the Church Council that a process be initiated to study the possibility of First Church becoming a Reconciling Congregation. It would be a slow process, but one that was faithful to the congregation's vision.

The trial became a hot topic in the news once again. In addition to the Nebraska media, the national media—including the *Los Angeles Times*, National Public Radio, and CNN—called me for interviews. Our living room on Jackson Street became a studio for videotaping interviews and meetings with reporters. At the end of one telephone interview, a reporter for a radio station from somewhere in the middle of Nebraska said, his voice choked with tears: "This is off the record, but I want you to know how much I appreciate what you've done. I'm not out, and can't be. But your support means a lot to me personally and to my community."

Chapter 10　　**THE CHURCH ON TRIAL**

"Good morning, Jimmy, this is Bill Finlator.[1] How are you?" Bill was calling from Raleigh early on Wednesday morning, March 11. Chris and I were in Omaha, packed and about to leave for Kearney. The pretrial meeting was to begin at noon. Chris had answered the phone, chatted briefly with Bill, and then handed the phone to me. My mind was on the trial, and I was anxious. Bill's familiar and cheerful voice relaxed me immediately.

"I'm okay," I replied. "Nervous, but also calm in a strange way."

Bill asked, "Did Mahan ever tell you his story about what he said when he was asked if he had a particular Bible verse that comforted him during the controversy at Pullen?"[2]

"No, I don't think so," I replied.

"Well, Mahan says he thought for a moment, then answered, 'Well, yes, the twenty-third psalm. You know, the Lord is my shepherd, so . . . what the hell!'" Bill chuckled, and I laughed with him.

It was a welcome gift of humor and wisdom on the eve of an ominous three-day ordeal. Bill's story helped to put my part in the trial into perspective. I knew that the trial, and the bigotry within The United Methodist Church and our society that had led to it, were much bigger and more important than I was. Whatever might happen to me was much less important than what the church decided. I wasn't really the one on trial. The United Methodist Church was.

"Don't worry about a thing," Bill said. "You've done the right thing, no matter how all this turns out."

My strange calmness continued as Chris and I drove to Kearney, even though I expected to be found guilty. Perhaps it was because the long ordeal of waiting was finally coming to an end. I knew I had the easiest role, while Mike and Doug had all the work to do for our side and felt the emotional burden of success or failure. They had prepared diligently, and I had complete confidence that they would perform superbly. Chris could not have been more supportive and helpful. She was never anxious or despondent. She translated her feelings of anger, disappointment, and frustration into action, always working on something she believed would make things better. She had affirmed and stood by my decision to conduct the covenant ceremony, in spite of the potential consequences to her as well as to me. She encouraged me during the suspension, helping me deal with so much empty time at home in positive ways. She had worked hard with Supporting the Vision to keep things going at First Church and to mobilize support at the trial. And, though always busy, Chris never withdrew from intimacy with me.

Most of all, I was confident that what I had done was right, even though I didn't think I was perfect in knowledge or wisdom. I had acted with integrity, and I had no regrets. I would do it all again and in the same way, even knowing all the consequences in advance. I had only a slight hope that the jury would rise above the pressure from the bishop and angry clergy and lay people to make the right decision.

My trial had become the vortex of the intense debate about homosexuality raging throughout The United Methodist Church like a midwestern tornado. By coincidence, that same week a final report was released by a convocation of liberal and conservative church leaders that had met twice, once in Nashville in 1997 and once in Dallas just a month before my trial. The convocation, sponsored by the United Methodist General Commission on Christian Unity and Interreligious Concerns, was intended to be, as the report explained, a "dialogue on theological diversity within The United Methodist Church."[3] Entitled "In Search of Unity," the report said: "In recent years there has been growing tension within The United Methodist Church. Controversies over social issues have led to the realization that a deeper layer of tension exists concerning the role and authority of scripture and divine revelation. Today, some persons suggest that a split could occur in The United Methodist Church because of the depth of the conflict and the disturbing choices people feel compelled to make."[4] Regarding the issue of homosexuality, the report stated: "There are those who in conscience can accept the continuation of divergent points of view within the church structure and those who in conscience cannot."[5] It continues: "The challenges facing the church in the preservation of unity are daunting."[6] The contending passionate interests involved in my trial in Kearney certainly proved that point.

A snowstorm had hit Nebraska just days before the trial. Snow and ice still covered the ground in Kearney, and daytime high temperatures were just above zero. Nonetheless, supporters from all over the country, including a large contingent of First Church members, had begun to arrive in Kearney on Tuesday, the day before Chris and I drove there. They had taken vacation time, personal leave, and sick days from work to be there. Some brought their children. Some had been sent by their congregations, which had collected special offerings to cover their expenses. In many ways, the gathering at the trial resembled a church retreat or conference. Opponents of the covenant ceremony also came, including official representatives from the Confessing Movement and the Good News evangelical caucus.

The members of Supporting the Vision had been fully engaged in supporting me and preparing for the trial. They did so not only because they cared for me and about what could happen to me, but because they believed that God was calling First Church to become truly inconclusive. Joyce Elder, one of the group's leaders, told me later: "We were passionate about saving you, helping you, supporting you in all the ways that we could. If we saved you, then we saved all that we wanted to be as the church. Saving you became the one bold statement we could make about who we were as the church."

The group worked with the media, arranging interviews and writing statements and press releases. A graphic designer produced sweatshirts for supporters to wear, featuring a rainbow background over which was written: "Supporting All God's Children—First United Methodist Church, Omaha, Nebraska." The group had large buttons made up that read: "Supporting Jimmy—All God's Children." A suite at the Regency Inn served as a hospitality and command center, called Vision Central. It was equipped with a fax machine, copying machine, and computer, on which group members regularly sent trial updates out over the Internet.

Packets of information were available in Vision Central for the media and supporters coming to Kearney to observe the trial, including a "Guide to the Trial of Jimmy Creech" (a timeline of events leading up to the trial; biographies of the defense team members; a schedule of the trial; a piece on the Social Principles; the "In All Things Charity" statement; my written response to the charge against me; articles about homosexuality, a copy of Walter Wink's booklet, *Homosexuality and the Bible*;[7] and maps, lists of hotels and restaurants, and things to see and do in Kearney).

Chris and I arrived at the First United Methodist Church, Kearney, for the noon pretrial meeting with Bishop Hodapp, Doug and Mike, and the prosecution team. The parking lot was packed, and TV satellite trucks and reporters were everywhere. We had to park some distance away and walk to the church through the snow, with the wind chill temperature twenty-seven degrees below zero. Reporters spotted us coming up the hill and rushed out of the church, surrounded us, and followed us inside, asking questions along the way. The entrance was crowded with prospective jurors, people who had come to observe the trial, and church staff still preparing the facility for the trial.

In a small classroom away from the crowd, Bishop Hodapp reviewed the trial schedule and procedures with us. Jury selection would begin at one that afternoon, with a recess at five. If the jury selection was not complete by then, we would return that night to finish up. The trial itself would begin the next morning, Thursday, at eight and continue on Friday until a verdict had been rendered. There would be night sessions if necessary. Should the jury render a guilty verdict, the bishop explained, the penalty options included a simple reprimand, suspension, and the withdrawal of my credentials of ordination—as well as the most severe penalty, expulsion from The United Methodist Church. I knew the latter was one of the options, but I hadn't expected the bishop to include it in his instructions to the jury.

"Bishop," I asked, "do you mean I could be expelled from this church that I was baptized in, confirmed in, and have been a part of all my life and served as a pastor for twenty-eight years? You would instruct the jury to consider doing that to me?"

My question made Bishop Hodapp visibly uncomfortable, and he became quiet and pensive. After a few minutes, he said softly: "Well, this option is really for cases involving convictions of lay people, since that's about the only significant punishment the church could give them. In your case, however, I think it's not; so I'll not include this option when I instruct the jury."

Throughout the meeting, the bishop was decisive, reasonable, and considerate. He had been through this experience before, having presided over five other trials—all of which involved clergy accused of sexual misconduct.

He seemed to deeply regret that my trial had to take place. But since it was happening, he made it clear that he would do everything to ensure a fair process for everyone.

The church's Family Life Center, a large multipurpose room, had been transformed into a makeshift courtroom. A table was set up near the back wall for Bishop Hodapp, just beneath a basketball hoop. Just to the right of the bishop, two rows of chairs for the jury lined the side wall. A single chair to the left of the bishop was the witness stand. The defense and prosecution teams sat at two tables along the free-throw line, separated by a small lectern. Lauren Ekdahl and Warren Urbom sat on the right, while Doug Williamson, Mike McClellan, and I sat on the left. The rest of the room behind us was filled with several hundred chairs for observers.

As Chris and I made our way into the courtroom, television crews and photographers once again surrounded and followed us in. I kissed and hugged Chris before going to my seat at the defense table. Supporting the Vision had reserved a chair for her in the first row, right behind me.

"This is not a civil trial," Bishop Hodapp announced as he began the proceeding. "We are not bound by civil law. We are only bound by a process of fairness. And we'll do our best to follow that out. We put a small cross here," gesturing toward a small table in front of him, "simply to indicate that this is a church proceeding, and that we hope and pray that it may be done in the spirit of Jesus Christ, and that we may maintain that kind of order and discipline among ourselves, and that we may, both participants and onlookers, keep that spirit in all that we do over these three days."[8] With that, jury selection began.

A jury pool of thirty-five ordained United Methodist elders from all over the Nebraska Annual Conference, seated at the front of the audience, had been carefully selected by the eight district superintendents. Twenty-three of the thirty-five were chosen by lot to be interviewed as potential jurors. The defense and prosecution were to select from these clergy thirteen jurors and two alternates.

Lauren Ekdahl was the first to question the prospective jurors. He stood behind the lectern and asked a series of general questions, such as whether anyone knew me or Doug, or belonged to the Methodist Federation for Social Action or any organization outside the church that advocates greater rights for or service to homosexual people. He asked if anyone had already formed an opinion about my guilt or innocence. No one spoke up. Then he asked if the potential jurors could set aside any information or knowledge or relationship that they might have in order to make an objective decision based solely on the evidence presented during the trial. All of the prospective jurors said they could be objective. Lauren concluded by asking: "Is there any reason that you can think of that you might not be fair and impartial to both The United Methodist Church and Jimmy Creech in this case?" When no one responded, Lauren left the lectern and sat down.

Mike McClellan understood jury selection to be more than just picking thirteen clergy to serve. It was an opportunity to establish a relationship with the prospective jurors, to preview the defense, and to educate the jury pool and observers. Carefully prepared and coached by Mike, Doug stood directly in front of the potential jurors, rather than behind the lectern, and addressed them as a pastor rather than as a trial lawyer, showing himself to be gentle, engaging, and sensitive. As he spoke, he maintained constant eye contact with the potential jurors. He was relaxed and friendly, his tone not one of interrogation.

"We don't intend for this process to embarrass anyone," he said, "or to make you feel ill at ease, but we need to delve into any preconceived notions that might be floating around; and, hopefully, into your hearts and minds just a little bit. Now, that brings up a very sensitive subject: sex; or, rather, issues dealing with human sexuality. And there is no way to get around this subject. The United Methodist Church is prosecuting Reverend Creech for a reason that puts human sexuality, with all of its mystery, all of the different understandings about it, right at the forefront. To a large degree this trial is about human sexuality, and how the church deals with that subject. But, with your permission, I'd like to get off of the subject of sex for a moment. Is my face still red? No?"

Having eased the tension, Doug switched to questions about what he termed "mundane subjects." He asked for a show of hands of those who owned copies of *The Book of Discipline*, *The United Methodist Book of Worship*, and *The Book of Resolutions of The United Methodist Church*. He asked: "Have any of you considered the Social Principles at any time to be binding ecclesiastical law?" None had. "Have any of you ever filed a complaint against another United Methodist pastor?" None had. "Okay," he continued, "I'd like to shift to worship for a moment. How many of you would agree with this statement: 'United Methodist ministers can perform only

those rituals that are the official rituals of The United Methodist Church?'
Okay. So no one would agree with that."

"Now, I've noticed that your eyes are bleary," he said jokingly, "so gently
and gingerly I'm going to come back to sex. Has anyone taken a course or
a class dealing with human sexuality?" Doug asked everyone who raised a
hand what he or she had learned, and what of importance had come out of
the experience. This conversation continued for some time, with the prospective jurors reflecting on lessons learned in formal educational settings.

Doug had talked with the jury pool for nearly an hour when he asked:
"Has anyone here struggled with issues dealing with homosexuality anytime in your life or with anyone in your life, family members or friends?"

At first, no one responded. Then, slowly, hands began to rise. "Okay.
Thank you," he said. "I'd like to ask those of you who put up your hand to
say a little bit about it. I realize that some of the specifics may be hard to
talk about, but could you say a little bit about the issues with which you've
struggled?"

In this cavernous room, surrounded by nearly four hundred hushed ob
servers, the prospective jurors talked one by one about lesbians and gay
men they had known who had profoundly affected their lives.

The first person to speak said: "I have an older sister who is lesbian, has
had a partner probably for the last fifteen years. I see her every four to five
years. She lives in British Columbia. We talk a couple times a year. I know
that she has been hurt by the church because of her sexual orientation.
When she was here for my ordination, she went to church three times and
that was more than she'd been in twenty years."

"My best friend in high school called me about six or seven years ago, announced to me that he was gay," said another juror. "And in the last thirty-
five years or so, I hadn't had a lot of contact with him. Since he called, we
have had a lot of contact. And he is studying for the ministry. It did not destroy a relationship that we had. Matter of fact, it renewed it."

Another juror told about his freshman year in college when he "had a
friend who was homosexual and came from a very strict background, and
wanted to kill himself because his family believed that that was an abomination. I just went through that with him."

On and on the stories came, each making the next person more eager
to speak. There were stories about friends from seminary days, a former

husband, respected clergy colleagues and church members who were lesbian or gay. "In college," one woman said, "I developed a friendship with a young man who confided in me that he was gay. He was an extraordinarily bright and entertaining friend, and since I was going to college as a married woman, it was nice to have a young male friend with whom I felt safe and comfortable. And my whole attitude I think towards the issue of homosexuality changed basically the day that he confided in me that he was gay. We've remained in touch since college. He's been in a committed relationship for thirty-some years."

One potential juror told about "a clergy friend, a United Methodist, in another conference who has never told me she is lesbian, but I've been in the home, and she has a partner, so it bothers me that we have never talked about it. I think I've waited on her to say it, you know, struggled with the fact that I've not said it to her. And I understand why, because of our denominational rules, that she won't necessarily self-avow."

Doug asked: "Have you—and I realize that this is a difficult question, a delicate question—have you considered, since you seem to be fairly certain about it, have you considered asking her to turn in her credentials, or filing charges against her?"

"No. No," she responded. "I've—I've considered asking her why we haven't talked about this."

"Okay," Doug said. "And you're aware of our denominational rules?"

"Yes."

"What is more important than the denominational rules in this case for you?" Doug persisted.

"Our friendship."

"Is she in your opinion an effective pastor?"

"Yes. Very effective."

Another prospective juror described how she now felt that she had failed a friend who had reached out to her: "I was part of a very conservative religious group about twenty years ago, and I had a friend in the midst of my wedding preparations confide that she was beginning to struggle with her sexual orientation. And I realize, in reflecting upon that many times over the years, that I failed my friend. Because I allowed the busyness to separate us. And she was not in a safe enough place where she could reach out to others and I was moving away and getting married. And so I've had to reflect back on those conservative circles I was in at the time and how that caused me to react to a friend—and cost me a friendship."

Doug asked: "When you talk about not being in a safe enough place for her to reach out to you, would you be willing to say a bit more about what you mean by that? What made it unsafe?"

She replied: "The church was very ultraconservative. Nowadays, I would call it fairly fundamental. And the preaching from the pulpit and the re-action of other people would be very condemning to her if she had made that known publicly. As it was, she approached me one-on-one and I didn't reciprocate."

"It sounds as though this was an important experience in your life," Doug observed. "Has it shaped your ministry with gay men and lesbians in any way?"

"I think it's affected my empathy for other people and realizing that the people around me at times have an effect on my theology and my theology affects the way I live things out. And the theology I've come to in the last number of years by reflecting on that experience. I couldn't have articulated it at the time."

"What would be the one thing you would do differently at this point in your life, if you could live that situation again? What would be the one thing you might do differently?"

"I would love her no matter what. And be there for her."

Nineteen of the twenty-three potential jurors had had at least one person who was gay or lesbian who had influenced their lives, someone who would be in their minds throughout the trial, someone they could not ignore or dismiss, someone whose dignity and integrity they could not deny, some-one they were accountable to in a deeply personal and pastoral way. They had told their stories with care and consideration, each as if he or she was alone with Doug and speaking only to him, sometimes almost in a whisper. On two occasions Bishop Hodapp had to ask prospective jurors to speak up. "I'm sorry, I'm still straining to hear," he pleaded. "Let me advise you, you're a bunch of United Methodist preachers and I'm sitting on about where the fourth or fifth pew would be in your churches and I can't even hear you." But we all heard and felt the emotional power of the stories, and the trial was transformed.

Bill Kelly, covering the trial for the Nebraska Educational TV Network, passed a note to Doug as he returned to his seat after the stories were told. "If verdicts were based on jury questioning," the note said, "you'd be drinking champagne right now!"

Recognizing the impact of the stories, Lauren asked the jury pool a follow-up question: "You've given us some very moving stories of relationships that are important to you. Do you think that they will color your attitude or your opinion as you listen to the evidence in this trial?" No one said that the stories would influence their judgment, but we all knew that everyone—jurors, judge, prosecution, and defense alike—were now accountable to the invisible witnesses they had invoked.

Of the twenty-three in the immediate pool, eight were eliminated, leaving the remaining to serve as the jury and two alternates. If anyone had had any illusion that the trial would be a dispassionate deliberation on church law, that illusion had been dispelled by the jury selection process.

The next morning, I felt very different as I took my seat at the defense table. The day before, the attention had been on the jury and I had been a bystander. But this day, I knew the attention was squarely on me. "Today," I thought, "the whole United Methodist Church, with all of its resources, intends to prove me guilty of disobedience and punish me for honoring the love of two people." It was surreal.

After calling us to order and giving an opening prayer, Bishop Hodapp looked at me and said, "Jimmy, the charge against you is disobedience to the Order and Discipline of The United Methodist Church. How do you plead?"

"Not guilty," I responded.

Bishop Hodapp instructed the jurors on their duty, explaining that the burden of proving me guilty, "by clear and convincing evidence," was on The United Methodist Church. He then called on Lauren Ekdahl to make his opening statement to the jury.

Lauren reviewed the charge against me and told the jury that the evidence would prove I had created an "illegal" ritual and conducted a "homosexual union" in "disobedience" to the Church. "Let me hasten to say," he said, "that this trial is not about the nature of homosexuality, whether it is a chosen or genetically determined sexual preference. This trial is about an action taken by Jimmy Creech that is clearly forbidden by the current *Discipline* of The United Methodist Church."

Doug Williamson responded in his opening statement: "The Counsel for the Church has told you that the issues of homosexuality and sexuality are not issues in this trial. But, if you read the charge, you will see terms clearly related to sexuality." Doug argued that, instead of being irrelevant, sexuality, gender, and sexual orientation were "at the heart" of the trial.

Lauren called me to the stand as his first witness. He asked if I had celebrated a "homosexual union" for two women at First Church on September 14, 1997. He was startled when I replied, "No." He pressed me to explain, and I said that I didn't understand the term "homosexual union," it was not defined in *The Book of Discipline*, and it had no meaning to me. I had conducted a covenant ceremony for two women, I said.

Lauren asked if the ceremony was essentially the same as the service of Christian marriage found in *The United Methodist Book of Worship*, with an exchange of vows and rings. I said that it was. He asked: "You offered a prayer of blessing upon them and expected they would then create a home together. Do you agree that there was a union?"

"Yes," I replied. "There was a spiritual union that was actually confirmed and celebrated by the covenant ceremony."

"Was there any difference between their ceremony and a marriage ceremony?" Lauren asked.

"Yes, a very significant difference," I explained. "A marriage ceremony involves two parts. There is a covenant ceremony that is a celebration of the spiritual commitment of love and fidelity by two people to one another. Then, clergy act as agents of the state to give legal recognition to that spiritual union, so that it becomes a legal contract recognized by the state. The legality, the legal sanction was not a part of this covenant ceremony."

"So the primary difference between this and the normal ritual of marriage," Lauren said, "was that it would not be recognized by the state and it involved two persons of the same sex. Would that be correct?"

"That is correct," I said.

When Doug cross examined me, he addressed issues raised in Lauren's opening statement and questions to me on the witness stand. Lauren had accused me of breaking covenant with my colleagues, The United Methodist Church, and *The Book of Discipline*. Doug said: "We've heard some conversation about covenants that are important, covenants that we have with each other as clergy, with our local church. Would you talk about some of these covenants that shape your ministry?"

"I think the baptismal covenant is prior to all covenants for us as Christians and as United Methodists," I answered. I explained that when we are baptized, "among the first questions asked of us is, 'do we accept the freedom and the power that God gives to us to resist evil, injustice, and oppression, in whatever forms they take?' I take that very seriously. 'In whatever forms they take,' and wherever they may be found."

Another covenant that's important to me as a pastor, I said, is the one with the local church, the parish: "I take the covenant with the local congregation very seriously. I think ministry grows out of the context of a congregation and the covenant that exists between pastor and people. I understood the covenant ceremony to be a living out of the covenant that I have with the congregation. The two women were members of First United Methodist Church in Omaha. I was responding to them as their pastor to give them pastoral support and care, to be a witness to them of God's grace, God's love."

Lauren's next witness was Bishop Kenneth Hicks from Little Rock, Arkansas. (All of the witnesses, except for me, were sequestered in a room in another part of the building, unable to hear any of the trial that preceded their testimony.) Bishop Hicks was well known and respected in Nebraska. He had been ordained and served churches there until he was elected to the episcopacy in 1976. He had retired in 1992. Lauren questioned him about what pastors should do if they find themselves in disagreement with the church and *The Book of Discipline* and, specifically, what would be "the appropriate response" for a United Methodist pastor if asked to conduct a "homosexual union"?

"I feel that, as a United Methodist minister, I am bound and have committed myself to uphold the covenant of the ministry in The United Methodist Church, the Order and Discipline of the church," Bishop Hicks replied. "Inasmuch as I am a United Methodist minister, I will uphold the position of the church. I feel bound to adhere to the guidance, to the law, as well as to the support of the church of which I'm a part." In light of the prohibition, he said, "a pastor would need to say to himself or herself, 'How much do I want to be a United Methodist minister?' and, 'Do I want to be a United Methodist minister, you know, regardless?'"

Bishop Hicks said it would be appropriate, if asked by two women or two men to conduct a covenant ceremony, to refer them to another denomination where such ceremonies are accepted. Even so, the couple should be invited "back into the life of The United Methodist Church. I can't think of any circumstance where it would be the Christian thing to exclude anyone from the ministry and from inclusion in The United Methodist Church."

Lauren had a final question for the bishop: "If a pastor informed you that he or she planned to perform a ceremony for a homosexual union, what would you advise that pastor?"

"I would tell that pastor that that kind of service should not be held," Bishop Hicks replied. "It would bring considerable dissension and strife to the pastor and to the life of The United Methodist Church. It would, it seems to me, contribute to the unraveling of the fabric that makes our church as strong and as effective as it is. I would indicate to the pastor to continue to be supportive to the individuals. No sincere pastor wants to make decisions that would be hurtful to anyone. But, given the nature of our church, this is what I feel they must do in order to be faithful. And I think there's some responsibility on the part of the people who have come asking for that service to assume their share of the responsibility that the pastor is not able to do this at this time."

In his cross-examination, Doug asked Bishop Hicks, if, given the fact that the introduction to the Social Principles says that they "are intended to be instructive and persuasive in the best prophetic spirit, and there's no distinction made between them," the bishop said he thought putting the prohibition in the Social Principles created ambiguity about its legal status.

"The Social Principles as a whole are, as you indicate, instructive," the bishop answered. "Once in a while there does creep into them something that the General Conference clearly has indicated to be a mandate, and therefore, it must be adhered to and enforced. Yes, there are some ambiguities. However, the statement itself, you know, is very clear."

"Do all our bishops agree with you on your opinion on this matter?" Doug asked.

"I do not know," Hicks replied. "I have not talked with them."

The prosecution called no other witnesses. My testimony and that of Bishop Kenneth Hicks was all the evidence the prosecution thought it needed to convince the jury of my guilt. What evidence had Lauren Ekdahl established? That I had conducted a covenant ceremony for two women, virtually identical to a United Methodist marriage ceremony, and that at least one bishop of The United Methodist Church believed that the prohibition of "homosexual unions" was an enforceable mandate of the church in spite of its location within the Social Principles. In addition, Bishop Hicks had argued that the policies and laws of the church take precedence over individual conscience, and that a pastor who doesn't agree with the church should leave it.

With the church having rested its case against me, it was time for us to present our defense. Doug's first witness was the Reverend Glenn Loy. It was evident that Glenn did not want to be at the trial, much less be questioned. Doug's questions were straightforward and civil, yet Glenn glared at him with apparent annoyance and hostility throughout his testimony.

When asked to explain his understanding of the Social Principles, Glenn said that not all of the principles were church law, but when "General Conference takes a vote on something and puts the word 'shall' and 'shall not' in, it's pretty clear what they intend for you to do with it." Glenn filed the complaint, he said, because he believed I had broken a church law when I conducted the covenant ceremony. When Doug asked him to describe the ceremony, Glenn angrily responded: "Well, there again, you know, I wasn't given all the details that afternoon, so I filed a complaint. But since then, I was right. Now, what do you want to do with that?"

"Why would you file a complaint against a fellow pastor if you were not certain what happened on that occasion?" Doug persisted.

"Because it is a matter of conscience to me that we follow *The Discipline*. And I knew that without being there. I know what you're getting at, you know, 'were you there?' No, I wasn't there. But he told the bishop's office what he was going to do, he did it, and I filed."

The irony of Glenn appealing to conscience was astounding, considering that he had dismissed my act of conscience as purely self-serving. But the conscience that Glenn appealed to was constrained by *The Book of Discipline*, not one free to follow a higher standard of justice.

Doug called the Reverend Don Bredthauer, my colleague at First Church, as his next witness. Don was among the most highly esteemed and trusted pastors in the Nebraska Annual Conference. He described his experience over the past ten years observing the transformation of First Church from "a tall-steeple church, perhaps a little bit aloof and exclusive" to one that had become "very intentional about living the gospel of Jesus Christ in the community, and sharing the good news of God's love and justice. At the same time that we've been more community-oriented," he said, "we've also taken very seriously an intentional spiritual formation ministry. We've tried to develop both areas of ministry at the same time, because we believe they're both important and they go hand-in-hand. You can't have one without the other."

Don went on to explain the process that the congregation used to develop the Vision Focus, which was completed after I came to First Church.

"Don, say a bit about what Jimmy Creech brought to this ministry, this vision?" Doug asked.

"Well," Don replied, "Jimmy brought integrity. He brought a sense of faithfulness to the gospel of Jesus Christ. He brought an ability to articulate that gospel. He brought spiritual depth. And I think what he did regarding the Vision Focus in particular was to instill within us who had developed this vision a sense of hope and possibility that we could actually bring this vision, which we believed was God's vision for us, into reality. And I have very much appreciated the kind of support that he's given to this vision and the kind of leadership that he's given to it."

"So, would you place the covenant ceremony within the context of a ministry faithful to the Vision Focus of First Church, faithful to the gospel?"

"Yes, I would. The covenant ceremony was a way to give support to a new family, as they sought to commit themselves together in love and faithfulness, seeking God's blessing, and to give a spiritual undergirding to the beginning of that new family."

Doug asked Don how First Church had fared during the controversy ignited by the covenant ceremony, and Don described the division within the congregation. He explained that some members had left, while others became inactive and withheld financial support. "On the other side," Don continued, "the majority of the active leadership of the church has been very, very supportive. It's been exciting to see how committed they are, how they are learning to be a church, to support its ministries, to take leadership in its ministries and how they have dug deeply financially to support the church. And so, for all the pain and distress that it has caused us, it's also been a very exciting time to be a part of First United Methodist Church."

It was Doug's intent to establish that my ministry was consistent with the Vision Focus of First Church. After Don had spoken about this as one of the church's pastors, three key lay leaders who had held the position of chairperson of the Staff-Parish Relations Committee were called in succession and asked about my ministry in the context of the Vision Focus. Joan Byerhof said: "I think the cabinet and bishop did a fine job of matching Jimmy Creech with our congregation. We were in need of leadership at that time, and he brought that leadership to us. We were in need of an awakening in ideas, and he brought that to us."

Joanie Zetterman said: "Our Vision Focus talks about inclusiveness of all people and I recall Jimmy saying in his first sermon at First United Methodist Church that he saw Jesus's message as one of peace, love and justice for all people. And I believe performing the covenant service follows directly with both of those, the church's Vision Focus, as well as what Jimmy had been preaching."

Bill Jenks said: "The thing that means the most to me, in characterizing Jimmy's ministry, and especially in relation to the Vision Focus, is that Jimmy lives his beliefs. He lives his faith. He lives our vision. He doesn't just talk about it. And it's been a revelation to me and to many in our church to see that, and to participate in it, and to follow him in that. He's very concerned with oppressed peoples, wherever they may be and in whatever way they are oppressed. People without a voice. That kind of thing he's very concerned about, and very effective at shining the light where it's been dark, so that we can all see that, and begin to do something about it. The church's treatment of gay people is an issue that we all have to face and grapple with. And it goes to the heart of what it is to be a Christian. We need to face this issue as Christians, and face our own fear, and that can't be done if somebody isn't doing it. If we only talk about it, we're only talking. Until we live it, it's not real."

After Bill's testimony, Bishop Hodapp recessed the trial for a break. It was mid-afternoon, and the day had been long and grueling. The testimonies of Don, Joan, Joanie, and Bill had touched me deeply, and I was emotionally drained. The break was a welcome chance to recover a bit. I was to be called as the next witness, and I badly needed to visit the men's room.

Each time we had taken a break so far, the media had rushed into the court area, trying to get a quote from me and other trial participants. I knew that if I lingered, I'd never make it to the men's room, so I quickly left my chair and walked briskly toward the rear door at the sound of the bishop's gavel. As I approached the door, television cameras flooded me with their glaring lights. "Folks, I'm on a mission," I said with urgency, "but I'll be right back to talk with you." They immediately understood. They had played this game before with me—I was always in a hurry for the men's room. This time, however, they decided to have a little fun and followed me down the hallway into the men's room, with cameras on their shoulders and lights still glaring, but without the video recording. Faces of others in the crowded men's room were flushed with horror and embarrassment. Zippers could be heard ripping upward, and the room suddenly emptied. I was standing alone at the urinals, laughing. The members of the media, delighting in their prank, stepped outside to allow me privacy and to wait for a brief interview.

When the trial resumed, I took the witness stand. Doug began by asking me to review for the court my history as a pastor in North Carolina. I talked about the four churches I had served there, and about my work with the North Carolina Council of Churches.

Doug asked me to tell how I was asked to be the senior pastor at First United Methodist Church in Omaha. I told about Susan Davies's telephone call, explained my immediate lack of interest in leaving North Carolina, and described how Susan had piqued my interest by telling me about the various ministries of First Church and its commitment to being truly inclusive. I told the jury that I had said: "Susan, I need to send you some information about me. Because I think if you're going to consider me, you need to know my history, my background. You need to know everything there is to know about me."

I then described my advocacy for gay men and lesbians while I was at Fairmont United Methodist Church, and the controversy that ensued. I explained how, after three years at Fairmont, I had suddenly found myself without an appointment. "I felt after that point in time that I would never again have a chance to be a pastor," I said. "And so when the invitation came to consider the church in Omaha, I was delighted because I feel I'm called to be a pastor, and have a passion for it. So, I sent Susan newspaper articles, things I'd written, things that I felt would inform her and the cabinet about my background. I tried to inform her of everything, so that she and the cabinet would be aware."

"Would you consider yourself to be a social activist?" Doug asked.

"No," I replied, "I'm a pastor. I believe that the gospel of Jesus Christ calls us to be responsive as Christians to all the needs of the world. We have a responsibility to address structures of injustice and oppression that exist in our world. Those are spiritual issues, as well as political issues."

"Then, pursuing that line of thought, do you understand your participation in the covenanting service of September 14th of last year to have grown out of a social activist role, or to have grown authentically out of your pastoral role?"

"It most definitely grew out of my understanding of what it means to be a pastor. It has to do with the integrity of the gospel, the integrity of the church, the integrity of the pastoral office that I'm called to serve."

"We have heard a great deal about events leading up to the ceremony," Doug said, "but could you just refresh our memory? Could you describe the most important events?"

I told the story of Adam's coming out to me at Warsaw United Methodist Church back in 1984, and the impact he had on my life, beginning my process of understanding the spiritual violence that lesbian and gay people experience in The United Methodist Church and society. I told about helping to start and giving leadership to the Raleigh Religious Network for Gay and Lesbian Equality. I continued:

And, in 1990, I celebrated for the first time a union ceremony for two men. And it was for me a very special gift, because these two men entrusted me with who they are, and the love they had for each other, and the commitment they had to each other, and gave me the opportunity to be a witness of God's love, to represent God's love, and to pray God's grace upon them.

Following that, I did several other covenant ceremonies, I think before coming to Nebraska at least a dozen, if not more. All of that prior to the language [the prohibition of homosexual unions] placed in our Social Principles in 1996 at the General Conference in Denver.

When the General Conference added that language, I was very disturbed. I was very upset. I knew that I could not, with the understanding that I have, and the experience that I have, with the commitment to the gospel of Jesus Christ that I have, I could not be guided by that language, and would not be guided by that language.

Following General Conference, Susan Davies called me to officially offer me the appointment to First United Methodist Church. I had prepared for her call, because I was again concerned that there be no misunderstanding about my understanding of ministry and what it means to be a pastor.

And, so in that conversation I said, "Susan, I need to tell you and you need to understand that I'm really upset about what the General Conference has done. I think it's wrong. I think it's unjust. And you should know that, if I am asked to do a covenant ceremony, I will. And if that makes any difference in your offer of the appointment, then that needs to be known now."

And Susan said, "Well, we will walk that road together when it comes."

So, all of that was preparatory for my signing "In All Things Charity" in January of 1997, and being willing and ready to say, "Yes" when two people who were a part of the congregation came to me and gave me the invitation and opportunity to celebrate with them their commitments to one another.

I continued the story, explaining how I had informed Bishop Martínez in January 1997 that I had signed "In All Things Charity," and his telling me in April: "I don't know what I will do. I don't know where I am on this issue, but all I ask is, let me know if and when you agree to do a covenant ceremony."

I said: "And I agreed to let him know. I felt that it was very important, because he was my bishop, and Susan was my district superintendent, that I be completely open to them about my intentions, and also about when I would agree to do a covenant ceremony. I thought not to be open to them would be a way of complying with the guidance that's in the Social Principles. Because it would be hiding, essentially. It would be doing it in secret, and in a way that would be recognizing the prohibition, the prohibitive language that is there, and giving it power and credence. So, I wanted to be open about it completely."

I explained how Mary and Martha had come to me first in the spring and finally in July to request a covenant ceremony, and that I had immediately written to inform the bishop of my intentions. I said that he had not responded until less than two weeks before the ceremony, and that he had then said that as my bishop, he would have to instruct me not to perform it. Nonetheless, I explained, I conducted the ceremony on September 14, 1997, as scheduled.

Doug returned to my experience in North Carolina of suddenly finding myself without an appointment and the pain I felt because of "being asked to pack up and leave." He asked: "We heard one possibility for you this morning from Bishop Hicks; and that is, if you can't live with us, leave. Go to another denomination. Why stay United Methodist?" I replied:

I grew up in The United Methodist Church. It nurtured me. I am who I am because of The United Methodist Church. I was taught the church is here to be a continuing witness to the ministry of Jesus Christ, a ministry that spoke of God's love for all people, that worked for justice, that was compassionate, and sought to offer mercy. And that teaching shaped me, gave me the fundamentals of my faith. I love the tradition of The United Methodist Church that combines spirituality with social justice.

It would be extremely painful for me to leave The United Methodist Church. It would be like leaving family. And I have to tell you that I don't leave family very easily. And I will have to be told to leave. I will not leave voluntarily. I love this church. I hate to see it spiritually crippled by bigotry toward gay people.

I think in order for me to truly serve this denomination, I have to address this issue as clearly as I possibly can, and try to help this family that I'm a part of regain integrity.

"Could you identify for us," Doug asked, "the most important theological point that influenced your decisions? We've heard a lot about law this morning. Can you talk about the theology of ministry that led you to conduct the covenant ceremony?"

"The ministry of Jesus Christ was a witness to God's grace and love for all people without condition," I said. "Jesus went to those whom society considered unfit to be in communion and fellowship with God. Jesus Christ proclaimed the presence of God's realm in the midst of all people, where everyone sat at the same table, where all are equal. To me, that's the essence of the gospel. I believe we are still being driven by the Spirit of God to open doors to communion with God for everyone, to welcome all to the family table. That's the ministry I have as a pastor and the reason I conducted the covenant ceremony."

"Jimmy, has there been any hurt and pain from the reactions to the covenant ceremony?"

"Yes," I replied. "We live in a culture strongly affected by a heterosexual bias. It's a very deep and emotional issue for us, and difficult to understand. Because of that, there have been a number of members of First United Methodist Church who found the ceremony to be offensive, disagreed strongly with it, and felt betrayed by me. And so, yes, there has been pain, but I don't want to put the responsibility for it on the covenant ceremony. Pain was caused by the heterosexism that we are all struggling with. The challenge to see things in new ways, to accept people who we haven't accepted before. While there was immediate pain by some who found this offensive, there had been years of pain for other First Church members because of the church's denial of dignity and respect to gay men and lesbians. Consequently, the covenant ceremony was a sign of hope, an announcement of the 'Good News' [that] the oppressed are free, the captives are at liberty. It was a jubilee event. But, most of all, there were two women who felt the love of God, as they spoke their vows of love and fidelity to one another with their friends and family in the church where they worship and are spiritually nurtured."

Doug had finished his questions to me. It had taken about forty-five minutes, but the time had passed quickly.

Lauren began his cross-examination, asking if I had considered referring the two women to a clergy colleague of another denomination. "No, I did not," I replied. "That would have been telling them they really didn't have a place at First Church, that the ministry and grace of God that is available to members of First Church would not be fully available to them, that they were second-class members; that they really were not accepted. That is what our denomination is communicating to lesbians and gay men, bisexual people and transgender people, and I don't want to be complicit in that message."

"So," Lauren challenged me, "you took it upon yourself to make that decision and not obey the current *Discipline*. Is that right?"

"My decision was to respond to two women when they were prepared to make a commitment of love and fidelity to one another," I explained. "I was not prepared to tell them that they had to wait four or eight or twelve years until the General Conference decided to change its position. I think that would be unconscionable."

"I think it's important for us to know, if you're allowed to come back to First United Methodist Church, do you intend to continue doing covenanting ceremonies?" asked Lauren.

"Yes, I do," I answered.

At five forty-five, we recessed for dinner, reconvening at seven. Doug called the Reverend Dr. Roy Reed, a retired professor of worship and music who had taught at the Methodist Theological School in Ohio for thirty-four years. The formal charge against me claimed that I had disobeyed the Order and Discipline of The United Methodist Church by conducting a ritual not authorized by the General Conference.

"Dr. Reed, to the best of your knowledge," Doug asked, "are there any laws in the church against using ceremonies or rituals other than the official ritual of The United Methodist Church?"

"Not that I know of," he replied.

"Do you understand, from what you've heard, and in discussions with me, that The United Methodist Church is attempting to prosecute Pastor Creech on a charge of using a ritual other than the official ritual of the church?"

"The covenant ceremony certainly is a departure from what's in the official ritual of the church," Dr. Reed answered. "But, then, vast numbers of Methodist clergy depart from the official ritual of the church. As far as the Service of Marriage is concerned, you're dealing with a liturgy that . . . many pastors make more changes [in] than they do in any other liturgy. To single out one thing and say, 'This is something you must do; all the other things you can change,' is just a capricious decision, it seems to me. And to say that there's one thing you can't change, where other things can be changed, certainly within the context of the liturgy itself, doesn't seem to me to be an appropriate conclusion."

"Let me make sure I understand," Doug said. "Just to single out the 'man-and-woman' designation and say you can't change this but you can change other things, you say that's a capricious decision?"

"I think so," Dr. Reed replied, "because I don't see the Methodist Church standing up for other elements in the liturgy in that same way. And, believe me, there are Methodist ministers who change virtually everything in that service."

"If the church charged pastors for using unauthorized ritual or changing authorized ritual, would you hazard an opinion on how many United Methodist pastors would have to be charged?"

"Well," Dr. Reed answered, "almost everybody."

Doug then asked Dr. Reed: "Would you officiate at a covenant service such as the one that Jimmy Creech did?"

"I would," he said without hesitation. "It might not have the same shape. But, yes, I would do that."

"On what authority would you do that?"

"On the authority of the gospel, because of Jesus Christ," Dr. Reed explained. "St. Paul can lay down the norms of the culture of his own day, and we can read in our New Testament the dictums about the life of the church that reflects his culture, given to us by this greatest preacher and theologian the church ever had. Nevertheless, we don't adhere to them [and that is] because of the loving compassionate God we perceive, we see, we hear about, we have been seized by, so to speak, and our understanding, our hearing, and our spirits are moved by this Jesus, who speaks to us in his parabolic teaching, these strange ways in which he doesn't tell us what the kingdom of God is, but shows us what it is in stories, and the life of sacrificial compassionate love that Jesus leads. It's very uncomfortable, these collisions in the life of the church, these collisions of the gospel and the system. The gospel will win out in the Methodist Churches, eventually. And I think that this issue will work itself out for the gospel's sake, and on the gospel's side, in God's good time, in the Methodist Church."

I was blown away. Dr. Reed was wise and authentic, and his testimony was moving and inspiring. He could not have been a better witness to talk about liturgy and theology.

Lauren challenged Dr. Reed in his cross-examination: "When a pastor rewrites the ritual and uses it for a service other than for that which it was intended, what would you call that?"

"Creative writing," Dr. Reed replied.

"Even though it is the authorized ritual of the General Conference of The United Methodist Church, which holds the sole authority . . ."

"Happens every day," Dr. Reed interjected.

Lauren continued: ". . . to determine what ritual is within The United Methodist Church? You're talking about rewriting the rituals, but you're also talking about using it for a purpose other than that for which it was intended."

"But people make changes in the liturgy according to purpose all the time," Dr. Reed insisted.

"My assistant counsel has given me what I believe is a very blunt question to you," Lauren said. "If you use a communion service to worship Satan, is that okay?"

"It is not okay," Dr. Reed said with disgust. "It's not only a blunt question, it is — I guess the words I'd choose to use to describe your question, I better not use."

It was an obscene question. I wished Dr. Reed had said what he thought. It was scandalous to compare changing the Service of Marriage to a covenant ceremony with changing the purpose of Holy Communion to the worship of Satan. Are gay people to be equated with Satan, with evil? The comparison was appalling.

Doug had one more witness for the evening session of the trial. Roy Wright had been "driving everyone nuts," as Betty Dorr put it later, waiting his turn in the witness room. She said that he couldn't sit still and talked continuously. "I knew I was doing something big for The United Methodist Church and for Nebraska," Roy told me later. "There was a pastor I loved and respected who was being put on trial for doing something in his heart he believed was right, something that I supported. So I volunteered to stand up and fight for my pastor out of that love and respect. Then again, I felt I had to be a voice for the gay community. So I testified. I was nervous, but I knew what I was doing. My name was going to be out there now. But I didn't care."

"Roy," Doug began, "I have to ask you a sensitive question. Are you willing to identify your sexual orientation for this trial court?"

"Sure. I'm gay." Roy described how at the age of

seven or eight, I just knew there was something different about me, but I wasn't quite sure what it was, because I didn't have the name for it. When I was about fourteen, I started understanding more and knew what I was. I knew I was homosexual. When I really understood what it meant to be gay, and understood the impact of what that meant, I didn't want to be gay. So, I started getting involved in church, going to some Bible studies and meditating on scripture.

A few years later I went to a Pentecostal church, where they said I was teamed up with the devil, so I was exorcised twice to get demons cast out of me. I prayed, I fasted, and at the same time I was told that, because I was still struggling with this in me, my heart wasn't right with God and that God didn't love me, because I was still struggling with this.

There were many, many sleepless nights. A lot of nights I would cry my eyes out, literally for hours, because I didn't want to be gay. And I knew that I had come to a point when I had to admit to myself that I was gay, because I was at a point of committing suicide. But it was faith in God that got me through that. I knew God made me who I am.

"Why were you trying to convince yourself that you were not gay?" Doug asked.

"Well, because I knew the way society reacted to gay people. I knew the way the church reacted. I knew I just had to try to fit in the best I could, if that meant lying and covering up, then that's what I had to do in order to survive. Because I knew if I didn't do that and if I were to admit who I really was, I knew I would be rejected. It was a struggle with my family because of the lies. I really didn't have any close friends either, but I had to lie, and I had to do that to protect myself."

"Roy, are you a Christian?"

"Yes, I am. That's been an important part of who I am ever since I was a young kid. As a boy, walking to the store, looking at the stars, listening to birds sing, I always said, 'Oh, God, you know, I just want to be closer to you. Just give me something to know who you are.'"

"What attracted you to First United Methodist Church in Omaha?" Doug asked.

"The Vision Focus that said they wouldn't discriminate against people for sexual orientation," Roy explained.

"How have you found the church? Is it accepting?"

"It's a mix. There are people that do accept me, but there are people who will look at me, roll their eyes, turn their face, and walk away. So, it's a mix. Jimmy Creech, my pastor, has done everything he could to make me feel comfortable being a member of the church. He let me know that anything I wanted to do as a member is open and available to me."

"Are there similarities between your identity as a black person and your identity as a gay person?"

"Yes, there are. Both are part of who I am as a human being. Because to accept me, you have to accept all of me as who I am."

When Doug reminded Roy that The United Methodist Church says it welcomes gay people, while claiming homosexuality to be "incompatible with Christian teaching," Roy said: "You know, that's where I'm really confused. On the one hand, you tell me that you've fully accepted me as a person, but on the other hand, a part of me is not accepted? We go back to where everything is a part of who I am."

Roy had spoken slowly and softly, in contrast to his characteristic boisterous enthusiasm. His dignity, integrity, courage, and sincerity were compelling.

Lauren understood the poignant power of Roy's testimony and in his cross-examination sought to weaken it: "Roy, I'm sure that you have come to appreciate Pastor Jimmy Creech a great deal. Do you understand we're not questioning the character of your pastor in this trial?"

"Would you repeat the question? I'm sorry," Roy replied.

"We're not questioning Jimmy Creech's character. We think he's a good person. And a good pastor. He may have exercised misjudgment by undertaking an action that has not yet won approval of the General Conference of The United Methodist Church, but he's a good person. And obviously you're experiencing him as a good pastor in your life. So, I ask you, do you understand that we are addressing an 'Order and Discipline' question in this trial?"

"I'm sorry, would you repeat that question one more time?"

"I guess I'm stating that we're addressing the issue of disobedience to the Order and Discipline of the Church and that's the issue that we intend to focus on here. And we appreciate your being here to share your testimony. Thank you."

Lauren's attempt at subtle distinctions, pitting "a good pastor" against "a disobedient pastor," separating my character from my action, didn't succeed with Roy. It was the typical "love the sinner, hate the sin" talk. Lauren wanted Roy to set aside his experience of me as his pastor and focus on my disobedience. However, a good pastor to Roy was someone who didn't discriminate. From Roy's point of view, I was being prosecuted precisely because of my character, because I had been a good pastor. No good pastor would have discriminated against Mary and Martha by refusing to honor and bless their love and commitment. Roy had stated clearly that he considered the church's policies on gay people to be discriminatory. Suggesting that I could be guilty of disobedience because I did not discriminate was so incomprehensible to Roy that Lauren's question made no sense to him.

This wasn't Roy's failure in understanding, it was Lauren's. He approached the trial from a technical and legalistic point of view, with no sensitivity to Roy's struggle as a gay person to fully accept himself and be accepted by others, and to claim his place in the world in spite of the church's discrimination against him. Lauren didn't grasp the contradictions and conflicts with which Roy was forced to live. When Lauren said "the issue of disobedience ... [is] the issue we intend to focus on here," he was not only dismissing my character and my ministry as a "good pastor," he was dismissing as irrelevant Roy's experience as a gay person in The United Methodist Church. It was a fitting and revealing exchange to end the first day of the trial.

Mike, Doug, and I recognized that the trial was an opportunity to spotlight The United Methodist Church's spiritual violence against gay people. It was an extraordinarily public venue to discuss issues related to sexuality, the inherent dignity of gay people, and the true ministry of the church. Determining my guilt or innocence was of much less importance. To accomplish this, we had invited expert witnesses to testify, in addition to Roy and the leaders of First Church. The Reverend Dr. Roy Reed had been the first of these witnesses. The Reverend Dr. J. Philip Wogaman would be the next, and the first to testify on Friday morning, March 13.

Most of Dr. Wogaman's ministry had been in teaching. He first taught Bible and Christian ethics at the University of the Pacific, a United Methodist school in California. Then, for the next twenty-six years, he was on the faculty at Wesley Theological Seminary in Washington, D.C., part of this time serving as the seminary's dean. He left Wesley to become senior pastor at Foundry United Methodist Church in 1992. During his career, he had been an eminent United Methodist leader, serving as a delegate to three General Conferences and a member of the World Methodist Council. He was a member of the special Commission to Study Homosexuality, appointed by the 1988 General Conference, and was one of the fifteen original signers of "In All Things Charity."

Dr. Wogaman was relaxed, pastoral, and reflective. He was pedagogical without being pedantic or condescending. Doug asked Dr. Wogaman to talk about his experience with the Commission to Study Homosexuality. He responded:

> Well, I was eager for that study to occur. There was so much acrimony, so many inflammatory statements before the General Conference of 1988. Our concern was that there be a serious study that would take advantage of the best available resources and consultants, and that the committee would include people of varying opinions. And I hoped that out of that there would come some kind of closure on the scientific questions. You know, what is homosexuality? Why is it some people are and some people aren't? And I was disappointed. We discussed the matter with numbers of scientists and discovered there is no generally accepted theory. So, that was the biggest disappointment to me personally. I like to see things tidy.
>
> What we discovered in the process, though, may have been even a greater gift, and that happened in meeting with numbers of gay and les-

bian people. We discovered the humanity of gay people. And I ended that process thinking, "Isn't it interesting? We started this study process hoping that the scientific experts would tell us all about it, and we wind up discovering that the truth is all there right in the church, right in our backyard, with the people we're ministering to. It's there and we just need to open our eyes and see it." That to me was a great gift.

Doug asked him to talk about his parish, Foundry United Methodist Church, located in the center of Washington, D.C., about a mile north of the White House. Dr. Wogaman described it as "wonderfully diverse" racially, culturally, and economically. It had a "substantial number of gay members," he said, who "want to be United Methodists" and who want "to have a normal church experience. They want to be affirmed as the human beings that they are and cared for. And they want to participate in the mutual caring with others in the congregation."

"What's the fundamental challenge for ministry in such a diverse congregation?" Doug asked.

"To be a channel of God's grace," Dr. Wogaman responded. "The church is always better at loving than it is at judging. I mean, we have to judge. We have to arrive at decisions, and we have to sort things out, and we have to criticize, and be prophetic in various ways. But, the prophet's role is always to be grounded in grace. And that's the fundamental message. If we get that one right, other things are more likely to follow. If we don't get that one right, then nothing else will follow. I'm convinced of that. That's the fundamental thing. And to be pastoral, to know that you're there for people. And you make mistakes. You may not get it quite right. But the most important thing is to communicate love. Love covers a lot of other mistakes, but if there's not a climate of love and caring, sensitivity, then you can get everything else right and it won't matter."

When asked to talk about the Social Principles, Dr. Wogaman said that they

had always been understood as a teaching document that speaks to the conscience. It's pretty hard to speak to the conscience at the same time you're issuing some kind of a threat. The Social Principles ask us to reflect deeply on the meaning of our faith, and its relationship with the world, and for them to be used as clubs utterly distorts the spirit of those principles. And, particularly, if there are people who, in conscience, find aspects of the Social Principles that they are in disagreement with, the church must not put them on a collision course. I think it would send a wonderful message, a very clear message to the whole church if, here in Nebraska in this trial, the fundamental intent of the Social Principles was protected and the integrity of the ministry of conscience upheld.

You know, I have to say that what happens here is going to affect the people I minister to, the message about the church they get. Because we're all one church. And far better, in my opinion, for that decision to register at the level of the annual conference where it's peers and pastors and not at the level of the Judicial Council, where it's church lawyers. Far better here, now.

It's the responsibility of the court to make a very broad judgment and not think in a narrow, legalistic way. You know, to me that's the heart of what this trial is all about. Does the gospel exist for the sake of the law? Or does the law exist for the sake of the gospel? That's why a jury is formed of peers who can make broad judgments about the ministry of somebody, and the pastoral context, and the applicability of one part of *The Discipline* over other parts of *The Discipline*. And to treat this language as a very narrow thing and to turn the church over to lawyers is the worst thing for the gospel.

Dr. Wogaman had spoken as a teacher and a church leader. But most important, he had spoken to the jury as a pastor to pastors. He understood that ministry could not and should not be defined narrowly by church laws, and he was sure that the jurors understood that, too. He spoke to the jurors' caring and compassionate instincts. This trial was about ministry, and ministry is understood only in settings where people live their lives, where they struggle with the ambiguities of right and wrong, of good and bad. Ministry is not to be defined in a trial. Carrying God's love and grace to the world cannot be legally bound or determined. It's the spirit, not the law, that compels, leads, and confirms ministry.

Our next witness was Dr. Gregory Herek, a research psychologist at the University of California, Davis. He conducted research in a number of areas, all of which related in one way or another to sexual orientation. He had published widely in professional journals and had co-edited five textbooks and was currently writing a book on the topic of heterosexuals' attitudes toward lesbians and gay men. He had advised the American Psychological Association regarding research on sexual orientation and had testified before the U.S. House Armed Services Committee concerning the military's policy on homosexual personnel.

"Given your area of expertise, can you provide for us a definition of the word *homosexual*?" Doug began.

"In defining *homosexual*," Dr. Herek said:

I think it would be useful to broaden that concept a bit and talk not only about homosexuality and homosexual, but the more inclusive term of "sexual orientation," which also includes heterosexuality and bisexuality.

When we talk about sexual orientation, we're really talking about a very complex phenomenon, one that has many different dimensions to it. One of the components of it is sexual attraction, feelings of desire or arousal or attraction that a person has for someone else of a particular sex. We're also talking about what I would call romantic or emotional attraction, feelings of an affectional nature that may or may not be related to sexual attraction. We're also talking about sexual behaviors that result in some sort of sexual gratification or orgasm.

When we're talking about homosexuality, we are talking about people for whom those attractions or behaviors involve someone of the same sex. When we're talking about heterosexuality, we're talking about people for whom those attractions and behaviors involve someone of the other sex. And we also have the category of bisexuality, which refers to people who have the attractions and behaviors toward people of both sexes.

Doug turned next to the language in *The Book of Discipline* that states: "Homosexual persons no less than heterosexual persons are individuals of sacred worth . . . Although we do not condone the practice of homosexuality and consider this practice incompatible with Christian teaching, we affirm that God's grace is available to all." He asked Dr. Herek to distinguish between "homosexual practice" and "homosexual orientation."

"I've heard that distinction made before," Dr. Herek said, "and I think it's a false dichotomy, a false distinction. I think you have to realize sexual orientation is a characteristic of the person as a whole, not a little segment or little compartment of a person. To try to distinguish between practice and orientation or to separate them is not very meaningful. If you would allow me an analogy, I think it might be comparable to someone saying, 'I am absolutely opposed to the practice of Methodism, but I don't have anything

against Methodists as long as they don't engage in Methodist practice.'"
Laughter erupted in the courtroom. Dr. Herek continued: "I say that not
to get a laugh, but just to draw an analogy. I think there's a similarity in the
sense you have a characteristic [that] individuals really perceive as a part of
themselves and to somehow make a distinction between 'being' and 'doing'
is really a false distinction."

Doug next asked Dr. Herek to address some of the popular misconcep-
tions about homosexuality and homosexuals: "Is homosexuality a mental
illness?"

"First, a short answer, 'no,'" Dr. Herek responded:

And then to explain that it's useful to understand a little bit of the background here. Historically, for the last several millennia, it was primarily
religion that set norms for social behaviors, especially in Western soci-
eties. There is debate about the first millennium or so of the Christian era
whether homosexuality was condemned or not, but it looks pretty true
to say that during most of the second millennium the church has defined
homosexuality as a sin, more or less, depending upon the denomination.
A few hundred years ago, that absolute authority of the church was taken
over in some respects by civil society, secular society, and many of the
same values were translated from church law into civil law, so that we
saw homosexuality moving from being a sin to being a crime. I say that
as background, because I think it's important to realize that it's only been
in the last hundred years or so that medicine, psychiatry, and psychology
have come to have a strong say in this area. And when that happened, one
of the early developments was that homosexuality shifted from being a
crime to being viewed as a sickness. In each case, I think that what you
had were people basically saying they disapproved of homosexuality, but
using the labels that were associated with religion, civil law, and medicine.

In the early 1950s, when psychiatrists and other people from the
medical establishment came together to try to develop an authoritative
manual on mental illness, they included homosexuality. And that was
really a translation of their earlier beliefs because there really hadn't been
research done to try to examine whether or not homosexuality was linked
to other forms of mental illness. It was really going from the sin-crime-
sickness model, and just adopting that.

When that book was revised in the early 1970s, there was some serious questioning of homosexuality being included as a mental illness. One of the main reasons was by that time there had actually been scientific research conducted which consistently failed to show there was any sort of linkage between being homosexual and being psychologically impaired in any way.

So, in 1973, the American Psychiatric Association removed homosexuality from that big book, the *Diagnostic and Statistical Manual of Mental Disorders*. The American Psychological Association strongly endorsed that move. And in the last twenty-five years, both the psychiatric and psychological professions have been trying very hard to undo some of the damage that was done in the name of psychiatry and psychology earlier, trying to explain to people that, no, homosexuality is not a mental illness.

"Is being homosexual a choice that can be changed?" Doug next asked.

"That is a question that has aroused a great deal of controversy, especially recently," Dr. Herek observed. "As we come to understand sexual orientation more and more, what we've come to realize is that people arrive at a sexual orientation as an adult through a variety of different paths. When we ask people about their sense of their own sexuality, what we see is that the majority will say that they don't perceive that they have made a choice, and indeed the majority says that they've just always been this way. And that's consistent whether you ask people who are heterosexual or homosexual. Now, there are some people who do feel that they have made at least some degree of choice in this. And interestingly, we see a bit of sex difference here, with women more often than men saying that they have experienced a greater sense of what I might call plasticity or fluidity or possibility of change in their sexuality. But we're talking about a minority of people. Most people don't believe that their sexuality is a matter of choice. With sexual orientation, our research shows it's not something that can be readily changed in either direction, from heterosexual to homosexual or homosexual to heterosexual."

"Are homosexuals child molesters?" Doug asked.

"There is no greater likelihood of a person who is homosexual [being] a child molester than the person who's heterosexual," Dr. Herek explained. "Child molestation is something that's completely independent of sexual orientation. People who are child molesters frequently are people who don't really have what we call an adult sexual orientation. They've not developed a capacity to relate to other adults, either of their same sex or the other sex, in a romantic or sexual way. For them, the focus is simply on a child or youth, and in many cases they're rather indiscriminate about the sex of the victim."

Shifting the focus, Doug asked: "How can the policies of an institution such as a church affect the way that its members respond to gay men and lesbians?"

"One of the principal findings from my own research," Dr. Herek said, "is that one of the most potent motivators for accepting people from any minority group, or rejecting one's past negative attitudes toward them, is to have personal contact with people from the group. And not only is it important that heterosexual people know someone who's gay or lesbian, or have a relative who's gay or lesbian, it's important that they've actually discussed that fact with the friend or with the relative. So it's not just enough to know that Uncle Joe is gay, but it's important also to have talked to him about it, at least to some extent. To have some sense of what it's like for him to be gay, and to know that this is part of his world, and to have that out in the open, to have talked about it. What we see when institutions adopt policies that set apart people who are gay, or people of other minority groups, where it's possible to hide one's identity in that group, as it is when you're gay and lesbian, is that those institutional policies tend to prevent that sort of open disclosure and open discussion from occurring. And so, in that sense, institutional policies that push people to remain hidden, like people who are gay or lesbian, have a way of perpetuating those negative attitudes, because they prevent personal contact, personal discussion from occurring. It's that personal contact and personal discussion that would have the most significant effect on changing attitudes."

Doug read aloud the following statement from the Social Principles and asked Dr. Herek to comment on it as a social scientist: "We recognize that sexuality is God's good gift to all persons. We believe persons may be fully human only when that gift is acknowledged and affirmed by themselves, the church and society." Dr. Herek answered:

Well, I would say that it's very consistent with the findings of social and behavioral scientific research. What we have found is that people who are gay or lesbian, or heterosexual or bisexual, are best able to function psychologically and socially when they are accepting of their own sexuality, when they are able to use that sexuality and their sexual orientation as a way of relating to other people in a positive way, when they're in more positive and intimate relationships with other people, and when they are able to live their lives in a way that allows them not to have to make an issue of it, or not to hide their sexuality, but rather to go on with their lives. It's in those circumstances that people manifest the greatest psychological well-being, and the greatest ability to function socially.

I would say, too, that it's under those conditions that people of the majority group, people who are heterosexual, are also going to benefit in that, if there is not this strong stigma attached to being gay and lesbian, we find that that often has a very positive advantage for people who are heterosexual as well, because it ends up allowing them to feel more free to, for example, violate gender norms. For a man to feel that he can put his arm around another man, and not be thought of as being homosexual, or not being accused of that.

Dr. Herek had turned the courtroom into a classroom. He wasn't just testifying, he was teaching. His responses to Doug's questions exposed The United Methodist Church's policies about homosexuality to be unscientific, unethical, and harmful.

Our final witness was Betty Dorr. She had been in the witness room since the start of the trial, and alone there most of the morning. Betty began her testimony by telling about her history with First United Methodist Church in Omaha, where she had been an active volunteer and held various leadership roles. She also talked about her involvement with PFLAG.

"Betty, at this point I need to ask a sensitive question," Doug said. "Do you have a family member who has shared with you that he is gay or she is lesbian?"

"Yes," Betty answered. "In fact, I have three that I am blessed with. My brother came out in 1959; my brother-in-law came out in 1966; and our youngest son came out in 1992."

"Could you describe some of the pain and some of the joys that have come into your life as a result of having gay men who are family members?"

"When I first discovered my son was gay, I was angry. I went through denial, guilt, shame, being afraid and worrying about my son, mainly because of knowing about my brother and brother-in-law who had to grow up in a world where we didn't know anything about homosexuality or gays or lesbians. I wasn't angry with my son — I loved him very much. But I was angry with society, and I think this is why I've gotten involved with trying to educate and inform people that these are people who need our respect and need our acceptance."

"Has the ministry of First Church changed positively towards gays and lesbians during the time that you've been a member?"

"When our son came out to us in '92, the first person I talked to at the church was Don Bredthauer and he was very supportive. He let me know that it was okay, and that God did love my family, and that helped tremendously. I think having ministers that you can go to in this situation is wonderful because I've met many parents throughout the United States that have been told by their ministers that they and their children are not welcome [in church]."

"Would you talk about the current controversy about the covenant ceremony and how it has made you feel?"

"I have felt sadness and joy. The sadness was because of the comments that have been made to us as a family. We have received unsigned letters denouncing our son. We were told that it was great that he lived in Chicago, but just please keep him in Chicago, and [do] not ever bring him home.

"But then, in the midst of this, there has been joy because a group of members we call Supporting the Vision has really been there for us, and it's been wonderful, and they've shared their unconditional love with us, and supported us, and our gay family members, and have always made them feel welcome. I know my brother feels very welcome in the church. And the sermon that Jimmy gave on accepting gays and lesbians was my dream. My dream had finally come true, that I had a minister in my own church that would stand in the pulpit and tell my family that it was okay. And that's still hard for me to talk about, because it's something that I thought never would happen in my lifetime.

"And I am hoping and praying for one day when the whole United Methodist Church will open its doors and welcome our family. And my biggest dream is that one day my gay son will be able to come home to his church and to have a commitment service with someone he loves. Because our other two sons are allowed to be married and they're happy. The one dream I've always wanted is for Mike to be able to find someone that he cared for, and that would care for him, and that we could celebrate as we did for our other two sons. And I'm hoping and praying that one of these days that will happen."

Betty's testimony brought the focus back to the pain and promise at First United Methodist Church. The pain was caused by bigotry within the congregation and the denomination; the promise, articulated in the Vision Focus, was that all people, gay and nongay alike, would be welcome and accepted into the membership. The trial wasn't only about my violating one of the Social Principles, whether or not that was law. The trial was about whether or not a United Methodist congregation could offer the full ministry of grace to lesbian, gay, bisexual, and transgender people.

The trial recessed for lunch. During the break, the Reverend Alice Knotts, from Montana, distributed a press release announcing that ninety-two United Methodist clergy from around the country had signed a "Statement of Commitment," publicly vowing to "celebrate rites of union with all couples, regardless of gender, as part of the pastoral responsibilities consistent with the gospel and spirit of Jesus Christ, entrusted to us by The United Methodist Church."[9] The timing of the press release was intended to coincide with the announcement of the verdict, no matter what it might be. The statement was a clear message that I was not the only member of the United Methodist clergy committed to full ministry to lesbian, gay, bisexual, and transgender people. The trial might remove me from ministry, but others stood ready to actively defy the church's bigotry.

The trial reconvened at one, and Lauren began his closing argument: "I have to tell you, I'm scared to death. I have preached a lot of sermons. I'd like to think that there's a lot riding on every word we say when we're preaching. That may be a fantasy, but there's no fantasy about the fact that there's a lot riding on the words I share this afternoon here in these closing arguments." Lauren was obviously nervous. The closing argument was his last chance to convince the jury, and desperation was in his voice. He continued:

We need to remember that this process was not started or initiated by Reverend Loy, nor was this process initiated by Bishop Joel Martínez. This process was initiated when a decision was made by Jimmy Creech to do something that he knew was in disobedience to the Order and Discipline of The United Methodist Church. The defense goes something like this: The Social Principles don't mean what they say. The "shall not" means, "unless I think better of it." "Shall not" means "shall not." Jimmy Creech decided that that particular part of *The Discipline* was no longer palatable to him and no longer served his function in ministry, and so he decided to ignore it.

Dr. Reed, who admits he's not an expert on *The Discipline*, would simply push it aside in favor of everyone doing their own thing. Except he finally admitted that purpose is important when developing rituals. It was a shame I had to ask that last question that so upset him. But I did it, and it did cause him to admit that it is important to use a ceremony, a ritual, a liturgy, for its intended purpose. It is important.

Dr. Herek this morning gave an interesting and informative lecture about human sexuality—I would correct myself, because I was listening, I was listening, and it's about sexual orientation. But was it designed to clarify or to confuse?

Finally, the defense put before us a long list of people telling us about Jimmy Creech. His defense is that he is a remarkable pastor in a remarkable church and thus is exempt from the law. Jimmy Creech is not above the law of The United Methodist Church. We could have matched person for person, in a debate of sorts up here, persons who would tell you quite a different story about their relationship with Jimmy Creech at First United Methodist Church in Omaha. We could have found those persons, had we searched for them. We wouldn't have had any trouble finding them. They're available. Some of them would have volunteered right here on the spot. Some of them are with us. But it was our decision not to pursue a course of acrimonious debate about Jimmy's leadership and pastoral style and rather to focus on the charge and the supporting specification.

It's been a long time, hasn't it? Seems like you've been sitting in those chairs forever. And I have to tell you, for me it's going to be good to get back to some normal sleep hours again, once we're done. We had the expert defense witnesses here. Now, they provided some interesting opinions, and the church members that came before you provided evidence that some of the members at First United Methodist Church in Omaha feel genuinely served by Jimmy. Thank God for that. We're thankful for that. But that's not the issue of this trial.

And understand that, regardless of the media spin on this, it is Jimmy Creech that is on trial here. This charge is not a charge against The United

Methodist Church. I've heard it said, "Jimmy's only a minor player in this; it's The United Methodist Church that's on trial." That is not the truth. It's Jimmy Creech that has been called before this trial, and Jimmy Creech who appeared before the Committee on Investigation, and it was because of the Committee on Investigation that this trial came into being.

And this trial court has a decision. The facts are that Jimmy Creech engaged in an act that places him in disobedience to the Order and Discipline of The United Methodist Church when he officiated at a covenanting ceremony that celebrated a homosexual union on September 14, 1997, at First United Methodist Church in Omaha, Nebraska. I remind you again that virtually every word of the specification supporting the charge Jimmy has agreed happened. The only word that he took issue with was the word homosexual. And I have sat here with a commonsense approach to that definition, and one that I believe values the church's capacity to look beyond the simply scientific or the simply technical aspects of relationships, and that will embrace a broader understanding of what those relationships mean, and how they are composed. So, in offering this unauthorized ritual, this unauthorized liturgy, this unauthorized ceremony, Jimmy was in fact going beyond his pastoral authority, and placed himself in disobedience to the Order and Discipline of The United Methodist Church.

We have attempted, even with the calling of two witnesses, remembering that Jimmy Creech was our first witness, and perhaps the only needful witness in the midst of this undertaking—we have given you the facts. And now it is your duty to deliberate and render a verdict. As counsel for the church, I want to share with you The United Methodist Church believes that that verdict should be guilty. Thank you.

The fright that Lauren had spoken of as he began was evident throughout his closing argument. He wasn't organized; he rambled as if trying to discover the persuasive, winning argument as he spoke, like a beaten boxer wildly flailing to land a knockout punch. He and Warren Urbom had not conducted a strong prosecution, and they knew it. Overconfident before the trial, Warren, a federal district court judge, had boasted that proving my guilt would be a "slam dunk." Now they clearly regretted not having been more aggressive and not having provided more witnesses against me.

Next was Doug's closing argument:

There's no question that the task before you, deciding the innocence or guilt of Reverend Jimmy Creech, has immense significance. Your decision today will shape the course of events in not only the life of Reverend Creech, but also in the life of First United Methodist Church in Omaha, and in the lives of the Nebraska Annual Conference. But that decision will also shape United Methodism as a whole, perhaps for generations.

We have heard over and over again about what a good match Jimmy Creech has been to the life and ministry of First United Methodist Church, Omaha. Three chairs of the Staff-Parish Relations Committee, the elected leaders of the church, a colleague in ministry, widely respected across this annual conference for years and years, and two other lay people who have been deeply touched by Jimmy's ministry have affirmed his ministry with and among them: his pastoral care; his adept administration; his powerful preaching of the gospel; and his prophetic voice and action, among other things. But most importantly, his inclusive vision of the church, and his genuine love for all people.

Why is this important? Because some among us are trying to get rid of Jimmy. Why? For showing the mercy and compassion of Christ to two people to whom he was a pastor. It has been suggested that Jimmy should have left our denomination rather than perform a covenant service. Similarly, it has been suggested that the two women involved in the covenant service, or for that matter gay and lesbian people in general, should not seek full inclusion in the nurturing ministries of The United Methodist Church. We've learned in the past three days of gay and lesbian brothers and sisters in Christ who are hurting, and who are in need of the full range of pastoral care offered by our Church. I cannot believe that the hearts of United Methodists are so cold as to fail to embrace completely our gay and lesbian family, to embrace all of God's children.

I tremble to think of prosecuting United Methodists for violations of the Social Principles, something that has never been done before in the history of our church. Over a period of ninety years, until this trial, we have not prosecuted anyone under the Social Principles. This trial is about fair process, to which all United Methodists are entitled. Is it fair process to say that our Social Principles are instructive and persuasive guides, not rules, without qualification, and then use them to prosecute?

What you are about today will take courage. We know you have to return to serve local congregations. Dr. Wogaman said, "Have courage. Do not make a big deal of this." That's very hard for me, after spending four months of my life preparing Jimmy's defense. But Dr. Wogaman said, don't be afraid to say that we can be loving rather than judgmental. We can have the courage not to use the "homosexual union" language as a club. We can have the courage not to establish a dangerous precedent that might affect the teaching of the church. We can have the courage not to allow legalism to dominate our life and ministry. We can have the courage to get past stereotypes and begin dialogue. Because of our faith in Jesus Christ, we can have the courage to say, as Dr. Wogaman said, that a church law has never solved a problem, and enforcing a Social Principle as law does not settle a disagreement. We can have the courage to support our freedom of conscience, our freedom to consider faithfully in prayer, study and dialogue our Social Principles and to act accordingly.

I believe there is hope for the church on the issue of homosexuality. Please be of good courage so that you can find Jimmy not guilty. It is in that verdict that there is hope for the church. Be of good courage. Be of good faith. And may the peace of God be with you all.

When Doug sat down, Bishop Hodapp began his instruction to the jury:

Now, I need to give you this charge about your deliberations. *The Book of Discipline* provides that the respondent[10] is presumed innocent until the time that nine or more of you find him guilty of the specification and charge. The burden of proving the respondent guilty has been on the church and unless you find a specification or charge to be proved by clear and convincing evidence, you must enter a finding of "not guilty" to that specification or charge. Fewer than nine votes will be considered an acquittal. The question you must decide on the specification is, did Jimmy Creech, a minister of First United Methodist Church, perform a covenanting ceremony that celebrated a homosexual union between two women?

The question of the charge is, if you find that Jimmy Creech did perform this ceremony as described, by doing so did he disobey the Order and Discipline of The United Methodist Church? If your verdict is "not guilty," our time together is over. If it is "guilty," you will hear additional arguments, and then deliberate about a penalty, and I'll give you instructions prior to doing that.

The jury left the gymnasium, moving to a private room for their deliberations. Bishop Hodapp recessed the trial, announcing that he would call
it back in session as soon as a verdict had been reached. It was twelve past
three in the afternoon.

The trial we had been anticipating for so long had ended—at least our
part of it. We would still need to make an argument in the penalty phase
of the trial if I was found guilty, but at the time that wasn't on any of our
minds. Our defense had been comprehensive, solid, and persuasive, and
the opposition knew it. There had been a lot of grumbling over the two
days of the trial from the opposition about the prosecution's poor performance. Lauren Ekdahl and Warren Urbom had offered no theological basis
for the charge against me, and no theological reflection on the nature and
mission of the church, or on Christian discipleship and ministry. Nor had
they given a theological defense for the institutional discrimination against
gay, bisexual, and lesbian people by The United Methodist Church. They
had acknowledged it without apology or regret and had essentially said:
"That's the way it is; we have to live with it." They had appealed only to
what they alleged to be church law and a collegial covenant to conform to
the status quo. Although this was a church trial, there had been nothing
uniquely churchlike about the prosecution. It had been all about order and
regulations, conformity and loyalty. While law is essential to maintaining
the organizational integrity of the church, grace is what gives it purpose and
power for ministry. Without God's grace, the church is no different from
other institutions.

When Bishop Hodapp recessed the trial, there was no sigh of relief in the
courtroom. Instead, those present seemed to take a deep breath and hold it.
We now had to wait for the jury's verdict. In spite of our strong defense and
the church's weak case against me, we had no idea what dynamics would be
at play in the jury room. Each juror was a pastor serving a local congregation
under Bishop Joel Martínez's appointment power. The great majority of lay
people throughout the Nebraska Annual Conference had been outraged
by the covenant ceremony. We had heard from a number of pastors who
said they supported me but couldn't do so publicly because of potential
repercussions within their congregations. Some lay people had threatened
to withhold financial contributions to their churches if I should be acquitted. And Bishop Martínez had pushed the judicial process from the outset,
even providing the language for the official complaint and the subsequent

charge from Lauren Ekdahl. There was no question that the bishop wanted me found guilty, never to return to First United Methodist Church.

How free could the thirteen clergy on the jury really be, I wondered. If they believed that the church had not provided clear and convincing evidence to convict me, would they be brave enough to vote against the outraged wishes of their church members and the will of the bishop? The ballot would be secret, but how could they be sure they would not be found out if they voted to acquit me? If the jurors who voted guilty went public, the process of elimination would reveal who had voted not guilty. Jurors who voted to acquit me would have to tell the truth or lie. If they told the truth, it could lead to conflict and disruption in their congregations, and retaliation from the superintendents and the bishop. I was an outsider, now perceived as a troublemaker who was not worth the turmoil that an acquittal would create. The jurors didn't know me personally, didn't have a bond with me. If the covenant ceremony had caused so much discord and controversy, it was not hard to imagine what an acquittal would cause. The grief that my conviction and removal from ministry would bring to First Church, Chris, and me would be minor compared to the chaos that an acquittal would create in The United Methodist Church.

I found it hard to believe in the objectivity and independence of the jury. It was reasonable to assume that fear had more influence in the jury room than clear and convincing proof. I was not the only one who would be affected by the verdict. It would affect every juror, the district superintendents, the bishop, and the lay people in the Nebraska Annual Conference and throughout the denomination.

The judicial process of The United Methodist Church was designed to be fair, but it had been corrupted by the politics of the church and gave an advantage to the prosecution. The playing field was not level. The presumption of innocence and the role of due process were nominal. The only hope we had was that a guilty verdict required more than a simple majority of the jurors. Would at least five of the thirteen be free enough — fearless, courageous, and faithful enough — to affirm that the Social Principles were meant to be instructive and persuasive rather than law, and to vote not guilty? In spite of the odds against it happening, in spite of our experience with the bishop and the Committee on Investigation, we hoped that would be the case.

Beyond that, we were sustained by our confidence in the Vision Focus, and by our conviction about what was just, compassionate, and faithful, about what it meant to be a follower of Jesus Christ. Even if the jury declared me guilty, we were convinced that The United Methodist Church was wrong in its teachings and policies against lesbian, gay, and bisexual people. We were sure that First Church would continue its faithful journey and that I would survive. I knew this could be the end of my ordained ministry in The United Methodist Church, but I also knew what happened to me if I were found guilty would be much less important than what that verdict would do to the whole church. A guilty verdict would be a defeat for The United Methodist Church because it would more deeply entrench its policies that mistreat gay people, their families, and their allies. It would be a defeat for pastoral ministry, allowing law rather than grace to determine compassion and justice. If the verdict was guilty, we would weep not for ourselves, but for the church of John Wesley and for the gay people of God who had been forsaken by that church. Our hopes were not just for me and First Church. They were for the emancipation of the entire United Methodist Church from the bondage of bigotry.

We gathered with supporters in the choir room to wait for the verdict. The chairs that were normally there had been moved to the gymnasium for the trial, so we sat on the floor. The room was filled with people from all over the United States, strangers before the trial but now tightly bonded together. Coyner Smith passed out a collection of hymns he had brought from Omaha for just such an occasion. Alice Knotts sat down at the piano, and we began to sing. Between hymns, we prayed together and shared stories. Emotions were full and freely expressed. We were in pain, but we were also joyous. We cried and we laughed.

Chris and I held each other tightly, tears sometimes streaming down our cheeks as we sang and listened to people's stories. She had been with me and supported me through so much. The seven months of waiting had been as agonizing for her as for me. We knew this could be the end for us in Omaha and in The United Methodist Church. We had come to Nebraska to fulfill a dream that we now feared was over. We hurt deeply and badly. We were emotionally and physically drained. But the loving spirit in that room surrounded, strengthened, and sustained us.

A little before six thirty in the evening, we got word that Bishop Hodapp was ready to reconvene the court. After more than three hours of deliberation, the jury had finally reached a verdict. The gymnasium filled quickly, and the bishop called us to order. The room was unnaturally silent; the apprehension, palpable. Mike, Doug, and I sat at the defense table, looking at Bishop Hodapp in front of us and at the jury to our right. Chris sat just behind me. Bishop Hodapp asked the Reverend Grant Story, the jury's foreperson, if the jury had a verdict.

"Yes, we do," Grant said, "but we have a statement to share with folks who are gathered here before we share the verdict: 'We've gathered in prayer, in silence and in respectful dialogue. Our vote reflects the difficulties the general church has experienced with this issue. We have struggled together in a spirit of love — no, not just struggled, but agonized — and our hope is that United Methodists everywhere will receive our verdict in that same spirit of love and respect.' As to the specification, the trial court returns the following verdict: eleven persons voting 'guilty'; two persons voting 'not guilty.'"

The jury had agreed with the prosecution that I had conducted a covenant ceremony for two women, or — to use the church's term — a "homosexual union." I was surprised that two jurors had voted "not guilty." I expected a unanimous vote on the specification. Grant continued: "As to the charge of 'disobedience to the Order and Discipline of The United Methodist Church,' the trial court returns the following verdict: eight persons voting 'guilty'; five persons voting 'not guilty.'"

For seconds that seemed interminable, everyone in the gymnasium sat uncomprehending, suspended in silence. Grant's words hung in the air, no one immediately grasping what they meant: "eight persons voting 'guilty'; five persons voting 'not guilty.'"

We waited, expecting Bishop Hodapp to say something like, "Jimmy Creech, the court finds you guilty" or, "Jimmy Creech, the court finds you not guilty." Instead, he looked toward the jury and simply said: "Thank you very much for all of your efforts and difficulty. You're now dismissed." Then, addressing everyone else, he said: "And we are all dismissed."

Without further comment, Bishop Hodapp unceremoniously rose from his seat and began carefully putting documents into his briefcase as if nothing of consequence — neither the trial nor the verdict — had just happened.

The courtroom was hushed, still uncertain of the verdict. I heard Mike McClellan mutter softly to himself in disbelief: "Is that all?" I felt my heart stop. "Is that all?" Mike's words echoed in my mind, and I assumed they meant he was disappointed in the verdict. Instead, Mike's disappointment was with the small number of "not guilty" votes. He had expected more.

Betty Dorr was sitting next to Dr. Wogaman. He grabbed her hand and said, "We won!" Instantly, Roy Wright, sitting on Betty's other side, jumped up in the air and shouted at the top of his lungs: "We won! We won! Praise the Lord, we won!"

Suddenly bedlam broke loose, and the gymnasium thundered with cheers, applause, and joyous weeping. Supporters were hugging each other, jumping up and down all over the room, and running toward the front to congratulate us. The media rushed in from the entrance doors to get statements and videos of anyone and everyone they could.

CNN, which had been broadcasting live, regular updates on the trial throughout each day, interrupted its regular program to broadcast this moment live around the world.

I hugged Mike and Doug and thanked them for the extraordinary gift they'd given The United Methodist Church. I embraced Chris, and we melted together in tears, our hearts pounding.

The improbable had happened. Five jurors had defied political expediency and used clear, sound judgment. They had refused to let fear keep them from making what they believed to be the right decision. They had been courageous.

I stood on a chair, quieted the crowd, and said: "We have a victory to celebrate, a victory for the church! The United Methodist Church won tonight. This is a victory for both sides. No one lost. The jury showed great courage, affirming the grace of God to all people and the integrity of pastoral ministry. It has said we are guided more by God's grace than by institutional regulations. I have to say, however, even in the midst of this celebration, there's a lot of work ahead of us. I am hopeful tonight's decision in this trial will help us turn around The United Methodist Church and end its mistreatment of gay men and lesbians. I am grateful for your support more than I can say. Thank you! Blessings on you all!"

Of course, not everyone was elated. Mel Semrad told Gus Niebuhr of the *New York Times* that the verdict "sends the message across the country that culture has triumphed over church doctrine and rules."[11] Another member of First Church, who didn't want to be identified, told the *Washington Post*'s Jon Jeter, "This is a sad day for the Methodist church. A minister shouldn't be allowed to make up his own rules as he goes along."[12]

John Grenfell of Good News told Yonat Shimron, the religion editor for Raleigh's *News & Observer*: "There will be many people who will walk with their feet. There will be some churches that will walk with their purse . . . This is blatant disregard of the rules, regulations, and responsibilities prescribed and enjoined by the General Conference. If these people do as they please, why should local churches give heed to the Order and Discipline of The United Methodist Church?"[13]

According to the *Omaha World-Herald*, some people approached Bishop Hodapp after the verdict and said, "You just made sure I won't be Methodist."[14] Helen Howell told a reporter: "No longer will I be a Methodist. I'm disenfranchised from the church because of the egocentricity of one man."[15]

While I was speaking to reporters, Robert Howell walked up to me and said, "You ought to be happy, because this is the second church you've ruined." He told Linda Story, director of communications at First Church: "It's the whole situation of having to accept the gay and lesbian lifestyle. I probably won't be coming back. Jimmy has left us out." When Linda asked what I had done to exclude him, Robert said: "Well, yes, Jimmy always talked to me. But he wouldn't do what I asked."

Bishop Martínez entered the gymnasium. He appeared to be in shock, his face ashen and hands shaking. He was about to do what he had never dreamed he would have to. When he meekly extended his hand to me, I took it, leaned toward him, and softly said: "Bishop, this is a great night for the church. This is a victory for the church." He looked puzzled, as if I had told him something ridiculous, like the earth was flat. Clearly, he hadn't fully prepared himself for what had happened and for what he was about to say. The crowd hushed as he began to read a statement, surrounded by the media's lights, cameras, and microphones: "A jury of his peers has acted to acquit Reverend Jimmy Creech of all charges. The church and its officers must respect the judgment handed down by the trial court. Reverend Creech was subjected to the judicial review process of the church and cooperated with it throughout. This jury trial was the concluding part of his judicial review. He is now returning to his clergy duties at First United Methodist Church in Omaha. This is his appointment."

His words were greeted with applause. Members of First Church and supporters who had come from around the country joined hands in a large circle and began to sing "Hallelujah, Hallelujah," a soft, prayerful song—not Handel's exultant chorus, although that would have been appropriate, too. The struggle had been long and arduous. Now, the Vision Focus and my ministry had been vindicated. The trial was over, and suddenly we found it hard to leave one another, or that moment and that space. It seemed as if an epiphany had occurred there, and divine sparks still filled the air.

Mel White, who had returned to his hotel, watched as CNN continued its coverage of the trial's end. In an e-mail to supporters across the country, he wrote:

> I'm back in our hotel room. Gary is packing away our long johns. (It's 54 degrees, not a bad jump from yesterday's 9 degrees.) Today we drive to Omaha and Sunday we fly home to Laguna Beach . . .
>
> CNN is still broadcasting from the courtroom. Someone from Jimmy's Church who disapproves or dislikes homosexuals has just informed the media that "he's not going to be my pastor." Already the celebration has ended and the work of reconciliation has begun. Jesus said, "Love your enemies." George Burns replied, "It will drive them crazy." Gandhi added, ". . . and set you both free."
>
> If you think the Christian religion has been the enemy of God's lesbian, gay, bisexual, and transgender children, you're correct. If the thought of going back to your church or to any church (or synagogue) makes you crazy, it's OK. I understand. But something happened today in Kearney, Nebraska, that made me feel hope again, hope that truth will triumph, that old prejudices will die, that ignorance is losing its powerful hold, not just here but across the nation and around the world. But it cannot happen without us.
>
> On the TV behind me, on CNN, in a courtroom in Kearney, Nebraska, [a] young, gay, African American from the Midwest who has been a victim of religious racism and homophobia all his life is hugging a privileged white Southerner from Raleigh, North Carolina. TV cameras broadcast the scene. "You did it, Jimmy," the young black man says grinning up at his pastor in complete disbelief. "We did it, Roy," Jimmy replies, "together."
>
> For a moment, Jimmy Creech just holds the young man. Tears stream down both faces. Their smiles light up the room. Then Reverend Creech adds quietly, "Now the work begins."[16]

"The Reverend Jimmy Creech was treated as a hero Sunday as he returned to First United Methodist Church. Church members greeted him with a standing ovation as he entered the sanctuary. They hugged and kissed him in the halls, and they gave him words of encouragement. For Creech, who Friday was acquitted of charges that he disobeyed the church by performing a covenant ceremony for two Omaha women, the greeting was heartwarming," the *Omaha World Herald* reported.[1]

Chris and I had left Kearney on Friday night after the celebration and arrived home in the wee hours of Saturday morning. I was up before daylight, unable to sleep. Don Bredthauer called early to encourage me to preach on Sunday, but I had made no preparations for that because I had not expected to be acquitted. I wanted to be in the First Church pulpit more than anything, but my mind and body rebelled.

"Thanks, Don, but I'm not ready. I'm emotionally and mentally exhausted. I don't believe I can think clearly enough to prepare a sermon."

"Just speak from your heart," he persisted. "We need you in the pulpit tomorrow." I finally agreed.

I was numb. I badly needed solitude to reflect on all that had happened, not just in the trial but since the September covenant ceremony. Quiet reflection was impossible, however. Friends were calling to congratulate and welcome me back to the church. Media from all over the country—even the BBC and a reporter from Australia—were calling, and reporters from local TV stations were coming by for interviews. Because the trial held such public interest and significance, I felt obligated to talk to everyone. Chris tried to screen the calls and let me have some time to myself, but I couldn't ignore them. There would be time later to process it all, I told myself. There never was, of course.

Finally, late Saturday afternoon, I got my notebook and Bible and sat down to prepare a sermon. What would be the appropriate subject for this particular Sunday, I wondered. What should I say? What is the meaning—the message—of the trial just finished, of the experience of the people of First Church?

So many emotions and thoughts flooded my mind that I couldn't focus: gratitude, relief, joy, covenants, baptism, diversity, hospitality, God's unconditional love, peace, human dignity, God's open arms for all people, with no exception. For the scripture reading, I chose the story of Noah in the book of Genesis. I wrote a simple outline of the points I wanted to make, and then I tried to rest, trusting in God's spirit to carry me and in the congregation to be gracious and forgive my lack of preparation. After all, preaching a polished sermon would not be most important that morning. Being back with the people for worship again, hearing the choir and congregation sing, standing with Chris and greeting folks at the door after four months of separation would be much more important. Being together again in itself would be an eloquent affirmation of God's grace. Words hardly needed to be spoken.

As had been my practice for twenty-eight years, I went to the church before daybreak on Sunday morning for quiet time to center myself for worship. On my desk were congratulatory messages that had come in since the trial's end. One said: "Congratulations! I now know it's possible to be both Methodist and Christian at the same time!"

The sermon I preached, simple and conversational, was about God's covenant with all creation, a promise of peace and protection whose sign, like a divine signature on a heavenly contract, was the rainbow. It was a joyous homecoming. I had thought I was completely emotionally drained, but during worship I discovered I had tears in reserve to weep.

The trial was over, but not the controversy. Bishop Martínez sent a cautionary letter on Monday, March 16, 1998, to all pastors and lay leaders in the Nebraska Annual Conference saying: "It must be stressed that this verdict does not have any bearing on any future proceeding. It speaks *only* to this particular case. It does not change my position on the matter. My instruction to all pastors will be the same as it was earlier. If a pastor proceeds to officiate at a same-sex covenanting service and a complaint is brought forward, I will process whatever complaint arises in the same manner as before."

It had been my hope that the verdict would free clergy from the fear of prosecution for conducting same-gender union ceremonies. After all, if the Social Principles were not deemed to be church law in my case, why should they be in another? Why would a bishop prosecute other clergy when the outcome would be the same? My optimism was dampened by the bishop's letter.

In strident chorus, bishops across the country condemned the verdict, declaring that it neither set a precedent nor changed church law, and strongly stating their intentions to enforce the prohibition of "homosexual unions" by prosecuting clergy who conducted them. Bishop Ray Chamberlain of Knoxville, Tennessee, wrote to members of his annual conference:

> While so many are obsessed with the church trial of a pastor in Nebraska, most of you have remained focused on Jesus Christ. There will always be persons, events, things, positions to distract us. We have 38,403 clergy persons in United Methodism. One of these clergy persons was charged with violating church law by officiating at a covenant service for two women. It is reported that more than one who voted for acquittal did so, not because they supported the action of the pastor on trial, but because they understood the Social Principles to be guides and, therefore, not to have the weight of church law. Every one of us has seen persons acquitted in civil courts over a narrow interpretation of the law or over a technicality. This is always frustrating.
>
> The key issue here is that the "church has not spoken" anything new in this trial. It was a jury that spoke and not the church. The position of the church is precisely the same today as it was yesterday. This trial is an aberration and hardly worthy of a great deal of energy and attention.
>
> I asked a group of pastors recently how many of them had gay people attending their congregations. Only about 10% of the pastors responded affirmatively. Then I asked how many pastors had members who were adulterers. All pastors raised their hands. We don't have to go to Nebraska to find sins/needs to address. We have our hands full right here at home.

While the covenant ceremony had caused convulsions of anger throughout The United Methodist Church, the trial's outcome not only exacerbated the outrage, it provoked panic that the church would be destroyed by the verdict. "The end of the church trial was the beginning of a firestorm of response," wrote Cheryl Hahs Edwards, director of communications for the Nebraska Annual Conference, which "overwhelmingly . . . opposed . . . the verdict and questioned what it means for the future of the denomination."[2] The *Nebraska Messenger*, the monthly publication of the Nebraska Annual Conference, printed numerous letters from clergy and lay people with headlines such as "Church Fails to Do Job," "Christ Is Weeping," and "Feeling Betrayed."

The *Wall Street Journal*'s editorial page declared the verdict to have been "A Methodist Misstep," saying that it had "sparked a conflagration that is sure to divide the church."[3]

Good News issued a press release condemning the verdict and demanding that the Council of Bishops convene a special session of the General Conference "as soon as possible to address the present crisis in The United Methodist Church." "We believe that this crisis is so severe," the Board of Directors of the Confessing Movement said, agreeing with the need for a special session, "that it threatens the connection and the ties that bind us together in worship and ministry."

Newscope quoted Maxie Dunnam, president of Asbury Theological Seminary in Kentucky: "Clergy across the nation will move now to follow suit and the unity of our church and the future of the connection are gravely threatened. If the practice of same-sex marriages is allowed to stand in the public eye as 'the mind of the church,' our beloved denomination will be seriously fractured if not completely divided. I sense we are at the 'breaking point' and if something is not done about this particular situation, we may be pushed 'over the edge.'"[4]

An editorial in the *United Methodist Reporter* proclaimed:

> The default acquittal in the trial of the Reverend Jimmy Creech: has widened the theological rift; has split the congregation of First United Methodist Church in Omaha, Nebraska, which has lost tens of thousands of dollars in revenue, and some 150 members; has fueled zealots across the church to push aggressively for their causes; has confused pastors who are sworn to uphold the Order and Discipline of The United Methodist Church . . .
>
> As a church mandated by our membership vows to live in covenant

with each other, United Methodists cannot tolerate the actions of pastors who disregard the church's *Book of Discipline* as a matter of conscience. To do so in the name of "justice" creates injustice to those who live in covenant by the rules and intentions which our representative governing bodies have enacted . . .

What saddens us most about the church's overwhelming preoccupation from both extremes — with this trial in particular and homosexuality issues in general — is how this battle diverts energies from needed ministries . . .

In light of Jesus' instruction that we love one another so that the world might believe, we call for a truce in this no-win battle of disregard for the church's order followed by emotional legal actions and spiteful protests.[5]

As the major weekly source of news about The United Methodist Church, the *Reporter* had given an appallingly shallow apology for institutional idolatry.

There were several protests around the country related to the trial's outcome. The Evangelical Renewal Fellowship of the California-Nevada Annual Conference issued a statement that said: "We humbly and strongly ask our annual conference leaders to join with us in seeking a just way in which we might allow evangelical pastors and congregations the choice to separate from the annual conference."[6] The request was denied. Nonetheless, some congregations and pastors withdrew from the California-Nevada Annual Conference, including Kingsburg United Methodist Church, which voted unanimously to leave The United Methodist Church the following June.

Two of Atlanta's largest United Methodist churches, Acworth and Mt. Bethel, along with First United Methodist Church of Marietta, Georgia, announced that they would withhold payments on apportionments for churchwide causes "in response to the Creech trial verdict."[7] Lindsey Davis, the bishop of the North Georgia Annual Conference, said: "The failure of our judicial system on this one case has spread life-threatening frustration and confusion in our church. Our people deserve to have this issue clarified as soon as possible."[8]

Other churches around the country followed the example of the Georgia congregations. The DeWitt United Methodist Church was one of several churches in Nebraska that decided to withhold payments on its apportionments until the legal status of the prohibition of "homosexual unions" was clarified.[9] Grace United Methodist Church in Marcus, Iowa, sent letters to over five thousand clergy and lay leaders urging them to not pay their annual conference apportionments.[10]

In April, James V. Heidinger II sent out a fundraising e-mail for Good News that encouraged people to sign a petition for a special session of the General Conference: "If a clear resolution does not come from a special session, many local United Methodist churches have said they may be forced to withhold certain church apportionments. Good News is on record affirming the right of persons and congregations to exercise their consciences financially without fear of reprisal or punitive actions against them or their pastors." Within The United Methodist Church, not paying apportionments is an act of mutiny by a local church. If the refusal to pay spreads, it's anarchy. Heidinger was promoting a transgression that he accused me of committing: violating the Order and Discipline of The United Methodist Church. Not only that, but he justified this action on the basis of conscience, a basis he did not accept for my act of ministry.

A dramatic picture of the sinking *Titanic* was on the cover of the May–June 1998 issue of *Good News*. "Will homosexuality sink United Methodism?" was written across the bottom of the cover. The issue included a letter to the editor from David Spence of Reedsville, West Virginia, who wrote: "The United Methodist denomination is beginning to resemble the *Titanic*. Incredibly, a jury of thirteen United Methodist ministers found Creech not guilty. The evidence was strong, but the jury was weak. United Methodist ministers are not known for bravery. The damage is irreparable. The ship is slowly sinking. The United Methodist denomination must split. Nothing matters anymore. Boards, programs, agencies, General Conference, Jurisdictional Conference, the children's initiative, Africa University—it's all a mere rearranging of the deck chairs on the *Titanic*. If you were on a ship that you knew was going to sink, would you stay on the ship? Or would you get in a life raft?"[11]

In addition to condemnatory messages in the printed media, I was deluged with hundreds of letters like the following from clergy and lay people around the country:

Jimmy Creech, *not pastor*. No, the Methodist Church didn't win, the devil won. The devil is now preaching in a church through you. Congratulations, one more way the Methodist Church is going down the drain, men like you.

—A lay person from Green Bay, Wisconsin

You are indeed a fag lover . . . hand in hand with Satin [sic] himself . . . Your church will grow because of all the humanists out in the world and all the homosexuals that will support you, but you are driving the faithful, God fearing, Bible believing people from their church home. God can only be angry as you stand before the cameras and flaunt [sic — I think he meant taunt] His precious Word. May God convict you and have mercy on your soul as you have joined Satan's march to destroy America.

—A lay person from Murray, Kentucky

Of course, not everyone was unhappy with the trial's surprise ending. Positive responses accompanied the expressions of anger. The Reconciling Congregation Program issued a statement on March 16, 1998: "While we regret that The United Methodist Church is unable to unequivocally welcome lesbian, gay and bisexual persons and their families at this time, we believe that God's Spirit is moving the church toward such a fuller understanding of the inclusive and compassionate gospel of Jesus Christ. The outcome of the Creech trial is one sign of this progress. However it is distressing to hear voices of those in the church who threaten withdrawal or reprisals because others on the margins of the church are being invited to join them at God's table. God's table is bountiful with room enough for all."

The Reverend Kenneth Chalker, pastor of First United Methodist Church in Cleveland, Ohio, and the chairperson of the Host Committee for the upcoming 2000 General Conference, made these observations in the Cleveland *Plain Dealer*:

One of the things that is so troubling to me in the controversy surrounding Creech's trial is that it points up how selective we are when it comes to identifying sins and wanting sinners punished. It is a chargeable offense for a heterosexual pastor, for instance, to become sexually involved with any person other than that pastor's spouse. How many church trials have been held on that issue? Not many. Usually, such instances of clergy misconduct are quietly dealt with and the pastor, even if guilty, is reassigned. It also is a chargeable offense for a pastor to be lazy in the performance of the duties of that office to the point that it destroys a church. The fact of the matter is, there are ministers serving in churches right now who have destroyed a string of churches over the course of their "ministry" and no charges have ever been brought against them. Now here comes an extraordinarily dedicated and gifted pastor in Nebraska who celebrates the love and commitment between two people of the same sex. He is put on trial. Imagine, this pastor has the audacity to pray for two people and ask God to bless them. What a terrible crime against the church. What are we coming to when such an act is not punished? For heaven's sake, he is eating with sinners and healing lepers. We should crucify him! Crucify him! Oops, sorry. Wrong story.[12]

Sara Ellen Mamlin of Indianapolis wrote to the *Hoosier United Methodist News*: "Traveling in East Africa, I heard a brief radio report of the decision in the Reverend Jimmy Creech trial and gave thanks another door was not shut on dialogue about the issues his trial raised. As the Christian community in the last century wrestled over the problem of its day—slavery—today our church is called to reason together over the issues of authority and sexual concerns. May we each be equal to the challenge of hearing one another fully and clearly while discerning God's action and word in our midst."[13]

In the *Social Questions Bulletin*, published by the Methodist Federation for Social Action, George McClain commented:

Rarely have I been so emotionally involved in an event as I was with this trial. I felt that so much that we value was on trial. Inwardly, I felt very vulnerable and still do. I believe many others have been similarly affected, whether present in Kearney or not . . .

In Kearney, we saw a microcosm of our larger church, deeply pained about the underlying struggle over what kind of church we want to be. The parallels to the days of the civil rights movement are numerous. Change in church and society is messy. Sometimes extraneous issues threaten clarity of vision. People get caught between conflicting "goods." Some nearly get ground to pieces. The pain is everywhere and none of us may escape it. There is such a need for compassion, forgiveness, and tenderness with each other, whether within camps or across "battle" lines.

The closer things come to changing, the hotter gets the struggle . . . We hear cries of protest, pledges to withhold funds from the general church, cabinet declarations that nothing has changed and panicky calls for an emergency session of General Conference. Understand: These are signs that the change we seek is under way. The old order is threatened.

We've met disappointment around the gay issue in every General Conference since 1972. We will meet it again, and again. But, as we shared in Kearney, it became so clear that we're in this struggle for the long haul. We know society doesn't change in just a few years, nor does a church . . .

The difficult work to build reconciling congregations and conferences, to do basic education, to come out as gay or gay-friendly—it all adds up. Jimmy's acquittal is a product of a vast movement. All who have contributed to the church's slowly but profoundly changing dynamic should feel that they helped make this come about. May these scattered (but very connected) works of justice continue and flourish![14]

I have no idea how many sermons were preached in Nebraska about the trial on the Sunday immediately after it ended, but I have no doubt that there were many. Fortunately, I didn't have to hear them. I did listen to one, however. In the week following the trial, I received an audiotape by mail in a manila envelope with no return address. The sermon on the tape, "Living Right in an Upside Down World," had been preached by the Reverend Les Beauchamp, pastor of Trinity Church Interdenominational, a megachurch of more than three thousand members and one of the fastest growing churches in Omaha. He began by explaining that "God had circumvented" his planned sermon on "The Basic Laws of Marriage" in favor of this one, which he had worked on throughout the day before he delivered it.

Holding up a copy of Saturday's *Omaha World-Herald*, he asked: "Did you get the news that Creech was acquitted?" Then he launched into a harangue damning the verdict, me, First Church, The United Methodist Church, and homosexuals: "This is a blind pastor leading blind people over the cliff to destruction. The United Methodist Church is sick. Homosexuality destroys people. It's an abomination to God. It ruins humanity. It ruins society. It is the downfall of great nations. Did you know what The United Methodist Church has done to your fair city? They have taken an avowed gay rights activist pastor and put him in your city. I would guess they knew what he was going to do. If the vision of First Church is to be inclusive, they're fulfilling it. It has grieved God in this city. And I believe there's very little if any Holy Spirit in that church this morning."

Beauchamp urged his congregation to write letters to the local newspaper to protest the verdict and any accommodation to homosexuals. He charged them to write and call their state legislators to urge passage of the Defense of Marriage Act, which would not recognize same-sex covenants in Nebraska. He told them that they needed to get involved to protect the city, the state, and the nation, and that if they didn't, they were failing God.

I received printed copies of two other sermons, both dramatically different from Beauchamp's and both preached by members of the Committee on Investigation that had sent me to trial. The Reverend Dr. Aaron Black, pastor of First United Methodist Church in Lincoln, titled his sermon "Let the Healing Begin!" He acknowledged the outrage provoked by the verdict and then called for healing, challenging his congregation to go beyond conventional opinion to a deeper and informed understanding of human sexuality.

The Reverend David Lux, chairperson of the Committee on Investigation and pastor of First United Methodist Church in North Platte, preached an extraordinary sermon with the ambitious title of "The Bible, Homosexual Practice, and Our Response." He closed his sermon with a personal story, revealing the deeper reason for his openness to lesbian, gay, bisexual, and transgender people:

> I know two women who have lived together for over fifty years. They are a part of my family. They met in college, but got jobs in a same small community in another state and moved there together. They are Christians, each involved in a different church. They have both contributed greatly to the community in which they live. They have never said to us whether they are homosexual or not, and frankly I don't care whether they are or not. It would make no difference in how I treat them or how they have treated me and my family over the years. Their sexual preferences and practices are between them and God. As far as I know they have never had a commitment ceremony, but at some point in their lives they made some sort of commitment to live together, to care for each other, to be a part of each other's families. They have been good for each other and a blessing to our family. One of them now has Parkinson's Disease and has trouble getting around by herself. I thank God that they have each other.

After four months away, I was finally back at First Church, and there was little opportunity to ease back into my ministry. Though exhausted, I was ecstatic to be back and plunged into my work with enthusiasm. One of the first things I wanted to do was meet with each staff person and the elected lay leadership so they could bring me up to date on the state of the church. Frank Rathbun, the current chairperson of the Church Council, was at the top of my list. I always worked closely with the council chairperson. In addition, Frank was the opposition's key person at the church. I expected there to be a period of negotiation and testing, a time for us to figure out just how we might relate. I was wrong. Instead of meeting with me, Frank sent in his letter of resignation. The opposition now had little influence at First Church. Even so, it remained determined.

On Thursday of that week, I received a flier that had been sent to members of First Church by the opposition announcing a "First United Methodist Church Laity Rally" to be held in a local high school auditorium on the coming Sunday. Patricia Miller, executive director of the Confessing Movement, issued a national press release describing the rally as an effort "to minister to members of the laity of First United Methodist Church of Omaha," clearly implying that this special service was necessary because the clergy at First Church were not able to minister to the disaffected members of the congregation. The opposition was representing itself as "First Church in exile," although the exile was self-imposed.

On Saturday, the *Omaha World-Herald* carried an article about the planned service, "a chance for members of First United Methodist Church who have been 'shunned and left out' by their pastors to come together and be ministered to, said [Mel] Semrad, one of the organizers. Organizers say the three pastors are unable to minister to congregants who uphold traditional Methodist Church teachings that the practice of homosexuality is incompatible with Christian teaching. 'This was the only way to have our voices heard,' [Semrad] said. 'Jimmy wouldn't respond in any way to our concerns. He listened but did not hear.' Rathbun said that while Creech's legal problems in the Church are behind him, he is not home free. 'His real trial started last Sunday,' the day Creech returned to his pulpit, Rathbun said."[15]

District Superintendent Marv Koelling, who earlier had been assigned by Bishop Martínez to supervise First Church along with Susan Davies, attended the laity rally and received an enthusiastic welcome. Mel Semrad extolled Koelling's presence as evidence that "we're doing nothing wrong in the eyes of God." The Reverend Dr. Ira Gallaway—the associate director of the Confessing Movement, who had flown in from Arizona—preached.

When he closed the service, Mel announced that the Reverend Dr. Bill Hinson, pastor of First United Methodist Church in Houston, "the largest United Methodist congregation," and Dr. Maxie Dunnam, the president of Asbury Theological Seminary, had sent greetings to the gathering. The *Omaha World-Herald* reported that "an estimated 300 people attended."[16]

That evening, the opposition held a discussion session at the high school, equally well attended. Marv Koelling spoke to the gathering several times, offering support and indicating that he was on their side. At one point, when answering a question about how the bishop appoints ministers to churches, he wryly remarked: "We all know a lot more now about Jimmy than we did." He explained to the Associated Press that "he was there to let members know that the church still cared about them. 'I think these people needed a time together, and the message wasn't divisive,' he said . . . They are good people and good United Methodists."[17]

By phone the next morning, Mike McClellan questioned Marv about his attendance at the two events and his public support of the dissident faction. Marv told Mike that his role there was only as an observer, that as the "eyes and ears" of the bishop, he needed to keep informed. He said that neither he nor any other member of the bishop's cabinet had talked with Mel about the rally ahead of time or had given permission or authorization for the rally to take place. However, Ira Gallaway told the *United Methodist News Service* that "he contacted the district superintendent before accepting the invitation to speak and was encouraged to participate."[18]

Marv's attendance at the rally was a stupendous blunder. He would not have been there without the direction and consent of Bishop Martínez. By attending, Marv had undermined my ministry and that of First United Methodist Church, legitimized the laity gathering outside of First Church, and strengthened the opposition's cause against me. At the same time that he was placing the full responsibility on me to reach out and reconcile with them, the bishop was encouraging the opposition to resist all attempts at reconciliation. Why shouldn't they? The bishop's and Marv's sympathies clearly were with them. All they needed to do was hold out until I was gone. Whether by ruthless intent or ineptness, Bishop Martínez and Marv Koelling had blatantly increased the dissension within The United Methodist Church, once again abandoning and isolating the active members of First United Methodist Church.

On the night of March 24, I met with the Staff-Parish Relations Committee for the first time since my return. In spite of the euphoria over the trial's verdict and my return to First Church, we felt uncertain about the bishop's willingness to reappoint me, in spite of his vow to do so should I be acquitted. The committee voted unanimously to send a letter to Bishop Martínez, with copies to all the members of his cabinet, expressing unqualified support for my reappointment.

The committee would not hear back from Bishop Martínez for nearly a month. And even then, in a letter dated April 22, the bishop made no commitment, saying only that the cabinet was "aware of the First Church Staff-Parish Relations Committee's position on re-appointments." He added that "we have discussed the issues in some depth during these past weeks." Although he had promised to be in close communication with First Church, just as in the past, he had not been. Usually appointments and reappointments are announced in late April. The congregation, its leadership, Don, and I faced prolonged uncertainty.

In an effort to initiate dialogue, I wrote to the key leaders of the Laity Group, the name officially adopted by the opposition, asking them to meet with me. By then it was clear that their rallies would continue until some concession had been made, by either me or the bishop. I wrote the group's leaders: "There are at least two things we have in common: our faith in Jesus Christ and our love for First United Methodist Church. It is my hope that we can build a constructive and helpful conversation upon this common ground. I know that you have strong feelings and beliefs. I know that you are hurt and angry. I want to hear from you. I believe that the common ground we share is sufficient for us to remain together in community, even when we have irreconcilable differences on other issues. But, this requires talking and listening together. I hope that you will join me."

Most of the leaders did not respond. Only Robert Howell and Mel Semrad were willing to meet with me, explaining they represented the others I had invited. They came expecting me to make some kind of deal to get them and those attending the rallies back to First Church. They insisted that the Laity Group have unhindered access to the First Church facilities for weddings, funerals, and baptisms, without any of the First Church clergy involved. I told them this was not possible, explaining that *The Book of Discipline* held the pastors of First United Methodist Church responsible for the pastoral care of all its members. An outside pastor could assist us in such services, I explained, but the invitation to any guest pastors would have to come directly from Don Bredthauer or me. Mel and Robert were angry at my response. The meeting lasted less than fifteen minutes, and they refused to sit down at any point. My effort to connect with the Laity Group had been rebuffed. Reconciliation was clearly impossible.

Richard Armstrong, an active member of the opposition who had been gravely ill, died in Methodist Hospital. He and his family refused to allow Don Bredthauer or me to visit him during his illness and sent word that we were not to conduct or attend his funeral. The family told me the hospital chaplain, who had provided constant pastoral care to Richard during his long stay at the hospital, would conduct the funeral at a local funeral home. Ironically, the chaplain, unbeknownst to Richard and his family, was gay.

Susan Mullins called to invite me to lunch at Goldberg's, a popular lunch spot on Dodge Street in the Dundee neighborhood, not far from First Church. This would be the first time we had talked since she began her spiritual growth leave on January 21. At lunch, she told me she had decided not to continue as a church pastor after June. The stress she had experienced in the fall had been far too painful for her and had taken a terrible toll on her spirit and her body. The intensity of the anger and hostility that exploded after the verdict reinforced her apprehension about continuing at First Church. She would return at the end of her leave on May 21 but stay only through June, the end of the appointment year.

It was hard for her to tell me this, and hard for me to hear it. Susan had been a wonderful colleague. She was an exceptionally able and caring pastor. While our friendship never had the opportunity to develop beyond professional respect and trust, what we had experienced together created a strong bond between us. Her departure from First Church, and especially from ministry altogether, would be an enormous loss.

On Sunday, March 29, the *Omaha World-Herald* published an ad that covered the entire back page of the first section. "Where We Stand" was written across the top, and under that were images of roses, wedding rings, and two interlocking symbols for female. Beneath the rings was "an open letter to the residents of the greater Omaha area." The letter read:

> As pastors and Christian leaders of churches in the city, we feel compelled to respond to the recent events surrounding Pastor Jimmy Creech and First United Methodist Church. We also believe that the exoneration of Pastor Creech has left many people bewildered and wondering

where other local churches stand on the issue of single-sex marriage and/ or covenants of commitments. We, therefore, wish to affirm our categorical commitment to marriage as a sacred and lifelong covenant instituted by God exclusively between a man and a woman. We also affirm our commitment to Holy Scripture as interpreted in the historic Protestant, Catholic, Orthodox, and Jewish traditions as exclusively limiting such a covenant to heterosexual relationships: "therefore, a man leaves his father and his mother and cleaves to his wife, and they become one flesh" (Genesis 2:24). We view any attempt to redefine marriage to include same-sex unions as violating Holy Scripture and therefore displeasing to God.

The names of 106 churches were listed at the bottom of the letter—mostly Pentecostal, evangelical and Baptist, with a few Lutheran and Presbyterian congregations and one Episcopal church, but no United Methodist churches. The ad was sponsored by a group called "Metro Area Leaders Network." Immediately after the trial, this group had met, drafted the ad, and sent it out to solicit church endorsements, as well as contributions to cover its $6,869 cost.

While the ad specifically addressed the covenant ceremony, the trial, First Church, and me, other clergy and churches in the Omaha area felt it implicated them as well. A group of clergy who saw the ad as especially offensive and harmful met almost immediately and drafted a response that was published in the *Omaha World-Herald*:

> The controversy surrounding the Reverend Jimmy Creech's actions affirming committed gay and lesbian relationships has challenged many people of faith. We are distressed that some Protestant church leaders, in their *Omaha World-Herald* advertisement of March 29, claimed: "We also affirm our commitment to Holy Scripture as interpreted in the historic Protestant, Catholic, Orthodox, and Jewish traditions . . ."
>
> The statement clearly does not reflect the thought of all faith groups. Our interpretations of scripture are not uniform and we cannot claim to speak for each other without consultation. No members of the Catholic, Orthodox or Jewish traditions signed the statement. We cannot find representatives from these traditions who were ever consulted.
>
> Misrepresenting some of our traditions is serious, but more grievous is the tone of the advertisement which we found to be a slap in the face to

gay and lesbian persons, many of whom are faithful members and leaders of our congregations. We must strongly protest . . .

The clear and painful lesson of history is that quoting scriptural proof-texts out of context to defame any group of people is always wrong and frequently leads to discrimination, violence and murder.

Scripture has been used to justify slavery, violence against women and children, the Holocaust against Jews and racial segregation. It has been used to silence people of science and to oppress the poor. Invoking God's name to convey reproach for any person is an action about which we cannot be silent.

A growing number of people of faith are being led to the conclusion that judging people solely on the basis of their sexual orientation is wrong.

We are shaped by faith and grounded in tradition. We base our faith in holy scripture, our experience of God's love for all people and the commitment to justice that this demands . . .[19]

The commentary was signed by seventy-seven clergy, including thirty-five United Methodists, and ninety-nine lay members of congregations in the Omaha and Lincoln areas associated with Reform and Reconstructionist Judaism, the Evangelical Lutheran Church in America, United Church of Christ, Baptist, Roman Catholic, Christian (Disciples of Christ), Episcopal, Metropolitan Community Church, Presbyterian (USA), Unitarian Universalist, and Unity denominations.

Supporting the Vision understood that we faced a crisis after the trial, just as we had in the fall of 1997 — except that this time, the crisis was not a matter of pending disaster, but rather of imminent opportunity. It would be a grave error to quietly withdraw into the confines of church programs and ministries for shelter from attacks and in search of relief and healing, satisfied that the trial had in some sense restored order to First Church. Instead, we opened our doors, inviting the world to see the truth: we were stronger and more committed to the Vision Focus than ever before.

In a letter to the congregation, Supporting the Vision offered this challenge: "We have a lot of building to do. The covenant ceremony and the trial have provided us with *incredible* growth experiences. We have again affirmed our vision of being open to ALL God's children. Now comes the hard work. For a long time First Church has been known as a high steeple church, distant from real people. We need to do more than lip service to our vision. We need action now, not in a couple of weeks. We need to capitalize on the momentum from the trial and move forward with clear action steps to build inclusivity, membership and our finances. We have made a clear statement to Omaha that we are intentional about including all God's children."

We initiated a major public relations campaign aimed not only at Omaha, but at the nation. We wanted everyone everywhere to know that First Church had done more than simply survive, and that we were standing behind our vision. We began running large ads each week in the *Omaha World-Herald* announcing our programs, emphasizing our diversity, and inviting people to join us. On Saturdays, church members conducted door-to-door visits within the neighborhood surrounding the church, telling our neighbors about the vitality of First Church and inviting them to visit us during the upcoming Holy Week and Easter services and programs.

We organized a community rally and open house at the church for mid-April. Displays were set up by the various committees and programs all around the First Church facility, each staffed by lay people eager to share information with visitors. The youth led a "spirit service" in Mead Chapel, and the choirs performed in the sanctuary. A large tent was put up on the front lawn, offering games and activities for children. Balloons of every color floated in the air. Church members baked brownies, cookies, lemon bars, and other goodies for everyone's enjoyment.

The print and television media, both local and national, gave the event extensive coverage, reporting around the country that First Church was very much alive and well. The open house and rally were a huge success, energizing the congregation as well as enlightening the Omaha community.

As if to accentuate its courageous commitment to its vision, First Church formally began the process of becoming a Reconciling Congregation at a Church Council meeting the following Tuesday night. The congregation was looking forward, not backward. It had survived too much pain to be afraid. It truly was Easter time at First Church, with life reigning supreme over fear and death.

The crisis within The United Methodist Church wasn't just a consequence of progressives on one side clashing with conservatives on the other. People on both ends of the spectrum located the crux of the crisis in the Council of Bishops, which, at best, didn't know how to lead the church or, at worst, was afraid to lead. There were exemplary bishops who were strong leaders, but as a group, the Council of Bishops operated by a code of consensus that crippled it. The council put preserving The United Methodist Church as an institution above bearing witness to the gospel of Jesus Christ. Had the bishops not been so weak, the Good News evangelical caucus and the Confessing Movement would not have had the power and leverage to manipulate the membership of the church and its General Conference over the past thirty years.

Methodist bishops have limited power but great authority. They are "set apart for a ministry of general oversight and supervision" and "authorized to guard the faith, order, liturgy, doctrine and discipline of the Church."[20] The Good News and Confessing movements, which wanted the church to adhere to a strict orthodoxy, denounced the bishops for allowing diversity.

Although the bishops were supposed "to be prophetic voices and courageous leaders in the cause of justice for all people,"[21] they were too divided to speak with one voice about the persecution and oppression of gay people. This was especially difficult for them because prejudice against lesbian, gay, bisexual, and transgender people was endemic to the church, and supported by as many bishops as opposed it. One bishop had told me in 1993 that the bishops would not talk even among themselves about the issue of homosexuality because they were afraid of it, afraid of having to take a public stand on the issue and of the fallout that such a stand might cause. They kept their collective head in the sand, hoping the issue would be resolved without their having to act.

The Book of Discipline charges the bishops "to seek and be a sign of the unity of the faith,"[22] and the facade of unity had become their golden calf. The Good News and Confessing movements were pulling The United Methodist Church hard to the right, and the progressives were resisting. Caught in the middle, the bishops were desperately trying to hold the church together.

On April 26, just six weeks after my trial, more than a hundred United Methodist bishops from around the world arrived in Lincoln, Nebraska, for the annual five-day spring meeting of the Council of Bishops. This year, the world was watching. It was a coincidence that this meeting took place in Bishop Martínez's jurisdiction, as it had been scheduled long before the controversy sparked by Mary and Martha's covenant ceremony. There was great pressure on the Council of Bishops to call for a special session of the General Conference and to make some response to the verdict at my trial.

On the fourth day of the council's meeting, the bishops unanimously adopted "A Pastoral Statement," which read in part:

We acknowledge the concerns regarding The United Methodist Church's stand on issues, particularly homosexuality and homosexual unions, and the church's ability to maintain discipline, order and unity. While recognizing the importance of these issues, we challenge the church to remain focused on the mission of God and our unity in Christ and to set its priorities accordingly. Issues within the church must not be allowed to distract us from the missional needs of the world and our call to make disciples of Jesus Christ.

We continue the commitment we made in our consecration as bishops "to guard the faith, to seek unity, and to exercise the discipline of the whole church; and to supervise and support the church's life, work, and mission throughout the world." In covenant with one another, we are committed to uphold the General Conference's action on the theological, ethical and policy matters defined in *The Book of Discipline*, including statements on homosexuality and all specified issues contained in the Social Principles including the prohibition of ceremonies celebrating homosexual unions by our ministers and in our churches.

At the same time we also affirm our pastoral responsibility to all peoples including those who feel excluded from the church. We acknowledge the desire to resolve current conflicts around issues of homosexuality. We have prayerfully considered the appeal to resolve legislatively the tensions through a called session of the General Conference. In anticipation of deliberations of the Judicial Council and the need for continued discernment and Christian conferencing on these matters, the calling of a special session does not seem wise at this time.

Just days before the bishops had convened, the Judicial Council had announced that it would meet in August to make a declaratory ruling on the legal status of the "homosexual unions" prohibition. So there would be no special session of the General Conference. That was the only good news in the entire bishops' statement.

The bishops had said nothing new or helpful. They had shown no prophetic insight. They had reiterated without critique the offensive, judgmental, and violent language aimed at gay people in *The Book of Discipline* and said that they intended to enforce it, entrenching themselves as guardians of the status quo. I knew that some bishops did not agree with or support The United Methodist Church's teaching and policies regarding homosexuality, and I found it incredible that the statement had unanimous support. I thought the statement was scandalous, offensive, and irresponsible. Rather than being a "pastoral" statement, the document was blatantly political, sacrificing moral leadership in order to pacify the outraged and try to resolve the growing discord within the church. In no way did it deal with the church's injustice toward gay people.

The pain that the bishops had responded to was the recent pain of those outraged by the covenant ceremony and my trial's verdict, those who were intent on closing the doors to openly self-affirming lesbian, gay, bisexual, and transgender people. The bishops were not responding to the pain inflicted by the Christian church upon generations of lesbian, gay, bisexual, and transgender people and their families. This selective pastoral attention was despicable and cowardly. I was particularly incensed at the comment very early in the statement that "issues within the church must not be allowed to distract us from the missional needs of the world." Clearly the bishops did not consider the spiritual, psychological, and physical suffering that the church caused lesbian, gay, bisexual, and transgender people to be of equal importance with the suffering caused by poverty, war, racial prejudice, and other social injustices. Because the violence done to gay people was being done by us, the church, the bishops implied that it should not be a distraction to our real mission. The statement even justified not holding a special session of the General Conference by saying: "As we respond to the crises in the world, especially among children and the impoverished and those who desperately need the gospel, a special called session might further distract us from our central mission."

At a press conference following the release of the statement, "the bishops who participated wouldn't say specifically whether they see the ban [on 'homosexual unions'] as law or guideline. Instead, Bishop Emerito Nacpil of the Philippines, president of the Council of Bishops for that year, would only say, 'What is in The Book of Discipline is binding to us, and we are committed to uphold it.'"[23] The statement was hailed by Bishop Martínez as "a strong statement" that "reaffirms the position of The United Methodist Church with respect to homosexuality [and] commits us to proceed against pastors if they conduct same-sex ceremonies."[24] What the bishops wanted, in addition to assuaging their right-wing critics, was an enhanced threat of disciplinary action to discourage clergy from conducting same-gender covenant ceremonies.

Surprisingly, many of those who had demanded a special session of the General Conference to save The United Methodist Church from pending destruction had only guarded praise for the bishops' statement. Steve Beard, editor of *Good News*, said: "We're disappointed that they did not deal with the Creech issue. The church needed something far more decisive on Creech."[25] However, the Good News movement executive committee said that "they were pleased with the Bishops' public commitment to uphold *The Book of Discipline*, including the Social Principles."[26] Likewise, a spokesperson for the Confessing Movement said: "We are grateful that the Council of Bishops has recognized the pain inflicted upon the membership of The United Methodist Church as caused by the performing of a same-sex union . . . and the verdict which failed to find the pastor guilty for violation of the Order and Discipline of the Church."[27]

Much was made of the fact that the bishops had reached consensus in their statement. But the unanimity of the Council of Bishops in that document was one of form, not substance. Soon after the bishops' meeting in Lincoln, Bishop Melvin Talbert sent out a letter to the California-Nevada Annual Conference, saying:

> While I agree with the statement as released, I want you to know that there is disagreement within the Council as to how various parts of *The Book of Discipline* are interpreted. Let me speak for myself. While *The Book of Discipline* is commonly referred to as "the book of law" for our denomination, all sections are not understood to be law. In the case at point, the statement regarding holy unions is found in the Social Principles. My understanding is that the Social Principles are not law. Thus, one performing a holy union does not violate the law of the church, even though such an act does go against the spirit of the Social Principles. So, as one bishop, I will hold to the principle that the Social Principles are not law, until instructed otherwise by our Judicial Council, which meets in August to deal with the issue of holy unions.[28]

Bishop Talbert was being consistent with the position he had held all along. He would uphold *The Book of Discipline* as interpreted by the Judicial Council, which had never ruled the Social Principles to be church law. While other bishops, the media, and people aligned with Good News and the Confessing Movement hailed the bishops' statement as a mandate to enforce the prohibition of "homosexual unions," using it to intimidate clergy and falsely reassure others, Bishop Talbert did not. What's more, he had made his view a matter of public record. Other bishops agreed with him, but none of them took such a bold public stand. Therefore, the state of affairs after the Council of Bishops meeting was no different than before the meeting.

The meeting ended on Wednesday, May 1. On Friday, Bishop Martínez's secretary called, asking me to meet with the bishop on Tuesday, May 5. I had no doubt that this meeting was about my reappointment to First Church.

I gave a speech about my trial and the Vision Focus of First Church at the University of Iowa in Iowa City on Monday night. I left Iowa City early Tuesday morning to drive west for my meeting with the bishop in Lincoln. True to my habit, I was going to be early for our meeting. To use up some of the extra time, I stopped at an outlet mall between Omaha and Lincoln to buy a dress shirt. As I looked through the shirts, another customer came over to me and asked, "Are you Reverend Creech?" When I said yes, she took my hand and softly said, "I'm lesbian, and I want to thank you for what you've done for us." There was no way that I could have conveyed to her how important her words were at that moment, when I was on my way to a meeting that could have a profound impact on my ministry in Omaha and perhaps on the rest of my life. Her words didn't ease my anxiety, but they gave me strength.

Bishop Martínez began our meeting by saying: "Jimmy, the cabinet and I have decided we're not going to reappoint you to First Church." He gave several reasons for the decision: the continuing deterioration of the situation at First Church; my inability to reconcile with the opposition; my failure to follow his advice not to conduct the covenant ceremony; my conducting the ceremony and intention to continue conducting same-gender union ceremonies; my refusing the conditions to end my suspension before the trial; and, finally, the continuing dissension within the Nebraska Annual Conference. I protested, arguing that First Church was not deteriorating but had developed into an amazingly strong and committed congregation, and that it was impossible for anyone to convince the opposition to return to First Church. I reminded him that the congregation emphatically wanted me to return. He listened but was unmoved by what I said. He had made his decision and wouldn't discuss it with me.

Before the trial, the bishop had explicitly promised the Staff-Parish Relations Committee, without condition, that he would reappoint me if I were acquitted. All the reasons he now gave to justify his decision not to reappoint me existed when he had made this promise, except that First Church was now stronger and thriving. But back then everyone had expected me to be found guilty, so he felt safe making his promise. He went back on his word — if he had really made the promise in good faith — because he simply didn't want to deal with me anymore. What the trial had failed to do, he would now accomplish: remove me from First Church.

Bishop Martínez told me I had three options. I could accept an appointment to another church in the Nebraska Annual Conference, I could look for an appointment in another annual conference, or I could take a leave of absence. I told him I needed time to think. As was his custom, he told me not to tell anyone about the decision and said that he would send an official announcement for Bill Jenks to read to the congregation of First Church on Sunday morning.

I was stunned. I had gone to the meeting knowing that I might hear what the bishop had told me, yet still hoping that I would be reappointed, the decision that I believed was best for him, the annual conference, First Church, and me. His long delay in making a decision — or at least in telling me what he had decided — had given me hope. It was, after all, too late to start looking for someone else for the First Church appointment.

Bill Jenks knew that I was meeting with Bishop Martínez that afternoon and called me early in the evening to ask what had happened. When I told him, he was irate, though not surprised. Other calls followed. The news spread quickly, and soon the media starting calling. The bishop's decision was reported on the ten o'clock TV news that night, and in newspapers across the country the following morning.

The next evening, the bishop met with the Staff-Parish Relations Committee at his office in Lincoln. The meeting went long into the night. Bill told a reporter afterward that the meeting "was a chance to air the feelings of the committee. We had no problems doing that. The decision is made. I'm still very saddened by it, very frustrated, but there's nothing I can do about it."[29] After discussing the decision not to reappoint me, the committee urged the bishop to appoint Don Bredthauer as senior pastor. Bishop Martínez made no commitment.

First Church members began frantically calling one another, many saying they were ready to leave The United Methodist Church. Someone suggested that there should be a meeting to talk this over, so one was quickly arranged for the next night in Mead Hall at First Church. The room was packed with people wanting to talk about the bishop's decision and what it meant for them individually and for the congregation, and to hear from the Staff-Parish Relations Committee. There was much anger at the bishop as well as grief. When several people said they were leaving not only First Church, but The United Methodist Church, Coyner Smith said: "Well, we thought we won. And if we give up now, they won. We cannot—because I know it's not over this building, but damn it, we can't give them the building. We can't give up. We've got to stay together." Then others echoed Coyner's determination to stay the course.

Bill Jenks said to the gathering:

At the meeting last night, the bishop told us what he'd told Jimmy, no more or less. We vented. He responded. He got defensive at times.

Here's the thing I have to keep telling myself: it's done. Nothing can change that. We have to accept that an injustice has been done and go on. That we are right doesn't change anything. All I can change is my attitude.

Walking away from where we find ourselves now dishonors Jimmy, ourselves, our vision. Jimmy's been a strong, steady light, and his light has exposed some ugly, hidden corners that make some people very uncomfortable, corners they would prefer to remain hidden. But his strong steady light has also revealed incredible riches and beauty that had also been hidden. It's the same light! The light is uncompromising. We have to be uncompromising. We have to see and acknowledge everything the light illuminates in ourselves: the beautiful woodwork and the dust bunnies, the flowers and the weeds.

This is hard to say, but the best way we can honor Jimmy is to not need him. To shine our own lights. To live our faith. I propose that we do that. I urge you to keep the faith, to stick it out, to stay together, and to stay at First Church.

We may yet determine at some point in the future, (and that could well come at different times for different people) that it can no longer work for us here. So be it. But for now, we must step into the dark void we perceive and begin to shed our own light on it.

When the evening was over, there was a shared appreciation and affirmation of all that they had gone through together. Only a few people still felt that they could not remain in the congregation. The others would stay as long as the Vision Focus was viable.

I had not prepared for any other possibility than returning to First Church. Now, because the bishop waited so long to act, I had no real options other than to take a leave of absence. I knew his suggestion of another appointment in Nebraska was a ruse. *The Book of Discipline* required the bishop to offer me another appointment, and he included that option only to meet the requirement. It was the first week of May, and appointments had already been decided, not only in Nebraska but in all the other annual conferences throughout the country. Even if there was a vacant appointment remaining in Nebraska, how could he appoint me? The very reasons he gave for not reappointing me to First Church would be reasons not to appoint me somewhere else. I would still continue to conduct same-gender unions. The controversy in the annual conference would continue. And what church in Nebraska would want me? As far as moving to another annual conference, it was too late to initiate contacts outside Nebraska.

On the following Friday, the bishop contacted Don Bredthauer and asked him to accept the position of senior pastor at First Church. Even though the Laity Group wanted Don removed, Bishop Martínez had heard the Staff-Parish Relations Committee's demand to have someone they could trust. Don was reluctant, but, with encouragement from the staff and lay leadership, he accepted. Don had wanted this appointment years before, but not this way and not at this price. He had been my stalwart friend and colleague and had wanted me to be reappointed as much as anyone. He accepted the appointment with deeply mixed emotions.

Susan Mullins returned from her spiritual leave on May 21. Finally, Don, Susan, and I were back together again. There were nearly six weeks before the end of June, when Susan and I were scheduled to leave First Church. Even though she was not seeking another appointment in The United Methodist Church, Susan was contacted by Saint Francis of the Foothills United Methodist Church—an energetic, creative, and vital Reconciling Congregation in Tucson, Arizona—and invited to be its associate pastor. Susan accepted the offer with great excitement.

My tenure at First Church would officially end on the last day of June. However, because Don was the senior pastor in waiting, it felt right for me to leave early and allow him and the congregation to begin the next part of their journey together. Lingering would be unbearable for me. I decided that June 7, the day following the end of the Nebraska Annual Conference meeting in Lincoln, when Don would be officially appointed senior pastor, would be my final Sunday at First Church.

Supporting the Vision planned a farewell party for us on the last Saturday in May at Mike McClellan's law office, located in one of the historic homes in downtown Omaha. Everyone wore their sweatshirts from the trial that read "Supporting All God's Children," and a large group assembled on the front lawn for a photograph. At one point in the evening, when presentations were made to us, Roy Wright put a lei around my neck, gave me a hug, and in his booming, exuberant voice shouted for all to hear: "Jimmy, you've just been 'laid' by a gay man. How was it?" "It was good, Roy," I replied. "It was good."

During the Nebraska Annual Conference meeting in Lincoln the first week of June, the Nebraska chapter of the Methodist Federation for Social Action held its annual banquet and presented the Gary Schlosser Justice Award, its highest recognition for those "who have shown particular conviction and effectiveness in Justice Ministries," to Supporting the Vision of First United Methodist Church, Omaha. It was a much deserved recognition.

On Sunday, June 7, I preached my last sermon at First Church. Each of the three services was packed. On Monday, the *Omaha World-Herald* reported:

> Tears flowed and hearts sank Sunday as the Reverend Jimmy Creech bade an emotional farewell to First United Methodist Church in Omaha.
>
> Creech told the members that he expected them to continue with their mission of inclusion and acceptance and to be a witness to the world. "The only consolation I have in leaving," he said, "is that you will continue the ministry you have begun."
>
> He said God doesn't expect people—including gays and lesbians—to live by other people's expectations, but to live creatively for justice and mercy. "Sometimes we confuse the creeds and rules with the real essence of loving God and each other," he said. "What really matters is not our creed and rules. In the end, what really matters is how we treat one another."[30]

On Monday and Tuesday morning, we finished packing with lots of help from friends, while a vigilant CNN camera crew and members of the local media recorded our every move. Tuesday afternoon, George, our cat, and I drove away in the largest truck towing the largest trailer that U-Haul had to offer. Natalia, now sixteen, followed in her car, with Chris bringing up the rear of our caravan in her car. We headed east through Iowa toward Ocracoke Island, North Carolina, more than 1,500 miles away.

In my last *Bread* column, published just after we left, I said to the congregation:

> It is difficult to express fully how grateful I am to have been part of First United Methodist Church, Omaha, for these past two years as one of your pastors. You are a wonderful community of faithful disciples of Jesus Christ. These years have been eventful, challenging us in new ways to be faithful. We have experienced struggle, pain, and losses. But, you have met the challenge and have grown stronger in spirit and commitment. To be in your midst is to be blessed! I celebrate your openness to grow in grace to become the community God is calling you to be. I am proud of your compassionate witness of love and acceptance for all of God's children. I am in awe of your willingness to work for justice and peace on behalf of those who are hurting in our world. I have confidence that you will continue to allow God's spirit to move you and lead you in these ways. Please trust that what we have experienced together and will continue to experience is the movement of God's grace in our time. This is God's history. It is moving toward the vision that Jesus announced and embodied. A vision of all of God's children equally welcomed and accepted, of a community of compassion and justice, of a reign of love and peace. Always let yourselves be open to it; do not resist it. Blessings on you always!

The Sunday after we left, Don Bredthauer met with the Laity Group following its worship service, now being held at the Scottish Rite Cathedral in downtown Omaha. Don took with him several of the key leaders of First Church, including Bill Jenks, chairperson of the Staff-Parish Relations Committee, and Deb Romberger, chairperson of the Church Council.

"They requested that I come to their place," Don later told me. "I was really reluctant, but I agreed to come with several of the church leaders with me. They got us all up front. They expressed their concerns to me. They questioned my own vision for First Church and I reaffirmed the Vision Focus. They asked me directly if they were to come back, could I assure them they would be placed in positions of leadership. I said that's not my decision to make. That's up to the Nominations Committee and the All Church Conference. Bob Leuder said, 'You're in a position to make that happen.' I said, 'I'm sorry, but I can't do that.' Probably that was the major turning point. We left without their making a decision about whether or not to come back."

The following Wednesday night, the Laity Group met at the Boys Town music hall. At the end of a two-hour meeting, the 175 who attended voted to leave First United Methodist Church and start a new church. Bringing together the two factions had not been achieved by removing me, nor could it have been. To no one's real surprise, the chasm was much too broad to bridge.

When we moved to Omaha in 1996, Chris and I had considered selling our Raleigh home because we intended to be at First Church until I retired (Chris was counting on ten years; I was counting on fifteen). However, our emotional attachment to the Raleigh house was strong, and we decided to keep and rent it out. This was fortunate for us. If we had sold it, we would have had no place to return to when we left Omaha.

Four young men currently were living in our home, and their rent was covering the mortgage payment on it. Because we had no income, we couldn't ask them to move out. So, we went to live at Maggie's on Ocracoke Island. Chris had earlier agreed to manage Maggie's as a boarding house for students who would come to the island to work during the summer. She would not be paid for her work, but we would have a free place to live. Chris, Natalia, and I shared one bedroom with a bathroom attached. The room had a full-size bed for Chris and me and a foldaway bed for Natalia. It was cramped but cozy. Chris took a day job at Rick's T-Shirt Shop, where she had worked before, and on weekends she and I cleaned cottages.

One week after arriving on the island, I drove to Norfolk, Virginia, to catch a flight to New York City. I was to preach at Riverside Church, the historic church built in 1930 by John D. Rockefeller Jr. for Harry Emerson Fosdick, the preeminent American Protestant preacher at that time. I had been invited to preach on Sunday, June 28, the day of the annual Gay Pride Parade in Manhattan.

In my sermon, "Free to Love without Fear," I told the story of Mary and Martha's long, painful journey preceding their covenant ceremony and reflected on its theological significance. I explained that their religious traditions had taught them that God was a monstrous power threatening to reject and condemn them because they loved women, not men. Ultimately, both turned their backs on this wrathful god, only to find the God of love in a tiny Metropolitan Community Church in Omaha, Nebraska. It was, I said,

> ... like a homecoming. Not a return to a home they had left behind, but a coming for the first time to a home they had been denied by the religious traditions in which they grew up.
>
> While they thought they left God, God never left them. God was the power within each of them that would not let them deny themselves, that nudged them to leave behind the dishonesty and embrace and honor their true selves as a sacred gift. This was God's active gracious love. It did not come from their religious training, nor from the expectations of family and friends. It came from the deepest place within their souls that knew the truth. This is what we Methodists call, "prevenient grace," the grace of God, the love of God that comes to us even before we know it's there, and claims, embraces, and empowers us to be whole.
>
> Mary and Martha's covenant ceremony was a victory of faith and love over fear and oppression. It was a sign that they had individually survived their long tortuous journeys and were finally able to love themselves. Once able to love themselves, they were able to love each other. Finally, they were free to love without fear.
>
> The Christian church must no longer demand that the Marys and Marthas of the world remain in the closet of fear, rejection, and self-hatred. No, the Christian church must join God in offering to all lesbian, gay, bisexual, and transgender people the assurance of what God has already done: blessed them and their loving with dignity and honor. When I prayed God's blessing upon Mary and Martha, I was only voicing what God already had done. By God's grace, they had been set free from fear and free to love.

I would preach this sermon many times in various forms in the months and years to come.

During that summer, I received invitations from other churches and groups all around the country to preach and speak. At first, I wanted to decline them all, thinking that I had to focus my attention and energy on what kind of work I could do to help us get back to Raleigh. Chris, however, understood that the story had to be told, and that many people wanted and needed to hear it.

One day, as we walked on the beach, she said: "Jimmy, you need to stop thinking about getting a job in Raleigh. You need to be free to travel and tell people about what happened in Omaha and why, tell people about how the church has mistreated gay people. And you need to write about it. You need to write a book. You can't do that if you get a regular kind of job working for somebody else. I'll get a job in Raleigh and support us. I'll support us so you can travel and write. We can make it." The strength of her passion and commitment convinced me. That's what we would do.

So my new ministry became that of an evangelist, something I had never wanted to be. I had never enjoyed being a guest speaker or preacher because it always felt like being more of an entertainer than a pastor. I knew this feeling was something I would have to overcome. I felt obligated to be a good steward of the role my trial had created, in what was a unique experience in the life of the church.

Eventually Chris was hired by the Center for Death Penalty Litigation, an organization that provided legal representation to death-row inmates in their appeals process. Chris's income and the honorariums I received for speaking engagements were enough for us to pay our monthly bills, making it possible for us to return to Raleigh at the end of August. Central Prison was a little more than four blocks from our home. Chris spent her time each day visiting some of the more than 120 inmates on death row who were waiting for decisions on their appeals, which would either set them free or move them toward the dreaded execution. She also corresponded with their families and attorneys. Her role was to counsel and support the inmates during their long wait.

I found myself speaking somewhere every weekend. Between September and December, I spoke in Pittsburgh, Philadelphia, Winston-Salem, Chapel Hill, Brooklyn, New York, Minneapolis, San Francisco, San Rafael, and West Hollywood. I led a retreat for the California-Nevada chapter of the Methodist Federation for Social Action, and I spoke at the Monday Club (an ecumenical gathering of clergy) at Christ United Methodist Church in New York City. I spoke on the campuses of Allegheny College, a United

Methodist–related college in Meadville, Pennsylvania; and Hastings College, a Presbyterian-affiliated institution in Nebraska.

In New York City, I met with a small group of students at Union Theological Seminary who were preparing for ministry in a variety of denominations. They were struggling with how to reconcile their understanding of the Christian gospel with being ordained in churches that discriminated against lesbian, gay, bisexual, and transgender people. I encouraged them, saying that this was an exciting time to be in ordained ministry because they had the opportunity to be part of what God is doing to bring about a change in the church to end the persecution of gay people. I told them that their calling was not to a job or a career. It was a calling to service, to ministry. I thanked them for being willing to take on the struggle.

At each place I spoke, I was received graciously. However, at Penn State, the archbishop of the local Catholic diocese instructed all of his priests not to attend my talk (one came incognito, wearing a polo shirt and khakis). In Lancaster, Pennsylvania, I was to speak at an event inaugurating a new social justice coalition of churches. The event was to be held at the local United Methodist church. The bishop of the area told the pastor of the church not to allow me to speak there. The event was moved to the local Reconstructionist synagogue, whose rabbi was a gay man. The infamous Reverend Fred Phelps, pastor of the Westboro Baptist Church in Topeka, Kansas, picketed outside the churches I spoke at in Tucson and Phoenix, Arizona, carrying signs that called me a "fag lover" and a "false prophet."[1]

Due to the many protests and anonymous threats that Hastings College received because I was coming to speak there, the administration secluded me in an undisclosed motel on the outskirts of Hastings, Nebraska, and kept a plainclothes police officer with me the entire time I was there. The college would not allow me onstage until the lobby was empty, everyone was seated in the auditorium, and the doors were secured. The auditorium was completely full, and the audience was most receptive. I commended the college president, who didn't necessarily agree with me, for standing up for academic freedom in the face of the protests and threats. It was a demonstration of his faith in the student body, I said. At the conclusion of my talk, I was kept locked in a room behind the stage until the auditorium and parking lot were completely empty. A police officer then escorted me to a car that quickly took me to my hotel, way out of town near Interstate 80.

It was inspiring to me to see firsthand the numbers of people around the country working on the front lines to end religion-based antigay teachings and policies. In most cases, those who came to hear me felt overwhelmed by the pervasive hostility toward gay people, but they were undaunted in their desire to end it.

During this time, I was also writing, putting my story on paper from Adam's coming out to me through my struggles at Fairmont United Methodist Church to First Church and my trial. It was painful to revisit the past. But each part of the story made me long more and more to return to being a pastor. It also made my current work that much more compelling. I was often asked why I didn't just transfer to another denomination that would welcome and support me. I certainly considered the possibility, but I just couldn't give up the struggle to change my church, The United Methodist Church. It would have been so much easier and more comfortable to be a pastor with the support of the church hierarchy. In such a situation, I could bury myself in the day-to-day work of parish ministry. But I felt that if I did that, I would be turning my back on the human and civil rights struggle for lesbian, gay, bisexual, and transgender people. I had to stay with the struggle, travel the country with the message, and write the story.

Over the next several months, there were new challenges to the antigay policies and teachings of The United Methodist Church, as well as efforts to protect and enforce them. The United Methodist Judicial Council's special session to rule on the prohibition of "homosexual unions" in the Social Principles was held in Dallas, Texas, on August 7, 1998. The South Central Jurisdiction College of Bishops had requested a declaratory ruling on the prohibition, and the bishops were at the session to argue that the ban should be declared to be church law. Because the defense in my trial had been based on the argument that the prohibition was advisory and not legally binding, the Judicial Council invited Doug Williamson, Mike McClellan, and me to make the opposing argument.

We presented our case before the Judicial Council in a very small room in the Harvey Hotel, just outside the Dallas–Fort Worth Airport in Irving, Texas. We were allowed a total of thirty minutes to make our case. Doug argued that the prohibition should not be considered law because it conflicted with the church's Social Principles, which declare homosexuals to be "persons of sacred worth" and which advocates for their equal civil rights.

He pointed out that the ban also conflicts with the United Methodist Constitution, which calls for inclusiveness without regard to "status."

Mike said that not all statements in *The Book of Discipline* are prosecutable, reminding the Judicial Council that the Social Principles were "intended to be instructive and persuasive." He went on to warn that a ruling that the prohibition was legally binding would result in witch hunts and the invasion of privacy within The United Methodist Church. I argued that the Social Principles, historically understood as guidance, should not become a straitjacket, restricting pastoral ministry by enforcing unanimity and conformity.

On the other side, Bishop Dan Solomon, of Baton Rouge, Louisiana, said that "the placement of the prohibition in the . . . Social Principles does not make it less a law."[2] Bishop Bruce Blake, of Oklahoma City, Oklahoma, argued: "When the spirit and intent of *The Book of Discipline* is violated, all of the book is violated. All of the book depends on each part of the book."[3] He went on to say: "The key to our connection is authority, not agreement."[4]

On Tuesday, August 11, the Judicial Council's decision was announced: "The prohibitive statement in the *1996 Discipline*: 'Ceremonies that celebrate homosexual unions shall not be conducted by our ministers and shall not be conducted in our churches,' has the effect of church law, notwithstanding its placement in [the Social Principles] and, therefore, governs the conduct of the ministerial office. Conduct in violation of this prohibition renders a pastor liable to a charge of disobedience to the Order and Discipline of The United Methodist Church."[5]

So there it was. The Judicial Council had made the ruling that I and many others had believed to be impossible. For the first time, part of the Social Principles had been ruled to be church law. I could not help believe that the fallout from my trial had played the central role in the ruling. Had the Judicial Council ruled before the trial, I am confident that their decision would have been different. This was a political decision, not a juridical one. While it threw into confusion how to treat the rest of the Social Principles, the Judicial Council was careful to say that this decision was narrowly focused only on the "homosexual union prohibition" and should not be interpreted to define the legal status of the Social Principles as a whole or any other part of them.

Because my trial was history, the ruling had no impact on its verdict.

However, it had a profound impact on how United Methodist pastors could minister with and to lesbian, gay, and bisexual people in the future. The institutional bigotry against them was so entrenched in The United Methodist Church that its highest judicial body would declare a single sentence in the Social Principles to be law in order to impose and enforce discrimination against gay people. It was a capricious and cowardly decision. In response to the ruling, I released a statement to the media in which I said:

The declaratory ruling of the Judicial Council gives legal, coercive force to the Social Principles prohibiting "homosexual unions," requiring pastors to discriminate against and contribute to the persecution of gay men and lesbians. The church of John Wesley, founded upon principles of social justice and piety, will now be prosecuting pastors for praying God's blessing upon same-gender couples who make covenants of love and fidelity.

It is a sad day for The United Methodist Church. Our witness to the grace of God has been compromised by bigotry and fear. The church has circumscribed itself into a closed, exclusive community that is in conflict with Jesus's vision of the realm of God where all are welcome, included and accepted . . .

This decision contributes to the church's long-standing assault upon lesbians and gay men, as well as upon their families and friends and the churches that seek to be welcoming, inclusive and supportive. It is an act of institutional violence and cannot be tolerated.

I appeal to United Methodist pastors to protest this decision through ecclesial disobedience by defying the prohibition and publicly celebrating same-gender covenants. The leadership of The United Methodist Church must then decide whether or not it will devote its energy and resources to prosecuting pastors who seek to be faithful to the gospel of Jesus Christ by providing pastoral and liturgical support to gay and lesbian persons. It will have to decide whether the enforcement of prejudice is of more importance than witnessing to the grace of God in Jesus Christ.

I also appeal to laity and clergy of The United Methodist Church who disagree with the antigay language in The Book of Discipline to begin organizing to change it at the 2000 General Conference in Cleveland, Ohio. We can no longer allow fear and prejudice to define who we are and how we behave as United Methodists. We can wait no longer. It is time to end the bigotry and stop the persecution.

It wasn't long before the Judicial Council's surprising decision was openly defied. On September 19, 1998, a little more than one month after the council's August meeting, the Reverend Gregory Dell, my friend and classmate at Duke Divinity School, conducted a holy union ceremony for Keith Eccarius and Karl Reinhardt at Broadway United Methodist Church in Chicago. The ceremony, planned long before the Judicial Council's ruling, was one of many that Greg had conducted during his ministry. At Broadway United Methodist Church, 30 percent of the congregation was gay, so conducting covenant ceremonies had become a rather ordinary part of Greg's ministry. In spite of the obviously greater risk now involved with the Judicial Council's decision, Greg hadn't flinched.

Bishop Joseph Sprague of the Northern Illinois Annual Conference filed a judicial complaint against Greg, and the Committee on Investigation formally charged him with "disobedience to the Order and Discipline of The United Methodist Church." His trial was scheduled for March 25, 1999, at First United Methodist Church in Downers Grove, a suburb west and slightly south of downtown Chicago.

When complaints had been filed against me after Mary and Martha's covenant ceremony at First Church, Greg Dell was the first person I contacted for advice. I e-mailed him asking for suggestions of clergy I might consult. Greg replied with some suggestions, and concluded with this note:

> I hope you're doing ok personally. As I've described our relationship to a number of folks who've asked I've said that you, Powers,[6] and I were this strange kind of three musketeers (or horsemen of the apocalypse) at Duke. I was the crazy ready-for-a-not-always-well-advised-fight confronter. Powers was the almost always supportive good ole Southern boy, and you were the voice of reason, compassion, gentleness and encouragement for dialogue where it would work. How ironic that you should be in the place where you are while I go blithely doing covenant services unchallenged and, in a lot of ways, being as crazy as ever. Not very fair. On the other hand, without discounting the personal cost to you of all of this, this may be the very best circumstance to test the apostate position of the church. But I return to my question above. How are you doing in your soul, guts, head and heart? And how goes it with your family?

Greg and I hadn't had a lot of contact since we left Duke Divinity School in 1970. Christmas cards, church newsletters, and an occasional phone call were pretty much it. We spent some time together once when he came to attend a seminar at Duke and I was a pastor in Raleigh, once in Atlanta when we both attended a seminar at Emory University, and twice when I stayed with him and his wife, Jade, while attending board meetings of the Reconciling Congregation Program. That's not much over a span of twenty-six years. Nonetheless, there was a strong bond of respect and loyalty between us. It was Greg who had first suggested to Susan Davies that I would be a good fit for First Church. His friendship was invaluable to me, especially during my trial. The more liberal environment of the Northern Illinois Annual Conference had been a safe place for Greg to have a full ministry to all people. But now that the Judicial Council had ruled the prohibition on covenant ceremonies to be church law, not even Chicago was free from the bigotry of The United Methodist Church. Chris and I flew there to be with Greg and Jade for the trial.

In the beginning, there was some hope that Greg's trial would be a step forward in the struggle to overturn the antigay policies and teachings of the church, and the legalistic restrictions placed on pastoral ministry. The Northern Illinois Annual Conference was perceived to be one of the liberal annual conferences in The United Methodist Church. In addition, Greg, a native of Chicago who had served in the Northern Illinois Annual Conference for all of his ministry, was held in high esteem and loved by his colleagues. It would not be possible to pick a jury without the majority being Greg's close friends. Even the church counsel, the Reverend Stephen Williams, talked about how grieved he was to have to prosecute Greg, whom he spoke of with respect. Perhaps in this context, a creative response to the complaint could be found that would challenge the prohibition and serve justice.

Both the prosecution and the defense presented straightforward cases. Stephen Williams argued that Greg had violated a law of the church and should be found guilty and punished: "'If the church cannot enforce [the law], the General Conference is stripped of its authority,' Williams said in his summation. 'To break this prohibition is to break a bond.' Failure to enforce church law in this case would open the church to increased disregard for discipline and order, he said."[7] Greg's counsel, the Reverend Larry Pickens, countered: "The church would have you believe this case is about the law and the letter of the law. This case, however, is about the people, the faces, the personalities, the real life stories of persons who have been affected by the ministry of Gregory Dell. This is not about a single act. This is a case that reflects a single ministry over thirty years, [a case] about whether we are going to allow ministry to be extended to persons in ways that are affirming and supportive."[8]

Greg said in his testimony: "I felt I did not disobey the discipline and order of the church, but rather was being obedient to it. I have been appointed to Broadway to serve all, including the 30 percent who are gays and lesbians. If I can't be a pastor to all I am appointed to serve, you don't want me as a pastor."[9]

The jury announced a verdict of guilty by a vote of ten to three and imposed the following penalty: unless he signed a statement promising never again to conduct a same-gender union ceremony, Greg would be suspended until the General Conference repealed the ban on "homosexual unions." The jury had chosen the most cynical and pernicious penalty, an indefinite suspension to begin July 5, 1999, and to last until The United Methodist Church repealed the prohibition on "homosexual unions" or until Greg signed a pledge to never again celebrate one. Knowing how unlikely it was that the church would repeal the prohibition anytime soon, the jury contemptuously ruled that Greg Dell must give up his integrity in order to continue as a pastor in the church. This was not only harsh, it was cruel.

Greg was not punished for celebrating a holy union for a same-gender couple. He was punished for refusing to promise that he would never perform another one. Stephen Williams, the church counsel, had said during the trial that he would be satisfied and say "let's all go home" if Greg would promise to never again celebrate a "homosexual union." That would be the end of it. There would be no need for a penalty. By imposing a penalty contingent on Greg's signing a pledge to never again celebrate a "homosexual union," the jury took essentially the same position.

Some friends and members of his congregation urged Greg to sign a promise not to conduct any more same-gender unions, but he said he could not. However, he appealed to the North Central Jurisdiction Committee on Appeals, and the jury's penalty was reduced from the punitive indefinite suspension from active ministry to a one-year suspension. Bishop Sprague promised Greg that he could return to his appointment at Broadway when the suspension ended.

Greg's trial had cost the Northern Illinois Annual Conference $123,000.[10] Of that amount, $107,955.82 was paid to the law firm that assisted Stephen

Williams. The balance was spent on security; travel expenses for Bishop Tuel, who presided as judge, and Williams; food and lodging for the jury; and other similar expenses. Courtney Cosgrove, chairperson of the Broadway's Trial Steering Committee, reported that the defense costs were $8,837.36.

Another dramatic challenge to The United Methodist Church began on Sunday, October 4, 1998. The Reverend Don Fado, pastor of St. Mark's United Methodist Church in Sacramento, California, preached a sermon titled "The Ugliest Word in the English Language: Exclusion." In his sermon, Don said,

> I find [the Judicial Council's] decision to be incredibly narrow and out of keeping with what The United Methodist Church has stood for over the ages: an inclusive ministry that welcomes all.
>
> My denomination now says to me that I am to minister to anyone and everyone, but leave out the gays and lesbians. Leave them out. As a United Methodist minister, I'm free to utter prayers and vows for any group I want, unless it happens to be two people of the same sex who wish to have vows of fidelity.
>
> I cannot remain silent in face of such an injustice. I have a choice between two options, it seems to me. I can leave the United Methodist ministry, or I can protest. I choose the latter, and the way I will protest is that I will . . . conduct a service of holy union, as an act of ecclesiastical disobedience. I will not do it in secret. I will do it in the spirit in which Martin Luther King, Jr., did his disobedience. I will do it openly in order to challenge the law.
>
> Most of the ministers in our conference, including those on the staff of your church, feel the outlawing of our vows to gays and lesbians to be unjust. My hope is that we can get fifty to a hundred of us to co-officiate at one service. We must demonstrate to the General Conference the folly of the exclusion.

After hearing Don's sermon, Jeanne Barnett and Ellie Charlton, members of St. Mark's, volunteered to be the couple for the ceremony he was prepared to conduct. Jeanne and Ellie were ideal. Both had long been active in the life of the church in California and were well known and loved. Jeanne was the lay leader of the California-Nevada United Methodist Annual Conference, and Ellie was a member of the conference's Board of Trustees.

As soon as they informed Don of their willingness, he sent out an invitation to clergy in the conference to join him in the public celebration of their holy union. The date would be in January at St. Mark's United Methodist Church. Immediately, clergy began accepting his invitation, not only from the California-Nevada Annual Conference but from all over the country. It quickly became apparent that St. Mark's sanctuary, even with its spacious seating capacity of four hundred, was too small to accommodate the growing number of clergy, family, and friends who wanted to attend. The organizers rented the Sacramento Convention Center for the event.

I was scheduled to speak in Seattle the weekend of Jeanne and Ellie's holy union, but I still wanted to participate. I e-mailed Don and explained my situation. He graciously indicated that I would be listed in the worship bulletin as a "co-officiant in absentia."

The ceremony took place as planned on January 16, 1999, most fittingly the weekend of the holiday honoring the Reverend Dr. Martin Luther King Jr. One hundred and sixty-three clergy were listed in the worship program as co-officiants, along with four former clergy who had been forced to surrender their credentials because they were gay or lesbian. Ninety-two of the clergy were from the California-Nevada Annual Conference and fifty-eight were from twenty-six other annual conferences around the country. In addition, thirteen clergy from six other denominations joined in. Seventy-two of the clergy participated in absentia, as I did.

The Reverend Charley Lerrigo wrote this report on the ceremony for the *United Methodist News Service*:

> The ceremony drew more than 1,200 invited guests to the Sacramento Convention Center, and at times it seemed more like a soulful "love-in" than a solemn worship.
>
> The couple, Jeanne Barnett and Ellie Charlton, were greeted with cheers and sympathetic tears as they declared their 15-year relationship would continue as a life partnership. Charlton's daughter-in-law and granddaughter paid poetic tributes to her courage as a lesbian. Charlton, a 63-year-old great-grandmother, broke into tears as she publicly affirmed her love for her 68-year-old partner.
>
> The service was the largest public holy union in the denomination since the controversy over such ceremonies heated up last year . . .
>
> During the press conference, Fado was asked what he would do if

charges were filed. "We are on the right side of history," he replied. "We are on the right side of God. We are committed to the struggle."

During the service, he referred to the prospect of charges arising. "If people are going to file charges," he said, "then let it be because of this prayer." He and the other ministers then read: "O God our Creator, Redeemer and Sustainer, we bow before you to ask your blessing upon Ellie and Jeanne, whom we now bless in your name. Their commitment to one another grows out of their commitment to you, whose love is revealed through Jesus Christ. We pray for you to guide and strengthen them, that they remain open to your spirit and continue to grow in love. We thank you for Jeanne and Ellie's love and faith, which they so readily share with us. We recognize in this service the place of family, friends, church and the entire human family. We are able to love because you first loved us. O God, our Maker, we gladly proclaim to the world that Jeanne and Ellie are loving partners together for life. Amen."[11]

On March 23, Bishop Melvin Talbert of the California-Nevada Annual Conference held a press conference to announce that complaints had been filed against sixty-eight of the clergy who had participated in the Sacramento ceremony.[12] It was an extraordinary press conference because Bishop Talbert, even while announcing the complaints, denounced The United Methodist Church's restrictive policies against gay people. He described Ellie Charlton and Jeanne Barnett as "two well-known and respected members of St. Mark's United Methodist Church, honorable, loyal and dedicated followers of Jesus Christ. Like other Christians, they are living out their faith in the name and spirit of Jesus Christ." He declared the Judicial Council's ruling that the prohibition of "homosexual unions" in the Social Principles was church law to be "an act of injustice" and said that the prohibition of same-gender holy unions was "unconscionable!" "I agree with those pastors who contend that such action is an intrusion into their priestly role as clergy to all their people," he said; "I contend that all clergy must be free to choose the appropriate pastoral responses they should make in the priestly roles. Therefore, I refuse to treat as enemies those who chose to violate this church law as an act of conscience. They are not our enemies. They are our sisters and brothers in Christ, in the same way that those are who hold opposing views. Biblical and theological debates are appropriate. But there comes a time when God's call to love must take precedence over any political or theological action or decision. I believe that is the case now with this issue. I will continue proclaiming that we all belong to God, and that we will have a space at God's table."

He concluded his statement with these words: "My referring this complaint is without prejudice to enable these colleagues to have their day in a court of peers. My prayer is that in the due process to follow, clergy peers will seek to do justice, and to act in a way that is consistent with the teachings and compassion of Jesus. I trust they will hold before them the vision for our church that is inclusive, with diversity and acceptance as its hallmarks. May God bless all of us as we seize this moment as an opportunity to model how Christians should deal with controversy in our lives and in our churches."[13] Significantly and prophetically, he identified "the teachings and compassion of Jesus," not church law, as the standard to follow when seeking justice.

Not long after Ellie and Jeanne's holy union, I received a letter from Larry Ellis and Jim Raymer inviting me to participate in their holy union on April 24. Jim was a research scientist; Larry, a college administrator. Larry had been a pastor until he openly identified himself as gay and had to leave church ministry. I first met Jim and Larry in the fall of 1998, when I preached at the United Church of Chapel Hill (United Church of Christ), one of the oldest and most progressive churches in Chapel Hill, North Carolina. The United Church regularly provided union ceremonies for same-gender couples as part of its ongoing ministry. Jill and Rick Edens, its pastors, were among the first of the few clergy to invite me to preach in their churches upon my return to Raleigh.

Rick and Jill originally were to officiate at the ceremony, Jim and Larry explained in their letter to me. However, due to an oversight in scheduling, Rick had to be out of town that weekend for a church activity. Jim and Larry wanted both a male and female minister, in the interest of diversity, to conduct the ceremony, so they asked me to officiate with Jill. I was delighted to accept their invitation.

I wrote Bishop Martínez to inform him. He wrote back saying that I would be breaking church law, and that charges would be filed against me if I conducted the ceremony.

In early April, Jim and Larry sent out invitations to family, friends, and coworkers. Not long after, I received a call from Amanda Lamb, a reporter with WRAL-TV in Raleigh. She said she had learned that I would be involved in a holy union ceremony for a "gay couple" and wanted to know if that was true and, if so, could she talk with me and the couple about it? I told her I would consult with the couple first and then get back to her. Jim and Larry were quite comfortable about being interviewed, so they contacted Amanda and set up an interview in their home on the Tuesday morning before their ceremony. They also invited Jill Edens and me to be part of the interview. After the story aired, other media picked it up, and the ceremony became a public event.

When Jim and Larry asked Amanda how she had learned about the ceremony, she explained that her TV station received an anonymous tip on the hot line on its website. Whoever sent the tip must not have known Larry and Jim or the date of their ceremony, but only that "Jimmy Creech was going to do another ceremony." The tipsters identified themselves only as "disgruntled Methodists."

The ceremony took place on a beautiful spring day. There is nowhere lovelier than Chapel Hill in the spring, called by admirers "the southern part of heaven." I was quite emotional as I prepared for the ceremony, very happy for Larry and Jim and about the public witness they were making and the gift I knew it would be for lesbian, gay, bisexual, and transgender people. The sanctuary was filled with friends, colleagues, and family members. Jim's parents had flown in from New York State. The atmosphere was electric with joyous excitement. Newspaper reporters and television crews were on hand to do interviews with Jim and Larry, as well as their family and friends.

Because Larry had been a minister, he took the lead in preparing the ceremony, carefully crafting it as a service of worship. It was very moving, with a strong emphasis on biblical readings and the celebration of Holy Communion. Jill and I took turns leading the various parts of the liturgy. I ended the ceremony with these words: "Larry and Jim, because you have promised your love to each other before God and these witnesses, and have exchanged these solemn vows and these symbols of your love and commitment, I now pronounce you life partners. You may now express your love with the kiss of union."

For the families and friends who had come to be with Larry and Jim, the ceremony was typical of other weddings they had experienced, both solemn and joyous, and containing traditional ritual, music, and symbols. But it was also profoundly different. For those who had never before attended a same-gender union ceremony, it was a demonstration that marriage is truly a spiritual bond predicated on neither sexuality nor law, but solely on a shared love, faith, and hope. And for the lesbian, gay, and bisexual people present, the highly public nature of this holy union was revolutionary and liberating. Two men who loved one another had made mutual commitments, not in hiding but publicly for the world to see, and they did so with dignity and pride. Larry later wrote about the ceremony for the *Chapel Hill News*:

> Someone asked me why, after four years, we are doing this now. Our answer is simple. We want to live our lives together with integrity and dignity. We want our relationship to be recognized as any other committed relationship. We are a family. We live our lives as any other couple.
>
> For example, when I became seriously ill . . . three years ago, it was Jim who rushed me to the hospital and sat by my side in the ER, answering questions. Jim cared for me night and day for the month after I came home after emergency surgery. We built a house, making the many decisions together. We shop for groceries, do the yard work, go on vacation and have family birthdays and holidays together.
>
> We decided over a year ago that we would spend the rest of our lives together. Now we wanted to stand before our church and friends and make a public declaration of that commitment. Did this act make us a family? No; our love and commitment make us a family.
>
> Unfortunately, gays and lesbians often make this commitment with no one else to witness the joining of their lives in spiritual union. There are no laws that bind us together. We make that decision in the face of opposition and society's objection . . .
>
> To force such a deep commitment underground denies a couple and their friends the joy and love that many straight couples take for granted.
>
> For us, and the many lesbian and gay couples like us, it is about God's love for us. It is about our right to live without fear of retribution from any person or church. It is our right to live as a family and be respected as productive citizens of our community. It is our right to worship God without condemnation.[14]

Jim said about the ceremony: "Unless someone actually goes through it, they don't really have a good sense of what it means. Going through it and making a public statement really can alter the relationship, really bring it to another level. People make choices all the time and we had made a choice quite some time ago to be together as partners. By making a public statement, that takes on a whole other level of commitment. When you have to stand in front of a group of friends and family and church members and your pastors and proclaim, 'This is the person I love, the person I want to spend the rest of my life with,' it just really has a profound meaning."[15]

I left almost immediately after the ceremony to catch a plane to New Jersey. I was to preach at Princeton University's chapel on the following day. As Chris drove me to the airport, we talked about the beauty of the service, the gracious support of Larry's and Jim's friends and families, and how healing and empowering the occasion had been. We talked about how one day in the not-too-distant future, such a ceremony would be a common, though still extraordinary, affair.

On June 3, I received a letter from Bishop Martínez notifying me that the Reverend Jim McChesney, superintendent of the Central District in Nebraska, had filed a judicial complaint against me. The complaint, as before, was for "disobedience to the Order and Discipline of The United Methodist Church" for conducting the holy union in Chapel Hill. I was surprised that Jim McChesney had filed the complaint. He was present for the interview I had with the bishop and cabinet when I had visited Nebraska for the first time in April 1996. That night, after I had shared about my experience of being expelled from ministry in North Carolina because of my support for gay civil rights, Jim was aghast. He had assured me then that such a thing would never happen in the Nebraska Annual Conference. He told me with deep emotion about how, when he had been outspoken in his opposition to the Vietnam War, members of his congregation had tried to have him moved. But his bishop, district superintendent, and clergy colleagues had stood by him. "We'll stand by you, too," he had assured me back then, with tears in his eyes.

I later learned that Bishop Martínez had asked his cabinet as a group to file a complaint against me, and the cabinet refused. Then he separately and privately approached five other district superintendents about filing a complaint, and each one turned him down, saying they would have nothing to do with it. Although reluctant, Jim McChesney was apparently the sixth and most pliant person that Bishop Martínez approached. In a subsequent cabinet meeting, the bishop simply announced that Jim had filed a complaint, and neither he nor Jim offered any explanation as to why he had chosen to do so. Jim's motive was never discussed. The bishop had wanted the complaint filed, and Jim was the one least able to refuse his request. The judicial process, as expected, had begun.

Controversy seemed to precede and follow me in those days. In late May, I flew to Washington, D.C., to receive an award from People for the American Way at its annual national banquet. In the Raleigh-Durham airport, just after checking my suitcase, I stopped at the shoeshine stand before going to the gate. Both chairs were occupied. As I waited, I listened to the casual conversation between the men shining shoes and their customers. It was pretty typical male talk about basketball and baseball teams, about why teams had lost the week before and why they would or wouldn't win the next games. Next to the cash register, I noticed a large glass jar with a handwritten sign that read: "Apostolic Church of God and True Holiness Building Fund. Contributions appreciated!"

Finally, one of the patrons stepped down, shoes gleaming, and gave the shoeshine man seven dollars. He stuffed a couple more dollars in the building fund jar as he left. I climbed into the chair and settled down while the shoeshine man began to brush my shoes. "Where you headed?" he asked.

"Washington," I replied.

"D.C.?" he probed.

"Yep."

"Business?"

"Yeah, well, it's related to my work."

"What kind of work do you do?"

"I'm a minister."

"You're a preacher?"

"Yep."

Silence. Then he said: "Thought so. You're Creech, that minister that's in the news so much around here, the one who married those two men?"

Oh, hell, I was caught! Sitting in this elevated, thronelike chair, my feet resting on iron supports as this sports fan, this evangelical Christian black male stopped brushing my shoes and looked up into my eyes, all I wanted to do was disappear. This was not a situation in which I expected to find understanding and support and I was stuck in this chair.

"Yep," I nodded, the word sticking in my throat.

My shoeshine man, turning to his partner who was now standing near the cash register, said: "Hey, this here is that Creech fellow, the minister who the church has been giving such a hard time because he married two men."

Turning to face me again, he said: "Why is the church giving you such a hard time? Why do some Christian people think they're so superior and treat other people so bad? Why can't people just let other people be? I don't know if it's right or wrong for two men to marry each other. I don't understand it. But it don't matter what I think. It's not up to me. That's up to God. We just need to get along. We need to stop judging one another and putting people down just because they're different, and let people be who they are. We just need to learn to get along. You're a real preacher. What you're doing is hard. But you're doing the right thing."

As I stepped down from his chair and passed the building fund jar, I stuck a ten-dollar bill in it. If his church taught what he believed, I wanted to give it my support. And if it didn't, I wanted him to have a lot of influence in it.

At the People for American Way annual banquet the next day, I received an award for "challenging bigotry and promoting tolerance within the church." It was an honor to receive this award. But I've never felt more humbled and honored than I was by the words of the shoeshine man. His understanding and grace, not just toward me but toward people whom he didn't understand, were profound. If the world had more people like him, it would have more justice, freedom, and peace.

The North Carolina Annual Conference met in Fayetteville, North Carolina, the next week. Even though I was no longer a member, I was a subject of concern. A resolution was introduced demanding that the Nebraska Annual Conference restrict me from preaching outside of Nebraska, an unheard-of restriction on a preacher. There was no vote on the resolution, however, because Bishop Marion Edwards explained that a judicial complaint had been filed against me. The Nebraska Annual Conference, he assured the delegates, will take care of Jimmy Creech without our resolution.

In the lobby of Memorial Auditorium in downtown Raleigh following a concert, a man I recognized as a minister and former colleague in the North Carolina Annual Conference approached me with a broad smile. He vigorously shook my hand and with great personal delight said: "You know, I've taken a leave of absence and no longer serve a church. I've got my own business doing financial consulting work. And you know, I can say whatever I want to now, and nobody can do anything about it." He'd never been friendly or supportive to me in the past, and I'd never known him to take a controversial stand on anything. I faked a smile and said, "Good for you." I felt pity for him. It was a shame that he had to leave the church to find the freedom and courage to speak his mind. The reality was that nobody in the church cared what he said now, because he'd left it. He had forfeited the opportunity to speak when it would have made a difference.

The same week that the North Carolina Annual Conference met, I spoke at the Methodist Federation for Social Action annual banquet in Washington, D.C., held during the Baltimore-Washington Annual Conference. When it was announced that I would be speaking, rumors started circulating that I was planning to stage a demonstration during one of the business sessions of the annual conference. Because of the alarm that this caused, the MFSA reassured the conference members in the organization's newspaper in an article titled "Rumors of Demonstration at Conference Untrue, MFSA Says."[16]

Back home in the rolling Piedmont of North Carolina, the *Hickory Daily Record* published an article with the headline "Creech Urges 'Revolution' for Change." The article reported on a speech I had given the day before in Newton, a small town very close to Hickory and not far from Charlotte. The occasion for my speech was a public event sponsored by the City of Hickory Community Relations Council, Building Community from Diversity, PFLAG of Catawba Valley, Lutherans Concerned/Charlotte, and the Unitarian Universalist Church of Catawba Valley.

In my speech, I had spoken about the similarities between African Americans' fight for civil rights and gay men and lesbians' fight for civil rights: "Just as the [African American] civil rights movement could no longer be denied, Creech said he does not believe the new movement can be denied. 'It will be resisted, but it will not be successfully resisted. For I believe, and this is from a theological perspective, this is a movement of God.'"[17]

Angry protests flared up because of the article and a similar one published in the *Charlotte Observer*. For weeks afterward, the newspapers in the area published commentaries, letters to the editor, and op-eds with headlines such as "Creech's Disputable Opinions Require Strong Counterbalance,"[18] "City Sponsored Pro-gay Propaganda,"[19] "Jimmy Creech or Christ: Whom Will You Follow?,"[20] "United Methodist's Creech Preaches Homosexual Gospel,"[21] and "Creech Spread Untruths about Homosexuality."[22] The few supportive published responses were overwhelmed by the much larger number of negative ones. The controversy began to subside in August, when the Hickory City Council said it would have to give prior approval to all future programs of the Community Relations Council.

Bishop Martínez scheduled a conference call on June 21 for Jim McChesney and me to discuss his complaint to see if we could reach reconciliation. "The issue is you disobeyed the Order and Discipline of the Church," Jim said to me during the call. "I agree with most of your views about the church's position being wrong but not with what you've done. You disobeyed the church. You've set the cause back. We were making progress on this issue before you caused all this controversy." He was using the old excuse of "you have broken a law," and he was blaming me for the unsettling controversy. Apparently, he considered the unjust nature of the law and the General Conference's responsibility in adopting it to be inconsequential. The controversy was all my fault.

In response, I again stated my position that the prohibition of "homosexual unions" was an unjust law that discriminated against gay, lesbian, and bisexual people. I told Jim that if he persisted with the complaint, he would be complicit in The United Methodist Church's violence against gay people and, by processing the complaint, the bishop would be complicit, too. I strongly urged Jim to withdraw the complaint. There was silence on the phone. Finally, Jim said: "I need to think about this some more." Bishop Martínez quickly broke in, saying: "It looks like we'll need to schedule another conference call. But if Jim withdraws his complaint, others will come forward because of your high public profile." Two weeks later, we talked again. This time, Jim was adamant about proceeding with the complaint, and there was no reconciliation. Soon after the second call with Jim, the bishop informed me that the Reverend Steve Flader would be the church counsel and would forward the complaint to the Committee on Investigation.

The Reverend Jill Edens was irate and wanted to intercede. Not only because I was under attack, but she recognized that the credibility and propriety of the worship of the United Church of Christ was also under attack by The United Methodist Church. After trying unsuccessfully to reach him by telephone, she wrote to Bishop Martínez:

> I have just learned that an investigation is under way of a worship service of my congregation that was held on April 24, 1999. This was a service of

worship of the United Church of Chapel Hill, United Church of Christ, at which I was the presiding pastor. The service included a service of the Word, a service of communion, and a service of covenant making, just as most of our services include these three elements of worship.

During the service of worship, I presided over a service of covenant between two members of my congregation, Larry Ellis and Jim Raymer. I invited Jimmy Creech[23] to participate in this service of worship as I have in the past . . . I had no reason to believe that inviting Jimmy to participate in a worship service of the United Church of Christ would precipitate an investigation of our worship or of members of my congregation since I understand he is an elder in good standing with the Nebraska Annual Conference of The United Methodist Church. Are your elders permitted to participate in the worship services of the United Church of Christ?

I was hoping to talk with you directly to understand why you are investigating the worship of my church so that you might clarify at what point an elder of The United Methodist Church may go to trial for worshipping with a United Church of Christ congregation and participating in the leadership of its worship at the invitation of its pastor. Having not received an answer to my phone call, I hope to receive a response to this letter.

Finally, I am asking that this investigation be halted immediately and that we as members of the United Church of Christ and of The United Methodist Church may continue to enjoy a fellowship free of fear and committed to the inclusive love of Jesus Christ.

Bishop Martínez wrote back, explaining that I had informed him of my intention to participate in the service and that he had advised me against doing so. "This matter has been referred through our disciplinary process as our *Book of Discipline* provides," he wrote. "We in the State of Nebraska, The United Methodist Church and the United Church of Christ, engage in many shared ministries in a variety of places and in addressing a variety of concerns." He concluded: "We have a long and honored history of cooperation and collaboration in ecumenical work and will continue to have that. I will not comment further regarding the matters related to Jimmy Creech."

There was no Reconciling Congregation among the United Methodist churches in the North Carolina Annual Conference, but there were many individuals who considered themselves to be Reconciling United Methodists (RUM). In 1996 or 1997, a group of them in the Triangle area of Raleigh, Durham, and Chapel Hill began meeting once a month for mutual support, the location of the meetings moving from one church to another. The meetings alternated between a Monday night support group and a Sunday afternoon service of worship. Many in the group said they had no other place to go for worship and the Eucharist where they felt welcome and comfortable. Over time, the group expanded, adding people from around the state.

The RUM group was scheduled to meet for worship at Calvary United Methodist Church in Durham on August 22. Calvary's pastor, Laurie Hays Coffman, a member of the group and a friend of mine, invited me to preach at the service. This wasn't the first time that Laurie had hosted the RUM gathering at Calvary. And she had included an announcement of the upcoming gathering in the worship bulletins for several weeks in advance without controversy. But when word got out through newspaper, radio, and television announcements that I would be preaching at Calvary, she started getting phone calls from members of the congregation who were upset.

When I arrived at Calvary, television crews were already there interviewing Laurie, church members, and others who had come for the service. Jim and Larry already were there being interviewed. The sanctuary was packed. The nine members of the Pastor-Parish Relations Committee and their spouses were there, along with the twenty or thirty RUMs. The rest of the two hundred or so people attending the service were from the community, the great majority of whom were gay, lesbian, bisexual, and transgender.

In my sermon, I related Mary and Martha's story and told how their newfound faith in God's love had empowered them to love themselves and each other. Then Laurie and I served the Eucharist. Many people cried as they received the bread and cup and paused to give us hugs and briefly speak to us. Some said that it had been a very long time since they had felt welcome in a church, a very long time since they could worship freely as themselves. Some said they had heard echoes of their own story in Mary and Martha's, and some said they longed for the same acceptance and freedom to love without fear that Mary and Martha had found.

It was an emotional time for Laurie and me. Tears streamed down our faces as we broke bread and offered the cup to those who spoke words of pain, longing, and gratitude. The spirit of God was palpable. Many in the RUM group, as well as those from the surrounding community, felt abused and abandoned by their religious communities. Gathering in this sanctuary of acceptance and support was both healing and empowering for them.

When the evening TV news headlined the service, members of Calvary who didn't approve were upset and angry. Some were embarrassed because neighbors, coworkers, and friends challenged them about being members of the church whose pastor had a worship service for gays and lesbians and allowed Jimmy Creech to preach. "How can you belong to that church?" they were asked.

On Monday morning, Laurie began receiving telephone calls from enraged members telling her they were leaving the congregation. Some of the key elected leaders resigned their positions and left. The next Sunday morning, the teacher of one of the adult Sunday school classes announced to his class that Laurie had desecrated "holy ground by bringing in all those perverts," and that he would not set foot in the church again as long as she was the pastor. He resigned, and his wife dutifully left, too. A few weeks later, the teachers of the remaining adult Sunday school left. From then on, every Sunday somebody else left: the head usher, the church historian, members of the Board of Trustees, the treasurer, the chairperson of the Finance Committee, and lifelong members of the church who had been staunch supporters. It seemed that nothing could stop the bleeding. Calvary United Methodist Church was in crisis because I had preached in its pulpit and lesbian and gay people had worshiped in its pews.

I was soon notified by David Lux that the Committee on Investigation would meet in Lincoln, Nebraska, to hear the complaint against me and my response to it on September 16, 1999. I wasn't sure what approach to take in my defense. This was a different situation from 1998, when the location of the prohibition in the Social Principles had created ambiguity. Then there was reason to challenge the legal status of the prohibition. Now the legal status was no longer in question. I could plead guilty, I thought, admitting that I knowingly and willfully violated a law of the church, and accept whatever punishment the jury would mete out. Or I could simply refuse to cooperate, turning my back on the trial as an abuse of power by the church. To do that, however, would allow the process to proceed unchallenged, leaving the church free of public accountability. Neither of these options felt right. They were easy outs. I had to do more. It was clear to me that should I defend myself and be either acquitted as before or found guilty, which was likely, I would be legitimizing the prohibition as if it were a just law. The focus would be on my conduct rather than on the prohibition as an expression of The United Methodist Church's bigotry against gay, lesbian, and bisexual people.

I decided that I would participate as little as possible in the trial. I would not have a defense counsel to represent me, would not participate in the selection of the jury, and would not offer a plea to the charge against me. Even to plead not guilty, I believed, gave the law legitimacy. I would not make an opening argument, call witnesses, cross-examine the church's witnesses, or participate in the penalty phase of the trial, if there should be one. In short, I would not defend myself.

My only participation in the trial would be to answer questions asked of me by the church counsel and to make a closing statement. The purpose of my closing statement would be to condemn the prohibition as unjust and illegitimate and call for resistance to it. Rather than offer a defense for breaking an unjust law, I would hold The United Methodist Church accountable for the law and the violence it does, not only to gay people but to the Christian gospel.

At the end of August 1999, another challenge to the "homosexual union" ban took place. On the street in front of Bering Memorial United Methodist Church in Houston, Texas, Eleanora Plombino and Linda Enger were united by speaking vows to each other in a ceremony of holy union conducted by the Reverend Troy Plummer, an ordained priest in the Orthodox Catholic Church who was on the staff of Bering Memorial. During the ceremony, the Reverend Marilyn Meeker-Williams, senior pastor, stood on the steps of Bering Memorial United Methodist Church, as a witness both to the ceremony and to the denial by The United Methodist Church of her freedom to conduct it. Following the ceremony, the couple and their guests came from the street up the steps into the sanctuary, where Marilyn and the Reverend Dr. Bruce Felker served Holy Communion. The event was announced to the media in advance and was widely reported.

Another significant challenge came later in the fall with the announcement that twenty retired clergy from the New England Annual Conference, led by the Reverend Dick Harding, were willing to co-officiate at covenant services for same-gender couples. In an article for *Crosscurrents*, their annual conference newspaper, the clergy stated:

We emeriti clergy members of the New England Conference of The United Methodist Church . . . are troubled that in our current social landscape homophobia grips our people . . . We believe that same-gender orientation is a divine gift. We believe that every child of God deserves to be treated with respect and challenged to become fully the person God is creating.

We believe that the church has a singular role in nurturing that process . . . We believe loving covenants between persons are rich and wholesome acts . . . We therefore covenant with one another to co-officiate when called upon by other clergy-members of our conference for the sake of pastoral care for all God's people. We believe God is calling us to faithfulness in this ministry.[24]

On Tuesday night, September 14, less than forty-eight hours before I was to meet with the Committee on Investigation in Lincoln, Nebraska, Hurricane Floyd was racing toward the North Carolina coast. The weather center was calling it the largest and most powerful storm to ever threaten the East Coast. Hurricanes are unpredictable, however, and can change course and intensity quickly. While its winds of 150 miles per hour had abated to 90 miles per hour by the time the storm hit the mainland, Floyd dumped heavy rain on North Carolina, flooding a large part of the state. Consequently, I was unable to fly out of Raleigh-Durham International Airport on Wednesday. Rather than reschedule the hearing, David Lux arranged, with my consent, to hold it via teleconference.

Steve Flader presented the church's case against me. He reviewed the vows that clergy take to uphold the "Order and Discipline of the Church" when they are ordained, the Judicial Council ruling regarding the prohibition of "homosexual unions," and the fact that I had informed Bishop Martínez that I planned to celebrate a holy union in April. He then said: "I call on the committee to support the church's position that Reverend Creech has committed a chargeable offense under . . . *The Discipline of The United Methodist Church* and is subject to trial for such offense."[25]

The committee members were the same as before, with only one or two changes. Since most if not all had read my response to the 1997 complaint, I didn't need to repeat what I had said in it. My brief response to the new complaint, sent to the committee members in advance of the hearing, was read for the record. It concluded with this challenge:

It is not in the best interest of The United Methodist Church for a trial to take place. I urge you to intervene in the judicial process against me by refusing to refer the complaint to a trial court. I ask you to do this for the sake of The United Methodist Church, not for my sake. I believe that a trial would be an act of violence against lesbian, bisexual and gay persons and a betrayal of the gospel of Jesus Christ. I am confident you do not believe that these should be either the purposes or consequences of any judicial process.

A trial would be an expenditure of resources (financial, time, energy and personnel) that should be used otherwise in ministry to the world in the name of Jesus Christ. I am asking you to act with courage to help end our persecution of gay, bisexual and lesbian persons and to not act in blind allegiance to an unjust law. I urge you to let the gospel of Jesus Christ and the Holy Spirit rule your hearts, minds and actions. In this way you will best serve the interests of The United Methodist Church and make a faithful witness to the gospel of Jesus Christ.

After my statement was read, the committee members questioned me about such things as the parts of the ceremony I led, about my relationship with Larry and Jim, and about how, since the prohibition was now officially church law, my defense would differ from that in 1998.

When I had answered all their questions, David Lux asked Steve Flader to make a closing statement. Steve reminded the committee that the issue had changed since the Judicial Council's ruling in August 1998, and that the issue was now the enforcement of the council's ruling. "I agree with Jimmy," Steve said, "that the issue is the law, it is precisely the law. If Judicial Council decisions are to be enforced, they will be enforced here."

In my closing statement to the committee, I said: "Let this be an opportunity for you to make a witness by choosing not to refer this complaint to trial. I'm asking you to set aside legalities and let the grace of God, the spirit of God, enable you to say, 'no, we won't do this, not because Jimmy deserves to be set free from trial, but because we as United Methodists are simply no longer going to participate in the persecution of gay, lesbian and bisexual people, their families and loved ones, by bringing pastors to trial because they have given pastoral support to lesbian and gay people.' I ask you to do this, not for me, but for the church."

After the hearing, the committee voted six to one to refer the charge to trial. I released a statement to the media that said: "The celebration of love and commitment between two people is a profound and particular embodiment of the gospel of Jesus Christ. If I am found guilty by a trial court, then The Order and Discipline of The United Methodist Church is in conflict with this gospel . . . I regret the Nebraska Annual Conference has chosen to take this action against me. The trial will more deeply mire The United Methodist Church into the sludge of bigotry and legalism. How can such an encumbered church witness to the grace of God?"

The trial was scheduled for November 17 and 18, 1999, at Trinity United Methodist Church in Grand Island, Nebraska. Retired Bishop William Boyd Grove, of Charleston, West Virginia, would be the presiding officer.

"Jimmy, I hope you're agreeable with this, but it doesn't matter because we're going to do it anyway. We're going to shut down your trial in Grand Island!" Mel White announced as he joined me for breakfast in the hotel restaurant; "We're going to surround that church, block the doors, and keep the trial from happening!" This wild inspiration had awakened Mel at four in the morning and he had immediately begun making plans.

It was October 24, 1999, and we were in Lynchburg, Virginia, for an Anti-Violence Conference with the televangelist Jerry Falwell. Because of Falwell's abusive rhetoric against gay people, Mel had initiated the event and brought two hundred gay, lesbian, bisexual, and transgender people and their allies with him from all over the United States to meet and have a dialogue with Jerry Falwell and two hundred members of his congregation. It was the first direct action of Soulforce, an organization that Mel and his spouse, Gary Nixon, had created. Using the principles of nonviolent resistance developed and practiced by Mohandas Karamchand Gandhi in South Africa and India, and later used by the Reverend Dr. Martin Luther King Jr. in the African American civil rights movement of the 1950s and 1960s, Soulforce embodied a new strategy in the civil rights movement for gay people by directly and publicly challenging religious sources of antigay bigotry.

Mel told me of his intention to shut down the trial just before he was to do a live interview on NBC's national Sunday morning news program. I was surprised by Mel's idea but endorsed it without reservation. Having Soulforce at the trial would draw attention to what The United Methodist Church was doing. It was fortunate that I thought so, because it wouldn't have mattered if I hadn't. In Mel's mind, he was already on his way to Grand Island.

Although the NBC News interview with him focused on the meeting with Jerry Falwell, Mel took the opportunity to announce the launching of a "national Soulforce campaign against spiritual violence" and to declare that the first action would be at "the trial of Jimmy Creech in Nebraska."

Mel and Gary had been with me in Kearney for the first trial as observers and supporters. This time, they would bring with them Soulforce volunteers from all over the country in nonviolent resistance to The United Methodist Church's prosecution of a pastor for providing ministry to two gay men. Many of the volunteers would come from the same group who were in Lynchburg. Others would join them. I had ridden to Lynchburg with Jim Raymer and Larry Ellis, and they had already decided to travel to Nebraska for the trial. They were excited that Soulforce would be there, too.

When we left Lynchburg, the trial was only twenty-four days away. To plan and organize a direct action in remote Grand Island, Nebraska, in such a short time was a monumental logistical challenge.

Because I was being prosecuted for conducting a holy union ceremony for two men, something unfamiliar to the general public, I asked Larry and Jim if they would be willing to renew their marriage vows on the eve of the trial, using their original ceremony, and they agreed without hesitation. I wanted the media and those attending the trial to witness the very act for which The United Methodist Church was putting me on trial. I knew the church would inevitably see this as an act of defiance, but I believed it was an important opportunity to educate the public and the media.

"It fully supports what Jim and I have attempted to do from the outset," Larry said. "That is to provide a witness to the world that we are people of integrity and dignity, and spiritual as well. Every single reporter we have talked to has asked us, 'what is a holy union? What do you do, what do you say?'" The renewal ceremony would be an answer.

We decided to use the original ceremony and follow it up with an invitation to all other attending couples in committed relationships to join in a renewal of their vows. Jill Edens was unable to come to the trial, so we asked the Reverend Nancy Wilson,[1] pastor of the Metropolitan Community Church in Los Angeles, to join me in conducting the ceremony.

The Lynchburg event with Jerry Falwell had given Soulforce international attention, with major coverage in such publications as the *New York*

Times and *Time* magazine, as well as worldwide television coverage. Consequently, Soulforce's announcement of a plan to conduct a direct action at my trial added to what was already significant media interest.

Mel sent out a press release, explaining to the church hierarchy and the public why Soulforce would try to stop the trial: "This trial is not simply a private legal matter between the United Methodists and one of their clergy. It is a highly visible assault on America's sexual minorities by an historic Christian denomination. They think the trial is about Jimmy Creech. We see it as an act of spiritual violence against all God's lesbian, gay, bisexual and transgender children."

Mel sent an open letter to Bishop William Boyd Grove, the presiding officer for the trial, and Bishop Joel Martínez, as well as all members of The United Methodist Church in the form of a newspaper ad. He wrote: "Whatever your verdict, this trial will further confuse and divide the church of Christ. It will support discrimination in public policy against homosexuals. It will help ruin lives, divide families and split churches. And it will justify fear, anger, bigotry and acts of violence against us. If you allow this trial to continue, you will break the heart of Christ, bring shame to His body, the church, and commit an act of spiritual violence against God's gay and lesbian children."

The planned Soulforce action generated widespread support from around the country and within Nebraska. Members of First Church in Omaha and clergy from the Nebraska Annual Conference began to make plans to attend the trial, along with people from distant states. For those who could not travel to Nebraska, prayer vigils were planned around the country in places like Chapel Hill; San Francisco; Bloomington, Indiana; Saratoga, California; Denver; Omaha; Miami Beach; Binghamton, New York; Pittsburgh; Seattle; Arvada, Colorado; Oklahoma City; Sacramento; Brooklyn; Madison, Wisconsin; Oak Park, Illinois; and Philadelphia.

Chris, Natalia, and I boarded our plane to Omaha around eight thirty in the morning on Tuesday, November 16. As we moved down the crowded aisle, Chris kept her eyes on the armrests for our seat numbers and didn't notice that ahead of her a neatly dressed businessman had folded his suit coat and put it carefully in the bin just above our seats. When Chris arrived at our seats, she put her carry-on bag in the overhead bin, assuming it was empty and unknowingly smashing the man's coat into the back of the bin. Having seen all this happen from several strides behind Chris, I took out the man's coat and neatly refolded it. As I was about to place it on top of Chris's carry-on bag, the man, seated just in front of me, saw me with his coat. Thinking I had messed it up, he yanked it from my hands, his face red with anger, and screamed, "Asshole!" Everyone on the plane looked at us with alarm. It was not an auspicious start for what lay ahead, I thought.

As we traveled to Nebraska, preparations for the trial were well underway in Grand Island. Mel and Gary were already there, greeting the more than one hundred people who had come to be a part of the Soulforce direct action, along with others from around the state and country. Mel was conducting training in Gandhi's principles of nonviolence for everyone who had come to do civil disobedience and "stop the trial."

Chris and I arrived at Grand Island's Holiday Inn Midtown just minutes before Jim and Larry's renewal of vows was scheduled to begin. I had just enough time to change clothes. As I put on my clerical shirt, chasuble, and stole, the awareness that this would be the last time I would wear these priestly symbols of ordination swept over me. Even though I was hurrying because time was short, I carefully considered each item as I dressed: the black shirt, the white collar, the tiny studs that held the collar in place, the full flowing white flax chasuble that I loved to wear, and the richly embroidered gold and white silk stole Chris had given me to wear for marriage ceremonies. I was experiencing a sort of dying, knowing that these tangible articles of clothing that I had worn so many times would soon be taken from me. For months, I had been preparing myself for the trial, certain that The United Methodist Church would find me guilty and remove my credentials of ordination. But I had not prepared enough. As I dressed for the ceremony that night, reality hit me hard.

Mel had asked several churches in Grand Island for permission to hold the renewal ceremony in their sanctuaries, but all had refused. The ballroom of the Holiday Inn was our only option. It was packed to capacity. Local, statewide, and national media with several television cameras were set up behind the rows of folding chairs where the guests sat, waiting for the service to begin. In addition, a score or more of officers from the Grand Island Police Department, the Hall County Sheriff's Department, and the Nebraska Highway Patrol were both inside and outside the room, providing security.

A communion table, covered with a white cloth, was centered in front of the chairs. Two candles, a plate of freshly baked bread, a cruet of wine, and two chalices had been placed on the table. A colorful image of stained glass was projected on the wall behind the table. Violin music accompanied the whispered voices of those waiting patiently for the ceremony to begin.

Jim and Larry in black tuxedos, the Reverend Nancy Wilson, and I entered, with Mel leading the way, and the ceremony began. "Tonight, Jim Raymer and Larry Ellis will renew their vows of commitment," Mel explained to the gathering, "using the ceremony they used in April to celebrate their holy union. We want you to witness the act The United Methodist Church is prosecuting Jimmy Creech for doing. This is a respectful, holy ceremony, a loving commitment between two people of faith that the church is so afraid of."

Nancy Wilson greeted the gathering, saying: "On behalf of Jim and Larry, I welcome you to this celebration of their commitment to each other. We are here to affirm intimate relationship in its many forms: the love of family, the support of friends. We are here to witness the making of a covenant expressed in solemn vows and promises, in dignity and integrity."

We repeated Jim and Larry's complete ceremony, including the Eucharist, through to the final blessing. Immediately afterward, the Reverend Gregory Dell conducted a renewal ceremony for all married and committed couples who were present. Then we cut a wedding cake adorned with the figures of two men holding hands, a gift I'd found for Larry and Jim on one of my speaking trips to San Francisco. The occasion was not only a renewal of commitment for Larry and Jim and the other couples, but a solemn and joyous demonstration of the ritual of loving covenant making.

Following the ceremony, we all went to Trinity United Methodist Church, where the trial would be held. The steps leading to the front entrance of the church were filled with Soulforce volunteers who were holding a candlelight vigil throughout the night. I spoke to the gathering, thanking them for their witness and asking for their prayers. It was below freezing and windy, and they wrapped themselves in blankets and snuggled close together to keep warm. During the night, the Reverend Jim Keyser, the pastor of Trinity Church; his wife, Cheryl; and other church members provided hospitality, bringing hot coffee and cocoa to warm the bodies and spirits of those keeping watch on the cold church steps.

It was a sleepless night for me. My heart was grieving, and my mind crowded with thoughts about what to say to the jury in my closing statement. I wanted to convince each member of the jury that the policies and teachings of The United Methodist Church about homosexuality were not only wrong but evil, and that the jurors' participation in the trial made them complicit in this evil. I wanted to persuade them to dissent and to resist this bigotry by refusing to render a verdict.

Since my early years in ministry, I had rarely spoken from a written text. With a few exceptions, I had always prepared for sermons and speeches by making and rehearsing outlines of what I wanted to say. That night, every outline was out of control, many pages too long. But after I decided that trying to sleep was more important than preparing a final outline, I lay awake staring into the dark. Shortly before daybreak, I sat down again with pen and paper, trying one last time to create an outline. There was one in my head, but each time I tried to put it on paper, it grew to an unmanageable length. As the sun rose, I drank coffee to combat my lack of sleep and began to dress.

At seven in the morning 150 Soulforce volunteers and allies gathered at Trinity United Methodist Church. Each wore a white sweatshirt bearing a large red stop sign on the front with "Spiritual Violence" printed underneath. On the back was printed: "The Trial of Jimmy Creech, November 17–18, 1999, An act of spiritual violence." Representatives of the media waited on the plaza in front of the church. The streets around the church had been blocked by the Grand Island police earlier that morning.

At seven forty-five a bus, escorted by police on motorcycles and carrying the jury pool of thirty-five Nebraska United Methodist clergy and Bishops Martínez and Grove, arrived at a side entrance to the church. Seventy-five Soulforce volunteers quickly moved in front of the entrance, standing in rows with locked arms. In the first row, in front of United Methodist clergy from all over of the country, six Nebraska pastors stood unyielding: Bill Finlaw, Mark Kemling, Michael McMurtry, Jay Vetter, Jim Wallasky, and Doug Williamson. Television camera crews, along with the other Soulforce volunteers who chose not to be arrested, stood on either side of the walkway between the bus and the church entrance. As the bishops and jurors left the bus and approached those blocking the entrance, silence fell over the scene.

Standing toe to toe with the front line of protesters, Bishop Grove asked them to step aside so that he and the jury could "do their duty." Bishop Martínez looked into the undaunted eyes of his own clergy. No one moved. No one spoke.

"Move away or be arrested!" shouted Captain Bill Holloway of the Grand Island Police Department, breaking the tense silence. Still no one moved or spoke.

The few minutes that passed seemed interminable. Finally, Captain Holloway announced, "You're under arrest!"

As the police removed those who were blocking the entrance, the crowd of Soulforce supporters broke into applause for the protesters' resolute nonviolent resistance and willingness to be arrested. Victoria Peterson emerged from the crowd of onlookers running to catch up with those being arrested. A member of First United Methodist Church in Omaha, and at seventy-three the oldest member of the Soulforce group, she had donated several hundred dollars to help cover the fines and court costs of those being arrested. Her niece, who once had been the choir director at Trinity, was among them. Victoria had not considered being arrested until that moment. When she saw the powerful witness of the seventy-five people who had blocked the way to the trial and who now were being led away under arrest, she couldn't restrain herself and rushed to be arrested, too: "Thinking I would regret it if I did not participate, I found myself . . . bringing up the rear."[2]

Those who had been arrested were taken to a nearby unused school for processing. Each was cited for trespassing, ordered to pay a fine of $25 and $23 for court costs, and released. They then returned to join the other Soulforce volunteers continuing the vigil on the church steps.

Kelly Anderson, Leigh Ann Scharp, Sue Rood, Betty Dorr, Victoria Peterson, and Bill Jenks of First Church were among those arrested. Bill was in the second row, his arms locked with those of his children, Dexter (eight years old) and Eliza (twelve years old), who stood on either side of him wearing oversized "Stop Spiritual Violence" sweatshirts and fuzzy black ear muffs. The police took Dexter and Eliza to the old school with the others but, because of their age, refused to arrest them. As Bill and the others were being processed, Dexter and Eliza waited in the hallway of the school.

Victoria described the setting as "a dark hall" with no heat or chairs: "As we got nearer to the officers processing the arrests, we could hear children's voices singing. I could see no children — it must be angels, I fantasized. Later, I saw the kids hovering in a hole in the wall near the outside door."[3]

Dexter and Eliza had begun singing to themselves as they waited, the sound of their voices echoing softly through the empty building. Their song of defiance and hope transformed the abandoned school into a sanctuary, and the processing into a sacrament. Soon their pure, sweet voices were joined by those of the people being processed, swelling into a chorus: "We shall overcome, we are not afraid, we shall overcome someday."

"I remember Dexter and me singing," Eliza said, "and then everybody singing. That was when I felt the most connected with everybody. We sang 'Amazing Grace' and 'We Shall Overcome' over and over and over."

"You know, it could have been sort of a canned experience," Bill Jenks said later, "because it was all planned and we knew what to expect, what was going to happen. But still, linking arms and standing up to the bishops and getting arrested, it was a real thing, a real thing that we wouldn't let them by. There was such a closing of the ranks there, physically and spiritually. It was awesome. And these two, Dexter and Eliza, singing over there, it was something!"

Jim Wallasky, one of the arrested Nebraska United Methodist clergy, told me later:

I'm very grateful that Soulforce allowed us to be in that first line. The trial was so wrong. I'd talked to a lot of other clergy who were frustrated with what was going on but were unwilling to do something about it. So when Soulforce said they were going to come and said what they were going to do, it was good that someone was organizing something because we weren't doing that here.

Some people did ask, "Why is this group coming from the outside?" So another reason it was important for us to be on the front line was to say, "This is not an outside group."

Everybody keeps saying that talk is cheap. It's one thing to encourage somebody else to go out and do something, but it's another thing to step out yourself, and this was my opportunity to step out and to say, "No, this is wrong and it can't happen." So I did it. I had no idea what the consequences might be. I took a risk. I was willing to let whatever would happen, happen. It needed to be done. I don't think I could have lived with myself if I had not done it.

There are times when you throw yourself into the fire, and you feel so peaceful about it. It doesn't mean that the fire doesn't burn, but it's still the right thing to do and there's a sense of peace in doing it. I couldn't do anything else. I'm very, very thankful that Soulforce did come.

Chris and I arrived at Trinity United Methodist Church shortly before nine in the morning, just after the Soulforce action. We went up the steps, lined on either side by Soulforce volunteers wearing their white sweatshirts and holding candles, and entered the front of the church. The sanctuary seemed dimly lit, but it could have been just the atmosphere created by its high ceiling of dark wooden beams and its many rows of dark, empty wooden pews. The space, being used for an unnatural purpose, had an impersonal feeling about it, quite unlike that during worship. A few people were making last-minute preparations, and only a quiet hum of conversation could be heard.

As we walked forward, I saw Bishop Grove standing behind a table in the center of the chancel area where he would sit to preside. To the left were fifteen chairs for the jury; to the right, a single witness chair. In my communications with him before the trial, I had found Bishop Grove to be gentle, gracious, and compassionate. I greeted him and then sat down at a table in front of the first pew on the left that had a small sign reading "Respondent." Chris sat behind me on the first pew. I clasped my hands before me on the table and rehearsed what I wanted to say. Steve Flader, the church counsel, sat studying his notes at a table across the middle aisle to my right.

At nine the jury selection began. Earlier, Bishop Grove had ruled that jury selection would not be open to the public, unlike in my first trial. After the jury pool was brought in and seated, I asked for permission to make a statement, and Bishop Grove consented. I said: "Bishop Grove, Bishop Martínez, jury pool, I believe the law that is the basis for the charges against me to be unjust and immoral. Consequently, I am choosing not to participate in the selection of the jury. The church has decided that this charge and this prosecution should move forward, so I leave it to the church to decide who should be involved in it. I don't want to be responsible for anyone being involved in what I consider to be an act of violence against gay, lesbian, bisexual, and transgender people."[4]

Nineteen of the thirty-five potential jurors were then selected by lot to be examined. Steve Flader asked them: "Is there any physical or spiritual reason to render you unable to serve on this trial court?" No one responded, except the Reverend Mark Richardson. "I don't know if this really answers that question," he said, "but I am a pastor of some churches that if I voted innocent, it would take an extreme amount of moral courage on my part. I think I have that courage, but I would rather not serve on the jury if I could."

He was excused. Steve Flader chose thirteen of those remaining for the jury, plus two alternates. Bishop Grove announced a recess. It was nine twenty-five in the morning.

At ten, we reconvened for the beginning of the trial. Jim and Larry took seats in the second pew just behind Chris. About three hundred people were in the sanctuary to observe. When Bishop Grove read the charge against me, he explained to the trial court that I had chosen not to enter a plea, so "we enter for him a plea of not guilty." He then called upon Steve Flader to make his opening statement. Steve was succinct and businesslike, telling the jury that the evidence would prove that I had taken part in a ceremony of holy union for two men, that this act constituted a violation of the Order and Discipline of The United Methodist Church, and that, consequently, I was guilty of committing a chargeable offense against the church. By his body language, demeanor, and concise statements, Steve indicated that he clearly understood he had a job to do and he was going to do it. The case against me was simple and unambiguous. He would make the prosecution just as precise and straightforward. The church counsel in my first trial had failed to convict me, and Steve wasn't going to let that happen this time.

Bishop Grove asked me to make an opening statement, and I declined. Steve then called me as the first witness for the prosecution. He asked if I had participated in a "ceremony of holy union . . . involving two men." I answered yes, and described the ceremony, reading aloud the pertinent parts that I had conducted. Steve asked: "Did you pronounce them life partners?"

"I did," I answered.

His final question to me was: "Will you continue to celebrate ceremonies of holy union for homosexual persons if requested?"

"There is nothing that would deter me from doing that," I replied.

The only other prosecution witness was the Reverend Jim McChesney, who was asked to read aloud his letter of complaint against me and then was excused. Steve then began his closing statement by reviewing the August 1998 Judicial Council decision declaring the prohibition of "homosexual unions" to be church law. He concluded by telling the jurors: "The responsibility of enforcing this decision of the Judicial Council rests with you. You have patiently listened to the evidence presented. It is now time for you to do your duty which you were sworn to do at the beginning of this trial. It is up to you, the trial court, to enforce the decision of the Judicial Council. As ordained elders, one of our duties is to administer the provisions of the

Discipline. Reverend Creech has broken his covenant and should be found guilty as charged by the Committee on Investigation." Steve sat down at ten thirty. The trial was moving quickly.

When Bishop Grove asked for my closing statement to the jury, I walked to the chancel area in front of them, looked into their eyes, and began to speak:

> My dear colleagues, members of the trial court, this is a sad day in the history of The United Methodist Church. You are honorable people, people of good will; and this is an honorable process. This judicial process is one that should be about upholding just, fair and honorable laws, laws that are intended to protect people, to ensure fairness and justice; laws that fairly order the way we live our lives as United Methodists as a part of the body of Christ.
>
> But the law that is the basis of the charge against me is a law that is unjust and immoral. And for that reason, this trial has been corrupted. The church is relying on your commitment to The United Methodist Church as ordained clergy to uphold a church law that is unjust and violent.
>
> But we must put our calling to serve God above all things. And if we blindly support laws that can cause injury and harm, that encourage violence against some of our sisters and brothers, then we are violating the prior call to be servants of God, to be witnesses to the love and grace of Jesus Christ.

I told the jurors about my experience working with gay and lesbian couples whose unions I had celebrated over the past eight years, about how they had been wounded by the church yet found the capacity to love one another and to believe in God's love. I talked about lesbian and gay people I knew to be concealed in painful, loveless heterosexual marriages in order to remain clergy in the church. I talked about Jesus's vision of a realm where all people are accepted, about Peter and Paul's radical act of welcoming gentiles into what was in their day a Jewish movement. I shared some of my experiences growing up in a racist society, and pointed out how the prejudice I witnessed then was much like what I saw now directed against gay people. I continued:

> There are those who argue that we need to wait for General Conference to change the church's law. I say that if we follow that advice, we are trivializing the pain of gay and lesbian people. We're saying it's okay for

them to suffer longer. That what is most important is that the church has a nicely run organization, that the institution has rules that everybody is following. I say to you that is idolatry.

To place the institution and its rules above the well-being of God's children is certainly not Christian. Any reading of the gospel tells us that Jesus always placed the well-being of God's children above the religious institution and its laws, for it is God's will that each child of God be whole and well and accepted as she or he is.

We must today begin to change the direction of our church. You have a decision to make. You must decide whether or not you will uphold this law by voting that I'm guilty. If you vote me guilty, you will be honoring this law. You will be saying that it is all right for our church to discriminate against gay, lesbian and bisexual people.

I'm not going to ask you to acquit me, because whether I'm declared guilty or innocent is not the issue. Because if you acquit me the law still stands unchallenged.

I would like you not to render a verdict, to vote neither guilty nor not guilty to take a stand and say, "We will no longer allow the legal power of The United Methodist Church and its resources to be used to prosecute clergy for being pastors. We will not allow the judicial power of the church to enforce unjust laws and we will not tolerate any longer the use of the church's resources and its leadership to persecute gay, lesbian and bisexual persons."

If you say you will not vote and will not legitimize this law, then you will be making a strong witness to help turn the tide so the church can begin to recover its integrity, its soul can begin to heal, the persecution can begin to end and we can all join together—gay, lesbian, bisexual, transgender and nongay people—in the witness to and service of Jesus Christ.

This trial is really not about what I have done. The trial is about what you are going to do. You are the ones who have the opportunity to make a difference. You are the ones who have an opportunity to say, "No more! We will not bring harm to our sisters and brothers who are lesbian and gay, bisexual, and transgender." You have the opportunity to turn away from institutional idolatry and to stand in the presence of Christ and in the spirit of God for what is true, for what is loving, for what is just and for what is compassionate. I hope that you will decide in this judicial process that what you are called to do is to rise above the law and give witness to the love, compassion and justice of Jesus Christ.[5]

I looked in the eyes of each of the jurors as I spoke, but I saw no clue to what they thought or whether what I was saying was making an impact. I felt that I had been brief, yet I had spoken for nearly an hour. Still I had left so much unsaid that I wanted to say. Frustration welled up within me. I felt that I had failed to meet the challenge before me. I wanted to do better, to speak more eloquently and convincingly. I wanted to see understanding and agreement in the eyes of the jurors. I wanted to see defiance of the hurtful law, or at least consciences troubled by it.

As I turned to walk back to my table, I heard the sound of someone clapping. Its lonely echo in the lofty ceiling grew quickly into a roar. I looked up, and the room was filled with people standing, clapping, and crying. While speaking, I had focused so intensely on the jurors that I had forgotten anyone else was listening. Frustration, futility, and grief consumed my soul. I sat down with tears streaming down my face. I held my head up, but I cried for the church and the victims of its sin. I cried for my inability to stop its violence against lesbian, gay, bisexual, and transgender people and their families. I cried for the mortal wound that the church had inflicted upon itself.

Two hours later, the jury rendered its verdict. The Reverend Jeffrey Kelley stood and said: "We the members of the jury, find the defendant, Reverend Creech, guilty of breaking the Order and Discipline of The United Methodist Church. The count was thirteen guilty, zero not guilty."

I had failed to convince even one juror to refuse to vote, protest the prohibition, resist the trial, bear witness against our church's persecution of lesbian, gay, bisexual, and transgender people. I was numb. The verdict served neither John Wesley's nor Jesus's legacies. It served only bigotry and misguided devotion to duty. Based on the Judicial Council's decision, the verdict was a proper application of law. Based on God's unconditional love, it was a travesty. The United Methodist Church had been on trial this day, not me, and it had proven itself guilty.

It was time in the trial to determine my punishment. Steve Flader addressed the jury: "I ask you to recommend withdrawal of Reverend Creech's ordination as a deacon and elder in The United Methodist Church, as is in your power and authority. The Church does not ask this lightly . . . , [but] Reverend Creech's blatant disobedience to the Order and Discipline of The

United Methodist Church must end. He has stated . . . he will not abide by the *Discipline* in the prohibition of ceremonies celebrating homosexual unions . . . [and] will continue to celebrate those ceremonies. This disobedience needs to end and it needs to end now."

Bishop Grove asked if I wanted to speak, and I declined. He then recessed the trial so the jury could decide my punishment. There was no telling how long the process would take. I didn't want to leave, so Chris and I sat waiting in the front pew. Most of the others in the sanctuary also waited. John Fletcher sat down at the piano in the chancel area and began to play hymns. Someone began to sing, and others joined in. Hymn numbers were called out, and soon we were all singing together. Observers in the sanctuary were divided between those supporting me and those wanting me punished. For the next two hours, however, we sang together. The division was invisible, the facade of unity restored.

Someone noticed a sparrow frantically flying near the vaulted ceiling. How it got in was a mystery; how it would escape, a greater one. We continued singing with eyes cast upward, following the desperate, futile flight of the sparrow among the wooden beams and organ pipes.

About three forty-five, the jury returned. Bishop Grove asked me to stand and invited any of the observers who so desired to stand with me. The division, invisible while we sang, reappeared. "How unstable a space was that sanctuary," John Fletcher later reflected. "One minute a place of praise and fellowship, the next a courtroom. Those moments seemed to me like the distillation of all your efforts. You brought the tensions within the community that is The United Methodist Church to a point of crisis and opportunity. Your trial showed us at once what we could be (a congregation singing as one) and how we are not yet there."

"Having found the Respondent guilty of the stated charge," Jeffrey Kelley said, "we then designate the penalty to be withdrawal of credentials of ordination, including both deacon and elder of the Respondent." Conferred upon me twenty-nine years before, my ordination had been taken from me, the blessing withdrawn.

Bishop Grove, visibly shaken, spoke:

This is a sad day for all of us, for our church. But we thank the jury for doing what they felt they must do and being responsive to the charge. I just now would invite you all to join me in prayer:

Merciful and gracious God, we thank you for your grace which you offer to us unconditionally in every circumstance. We all share, whatever our point of view on the issue before this court, in the sadness of the day. We all pray for Jimmy, pray for his family, for their comfort and their strength. We thank you for this jury pool that has done hard work today for you and has brought to us what they felt called to bring.

We pray for all those in this conference and across the church who are affected in any way by this decision. And we pray for our church, for grace, to bring us all together, to lead us toward a new day. We pray for all gay, lesbian, bisexual, and transgender people, that wounded as they will be by this verdict, they will know that they abide in your care and in your love.

Lord Jesus, each of us has heartache this day. We did not choose to do this. We were called by the church to do it. Hear our prayers and abide with our church and its children, all of them, everywhere.

In the name of the Father, the Son, and the Holy Spirit, keep you safe and bless you, now and forevermore. Amen. We are adjourned.

I picked up my briefcase and overcoat and turned to leave. Chris clutched my arm and we began to walk down the center aisle of the sanctuary. People in the pews, many weeping, waited silently for us to pass. Sara Sherrard, a transgender woman and Soulforce friend I had met in Lynchburg, led the way for us. She had been holding a large lavender candle through the night and throughout the day. Its flame had symbolized the presence of the spirit. When the penalty was announced, Sara carried the flame out of the sanctuary. "Can the Holy Spirit remain in a place where all God's children are not welcome?" Mel White whispered.

As I walked toward the exit, I was haunted by the words in the bishop's prayer: "the jury pool . . . has done hard work today for you ⌊God⌋," and "we did not choose to do this. We were called by the church to do it." Bishop Grove obviously was grieving over the trial's outcome. Still he felt compelled to equate the court's work with God's work and to absolve himself, the church counsel, and the jurors of all responsibility for it. Once again, good people were justifying evil in the name of God and the church; Pilate was washing his hands with his tears.

We emerged into the glare of the afternoon sun. The air was cool and fresh. Soulforce volunteers, many of whom could not bring themselves to enter the sanctuary to witness the inevitable verdict, still lined the steps and filled the plaza below in vigil. They now wore purple armbands, a sign of mourning. Betty Dorr, standing just outside the door, hugged Chris and me, and we began the descent to the waiting media at the edge of the crowd. It was very quiet.

As I stood before the microphones and cameras, the grief around me was palpable. I looked at the tear-streaked, anguished faces of the supporters surrounding me, the pain inflicted by the trial racking their souls. The children especially moved me. They gathered close and clung to me. Chelsea, Natalie, Dexter, and Eliza understood; just how much, I didn't know. But they understood enough to be hurt and to cry.

"The church began this process that has brought us to this moment," I said:

The church promised me nothing. It asked me to be obedient to God's call. It asked me to resist evil in whatever form it takes. It asked me to do justice. I have done what the church asked of me. It is the church that has betrayed itself.

The guilty verdict and punishment are harsh and hard to bear. The jury has sent a message to the world that The United Methodist Church supports the persecution of gay, lesbian, bisexual, and transgender people and will prosecute pastors who extend the full ministry of the church to them. It is the pettiness of the church, not the spirit of God, that has acted here today.

You who are lesbian, gay, bisexual, or transgender are people of inherent dignity. You are beautiful and holy creations of God. The church may deny this, but you must know God does not.

This trial is not the end. I grieve for my loss, but I also feel called to ministry more than ever. We're all part of God's movement in history. Ultimately, God cannot be resisted, not even by the church, and will prevail. One day, be assured, all of God's children will be welcomed and accepted and the church will be well and whole.[6]

When we returned to Raleigh, I wanted to hide myself away and grieve for a while. I didn't want to talk to anyone. I had been holding back my grief since the trial, and I desperately needed to let it out and begin healing. But there was a message waiting on the answering machine. Judith Powell urgently needed to talk with me. When I called, she told me that her sister was in the critical care unit at Rex Hospital. "Would you go see her?" Judith pleaded. "My mom's there, and they both need support."

"Of course I'll go," I said.

I hung up the phone and wanted to scream. My grief was intense, and I desperately needed time alone to deal with it. Judith knew what had happened in Nebraska. But her sister was in danger of dying, and Judith wanted me to be with her. I was torn. I was angry with Judith for not letting me deal with my loss. I wasn't a pastor any more. But I couldn't say no.

Judith's sister was alone in her room. IVs, tubes, and monitor cables were attached to her thin, fragile body, and her face was covered with an oxygen mask. She had been unconscious for several days. I stood for a while at her side, holding her hand and watching her breathe. I prayed softly, kissed her forehead, and quietly left. I stopped by the waiting room and visited with her mother.

On my way home, I thought about how what I had done was so usual and natural for me, the way things well practiced are for anyone. I had performed such acts thousands of times over the past twenty-nine years. I realized then that, while my relationship with The United Methodist Church had changed, I hadn't. I remained the same person I was before the trial. The church had taken from me only what it had given, my credentials of ordination. The clerical frock was truly an adornment, not an essential part of who I was. Being defrocked took from me a title I had worn, but not my identity or vocation, which were so much more than a covering, so much more essential than a title. I might no longer be a "Reverend," but I would always be a pastor. I called Judith to report on my visit with her sister and mother, and I thanked her for calling on me.

As the intensity of my grief eased, the significance of the trial for me and for The United Methodist Church began to clarify. Wanting to share my perspective on the trial and to say thanks, I sent the following message to those who had stood with me throughout the ordeal:

December 4, 1999
Greetings!

Two weeks have passed since the trial in Grand Island, Nebraska. While I still need more time to assess the significance and consequences of the guilty verdict and the penalty, both for me personally and for the movement toward justice and community of which all of us are a part, there are a few things I am clear about and want to share with you now.

First, I am immensely grateful for the support you gave to me, and for the witness that you made in various ways around the country on behalf of justice and to affirm the dignity of lesbian, gay, bisexual and transgender persons. I wish I had some adequate and personal way to say to each of you, "Thank you!" Your support strengthened and empowered me. I never felt alone. I was always clear that I was only one small part of a larger faithful community journeying together in this movement of God in history. You are for me the sign of our Easter faith, confirming our hope that justice, compassion and truth will prevail over bigotry, injustice and death.

The role that Soulforce played in exposing the truth about the trial was extremely important. The church wanted to reduce the trial to simply holding me accountable as a law breaker. You folks made that reduction impossible. You made it clear that the trial was about the oppression and persecution of lesbian, gay, bisexual and transgender persons by The United Methodist Church. This was a gift to the movement. You have opened the door and shown light into the church's closet of shame. You did this with your very bodies, with dignity, integrity and courage. No one else was willing to take the direct action that you took. What you did was historic!

The trial brought to an end a twenty-nine-year relationship that I have had with The United Methodist Church as an ordained minister. The ordination that was taken from me by the jury was given to me by The United Methodist Church. It belonged to the church and the church had a right to take it back. It was not mine to claim; it is not an entitlement. That is the basic meaning of ordained ministry.[7] However, the ordination that preceded it and cannot be reclaimed by The United Methodist Church is the one that came with my baptism and confirmed by my call to ministry. It belongs to me still and no institution, jury or person has the authority or power to take it away. I will continue to honor and live out this ordination in all that I do.

This is not to say that what the church revoked was unimportant to me. There is nothing I love more than being a pastor of a congregation. I know that I cannot be a United Methodist pastor now. I will not dwell on it, but be assured that I grieve for what has been taken from me.

But, I grieve more for those who are being rejected, oppressed, and persecuted by The United Methodist Church because of who they are and because of whom they love. The ordination that has been taken from me is one that The United Methodist Church has routinely denied and withdrawn from gay people long before it was officially required to do so in 1984. Many gifted persons called by God have been denied ordination because of their sexual orientation. Others have been denied fellowship, if not membership, in The United Methodist Church. Many have been spiritually and psychologically abused by vicious judgment and condemnation. I am only a casualty of the church's bigotry against bisexual, lesbian, gay and transgender persons. They are the true victims and martyrs. I have been punished only for what I've done. They are punished for who they are and whom they love. The difference is profound. My loss and pain trifles in comparison.

I also grieve for The United Methodist Church. It has wounded and crippled itself with bigotry, legalism and fear. Until these impediments are purged from its soul, The United Methodist Church cannot speak authentically of God's love in Jesus Christ. Every act and testimony toward that end will be smudged with the evil of its prejudice and persecution of gay people. We may be witnessing its death, at least the death of the church we have loved and served. We can mourn the church that dies; but, we cannot hold on to it if its soul is dead. Instead, we must look for the new reality of God's presence in the world, the new expression and experience of Christ's body.

I believe it is important to understand my trial as resistance within the church to the movement of God toward Jesus's vision of an inclusive and just community. The trial resisted but did not end the movement. Rather, it helped to bring clarity and definition to it. It was not axial, but only another movement in the redemptive process of God. It could be seen as a defeat, The United Methodist Church's further fall from grace, or it can be seen as a painful event that opens up new possibilities for change toward the new thing God is doing. I believe it is the latter.

I believe there is no way that God's movement toward justice, freedom, dignity and community can be successfully resisted and denied. I don't feel defeated. I am now among the laity of The United Methodist Church, called to the same ministry I've always been called to honor, called to "resist evil, injustice, and oppression in whatever forms they present themselves." Called "[a]ccording to the grace given to [me, to] remain [a] faithful member of Christ's holy church and serve as Christ's representative in the world."[8] When I was ordained, it was my privilege to serve the laity. It is now my honor to serve with the laity. And as time passes, I know God will call me to other ministries I've not imagined. God bless you! The journey continues, and we continue together!

"Cecil, I need to join a church where my membership won't cause any controversy. Will you let me become a member of Glide?"

In The United Methodist Church, clergy are members of an annual conference, not a local church. When the jury removed my credentials of ordination, I was effectively removed from membership in The United Methodist Church. Because I knew my presence at Calvary United Methodist Church in Durham had caused the defection of many of its members, I was concerned that if I joined a church in North Carolina, it might create controversy and cause similar harm.

So, soon after my trial, I called the Reverend Dr. Cecil Williams at Glide Memorial United Methodist Church in San Francisco and asked if I could become a member there. Glide Memorial is an extraordinary congregation, and Cecil Williams an extraordinary minister. And Glide's membership extends far beyond San Francisco. Without hesitation, Cecil said yes. The following Sunday, he announced from the pulpit that I was now a member of Glide. Once again, I was a United Methodist.

There's more to the story at Calvary United Methodist Church. Since the day I preached there in August 1999, the hemorrhaging of its membership had been steady and was nearly fatal. By mid-March of the next year, worship attendance had declined from more than one hundred to fewer than thirty, the congregation didn't have enough money to meet expenses, and the long-suffering valiant remnant began to talk about closing the church.

When news of Calvary's imminent demise spread, the RUM group began to attend worship there regularly on the second Sunday of each month, their voices filling the once nearly empty sanctuary with a hopeful sound.

They offered gratitude for Calvary's witness and encouragement in its peril—and they brought their checkbooks. Soon, many of the RUM group were coming every Sunday and becoming official members. Some of those from the Durham community who had found a safe haven there on that Sunday afternoon back in August also started attending regularly and supporting Calvary.

The Reverend Laurie Hays Coffman and the stalwart Calvary remnant were witnessing the fruit of their faithful journey through crisis, loss, and despair. Over the next two years, the worshiping membership of Calvary tripled in size. "It had to die to be reborn, to have a new identity, a new hope, a new vision," Laurie observed. "That's the only way it could happen."

On April 14, 2002, the membership of Calvary United Methodist Church unanimously voted to become the first Reconciling Congregation in North Carolina. "I learned to take neither the blame nor the credit for the death and resurrection of the church," Laurie told me. "It was just about trying to be faithful, trusting the Holy Spirit and moving forward on the journey."

Another surprising movement of the spirit occurred a few months after my trial. In the first week of February 2000, the California-Nevada Annual Conference Committee on Investigation held a three-day public hearing on the judicial complaints against the "Sacramento 68." Unlike the two hearings I had experienced in Nebraska, this hearing was viewed by the committee as a critical step in the judicial process that required careful inquiry into the merits of the complaints in terms of the meaning and context of ministry.

Each of the sixty-eight accused clergy spoke passionately about why they had participated in Jeanne and Ellie's holy union in January 1999. Scholars and church leaders spoke about how tradition within The United Methodist Church is dynamic and evolving, not static, and about how the California-Nevada Annual Conference had a tradition of ministry to and with lesbian, gay, bisexual, and transgender people dating back more than thirty years. The clergy discussed Christian ethics regarding human sexuality, the historical and cultural contexts of various biblical passages related to same-gender sexual behavior and their relevance to our current understanding of human sexuality, and how John Wesley and the early Methodist movement of the eighteenth century serve as models for those who today are seeking to open the church to gay people.

On February 11, the committee announced that the Sacramento 68 had not been "disobedient to the Order and Discipline of The United Methodist Church" in conducting Jeanne and Ellie's holy union. The complaints were dismissed, and Bishop Melvin Talbert declared the matter closed. There would be no trial.

The committee's decision was not so much an act of defiance against the General Conference as it was a recognition that ministry develops contextually and cannot be defined by legislation or imposed by laws. The committee had acted decisively, boldly, faithfully, and with extraordinary courage and integrity.

On February 15, 2000, just days after the "Sacramento 68" decision was announced, First United Methodist Church in Omaha held a special All Church Conference to vote on becoming a member of the Reconciling Congregation Program. A yearlong process of study and dialogue toward this end was initiated by the Missions and Social Action Commission of First Church on March 3, 1998. Because it wanted to give church members more time and opportunity to consider this important vote, the Church Council extended the process for an additional year. It also established a 66 percent or more affirmative vote in order for the proposal to pass, believing that a simple majority would not ensure sufficient congregational support. When the vote was taken, 112 voted in favor and 20 voted against — an 85 percent affirmative vote. First Church thus became the first Reconciling Congregation in Nebraska and took another significant step toward fulfilling its Vision Focus.

Unfortunately, the positive developments at First United Methodist Church, Omaha, and in the California-Nevada Annual Conference were countered by the larger church's regressive actions. In each of the General Conferences of The United Methodist Church since 1972, when antigay language first appeared in *The Book of Discipline*, progressive United Methodists had worked to end the church's mistreatment of gay people. In spite of their best efforts, the policies and teachings regarding homosexuality had grown increasingly restrictive, exclusionary, and punitive, with the 1996 ban on holy unions the most recent assault. The 2000 General Conference would continue that trend. It met in Cleveland, Ohio, May 2–12, with 992 delegates — divided equally between clergy and lay people — attending from the United States, Eastern Europe, the Philippines, Africa, and Puerto Rico, representing 9.7 million United Methodists.

Undaunted by the General Conference's intransigence over the past twenty-eight years, four progressive groups within The United Methodist Church—Affirmation, Methodist Federation for Social Action, In All Things Charity, and the Reconciling Congregation Program—formed a coalition named AMAR. The coalition was convinced that reason, intense lobbying, and personal testimonies could bring about positive change at this General Conference, at least slowing the legislative momentum in support of—if not ending—The United Methodist Church's persecution of gay people. AMAR's primary goal was removing the language in *The Book of Discipline* that says: "The practice of homosexuality is incompatible with Christian teaching." All of the United Methodist discriminatory policies against gay people were based on that one phrase.

On the other side, wanting to preserve if not reinforce the status quo, was UMDecision 2000, a coalition of the Confessing Movement, the Good News evangelical caucus, and their allies. It promised a massive walkout from the conference should the delegates support any weakening of the church's official proscriptions regarding homosexuality.

Added to these opposing United Methodist groups was Soulforce. Soon after my trial in Grand Island, Mel White began preparations for Soulforce to be present at the 2000 General Conference. If the conference failed to make positive changes, Mel announced, Soulforce would conduct a major act of civil disobedience to draw public attention to the church's violence against gay people.

By the second week of the General Conference, it was apparent there would be no positive changes. On Wednesday morning, with two days of the conference remaining, 191 Soulforce volunteers were arrested for blocking traffic outside the main entrance of the Cleveland Convention Center, where the conference was being held. Among those of us arrested were the Reverend James Lawson, a United Methodist pastor, legendary civil rights leader, and mentor to the Reverend Dr. Martin Luther King Jr.; Rodney Powell, MD, a civil rights leader in the 1959–1962 Nashville Student Movement;[1] and Arun Gandhi, the grandson of Mohandas Karamchand Gandhi.

On Thursday morning, additional arrests were made inside the General Conference. When the delegates voted 628 to 337 to reaffirm the statement in *The Book of Discipline* that says "the practice of homosexuality [is] incompatible with Christian teaching," about fifty members of AMAR came onto the floor of the hall and lined the front and main aisles where the delegates were seated. A hundred and fifty others stood around the edge of the auditorium floor and in the balcony, virtually surrounding the delegates. Bishop Dan Solomon, who was presiding at the time, pleaded with the AMAR protesters to leave the conference floor, but they refused. The delegates then voted to continue the ban on the ordination of "self-avowed practicing homosexuals," 640 to 317, and the ban on "homosexual unions," 646 to 294.

At that point, some of the AMAR protesters moved to the stage. Randy Miller and Sue Laurie spoke to the General Conference, charging The United Methodist Church with breaking faith with lesbian, gay, bisexual, and transgender members. "We are not strangers to this Church,"[2] they said, noting that they and other gay and lesbian United Methodists had been baptized and confirmed in the church, active in its programs, and faithful in worship and service as full members of the church. But, they told the delegates, when they discovered their sexuality and were open and honest about it, they were no longer welcome. The church had broken its covenant with them.[3]

Twelve bishops stood in solidarity with the AMAR protesters, along with about three hundred of the General Conference delegates. The protesters and their supporters — on the conference floor, on the stage, and in the balcony — began to sing "We Shall Overcome."

Finally, Bishop Solomon ordered police to arrest the AMAR protesters who refused to leave the stage. Horrified, supporters shouted, "Shame! Shame! Shame!" Bishops Susan Morrison and Joseph Sprague joined AMAR onstage and were arrested with them. Several other bishops moved from their seats to be close to those being arrested, offering words of solidarity. Twenty-nine United Methodists were arrested, several for the second time in two days.

A local newspaper reported: "'I think that the Church is horribly and painfully divided, irreconcilably so,' said the Reverend Kenneth W. Chalker, pastor of First United Methodist Church of Cleveland. Men and women wept openly. All day, hurt abounded. The Reverend Thomas Taylor, a former Cleveland district superintendent who sang from the balcony in support of gay-rights demonstrators, said, 'It's the saddest day of my life. This is a disaster.'"[4]

"I have shed so many tears this morning. I am grieving for our church. Cried on Jimmy Creech's shoulder on the way out. He was crying too. I have never shed so many tears," Sam Isley reported to friends back in Raleigh via e-mail.

Indeed, General Conference 2000 had been a moral disaster for The United Methodist Church. Reinforcing its persecution and oppression of gay, bisexual, lesbian, and transgender people, it had made no movement toward ending its spiritual violence against them, and the prospect of any such future movement appeared remote. The prohibition of "homosexual unions" was moved to the administrative law of the church, eliminating the scandal of deeming one sentence in the Social Principles law and all the rest guidance. All but one of the new members elected to the Judicial Council represented conservative constituencies. A new formula for electing future General Conference delegates was adopted, shifting the power base in the church to the more reactionary southeastern and south central jurisdictions and weakening the influence of the more progressive western, northeastern, and north central jurisdictions, presaging the continuation of the church's bigotry for generations to come.

United Methodist progressives were in a quandary after the General Conference about whether they should remain in the church and valiantly try to bring about change, or leave. Some refused to surrender to the re-actionaries now controlling The United Methodist Church, vowing to continue fighting for change through legislation. There would be other General Conferences, and those Methodists were not going to give up the struggle until gay people were welcomed with full rights of membership. Some, no less willing to concede the church to bigotry, vowed to remain and, instead of relying on the legislative strategy, create alternative ministries and structures within the church where all people, gay and nongay alike, would be included and accepted without condition. Others, bruised and weary, could remain no longer and left the church.

It would have been a sin against hope, however, to call the struggle lost. The overwhelming success of those protecting the status quo within the church may prove in the end to be a Pyrrhic victory because it will continue to provoke progressives and some moderates to publicly denounce and defy its antigay policies and teachings. What gives hope its power is the confidence that whatever the present situation is, it is not final. Injustice and evil are temporary, not eternal. The future is always open to change and new realities.

Until the Christian church ends its spiritual violence against gay people, we who believe in Jesus's vision of an inclusive, just, and compassionate community must strive relentlessly to make it a reality in our lives and in the world. We must be disciples of compassion and justice, not Pharisees loyal to church laws that serve fear, ignorance, and institutional survival. We cannot and must not wait for the church's permission and approval before doing what is right, moral, and just. People of conscience, committed to the vision of Jesus, must continue to actively and defiantly honor and bless the inherent dignity and goodness of gay, lesbian, bisexual, and transgender people and their committed relationships, regardless of the personal and institutional costs.

When my credentials of ordination were taken from me in 1999, I continued to travel around the country speaking and preaching for various churches and civil rights organizations, all the while writing this book. To supplement our family income, I worked in the specialty department of the Whole Foods Market in Raleigh, selling cheese, wine, and chocolates. As chairperson of its Board of Directors from 2000 to 2005, I was active with Soulforce, working closely with Mel White, its executive director and founder. We conducted direct actions, which most often included civil disobedience with arrests, against denominational meetings of the United Methodist, Southern Baptist, Presbyterian, Evangelical Lutheran Church in America, Episcopal, and Roman Catholic churches. In each case, we demanded an end to the spiritual violence against lesbian, gay, bisexual, and transgender people.

In 2004, when right-wing religious leaders pushed for legislation to amend the North Carolina State Constitution to define marriage as exclusively between one man and one woman "at one time," I helped organize the North Carolina Religious Coalition for Marriage Equality. The group collected the signatures of over three hundred North Carolina religious leaders on a statement opposing the constitutional amendment. We held a large rally at the North Carolina General Assembly opposing the amendment and carried the religious leaders' statement to all members of the legislature. In concert with Equality North Carolina, we have continued to work against antigay legislation, presenting a progressive, gay-affirming religious voice at the General Assembly. As of 2010, North Carolina was the only state in the South that had not passed an antigay constitutional marriage amendment.

In 2005, I collaborated with Mitchell Gold—a North Carolina–based furniture entrepreneur[5]—to create Faith In America. We conducted campaigns around the country—in Washington, D.C.; Baltimore; Indianapolis;

Colorado Springs; Ames, Iowa; and Greenville, South Carolina, as well as in Hickory, Taylorsville, and Greensboro, North Carolina—using a variety of media and town-hall meetings to educate the public about the history of religion-based bigotry against women, people of color, and other minorities, especially gay, lesbian, bisexual, and transgender people. I retired as the executive director of Faith In America in 2007 to devote full time to completing this manuscript and getting it published.

The course of my life changed when Adam came to my office in 1984. While my understanding of Jesus's life and teachings compelled me to challenge injustice and stand with the oppressed and disenfranchised, I always believed I would do this in the conventional role of church pastor. I am convinced that prophetic ministry is born in pastoral ministry. I would have happily remained in a local parish if I had been allowed to do so. But that was not to be. Adam's disclosure broadened my ministry beyond anything I ever imagined. Once my mind and heart understood the oppression and persecution of gay people by church and society, once I stepped off that curb, there was no turning back.

I don't mean to say I had no choice, because I did. But the alternative I had was to deny that gay people were being persecuted by the church I served and to turn my back on what I knew to be morally right and just. To make that choice was unthinkable.

Since then, I have had many unwanted departures and apparent failures. Yet each time I found an unexpected welcome and opportunity. I continue to mourn my absence from parish ministry even as I write, but I embrace what was for me a unique and rare opportunity to serve the truly human agenda of the Christian gospel, an opportunity that more than generously fulfilled what I always believed to be my call to ministry.

A final word about Adam: In January of 1990, the *News & Observer* carried a story about my activities with the Raleigh Religious Network for Gay and Lesbian Equality: "The dispute over the Reverend Jimmy Creech's stand on homosexual rights has divided one of Raleigh's most prominent Methodist congregations. About 80 unhappy members have sent a petition to the bishop, demanding that he rid them of their pastor. Attendance has plummeted. Contributions dropped by more than $25,000 last year, threatening the church's survival and causing the pastor to take a 30 percent salary cut. 'It has been a difficult and painful time,' said Creech."[6]

The day the article was published, Adam called me. He was in tears, just as he had been when he came to my office that morning five years before. "I'm so sorry I got you into this mess," he said; "I don't want anything to happen to you. I'm so sorry."

"Adam, you don't need to apologize," I replied through my own tears, deeply touched by his concern; "You told me the truth about yourself. You helped me begin to understand a truth about the church, a truth I discovered only because you told me. I'll always be grateful to you for that."

"Jimmy," he said, "one day when I retire and I can be open about who I am, I'm going to become an activist. I'm going to do everything I can to make the world a safe place for gay people."

That was the last time I talked with Adam. He died of a heart attack not long afterward, though he was only in his mid-fifties. Adam didn't live long enough to retire and realize his dream to be an openly gay man, working to make the world safe for his gay, lesbian, transgender, and bisexual brothers and sisters. But he had given me a most generous gift.

In 2000, I was on CNN's *Larry King Live* with Governor Howard Dean to discuss the civil union[7] legislation recently enacted in Vermont, which provided the same state benefits and rights to same-gender couples that non-gay married couples receive. When Larry King asked why Vermont was the first state to do this, Governor Dean gave this simple yet profound explanation: "Because we are a small state, so we get to know each other." He said the legislators found the gay and lesbian people who testified before them to be human beings the same as everyone else, not like the stereotypes the legislators had believed them to be. The hearts and minds of the legislators had been informed and changed by the essential humanity of the gay men and lesbians they got to know.

Gay, lesbian, bisexual, and transgender people will be successful in attaining full civil and human rights and social acceptance because of those among them who believe in their inherent dignity and integrity and have the courage to let the world know who they really are. This was the gift they gave to the legislators that made the difference in Vermont. And it was the gift Adam gave to me that changed my life and my world. It's a gift that all lesbian, gay, bisexual, and transgender people have to give. And by giving it, they change the world for good.

1. Adam

1. Adam is a pseudonym. Pseudonyms are used in this book for some people, to protect their privacy.
2. General Conference is the legislative body of The United Methodist Church. It meets every four years.

2. Orientation

1. Thomas A. Dooley's books are *Deliver Us from Evil: The Story of Vietnam's Flight to Freedom* (New York: Farrar, Straus and Cudahy, 1956); *The Edge of Tomorrow* (New York: New American Library, 1958); and *The Night They Burned the Mountain* (New York: Farrar, Straus and Cudahy, 1960).
2. Hogan and Hudson, *Completely Queer*, 194.
3. The Gospel According to Matthew 6:25–34.
4. Frederick Herzog, "The Political Gospel," *Christian Century*, November 1, 1970, 1380–83.
5. Herzog, *Justice Church*, 94.
6. The annual conference is the basic organizational unit of The United Methodist Church, often named for the geographical region or state in which it is located. United Methodist clergy have their membership in annual conferences.

3. Reorientation

1. Buttrick, *The Interpreter's Dictionary of the Bible* (*IDB*). This multivolume reference work is highly regarded for its scholarship and is generally associated with liberal Protestant theology. Contributors to the reference work include many of the most eminent biblical scholars of the 1940s and 1950s.
2. *IDB*, volume 4, 397.
3. Genesis 19:1–29; Leviticus 18:22 and 20:13; Romans 1:27; I Corinthians 6:9; I Timothy 1:8–11; and Jude 7.

4. All quotes from the Bible are from the 1952 Revised Standard Version.

5. Jordan, *The Invention of Sodomy in Christian Theology*.

6. Boswell, *Christianity, Social Tolerance, and Homosexuality*, 346–53.

7. Gold et al., *The New Testament and Psalms*.

8. Brundage, *Law, Sex, and Christian Society in Medieval Europe*, 57–58.

9. Ibid., 80.

10. Ibid., 580.

11. Tannahill, *Sex in History*, 159–60.

12. After earlier failed attempts, Pope Gregory VII prohibited clerical marriage, finally succeeding in the latter part of the eleventh century in making celibacy mandatory for priests.

13. The Social Principles are found in The United Methodist Church's *Book of Discipline* and *Book of Resolutions*, each revised every four years. They are not church law, but they are described in its preface as "a prayerful and thoughtful effort on the part of the General Conference to speak to the human issues in the contemporary world from a sound biblical and theological foundation as historically demonstrated in United Methodist tradition. They are intended to be instructive and persuasive in the best of the prophetic spirit. The Social Principles are a call to all members of The United Methodist Church to a prayerful, studied dialogue of faith and practice." *The Book of Discipline of The United Methodist Church* (BOD), Part III, Social Principles, Preface.

14. *The Book of Discipline of The United Methodist Church* (BOD), paragraph 65 (G).

15. Charles Keysor, "In the Aftermath of Atlanta," *Good News* (summer 1972): 37.

16. James V. Heidinger II, "Looking for Bold Leadership," *Good News*, January–February 1982, 38.

4. Stepping Off the Curb

1. Gustavo Gutiérrez, *A Theology of Liberation: History, Politics, and Salvation*, trans. and ed. Sister Caridad Inda and John Eagleson. Maryknoll, N.Y.: Orbis, 1973.

2. The Pastor-Parish Relations Committee, also known as the Staff-Parish Relations Committee, is comparable to a personnel committee. It is the body in a local United Methodist church that counsels and guides the pastor(s) and staff in their ministry to the congregation, and communicates with the district superintendent and bishop about the appointment of pastor(s) to the congregation.

3. "Just as I Am, without One Plea," lyrics by Charlotte Elliott (1789–1871), melody by William B. Bradbury (1816–68).

4. The Reverend Dr. Carter Heyward is a lesbian feminist theologian and priest in the Episcopal Church. She taught at Episcopal Divinity School in Cambridge, Massachusetts, from 1975–2006. She is the author of more than eleven books, including *Our Passion for Justice: Images of Power, Sexuality, and Liberation* and, *Touching Our Strength: The Erotic as Power and the Love of God* (see bibliography).

5. In the spring of 2008, the room at Fairmont United Methodist Church formerly used by the Wesley (Men's) Bible Class was remodeled and dedicated as a worship center for the Wesley Foundation in memory of Robert Bryant, who died an untimely and tragic death, demonstrating the progress made at Fairmont toward greater understanding and acceptance of lesbian, gay, bisexual, and transgender people.

6. The cabinet is the group of district superintendents.

7. When I worked there, its membership included the African Methodist Episcopal Church, African Methodist Episcopal Zion Church, General Baptist State Convention, Christian Methodist Episcopal Church, Christian Church (Disciples of Christ), Episcopal Church, Evangelical Lutheran Church in America, Moravian Church in America, Presbyterian Church (USA), Religious Society of Friends, Roman Catholic Church, United Church of Christ, United Methodist Church, Church of the Brethren, and five individual congregations of Southern and American Baptist Churches.

8. In North Carolina, engaging in anal or oral sex was a felony. While the law did not refer to the gender of those participating in such acts, it had the effect of making felons of gay men and lesbians by definition.

9. Quoted from minutes of the North Carolina Council of Churches House of Delegates meeting, May 5, 1993.

10. Ibid.

11. Every year thereafter, some Methodists attempted to restore the council's funding, unsuccessfully until 2002. Then the North Carolina Annual Conference voted 344 to 321 to restore funding ($16,000 at that time) to the North Carolina Council of Churches. The opposition to the UFMCC's membership had not weakened. What happened was that the Reverend Sam Brown surprised everyone with a motion from the floor. Even though those opposed made the usual arguments against restoring the funding, they were caught unprepared and lost on a close standing vote.

12. Six striking cotton-mill workers were shot dead and thirty wounded by deputy sheriffs at the Marion Manufacturing Company in Marion, North Carolina, on October 2, 1929. Sinclair Lewis wrote a booklet about it titled *Cheap and Contented Labor: The Picture of a Southern Mill Town in 1929* (New York: United Textile Workers of America and Women's Trade Union League, 1929).

13. Catherine Clabby, "Tar Heel of the Week: Social Worker Is an Angel for AIDS Children and Their Families," *News & Observer*, January 7, 1996.

14. The Reconciling Congregation Program, now known as the Reconciling Ministries Network, worked with individual congregations, annual conferences, and campus ministries to help them become inclusive and welcoming to gay, lesbian, bisexual, and transgender people. I was a member of its Board of Directors from 1992 to 1997.

15. The bishops were Judith Craig, William W. Dew Jr., Jesse R. DeWitt, Leontine T. C. Kelly, Calvin D. McConnell, Susan M. Morrison, Fritz Mutti, Donald A. Ott, Sharon

Zimmerman Rader, Roy I. Sano, Melvin G. Talbert, Mary Ann Swenson, Melvin E. Wheatley Jr., C. Dale White, and Joseph H. Yeakel.

16. *BOD*, paragraph 65.

5. A Pastor Again

1. Julia McCord, "North Carolina Pastor to Lead First United Methodist Church," May 14, 1996, *Omaha World-Herald*.

2. The fifteen were the Reverends Gilbert H. Caldwell, Minerva Carcaño, Ignacio Castuera, Susan P. Davies, Gregory Dell, Victor Paul Furnish, Stanley G. Hall III, William A. Holmes, Takayuki Ishii, George McClain, Richard S. Parker, Sharon Rhodes-Wickett, Tex Sample, Eugene Winkler, and J. Philip Wogaman.

6. Covenant Ceremony

1. Julia McCord, "Pastor Says He'll Unite Two Lesbians," *Omaha World-Herald*, September 10, 1997.

2. Julia McCord, "Three Lay Leaders Back Cleric on Lesbian Rite," *Omaha World-Herald*, September 11, 1997.

7. Hell Breaks Loose

1. Brook Weber, "Williamson Takes Stand on Homosexual Issue," *The Cornerstone*, February 13, 1998.

2. "Located" is a term in The United Methodist Church that means removed from ministry but without the loss of credentials. It is more than suspension, which is a temporary remedial action.

3. The magazine had a circulation of 70,000.

4. James V. Heidinger II, "United Methodist Pastor Calls Lesbian Union Ecclesiastical Disobedience," *Good News* (November–December 1997), 40.

5. James V. Heidinger II, "Church-busters Doing Irreparable Harm," *Good News* (November–December 1997), 9.

6. An apportionment is the amount of money that an annual conference assigns to a church as its payment in support of the annual conference and the denomination. The individual churches cannot pick and choose what part of the annual conference and general church budgets to support. First United Methodist Church, Omaha, had the largest apportionment in the Nebraska Annual Conference.

7. Julia McCord, "A National Debate," *Omaha World-Herald*, October 25, 1997.

8. Under Siege

1. Richard Taylor, "With All Due Respect: An Historical Perspective on Civil Disobedience," *Sojourners*, May 1983, 15–19.

2. Julia McCord, "Methodists Dissatisfied with Talks," *Omaha World-Herald*, October 13, 1997.

3. Ibid.

4. I went on First Church property only twice after the suspension. The first time was to attend Elizabeth Dinsdale's funeral. Elizabeth was hospitalized on November 9, the Sunday she was to receive one of First Church's 1997 Distinguished Service Awards. She died on the tenth, the day my suspension began. I sat in the very last row of pews, entering just as the service began and leaving immediately after it ended to avoid contact with church members. Elizabeth was not only a parishioner, but a friend and strong supporter of mine. It was extremely painful not to be allowed to be her and her family's pastor at that time. The second time was to attend the Boar's Head Festival, a choral program that First Church produced each year for the public during the week following Christmas. My son, Patrick, was visiting Omaha for the first and only time, and he accompanied Chris and me to the program.

5. Cindy Gonzalez, "Pastor: Celebrate Love Regardless of Gender," *Omaha World-Herald*, November 10, 1997.

6. LCSW stands for Licensed Clinical Social Worker.

7. Steve Nehrig, the church's building manager, audiotaped the entire All Church Conference. Quotes and descriptions of the proceedings are taken from the audiotapes, as well as from interviews with some of the people who attended.

9. Pretrial

1. BOD, paragraph 68(G).

2. Supporting the Vision had held protests at the bishop's office in Lincoln because of my suspension.

3. "Suspension Has Ended for Methodist Pastor," *Omaha World-Herald*, January 9, 1998.

4. Quotes are taken from the transcript of the hearing prepared by Cheryl A. Rooney, a court reporter with J. S. Wurm and Associates.

5. Gustav Niebuhr, "Pastor's Church Trial Attests to Divisiveness of Gay Issue," *New York Times*, February 15, 1998.

6. Charley Lerrigo, "California-Nevada Cabinet Supports Pastors Who Perform Same-Sex Unions," *United Methodist News Service*, March 3, 1998.

7. Ibid.

8. Ibid.

10. The Church on Trial

1. The Reverend Dr. William Wallace Finlator (known to his friends as W. W. or Bill) was a Baptist in the best of that tradition and a giant among religious leaders in America. He served Pullen Memorial Baptist Church in Raleigh, North Carolina, from 1956 to 1982. He was a rare combination of prophet and pastor, whose genuine compassion, gentleness, and humility complemented his passionate and unequivocal support for human rights, labor unions, and civil liberties and his opposition to

war, the death penalty, and racial inequality. The Reverend Mahan Siler succeeded Bill Finlator at Pullen, and the two were close friends.

2. In 1992 the congregation of Pullen Memorial Baptist Church voted to welcome lesbian, gay, bisexual, and transgender people into full membership and to provide holy union ceremonies to same-gender couples. This action led to significant public controversy and to conflict within the congregation and with other Baptists. Some members who did not support the vote felt compelled to leave, causing deep pain in the congregation. The local Baptist Association, the Southern Baptist State Convention, and the Southern Baptist Convention in succession severed ties with Pullen. See Mahan Siler, *Exile or Embrace?*

3. *In Search of Unity: A Conversation with Recommendations for the Unity of The United Methodist Church*, The General Commission on Christian Unity and Interreligious Concerns, March 9, 1998, cover. The dialogue participants were: Reverend William J. Abraham, Bishop Judith Craig, Ms. Mary Daffin, Reverend Maxie D. Dunnam, Bishop Marion M. Edwards, Mr. John Gardner, Reverend McCalister Hollins, Reverend Les Longden, Bishop Richard C. Looney, Reverend Donald E. Messer, Reverend M. Kent Millard, Reverend Joy Moore, Ms. Martha Morrison, Mrs. Shirley Parris, Reverend Bruce W. Robbins, Reverend Naomi Southard, Reverend Greg Stover, Mr. Ernest Swiggett, Reverend Linda E. Thomas, Reverend Mark Trotter, Reverend Eradio Valverde Jr., Reverend Phil Wogaman, and Bishop Joseph H. Yeakel. The dialogue was facilitated by Dr. John B. Stephens.

4. Ibid., 2.

5. Ibid., 6.

6. Ibid., 9.

7. *Homosexuality and the Bible* was first published in the *Christian Century Magazine* and subsequently available as a reprint from the Fellowship of Reconciliation, Nyack, New York.

8. Quotes from the trial come from the official transcript of the trial prepared by Linda P. Swanson, a court reporter with J. S. Wurm and Associates. The quotes have been edited and abridged for readability and brevity.

9. Clergy continued to add their names after the trial, and by November 1998 the statement had 350 signatures.

10. *Respondent* is the word used for defendant in the United Methodist judicial process.

11. Gustav Niebuhr, "Methodist Pastor Found Innocent of Performing Same-Sex Union," *New York Times*, March 14, 1998.

12. Jon Jeter, "Jury Acquits Pastor Who Performed Gay Marriage," *Washington Post*, March 14, 1998.

13. Yonat Shimron, "Minister Found Not Guilty, *News & Observer*, March 14, 1998.

14. Judith Nygren, "Pastors Acquit Creech," *Omaha World-Herald*, March 14, 1998.

15. Bob Reeves, "Creech Acquitted in Methodist Trial," *Lincoln Journal Star*, March 14, 1998.

16. Mel White's e-mail reports on the trial were published in "The Trial of Jimmy

Creech," *More Light Update*, May–June, 1998, 10–15 (material quoted found on page 14).

11. Aftershock

1. Alva James-Johnson, "Reverend Creech Returns to His Pulpit," *Omaha World-Herald*, March 16, 1998.
2. Cheryl Hahs Edwards, "Acquittal Stirs Controversy among United Methodists," *Nebraska Messenger*, April 1998, A1.
3. Melanie Kirkpatrick, "A Methodist Misstep," *The Wall Street Journal*, March 27, 1998.
4. "Reactions to the Verdict of the Jimmy Creech Trial," *The United Methodist Newscope, The National Weekly Newsletter for United Methodist Leaders*, April 3, 1998.
5. "We Mustn't Disregard our Discipline," *United Methodist Reporter*, March 27, 1998.
6. Cynthia B. Astle, "Evangelical United Methodists Ask to Separate from California-Nevada Conference," *United Methodist News Service*, April 6, 1998.
7. "Aftershocks Continue Following Verdict," *United Methodist Reporter*, April 17, 1998.
8. Mary Cagney, "Verdict Aftershocks," *Christianity Today*, June 15, 1998, 15.
9. Bob Reeves, "Methodist Bishops Arrive amid Turmoil," *Lincoln Journal Star*, April 18, 1998.
10. Julia McCord, "Methodist Bishops Gather," *Omaha World-Herald*, April 26, 1998.
11. David Spence, "Sinking Ship?," *Good News*, May–June 1998, 3.
12. Kenneth W. Chalker, "Trial Shows a Troubling Selectivity," *Plain Dealer*, March 21, 1998.
13. Sara Ellen Mamlin, "Viewpoints," letter to the editor, *Hoosier United Methodist News*, April 1998, 23.
14. George McClain, "The Creech Trial: What Does It Mean?" *Social Questions Bulletin*, March–April 1998, 1–2.
15. Julia McCord and Judith Nygren, "Divided Methodists Organize Response to Creech Verdict," *Omaha World Herald*, March 22, 1998.
16. Alva James-Johnson and Fred Mogul, "Parishioners against Creech Unite," *Omaha World-Herald*, March 23, 1998.
17. "Opponents of Minister Hold Ceremony," *Associated Press*, March 23, 1998.
18. "Opponents of Creech Gather for Sunday Rally," *United Methodist News Service*, March 25, 1998.
19. Rabbi Debbie Stiel, Temple Israel; the Reverend Tim Madsen, First Lutheran Church—ELCA; and the Reverend M. Winston Baldwin, First Central Congregational United Church of Christ, "A Struggle to Find the Truth," *Omaha World-Herald*, April 25, 1998.
20. *The Book of Discipline*, paragraph 404, 1.
21. Ibid.
22. Ibid.
23. Judith Nygren, "Bishops Vote to Reaffirm Stance on Gays," *Omaha World-Herald*, May 1, 1998.

24. Quoted in Stephen Buttry and Judith Nygren, "Bishop: Gay-Union Stance Clear," *Omaha World-Herald*, May 2, 1998.

25. Quoted in Mary Cagney, "Verdict Aftershocks," *Christianity Today*, June 15, 1998, 15.

26. "Bishops' Statement Draws Guarded Praise, Criticism," *United Methodist News Service*, May 11, 1998.

27. Quoted in ibid.

28. Bishop Melvin G. Talbert, "Letter to Clergy and Lay Members, California-Nevada Conference," *United Methodist News Service*, May 14, 1998.

29. Patrick Strawbridge, "Parishioners Air Feelings on Creech with Bishop Martínez," *Omaha World-Herald*, May 7, 1998.

30. Alva James-Johnson and Julia McCord, "Creech Gives Last Sermon," *Omaha World-Herald*, June 8, 1998.

12. New Challenges

1. Westboro Baptist Church's website is GodHatesFags.com. The Reverend Fred Phelps also picketed First Church on the Sunday I returned after the trial in Kearney, March 15, 1998.

2. Quoted in "Prohibition against Performing Homosexual Unions Ruled Enforceable," *United Methodist News Service*, August 11, 1998.

3. Ibid.

4. Quoted in Deborah Kovach Caldwell, "United Methodists Bar Gay Marriages," *Dallas Morning News*, August 11, 1998.

5. Judicial Council Decision Number 833. Judicial Council decisions can be found on UMC.org: http://archives.umc.org/interior_judicial.asp?mid=263.

6. Powers McLeod was a Duke Divinity School classmate from Florida.

7. Harry C. Kiely, "'A Triumph of Narrow-minded Legalism,'" *Christian Social Action*, April 1999, 4–8.

8. Ibid.

9. Ibid.

10. My first trial in Kearney, Nebraska, cost the Nebraska Annual Conference $20,000; the second trial, in Grand Island, $11,000.

11. Charley Lerrigo, "California-Nevada Clergy Celebrate 'Holy Union' for Two Women," *United Methodist News Service*, January 18, 1999.

12. Of the ninety-two clergy who participated in the holy union from the California-Nevada Annual Conference, twenty did so in absentia and were not considered to have been actually involved in conducting the ceremony. Consequently, there were seventy-two who were subject to formal complaints. Before Bishop Talbert announced the complaints, this number was reduced by three because of the serious illness of two and the death of one. Another would be removed later from the complaints because of illness, making the final count of clergy sixty-eight.

13. "Bishop Talbert Announces Complaint against 69 Pastors," *United Methodist News Service*, March 23, 1999.

14. Larry Ellis, "Like Any Other Couple . . . ," *Chapel Hill News*, June 20, 1999.

15. Quoted in Paul Lee, "Much Ado about Saying 'I Do,'" *Front Page*, June 18, 1999.

16. Dean Snyder, "Rumors of Demonstration at Conference Untrue, MFSA Says," *UM Connection*, June 2, 1999.

17. Allison Pennell, "Creech Urges 'Revolution' for Change," *Hickory Daily Record*, July 12, 1999.

18. Craig Brelsford, "Creech's Disputable Opinions Require Strong Counterbalance," *Hickory Daily Record*, July 11, 1999.

19. Mark Hilton, "City Sponsored Pro-gay Propaganda," *Hickory Daily Record*, July 20, 1999.

20. Ed Yount, "Jimmy Creech or Christ: Whom Will You Follow?" *Hickory Daily Record*, July 22, 1999.

21. Michael Barrick, "United Methodist's [*sic*] Creech Preaches Homosexual Gospel," *Charlotte Christian News*, July 28, 1999.

22. Larry H. Eckard, "Creech Spread Untruths about Homosexuality," *Hickory Daily Record*, July 29, 1999.

23. If a couple wants someone other than, or in addition to, their pastor to participate in a wedding or holy union, the protocol is for the couple to ask their pastor to issue a formal invitation on their behalf to the guest clergy.

24. Richard E. Harding et al., "Blessing Same-Gender Covenants," *Crosscurrents*, November 1999. The other signers of the article were Marie Bent, William C. Coleman, Earle R. Custer, Paul K. Deats Jr., F. Oliver Drake, Walter G. Hartley, Donald B. Hoyle, Evan R. Johnson, Franklin E. Kooker, John H. Lavely, Peter T. Misner, Sally P. Poland, Ruth E. S. Robinson, Robert Sammons, Donella Siktberg, Harry Soper Jr., Robert L. Treese, Wayne Underhill, and Thomas C. Whitehouse.

25. All references and quotes from the Committee of Investigation's hearing come from a transcript of the hearing prepared by Cheryl A. Rooney, a court reporter with J. S. Wurm and Associates. Direct quotes have been edited for brevity and readability.

13. Blessing Withdrawn

1. The Reverend Nancy Wilson was elected moderator of the Metropolitan Community Churches in July 2005, succeeding the Reverend Dr. Troy Perry, founder of the MCC.

2. L. Victoria Peterson, "Justice, Love, and Compassion on Trial: Why I Took Part in a Protest Demonstration," *EEWC Update*, Winter, 1999–2000, 4.

3. Ibid.

4. Quotes from the trial come from the official transcript of the trial prepared by Teresa M. Carpenter, a court reporter with the Elite Court Reporting Service Inc. The quotes have been edited and abridged for readability and brevity.

5. My complete statement to the jury was published as *Rise Above the Law*, in a limited edition of two hundred copies, by Swing Bridge Press, Omaha, Nebraska.

6. Quote taken from *In My Father's Church* (2004), a film by Charissa King-Obrien, a

documentary filmmaker. My statement to the media was video recorded and used in the film.

7. In some Christian churches, ordination to ministry is a sacrament and cannot be reversed, nullified, or withdrawn. That is not the case in The United Methodist Church.

8. The quotes are from the ritual of baptism found in *The United Methodist Book of Worship*.

14. Epilogue

1. James Lawson and Rodney Powell are profiled in David Halberstam's *The Children* (New York: Random House, 1998).

2. M. Garlinda Burton (UMNS), "Second Group Arrested in Protest of Church's Policies Regarding Gays," *North Carolina Christian Advocate*, May 30, 2000.

3. Ibid.

4. Karen R. Long, David Briggs, and Karl Turner, "Methodists Reaffirm Homosexuality Ban," *Plain Dealer*, May 12, 2000.

5. Mitchell Gold + Bob Williams, founded in 1989 by Gold and Williams, manufactures high-quality furniture and has signature stores throughout the U.S., as well as in Toronto, Mexico City, and San Juan, Puerto Rico.

6. Erin Kelly, "Homosexual-rights Stand Driving Away Pastor's Flock," *News & Observer*, January 21, 1990.

7. In 2009, the Vermont legislature replaced the term *civil union* with *marriage*, recognizing the inherent inequality of using separate terms for same-gender couples and nongay couples.

BIBLIOGRAPHY

Books Cited

Boswell, John. *Christianity, Social Tolerance, and Homosexuality: Gay People in Western Europe from the Beginning of the Christian Era to the Fourteenth Century.* Chicago: University of Chicago Press, 1980.

Brundage, James. *Law, Sex, and Christian Society in Medieval Europe.* Chicago: University of Chicago Press, 1987.

Buttrick, George Arthur, ed. *The Interpreter's Dictionary of the Bible: An Illustrated Encyclopedia, Identifying and Explaining All Proper Names and Significant Terms and Subjects in the Holy Scriptures, Including the Apocrypha, with Attention to Archaeological Discoveries and Researches into the Life and Faith of Ancient Times.* 4 vols. New York: Abingdon, 1962.

Creech, Jimmy. *Rise above the Law: The Appeal to the Jury, the United Methodist Church's Trial of Jimmy Creech, November 17, 1999.* Omaha, Neb.: Swing Bridge, 2000.

Gold, Victor Roland, et al., eds. *The New Testament and Psalms: An Inclusive Version.* New York: Oxford University Press, 1995.

Hartman, Keith. *Congregations in Conflict: The Battle over Homosexuality.* New Brunswick, N.J.: Rutgers University Press, 1996.

Herzog, Fredrick. *Justice Church: The New Function of the Church in North American Christianity.* Maryknoll, N.Y.: Orbis, 1980.

Hogan, Steve, and Lee Hudson, eds. *Completely Queer: The Gay and Lesbian Encyclopedia.* New York: Henry Holt, 1998.

Jordan, Mark D. *The Invention of Sodomy in Christian Theology.* Chicago: University of Chicago Press, 1997.

Scanzoni, Letha, and Virginia Ramey Mollenkott. *Is the Homosexual My Neighbor? Another Christian View.* Rev. ed. San Francisco: Harper and Row, 1996.

Siler, Mahan. *Exile or Embrace? Congregations Discovering Their Response to Lesbian and Gay Christians.* Cleveland, Ohio: Pilgrim Press, 2005.

Tannahill, Reay. *Sex in History*. Rev. and updated ed. Chelsea, Mich.: Scarborough House, 1992.

Wink, Walter. *Homosexuality and the Bible*. Nyack, N.Y.: Fellowship Bookstore, 1996.

Recommended Reading

Balka, Christie, and Andy Rose, eds. *Twice Blessed: On Being Lesbian, Gay, and Jewish*. Boston: Beacon, 1989.

Boswell, John. *The Marriage of Likeness: Same-Sex Unions in Pre-modern Europe*. London: Harper Collins, 1995.

Boykin, Keith. *One More River to Cross: Black and Gay in America*. New York: Random House, 1996.

Brown, Joanne Carlson, and Carole R. Bohn, eds. *Christianity, Patriarchy, and Abuse: A Feminist Critique*. New York: Pilgrim, 1989.

Brown, Mildred L., and Chloe Ann Rounsley. *True Selves: Understanding Transsexualism — For Families, Friends, Coworkers, and Helping Professionals*. San Francisco: Jossey-Bass, 1996.

Coontz, Stephanie. *Marriage, a History: How Love Conquered Marriage*. New York: Penguin Books, 2006.

Crompton, Louis. *Homosexuality & Civilization*. Cambridge: Belknap Press of Harvard University Press, 2003.

D'Emilio, John, and Estelle B. Freedman. *Intimate Matters: A History of Sexuality in America*. 2nd ed. Chicago: University of Chicago Press, 1997.

Geller, Thomas, ed. *Bisexuality: A Reader and Sourcebook*. Ojai, Calif.: Times Change, 1990.

Gold, Mitchell, ed. *Crisis: 40 Stories Revealing the Personal, Social, and Religious Pain and Trauma of Growing Up Gay in America*. Austin, Texas: Greenleaf Book Group, 2008.

Gomes, Peter J. *The Good Book: Reading the Bible with Mind and Heart*. New York: William Morrow, 1996.

Graff, E. J. *What Is Marriage For? The Strange Social History of Our Most Intimate Institution*. Boston: Beacon, 1999.

Greenberg, Steven. *Wrestling with God and Men: Homosexuality in the Jewish Tradition*. Madison: University of Wisconsin Press, 2004.

Griffin, Horace L. *Their Own Receive Them Not: African American Lesbians and Gays in Black Churches*. Cleveland, Ohio: Pilgrim, 2006.

Halperin, David M. *One Hundred Years of Homosexuality and Other Essays on Greek Love*. New York: Routledge, 1990.

Helminiak, Daniel A. *What the Bible Really Says about Homosexuality*. San Francisco: Alamo Square, 1994.

Heyward, Carter. *Our Passion for Justice: Images of Power, Sexuality, and Liberation*. New York: Pilgrim, 1984.

————. *Touching Our Strength: The Erotic as Power and the Love of God*. San Francisco: Harper and Row, 1989.

Hilton, Bruce. *Can Homophobia Be Cured? Wrestling with Questions That Challenge the Church*. Nashville, Tenn.: Abingdon, 1992.

Johnson, William Stacy. *A Time to Embrace: Same-Gender Relationships in Religion, Law, and Politics*. Grand Rapids, Mich.: William B. Eerdmans, 2006.

Kolodny, Debra R., ed. *Blessed Bi Spirit: Bisexual People of Faith*. New York: Continuum, 2000.

Lewin, Ellen. *Recognizing Ourselves: Ceremonies of Lesbian and Gay Commitment*. New York: Columbia University Press, 1998.

McNeill, John J. *The Church and the Homosexual*. Updated and expanded ed. Boston: Beacon, 1988.

————. *Taking a Chance on God: Liberating Theology for Gays, Lesbians, and Their Lovers, Families, and Friends*. Boston: Beacon, 1988.

Mollenkott, Virginia Ramey. *Sensuous Spirituality: Out from Fundamentalism*. New York: Crossroad, 1992.

Nelson, James B. *The Intimate Connection: Male Sexuality, Masculine Spirituality*. Philadelphia: Westminster, 1988.

Nissinen, Martti. *Homoeroticism in the Biblical World: A Historical Perspective*. Translated by Kirsi Stjerna. Minneapolis, Minn.: Fortress, 1998.

Pharr, Suzanne. *Homophobia: A Weapon of Sexism*. Inverness, Calif.: Chardon, 1988.

Rogers, Jack. *Jesus, the Bible, and Homosexuality: Explode the Myths, Heal the Church*. Louisville, Ky.. Westminster John Knox, 2006.

Rudy, Kathy. *Sex and the Church: Gender, Homosexuality, and the Transformation of Christian Ethics*. Boston: Beacon, 1997.

Scroggs, Robin. *The New Testament and Homosexuality: Contextual Background for Contemporary Debate*. Philadelphia: Fortress, 1983.

Weinberg, Martin S., Colin J. Williams, and Douglas W. Pryor. *Dual Attraction: Understanding Bisexuality*. New York: Oxford University Press, 1994.

White, Mel. *Religion Gone Bad: The Hidden Dangers of the Christian Right*. New York: Jeremy P. Tarcher, 2006.

————. *Stranger at the Gate: To Be Gay and Christian in America*. New York: Simon and Schuster, 1994.

JIMMY CREECH is a former United Methodist minister, now retired.

Library of Congress Cataloging-in-Publication Data
Creech, Jimmy.
Adam's gift : a memoir of a pastor's calling to defy the church's
persecution of lesbians and gays / Jimmy Creech.
p. cm.
Includes bibliographical references and index.
ISBN 978-0-8223-4885-6 (cloth : alk. paper)
1. Creech, Jimmy. 2. Homosexuality — Religious aspects — United
Methodist Church (U.S.) 3. United Methodist Church (U.S.) —
Clergy — Biography. I. Title.
BX8349.H66C73 2011
287'.6092 — dc22
[B]
2010039876